文化遗产新探

跨界话语研究

New Approach to Cultural Heritage :

Profiling Discourse Across Borders

程 乐 杨建平 蔡建明 主编

ZHEJIANG UNIVERSITY PRESS
浙江大学出版社

Foreword

The global rise of heritage studies and heritage industry in recent decades has been a story of crossing frontiers and transcending boundaries. The 2018 Association of Critical Heritage Studies (ACHS) Conference thus takes "borders" as a broadly defined, yet key, concept for better understanding how heritage is valued, preserved, politicized, mobilized, financed, planned and destroyed. Thinking through borders raises questions about theories of heritage, its methodologies of research, and where its boundaries lie with tourism, urban development, post-disaster recovery, collective identities, climate change, memory or violent conflict. Held in the city of Hangzhou, China, "Heritage Across Borders" has connected international participants with local issues, and in so doing opened up debates about the rural-urban, east-west, tangible-intangible and other familiar divides.

Since it was formed in the early 2010s, ACHS has held three conferences in Göteborg (Sweden, 2012), Canberra (Australia, 2014) and Montreal (Canada, 2016) with the number of participants growing. As the largest conference of its kind in Asia, the fourth edition attracted over 460 participants from different disciplines.

The 2018 ACHS Conference features one public speech delivered by Professor Michael Herzfeld from Harford University and five keynote speeches from: Professor David J. Bodenhamer at Indiana University-Purdue University Indianapolis; Professor CAI Jianming at Chinese Academy of Sciences; Professor CHENG Le at Zhejiang University; Professor Nelson H. Graburn at University of California, Berkeley; and Professor Michael Rowlands at University College London.

The conference program has held sessions and panel discussions on the following topics:

- Historical Approaches to Heritage in/from East Asia
- Heritage, Cultural Contestation and Government
- The Distributed Materiality of the Heritage of Migration
- Conservation of Private Gardens and Urban Futures
- Heritage Across Borders. Semiotic Strategies of Global Diasporas
- Conceptualizing Urban/Rural Heritage Connections
- "Across the Ditch": Advancing a Future for Critical Heritage Studies in Australia and New Zealand
- Borders Between Tangible and Intangible Museum Practice
- Toolkits Across Borders: Assembling Methods-futures for Critical Heritage Studies
- Design and Participative Methodologies for Heritage: Exploring the Notion of "Borders" Through Dialogic Digital Design Methods
- Heritage as Competitive Internationalism
- Heritage as Political Strategies? World Heritage Listing and Management in the Asia-Pacific Region
- Memorializing Movement: Celebrating Flows in an Age of Fixity
- Cultural Heritage Initiatives for Social Inclusion/Against Social Exclusion
- Downsizing Modernity: Heritage in Industrial Settings
- Contestations of Heritage-Formation in a Postsecular Age
- Occupation Heritage
- Cross-border Reworking on Difficult Memories and Places in Asia
- Bounded and Loose: Encountering and Transgressing the Conceptual Borders Between Planned and Unplanned Spaces of Heritage
- Atomic Heritage Goes Critical
- Museum Objects and Knowledge Across Borders
- The Europeanization of Realms of Memory and the Invention of a Common European Heritage
- Multiplicity and Polyphony of Cultural Heritage: Narrative, Visual and Vocal Ways

of Representing Heritage

- What does "Heritage" Mean in/for Pakistan? The South Asian Career of a Global Concept

- The Global Intangible Cultural Heritage Regime and the Politics of Community Participation in China

- Heritage and Religion in Asia

- Preservation of Boundary Resources: Languages and Cultural Heritages of Overlapping Communities

- Crossing Borders: From (Colonial) Heritage to Museum Exhibit. Challenging the Appropriation, Presentation and Communication of "Difficult" Heritage

- The "Unsafe" Museum: Negotiating Difficult Heritage

- Crossing Borders with Heritage Festivals

- Interweaving Cultures: Tangible and Intangible Heritage and Cultural Diversity

- Borders of Expertise and Professionalization

- Socialist Heritage Around the World: A Heritage Without Borders?

- Participatory Heritage and Civil Society

- Histories of Urban Heritage: Emotional and Experiential Attachments Across Time and Space

- Minority Arts and Heritage: Border Work and Contact Zones

- How Emergent Forms of Heritage Reconfigure the Discursive/Material Divide

- Conceptual Histories of "Heritage"

- What's in Asian Museology? Retheorising Contemporary Asian Museum Practices

- Unsustainable Heritage? Change and Adaptation Across Borders

- Heritage Across Linguistic Borders: Semantic Approaches of Intangible Cultural Heritage

- UNESCO Frictions: The Social Lives of International Heritage Norms

- Architectural Heritage Study, Preservation and Development from the Perspective of Cross-culture and Multi-discipline

- Earth as Text, River as Heritage: Textual/Linguistic Perspective in China's Heritage Studies
- Heritage and Leisure/Recreation/Tourism
- A European Heritage in the Making: External Borders and Internal Boundaries on the Move
- Blurred Borders of Knowledge and Action: Dilemmas of Practice and Research in the Heritage-making Field
- Traversing Disciplinary Borders—Theories, Methods and Ethics for Interdisciplinary Critical Heritage Research
- Applied Heritage and Research Across Sectors to Create Social Change
- Crossing Borders with Hopeful Heritage: Quiet Encroachment Towards Safe Spaces
- Intellectual Property and the Protection of Intangible Cultural Heritage: Emerging Themes and Challenges in Transboundary and Diaspora Contexts
- Gender Construction, Perpetuating Cultures and Heritage: Tackling Marginalization; Rewriting Histories
- The Challenges of Protecting Hybrid Natural-cultural Elements as Forms of Heritage
- Urban Conservation and Urban Governance: Sharing Responsibilities, Crossing Borders?
- Heritage Contestation: Politics, Management, and Sustainable Development Goals
- Heritage Resilience
- Gastronomy and Food Heritage Across Borders
- Heritage, Museum and Nation-building
- Decolonizing Heritage in City Space. New Epistemologies, Practices and Affects
- Heritage as an Enabler for Sustainable Transformations in Urban and Rural Areas

This book, based on the conference proceedings of the 2018 ACHS, is a collection of heritage studies from a critical perspective. The contributors cover a wide spectrum of issues in heritage studies, such as heritage management, accessibility to heritage, heritage conservation, heritage policy, heritage representation. The book addresses questions about theories of heritage, its methodologies of research, and where its boundaries lie with tourism, urban development, post-disaster recovery, collective identities, memories or conflicts. It also examines the various contexts within which heritage emerges and how heritage is constructed within that context. Explorations touch upon community involvement, landscape history, children's literature, endangered food, architecture, advertisement, allotment garden, gender and visual art. As heritage has always been a locus of contested verities, the book offers a variegated approach to heritage studies.

We thank the Zhejiang University Press for their generous support. We are also thankful to the program committee members and reviewers, without whose expert input this conference would not be possible. Finally, we thank the entire organizing team and all authors who submitted their work to 2018 ACHS conference.

CHENG Le
Zhejiang University
General Chair

YANG Jianping
Zhejiang University
Program Chair

Contents

1

Sharing Responsibilities in Managing a Residential Heritage Area: A Case Study of Darmo Area, Surabaya, Indonesia

Erika Yuni Astuti

School of Architecture, Planning, and Policy Development—Institut
Teknologi Bandung. Jl. Ganesha 10, 40132, Bandung, Indonesia.
CONTACT Erika Yuni Astuti: erika@ar.itb.ac.id

Abstract: Managing a heritage area requires strategic partnerships with the private sector for cross-funding possibilities. This is a scheme to understand how conservation works—a chain of regulations and legal support correlate with other factors: financial and economic incentives, and also inhabitants' social values. In order to conserve a heritage area within a rapidly growing city, the concept needs to keep the driving forces in balance. In the early definition of conservation (the Venice Charter of 1960), it simply meant to keep optimal conditions and prevent damage. In relation to the initial definition of conservation, this research indicates that the key to sustain a heritage area is to work hand-in-hand with the inhabitants to maintain the integrity of the place. The heritage buildings and their settings should not lose their attached meaning, but maintain the balance of their architectural values that need to be preserved. The attitude of the inhabitants to their heritage area is a response to its current condition, stimulated by law, regulations, and economic pressure. The main trigger for community engagement is an incentive from local authorities, which can be a direct or indirect advantage of living in the heritage area.

Keywords: community engagement in conservation, managing residential heritage area, shared heritage, Surabaya, Indonesia

Background: Sustainable Urban Heritage of an Emerging Asian City

Sharing responsibilities between central and local governments, as well as residents, is necessary when managing urban heritage (Turner and Tomer 2013:188). The task cannot be handled solely from the government side. The next question, in the case of the limited resources, is why government should prioritise conservation. Even though the heritage area is mostly a significant place that the municipality would like to preserve as part of the city's identity, its uniqueness, as well as the city branding the area, however, is in many cases barely profitable compared with non-conservation areas. It is widely known that conservation of the old part of the city in these times of rapid economic development requires a strategy and draws resources from citizens and interested parties. This preventive care would bring benefits not only for future heritage area preservation (Jokilehto 2002: 318) but also for the ongoing examples within the city. How to do this? The first attempt is to measure interests among the stakeholders. Hence, this is in line with the understanding of the historical value of the heritage building or the residential area (Pendlebury 2013; Kepczynska-Walczak 2015).

In some cases, not all the inhabitants appreciate the objects, which has to be the basic motivation for their willingness to preserve the buildings. The same trend could be seen in the study of the Darmo area (2012–2015); there was a similar level of interest in protecting heritage buildings. Family homes are the type of building that survived most (around 60%). Even though many of the buildings in that area have been modernised, the number of buildings that have survived has also decreased by around 10% since the listed programme was established in 2008. This is unlikely in the European context, where those buildings from the Second World War period are not favoured due to many people preferring other

2

types of buildings or stylish historical buildings; in this research setting, the buildings are highly appreciated by architects and academia due to their differences. For the public, especially the owner, it is not its character that caused the building to survive, but rather the family's social values. This is not to say that a person who has no family ties would not enjoy this type of typical building, but interestingly such a citizen also sees these buildings as being appreciated. It is important to underline this different response, which shows that the same object in a different context may be appreciated in different ways. These differences bring another advantage—the values that contribute to the sustainability of the city. This strength may lead to the last attempt of preservation in the midst of the rising economy within Asian cities, where investors would most likely firstly focus on the economic advantages. Since, in Indonesia, residential heritage areas are currently located in inner cities, the areas that are highly competitive due to the rapid growth of those cities.

Furthermore, the significant problem that has not yet been fully considered by the authority is that the daily lives of the senior inhabitants are threatened. The senior inhabitants do not live in particular homes for the elderly; their families take care of them, adhering to traditional Indonesian values. Meanwhile, the area starts to change its function into a commercial one, which severely impacts the surroundings due to its noise and traffic—the inhabitants have to put more effort into coping with the new surroundings, which becomes less convenient than before in which to live. This phenomenon has also happened in other heritage areas in Indonesian cities. It is important to reflect that conserving the area means not only giving attention to the built objects, but also preserving the inhabitants. Heritage conservation can only be considered to be a good example of its practice as long as it keeps the concept of place with integrity, here including the harmony of its inhabitants. Its history and meaning should be retained as part of integrity of place, such that it will be in the best position to sustain its heritage values for present and future generations. This is in line with Sir Bernard Feilden (2003: 3), who pointed out that the conservation of the built environment is an act of managing heritage objects in the dynamic of their purpose. Hence, in this context, this would be the transformation of built heritage in terms of the needs of the inhabitants, the citizens and the city itself—which needs to be allowed to grow for its existence. Since the earliest times of Surabaya's history, the city relies on its potential for trading; as a harbour city, this makes the growth of commerce demanding.

Transforming Meaning of Heritage Within Current Society

There is an example of transformation of the meaning of cultural heritage; the case of *baumkuchen* in Japan. This cake was brought by a German who happened to be a prisoner during the Second World War; the cake later became popular until, today, it is a symbol of prosperity or a wedding gift. The commodity can be found easily in Japan. This shared item of the past has been transformed, with a reinvented meaning in the current society and is loved for what it is—regardless of the history of how it was brought there. In the context of where this item was brought from—its origin in Germany—it might not be as popular there as it is today in Japan. The same analogy has occurred in cases of built heritage; many of them might be ordinary cases at the time of their origin, but later became extraordinary within different contexts. They demonstrate different structures and techniques of placing building materials and later the appropriation on the context. As commonly found in many examples of conservation of built heritage, their survival depends much on how the current society uses it. This is contingent on the contemporary understanding of heritage preservation.

Strategy for Managing Heritage: A Recognition That Cultural Heritage Is Formed by the Current Need

The city concept, context, and content determine the success of heritage conservation. These suggest that people should allow the conservation principles to be applied easily. This effort comes from their internal motivation—not as in most schemes, the top-down approach as seen in many examples of the European Union preservation heritage projects. Hence, in Asian cities, in the context of the Darmo heritage area in Indonesia, the strategy to engage people is a common purpose; the common needs of this community. This may refer to practical needs for neighbourhood security, cleanliness or the organisation of cultural events or festivals. In the heritage area, the inhabitants vary from long- and medium-term to short-term residents. Each possesses various needs, but generally the long-term residents are more likely to be engaged in the neighbourhood and maintain social relationships with other inhabitants.

In this research, a form of awareness was found, not only merely expressed in the good maintenance of the object, but also in people simply keeping the object as their own, because of some limitations of funding. Looking through the years of the evolution of heritage regulations, the development of the law over those years shows governance more concerned about heritage conservation because, in fact, the number of those heritage buildings has continued to decrease, affecting mostly those cases where investors have donations for new commercial purposes. Inhabitants whose buildings have remained as residential houses have challenges in maintaining it, due to the house being large and voluminous, which raises difficulties in managing costs. In addition, technical problems would follow, such as the plumbing system and the wooden roof structure. From this competitive usage of land, it is very difficult to preserve these old buildings as houses. It has been found that old buildings that have been changed to commercial use look well maintained compared with residential houses, but all rooms inside these buildings needed to be totally laid out again.

An incentive scheme for the owners of heritage buildings could be applied. The incentives should be given to the resident owners of houses, due to the issue of fairness. With rapid urban expansion, private owners may feel under pressure due to the duty to maintain their old buildings. Cultural institutions also play a role in the preservation of the city of Surabaya. By custom and tradition, inhabitants in the old part of the city are also willing to conserve the area. It has been found that they maintain the buildings without much economic advantage. A process of sharing responsibilities is only possible when the infrastructure of heritage is understood perfectly by the citizens. The table below shows the developing regulations of relatively new conservation. This is a chronological process of shifting concepts, and also the growth of the concept of major cultural heritage. Table

1 explains the context of cultural heritage in Indonesia. In the case study of the Darmo heritage area, the municipality preserved the area as an example of a planned residential area, because its quality might not be found in newer real estate in the city.

Table 1   Regulations and plans concerning heritage conservation, Surabaya, 1992–2014

Year	Regulation	Details	Process in this phase
1992	Law No. 5/1992 on Cultural Heritage Object (*Undang-Undang Cagar Budaya*)	Basic regulations of Indonesian cultural heritage protection; covers all heritage objects, both tangible and intangible. The regulations were then revised in 2010 (*UU No 11 Tahun 2010 tentang Cagar Budaya*)	Conservation in **developing** the concept
2002	Municipal Development Planning Board Plan on conservation cultural heritage objects in Surabaya city: Darmo residential area	Initial attempt to establish basic concept of Darmo heritage area and preliminary investigation report about the area	Conservation regulation **inventory** process
2003	Municipal Development Planning Board Plan on conservation cultural heritage objects	Aimed, firstly, to classify and invent cultural heritage objects; secondly to identify problems in conserving cultural heritage objects; thirdly, to build incentive scheme and strategy to conserve objects	From national regulations to local regulations: **adapting process** of conservation
2005	Surabaya Municipal Law No. 5/2005 on Conservation of Cultural Heritage (*Peraturan Walikota No 5 tahun 2005 tentang Pelestarian Bangunan dan atau Lingkungan Cagar Budaya*)	Darmo residential area was clearly defined as an heritage area in these regulations	**Establishing implementation** of heritage regulations
2007	Surabaya Municipal Law No. 59/2007 on Implementation of Conservation of Cultural Heritage (*Peraturan Walikota Surabaya Nomor 59 tahun 2007 tentang Pelaksanaan Peraturan Daerah Kota Surabaya No 5 tahun 2005 tentang Pelestarian Bangunan dan atau Lingkungan Cagar Budaya*)	Detailed implementation of cultural heritage regulations; announced two years after the establishment of the heritage area. All procedures of maintenance, listing and rehabilitation of heritage building including sanctions are clearly defined	**Details** of the regulated area

6

Continued

Year	Regulation	Details	Process in this phase
2007	Surabaya Local Regulation No. 3/2007 on General Spatial Plan (*Peraturan Daerah Kota Surabaya No 3 tahun 2007 tentang Rencana Tata Ruang Wilayah*)	Item no. 33 on heritage objects	Implementation process
2013	Surabaya Municipal Law No. 34/2013 on Tax Deduction and Cancelation (*Peraturan Walikota Surabaya No 34 tahun 2013 tentang Tata Cara Pengurangan atau Penghapusan Sanksi Administratif dan Pengurangan atau Pembatalan Ketetapan Pajak Bumi dan Bangunan Perkotaan*)	These recent regulations announced tax deductions for the owners of heritage buildings; to be granted this deduction the building needed to be retained in authentic form except for minor changes	Implementation process: research observes inhabitants' awareness of the impact of the heritage regulations
2014	Surabaya Local Regulation No. 12/2014 on General Spatial Plan (*Peraturan Daerah Kota Surabaya No 12 tahun 2014 tentang Rencana Tata Ruang Wilayah*)	Latest spatial plan, which mentioned heritage area as a part of the government city plan	Implementation process

Source: Astuti (2018)

First Form of Sharing Responsibilities: Managing Conservation Challenges by Engaging the Private Sector as a Strategy

To achieve sustainable heritage conservation, all actors need to contribute to its greater success. Stakeholder participation in heritage can be initiated by spreading information on the advantages of heritage preservation, which can lead to sustainability in the conservation area (Townsend and Pendlebury 1999; Rodwell 2007; Worthing and Bond 2008). The information from stakeholders can be forwarded to all inhabitants. This section aims to develop a concept of sustainable conservation, and also to analyse the essential contents in this research context. Preservation is not only about a remembrance of the past; it should also consider the current context with regard to its history, and the future, so that the conservation object can be sustained. This concept of revising what conservation actually is considers the appreciation of the context of the city. Then, it becomes necessary to combine both concept and context in the city when managing a heritage area.

7

Most family businesses with origins in Surabaya are motivated to follow the idea of conservation. Their rootedness in and bonds to Surabaya make them less calculating when weighing the issues between conservation and economic value. Some of the owners of the companies come from other islands or a particular ethnic group. Along with the growth of their companies and their adaptation to the place, the owners have also begun to identify as Surabaya people. Even though part of their ethnicity might express itself in a different cultural practice from that of Surabaya, most native Javanese people and their identity bring harmony to Surabaya city. I argue that their expression regarding their heritage building is also a way of being accepted into the local neighbourhood. The goal of their cultural consciousness is to adapt a typical Surabaya identity. This fact also confirms the concept of Hague and Jenkins (2005) that if there is a sense of identity towards a place, a willingness to conserve the heritage area will develop naturally.

In addition, Worthing and Bond (2008) suggest that there is a bonding of people to their place; a feeling towards historical places. Even though their research was formulated based on the settings of European cities, there is a similar indication of participation in the context of Surabaya heritage—a bonding of the people to their place. This research started with the idea that the motivation of inhabitants and/or stakeholders to conserve heritage may be developed by generating the aspects of emotional value, memory and attachment to places. In the Surabaya case of Darmo, most senior citizens in Surabaya have this attachment, and they will happily narrate their life stories and associate this with the place, as Darmo has been their setting since their childhood. In some informal interviews with Surabaya citizens, they mentioned, "I frequently used the steam tram each Sunday". This narrative between Surabaya citizens about the old area in Surabaya is a daily conversation.

Second Form of Sharing Responsibilities: A Cooperation Between the Private Sector, Academic Groups and Authorities

In the past fifteen years in Surabaya, heritage events initiated by Surabaya citizens have grown. The motivation to participate in such events is attributed to nostalgia for the old

8

cities, as well as consistent promotion of the events through social media, which draws younger audiences. These heritage events also spread to several cities such as Semarang, Magelang and Jakarta, but still, Surabaya is a unique case, because they started there purely due to the people's own initiative, without government influence. This demonstrates a strong form of participation. Several associations have shown interest in heritage preservation in Surabaya, both in tangible and intangible heritage.

Specialised organisations, such as the Surabaya Heritage Society (Sjarikat Poesaka Soerabaia) and Oud Rotherbourg Surabaya initiated this trend in the heritage movement around the year 2000. The interesting point about this movement is the establishment of permanent sponsorship. The movement receives no supplementary funds from the local authority. This demonstrates a form of awareness in heritage conservation and goes back to an old cultural system of Indonesian mutual help or *gotong-royong*. This system relies on donations from Surabaya families without any attempt to provide benefit to them. Those heritage societies work hand-in-hand with the donors (private-sector bodies); together, this network not only contributes to build heritage management, but also promotes the social aspects. Possible funding for private properties listed in the conservation area may come from individuals and/or businesses.

Private-sector corporations such as Wismilak and Sampoerna and banking corporations such as CIMB Niaga and Mandiri have shown interest in conserving heritage buildings in Surabaya, firstly, by retaining their old buildings, which are considered by Surabaya city as an example of best practice preservation. As discussed earlier, their awareness can be seen in their attempt to keep the heritage buildings in a well-maintained condition. The second attempt can be demonstrated in their cooperation with other relevant stakeholders or interest groups, for instance, academic institutions. Table 2 demonstrates private initiatives in heritage programmes, which can be seen as a form of participation. These organisations and the Surabaya municipality are working hand-in-hand to organise a festival on the theme of old Surabaya. It should be noted that "old Surabaya", in this case, dates back to the era of the War of Independence between 1945 and 1950, even though the city itself has been settled for 400 years.

9

Table 2 Support for the conservation programme in Surabaya by some private-sector bodies

Form of participation/activity	Institution	Form of support for heritage activities	Issues covered
Preserved built heritage including the social aspect	Wismilak Group	Preserving not only the built heritage area, but also supporting a cultural heritage event as an owner of one heritage building, Grha Wismilak, promoting urban heritage in the Darmo area	First company to hold a heritage event in Darmo
Promoting soft aspects/ cultural heritage	Surabaya Heritage Society	Characteristic of the society's aims for the whole cultural aspect of Surabaya's heritage. Initiator of heritage trail, together with Sampoerna Foundation	Academic group from Petra Christian University in Surabaya; Timoticin Kwanda focused his research on heritage values in Asia
Preservation of built heritage including the social aspect	Sampoerna Foundation Group	Initiated heritage trail from northern to southern Surabaya, including the Darmo area. This is an initiative to promote urban heritage in Surabaya	Sampoerna initiated the opening of the House of Sampoerna in the year 2000, one of the first successful preservations of a private building in Surabaya

Source: Astuti (2018)

Wismilak Group is involved in heritage events, including exhibitions of the Indonesian textile batik. This group converted their building in the Darmo area into a museum and funded the artists in the Surabaya sketchwalk. In cooperation with Surabaya Heritage Society (SHS), Wismilak Group organised a heritage sketchwalk along the main corridor of Darmo. This event is held twice a month, and the heritage area is documented through ink or pencil sketches. Wismilak Group was founded in Surabaya, and these events can be considered as an early private-sector initiative in built heritage conservation. Since then, their effort has continued in yearly events supporting heritage. The other group, Sampoerna Foundation, established a museum in the northern part of Surabaya that is one of the earliest examples of successful building conservation in the city.

Involvement of Academia and NGO

High participation was shown by engagement in support of the conservation programme, which shows that the stakeholders' involvement plays an important role. Academia's involvement in heritage, by creating the cultural programme, was also part of their contribution to the society. While stepping up this level of participation in urban heritage, conservation has been measured by this act (Peerapun 2011; Pendlebury 2009). Also, architects and planners from Surabaya educational institutions, namely Petra Christian University (PCU), Institut Teknologi Sepuluh Nopember (ITS) and University of Tujuh Belas Agustus (UNTAG) have been working hand-in-hand with the other actors for the urban conservation effort. Also, historians from the Airlangga University (UNAIR) and Universitas Negeri Surabaya (UNESA) have participated in heritage conservation. These members of academia have been proudly supporting the preservation of Surabaya city for a long time, not only by holding scientific discussions, but also engaging in heritage events.

SHS has a long track record in communicating the cultural heritage of Surabaya through the local media. In one of the most read newspapers in Surabaya, *Jawa Pos*, this organisation consistently promotes urban heritage and its events. Such events can be differentiated from the traditional culinary event in the old Chinese district in the northern part of Surabaya, from the batik event, Old Surabaya graphic art, etc. As the first event was organised without significant government support, it succeeded in gathering support from private companies, social media—newspapers, radio and television—and universities.

Third Form of Sharing Responsibilities: Inhabitants' Participation in Urban Conservation of Darmo

The perception and awareness of the inhabitants of a heritage area must be stimulated to influence a successful conservation programme, so that the inhabitants become involved in urban conservation. Perception is determined by subjective matters and influenced by people's life experience. At the same time, heritage is also selective with regard to the government listing certain buildings, without acceptance or consent of the owner. The

11

information about heritage regulations was sent via mail, followed by the regulations themselves; there were also some attempts to organise community meetings, but these were not a success. There was scepticism from the people, even though the Surabaya government has been one of the best in Indonesia. The worry of the building owners is partially because this programme has not given enough benefit to the people. Ideally, government incentives and benefits should apply to those who have property in the heritage area. However, even though the steps of participation seem easy to apply, the reality can be different. For example, some inhabitants have refused to preserve their buildings, simply due to preferring a new style. Table 3 shows indications of inhabitants' attitudes to heritage areas (adapted from Peerapun [2011] , to illustrate the process of participating in heritage conservation action.

Table 3   Inhabitant participation process in the management of Darmo heritage area

Step	Process of participation	Indicator in heritage area	Attitude	Remarks: how to manage
Inform	People affected by the authority's policy are well informed	The inhabitant understands the programme, guidelines, rewards and punishments in heritage area regulations	The houses in heritage areas are well preserved: they follow the height regulation and the setback regulation	Even though in this case not all of the regulations and policies are well communicated to Darmo's inhabitants, a form of participation—well-preserved houses—exists. This means that some active processes in conserving the heritage area have been carried out by the people
Consult	People affected by the authority's policy are invited to discuss their problem	The inhabitants may contribute their opinion to the decisions about programmes, guidelines and regulations as they apply in the heritage area	The communication is shown in an agreement between the inhabitants and the Surabaya government	Some invitations have been announced by the government

Continued

Step	Process of participation	Indicator in heritage area	Attitude	Remarks: how to manage
Involve	People affected by the authority's policy are invited to be more involved in discussing policy	The inhabitant is actively involved in the programme's events in the area	There may be a joint collaboration between the Surabaya government and the inhabitants: e.g. participation in city bazaars	This process of involvement needs to be designed so that the people participate in the right way

Source: Astuti (2018)

As the government is still in the process of communicating the heritage programme to the people and designing its regulations, levels of participation have remained mostly at the stage of consultation. Awareness plays a very important part in the three levels of participation in heritage discipline terminology. The phenomenon that has occurred in the area is that the process of consultation is still underdeveloped: communications between the authorities and the people have been rather one-sided, despite several attempts to organise a public discussion on heritage. As a result, there have been misunderstandings about the conservation programme between the inhabitants of the area and the government.

The participation in the conservation of urban heritage in the Darmo area can be described in the steps on information, consultation, and involvement, which are reflected in the model of the UNESCO (2005) convention. The convention stressed that urban heritage needs to be based on four components of sustainable development: natural and built environments, economic aspects, social and cultural aspects, and political aspects. Later, UNESCO (2011) suggested that public awareness must increase to achieve sustainable urban conservation, so that the development of capacity building and NGO involvement is necessary. Managing urban heritage can only be sustainable by sharing responsibilities between central and local governments, as well as residents (Turner and Tomer 2013: 188). Conservation is defined as an action to understand heritage and its elements; to know, to reflect upon and communicate heritage and its elements. Its history and meaning should be retained as part of the integrity of the place, such that it will be in the best position to sustain its heritage values for present and future generations. This is in line with Feilden (2003: 3) and his statement that the conservation of the built environment is an act of managing heritage objects in the dynamic of its purpose; in the context of this research, it would be the transformation of built heritage in terms of the needs of inhabitants, citizens and the city itself.

Concluding Remarks

In understanding heritage policies and regulations, the city's priorities and the dynamic investment of the city, some considerations for urban heritage conservation are as follows. Firstly, managing an urban heritage area depends on the synergy of the authorities, the people and the private sector. In the context of urban heritage in Indonesian cities, economic returns in value are simply not enough. Preserving the historical area also means preserving the community, by keeping the area alive with the current inhabitants. In the end, the people are social entities who need other people; in the case of an historic environment, the other people are the long-term neighbours. Management of a conservation heritage area in the city centre needs to consider the quality of life for residential use, and also to provide basic city infrastructure in the area. The local authority must maintain the function of the pedestrian pavements for street vendors, and also clean the drainage system of garbage, etc. In order to manage the quality of life in the residential area, the problem of traffic in the city centre needs to be solved; this aspect also plays an important role in the sustainability of the area's conservation. The conservation policy for the area should not only focus on the listed buildings, but also develop a holistic view on the other buildings in the area. The regulation system needs to be integrated with the policy of built heritage objects in a prime economic area. More detailed and precise regulations in the heritage conservation programme are also expected by inhabitants, especially the low-income groups. There is a need for better support mechanisms for specific private household owners in the heritage area, such as veterans, pensioners and the widowed. Similarly, incentives must also be addressed to commercial building owners.

Secondly, an important issue that has not yet been considered by the authority is the role of senior inhabitants who are living in this old area. They need to be integrated into the adaptive surroundings. This demographic phenomenon is also observed in other heritage areas. Again, conserving the area means not only giving attention to the built objects, but also preserving the inhabitants on site. Heritage conservation can only be considered to be a good example of its practice as long as it keeps the concept of place integrity, here including the harmony of its inhabitants.

Regarding harmonious living in the heritage area, there is a need for both residential and commercial activities. Hence, a balance between planning and the market is necessary. Drawing investments from the private sector is part of sustainable urban heritage conservation. For practical reasons, this idea needs to be implemented, and a scheme for incentives needs to be selectively observed. Managing the heritage area should provide an open opportunity to invite sponsors and third parties as donors for the heritage buildings. This finance model has been established for long-term investments; such a financing scheme is well established in Indonesia. In order to achieve a sustainable economic design of conservation management, there is a need for authorities to select investors very carefully and to have a vision of the future development of the heritage area. Some corporate entities have already demonstrated their sense of responsibility in the design of heritage conservation, for example, Sampoerna Group and Wismilak Group. Their awareness makes them exceptional within corporate circles in Indonesia.

Furthermore, appreciation from Surabaya citizens has been shown through their comments in several media reports and in their participation in the Old Surabaya Fest, a heritage event with a high level of participation. People's involvement in such events may be interpreted only on the basis of a good opportunity for recreation. Some media reported enthusiasm during the heritage event. Aside from this consideration, tourism frequently promotes heritage conservation strategies, but this is difficult in residential areas. Even though many of its buildings have become commercial units, the residential character still dominates the Darmo area, and requires particular conditions as a common residential area:

15

peace and calmness. Hence, it requires particular efforts to keep conservation alive.

In addition, aside from those management aspects of conservation, these acts will also help to protect the cultural wisdom for the society, because the area is a place where there are customs, traditions and moral values to be inherited. In that sense, conserving the heritage area acts not only as a favour for architects and planners in beautifying the city because of its physical value, but also morally: conserving the heritage area carries an important message for maintaining the sanity of society.

Acknowledgements

I express gratitude to the inhabitants of Darmo who gave me their time for interviews, Surabaya Heritage Team for the fruitful discussion, and Laboratory for Housing and Human Settlement of Institut Teknologi Sepuluh Nopember for the generous support during the fieldwork. I would like to thank the School of Architecture, Planning and Policy Development—Institut Teknologi Bandung (SAPPK ITB) and Architectural Design Research Group (Kelompok Keahlian Perancangan Arsitektur—KKPA) for the opportunity to continue research in urban heritage. I would like to express my great appreciation to the Research and Community Service Program (P3MI) 2019, Institut Teknologi Bandung for their assistance in supporting this work.

Note on Contributor

Dr.-Ing. *Erika Yuni Astuti* has been a Staff Lecturer at the School of Architecture, Planning and Policy Development in the Institut Teknologi Bandung (ITB), Bandung, Indonesia since 2010. Previously, she had worked as a Research Assistant and Junior Architect in the Laboratory for Housing and Human Settlement, Department of Architecture, Institut Teknologi Sepuluh Nopember (ITS), Surabaya, Indonesia (2001–2010). Her master's programme (2009) and bachelor's degree (2002) were obtained from the Department of Architecture, Institut Teknologi Sepuluh Nopember, Surabaya, Indonesia. She is also an awardee of a grant from the Swedish International Development Agency (SIDA) for the Advanced International Post Graduate Training Programme "Conservation and Management of Historical Buildings" in Sweden (September, 2006) and Egypt (February, 2007). She graduated from the Faculty of Architecture TU Darmstadt in 2018; her doctoral research was in an interdisciplinary field that included architecture, urban planning and social theories, where she explored public perceptions of heritage areas.

□ References

Astuti, E.Y. 2015. Local Perception of a Conservation Heritage Area, a Case Study of the Darmo Residential Area, Surabaya, Indonesia. In *Envisioning Architecture: Image, Perception and Communication of Heritage*, 132-141. Lodz: Lodz University of Technology.

Astuti, E.Y. 2018. Inhabitants' Awareness Toward Conservation of Urban Heritage Area Case Study of Darmo Heritage Area, Surabaya, Indonesia. Doctoral Dissertation, Technische Universität Darmstadt.

De la Torre, Marta. 2013. Values and Heritage Conservation. *Heritage and Society* 6 (2): 155-166.

Dick, H.W. 2002a. *Surabaya City of Work: A Socioeconomic History, 1900–2000.* Singapore: Singapore University Press, National University Singapore.

Dick, H.W. 2002b. Urban Growth and Crisis. Urban Development and Land Rights: A Comparison of New Order and Colonial Surabaya. In *The Indonesian Town Revisited*, edited by P. J. M. Nas, 115-116. Singapore: National University Singapore.

Feilden, Bernard. 2003. *Conservation of Historic Buildings.* Amsterdam: Architectural Press.

Hague, Cliff, and Paul Jenkins. 2005. *Place Identity, Participation and Planning.* London: Routledge.

Hebbert, Michael. 2005. The Street as Locus of Collective Memory. *Journal of Environment and Planning D: Society and Space* 23 (4): 581-596.

Hewitt, Lucy E., and J. Pendlebury. 2014. Local Associations and Participation in Place: Change and Continuity in the Relationship Between State and Civil Society in Twentieth-Century Britain. *Planning Perspectives* 29 (1): 25-44.

Jokilehto, J. 2002. *A History of Architectural Conservation.* Oxford: Elsevier Butterworth-Heinemann.

Jokilehto, J. 2010. Heritage, Values and Valuation. In *Measuring the Value of Material Cultural Heritage*, edited by M. Quagliuolo, 36-45. Rome: DRI-Fondazione Enotria ONLUS.

Kepczynska-Walczak, Anetta. 2015. Industrial Heritage Revitalisation as a Wordplay. In *Envisioning Architecture: Image, Perception and Communication of Heritage*, 39-48. Lodz: Lodz University of Technology.

King, Anthony D. 2004. *Space, Global Culture and Architecture*. London: Routledge.

Kusno, Abidin. 2000. *Behind the Postcolonial: Architecture, Urban Space and Political Cultures in Indonesia*. London: Routledge

Kwanda, Timotichin. 2009. Western Conservation Theory and the Asian Context: The Different Root of Conservation. In *International Conference on Heritage in Asia: Converging Forces and Conflicting Values*, 2-7. Singapore: The Asia Research Insitute (ARI) of National University of Singapore (NUS).

Kwanda, Timotichin. 2010. Tradition of Conservation: Redefining Authenticity in Javanese Architectural Conservation. *In Heritage 2010—Heritage and Sustainable D*evelopment, 141-152. Evora: Green Lines Institute.

Malpass, P. 2009. The Heritage of Housing: Whose Housing Heritage? In *Valuing Historic Environments*, edited by Lisanne Gibson, and John Pendlebury, 201-214. England: Ashgate.

Peerapun, W. 2011. Participatory Planning in Urban Conservation and Regeneration: A Case Study of Amphawa Community. *Procedia: Social and Behavioural Sciences* 36: 243-352. Accessed January 15, 2013. http://www.sciencedirect.com/science/article/pii/ S1877042812004946.

Pendlebury, J. 2009. Conservation in the Age of Consensus. London: Routledge, Taylor and Francis Group.

Pendlebury, J. 2013. Conservation Values, the Authorised Heritage Discourse and the Conservation-Planning Assemblage. *International Journal of Heritage Studies* 19 (7): 709-727. Accessed July 14, 2014. http://www.tandfonline.com/doi/abs/10.1080/135272 58.2012.700282.

Pendlebury, J., and I. Strange. 2011. Centenary Paper: Urban Conservation and the Shaping of the English City. *Town Planning Review* 82 (4): 361-392.

Rodwell, D. 2007. *Conservation and Sustainability in Historic Cities*. London: Blackwell.

Rojas, E. 2007. The Conservation and Development of the Urban Heritage: A Task for All Social Actors. *City & Time* 3 (1): 41-47.

Santosa, M. 2001. Harmoni di lingkungan tropis lembab: Keberhasilan bangunan kolonial. *Dimensi Teknik Arsitektur* 29 (1): 34-42. Accessed October 1, 2012. http://puslit2.petra. ac.id/ejournal/index.php/ars/article/view/15743.

Sullivan, Arthur. 2000. *Urban Economics*, 5th ed. USA: McGraw-Hill Irwin.

Townsend, T., and J. Pendlebury. 1999. Public Participation in the Conservation of Historic Areas: Case-Studies from North-East England. *Journal of Urban Design* 4 (3): 313-331.

Turner, Michael, and Tal Tomer. 2013. Community Participation and the Tangible and Intangible Values of Urban Heritage. *Heritage & Society* 6 (2): 185-198.

UNESCO. 2005. Four Dimensions of Sustainable Development for Urban Heritage Conservation. Accessed July 14, 2014. http://www.unesco.org/education/tlsf/mods/ theme_a/popups/mod04t01s03.html.

UNESCO. 2011. UNESCO Recommendation on the Historic Urban Landscape. Accessed July 14, 2014. https://whc.unesco.org/en/hul.

Wiryomartono, B. 2015. *Perspective on Traditional Settlements and Communities: Home, Form and Culture in Indonesia*. Singapore: Springer.

Worthing, D., and S. Bond. 2008. *Managing Built Heritage: The Role of Cultural Significance*. Oxford: Blackwell.

Accessibility of Castles: Reality, Imagination and Good Practices for Memory and Dissemination

Mariachiara Bonetti

Università degli Studi di Brescia Via Branze n.43, 25123 Brescia,Italy.

CONTACT Mariachiara Bonetti: mariachiara.bonetti@unibs.it

Abstract: The European Year of Cultural Heritage (EYCH) 2018 indicates the architecture of castles as an element of European culture recognition and guardian. The castle is configured as a privileged custodian of memory and "spirit" in which a community has formed and consolidated over time. In this perspective, access to culture and cultural heritage constitutes the core behaviour of a society which aspires to be inclusive and barrier-free.

The example, through some good practices, of multidisciplinary approaches applied to the Italian architectural heritage, can represent a first step for the sharing of solutions to common problems and obstacles. The first example refers to the International Summer School (ISS) held in Brescia starting from 2017 "Universal Design and Sustainable Tourism: Cidneo Hill and Its Castle in Brescia". The elaboration of different projects of preservation and restoration involved specialisations such as architecture, engineering, linguistics, sociology, communications and marketing.

The research was focused on the theme of accessibility to architectural heritage, the medieval fortress of the city, and its enhancement with an interdisciplinary and holistic approach in the perspective of Universal Design. The second example refers to the permanent exhibition "Signs of light", Cemmo, Capo di Ponte (Brescia-Italy), at Palazzo Zitti: the musealisation of a historical architecture that conforms to a castle, closed and inaccessible, through the realisation of an inclusive, multimedia exhibition that respects the artistic patrimony in which it is inserted.

Keywords: accessibility, heritage, architecture, castle, UNESCO, sustainability

The Need for an Accessible Cultural Heritage

The need to strengthen the knowledge and value of the cultural heritage for the local community needs to develop a strategy that can be functional in identifying a theme that is consonant, recognisable, shared by all and therefore accessible.

The European Year of Cultural Heritage (EYCH) 2018 indicates the architecture of castles is one of the elements of recognition and guardian of European culture[1]. The castle is configured as a privileged custodian of memory and "spirit" in which a community has formed and consolidated over time and is also intended as a custodian of cultural, urban and scenic identity. The *castellana* architecture is a physical tale of tangible heritage and represents its intangible construct, as identified by the Québec Declaration on the Preservation of the Spirit of the Place (ICOMOS 2008).

In this perspective, access to culture and cultural heritage constitutes the core behaviour of a society which aspires to be inclusive and barrier-free: sharing artistic and cultural testimonies which permeate architectonic historical heritage culture is the essential condition for a conscious participation to the foundation of modern society in which the interconnection of different layers of knowledge allows us to deepen, develop and increase awareness of the importance of cultural heritage (Arenghi and Bonetti 2018).

The address of the reflections emerged in the international debate is clearly exposed in some founding documents that indicate the key points of this necessary aspiration.

22

The Culture for Sustainable Urban Development Initiative (UNESCO 2015) seeks to demonstrate the link between the implementation of the UNESCO Culture Conventions and the achievement of the 2030 Agenda for Sustainable Development, an agenda to create a more peaceful, prosperous and equitable world (UNESCO 2016). Among the 2030 Agenda's 17 Sustainable Development Goals (SDGs), SDG 11 on sustainable cities and communities makes it clear that culture plays an essential role in realising sustainable urban development, particularly through strengthened efforts to protect and safeguard the world's cultural and natural heritage. This initiative brings together national and local governments, universities and research centres, NGOs, and civil society actors from across the globe to promote a culture-based approach. Goal 11 of Agenda 2030 for Sustainable Development (UN 2015) is aimed at better planning and management to make urban space more inclusive, safe, resilient and sustainable, with a particular reference to the right of persons with disabilities to social integration provided for by Article 15 of the Charter on Fundamental Rights of the European Union (UN 2006). In addition, a recent guide, the Culture and Local Development: Maximising the Impact (ICOM 2018), describes how museums and cultural heritage are powerful assets for local development. They can help attract tourists, bring revenues, regenerate local economies, promote inclusion, boost cultural diversity and reinvent territorial identity.

In this cultural effort the centrality of human being as the only possible actor, capable of establishing and substantiating valorisation as a bi-univocal relationship between person and cultural asset, is already present as the right of every person in the Faro Convention (CoE 2005) and strongly reiterated in the Zdrojewski's Report on structural and financial barriers in the access to culture (UE 2018) in which the rapporteur begins by stating: "This report is the first comprehensive report by the Committee on Culture and Education dealing directly with issues affecting access to culture. The rapporteur sees the problem of access to culture as the underlying issue for cultural policy from both a national and an EU perspective, and, most importantly, as the key issue from the citizens' perspective. Citing the fundamental importance of an active and accessible cultural sector for the development of an inclusive democratic society, the rapporteur stresses the need to foster and improve access to culture as one of the main priorities on the political agenda, and calls for cultural access and participation to be mainstreamed in other policy areas."

Under the theme "Heritage Across Borders", the 2018 Association of Critical Heritage Studies (ACHS) conference proposed a reasoning that has materialised in the concept of tangible and intangible heritage. Session 115 (Architectural Heritage Study, Preservation and Development from the Perspective of Cross-culture and Multi-discipline) made a specific reference: "a feasible and effective combination of humanities and social sciences (such as history, archaeology, cultural heritage, anthropology, sociology, folklore, arts), natural sciences (such as physics, chemistry) and engineering technologies (such as architecture, materials science) is predictable to have a significant role to play." Following this path, the example, through some good practices, of multidisciplinary approaches applied to the Italian architectural heritage, can be a useful contribution towards sharing solutions to common problems and obstacles.

The first remark refers to the *Castle* because it is a privileged custodian of memory and "spirit" in which a community, also understood as the guardian of cultural, urban and landscape identity, has been formed and has traversed the centuries. The *castellana* architecture represents and testifies, through its evolution, what happened to a particular place and to those who inhabited it. The castle is itself the physical narrative of a tangible patrimony and represents its intangible construct.

In this sense, the access to a castle does not mean merely approaching a historical place but involves drawing on an imaginary baggage that we possess since childhood. The idea of the castle evokes concepts related to inaccessibility, to the construct of archetypes and visions that refer to great battles, sieges, Machiavellian attacks, impossible and adventurous ventures, through impassable paths and walls. Reaching the castle presupposes the crossing of impervious lands and multiple adversities, after climbing on winding paths, overcoming armed guards and, finally, penetrating into a structure almost certainly, which will reserve other surprises. The artistic production has always undergone the fascination of these

24

landscapes that represent a kind of casket in which the great historical events that gave forms to the European culture were held, in which political events, military clashes were concentrated, and where lived great patrons and, as a result, great artists.

Our cultural education is permeated by these facts and we are unconsciously involved, since the first readings by dragons, princesses and knights. The major works of Western literature, where numerous semantic references overlap, are indelible testimony. The hypothetical setting of the Castle of Gradara, composing the verse 138 of the Hell of the *Divine Comedy*, uses the myth of the fortress of Camelot and the romance between Lancelot and Guinevere to narrate about Paul and Francesca: "Galeotto fu'l libro e chi lo scrisse." But the castle is also used as an immediate reference to certain romantic and popular concepts in various forms and artistic productions, both historical and contemporary. In historical and contemporary literature, the castle is the backdrop to romantic, popular, mysterious and dreamlike stories: Shakespeare sets between the bastions of the Royal Danish Castle of Elsinore, on a cold winter night, the vision of the sentinels Bernardo and Marcello and Hamlet's friend, Horatio, meet a person that looks like the deceased king. And again, a castle is the backdrop to what is considered to be the first Gothic novel, *The Castle of Otranto* by Horace Walpole (1963). Also film production uses in different forms the structure of the castle: in the famous British film of 1968 directed by Brian G. Hutton *Where Eagles Dare*, set during the Second World War, a commando of English paratroopers are instructed to liberate the American general Carnaby, captured by the Germans and held captive in a castle in the Bavarian Alps—it is interesting the method with which the protagonists succeed in entering the castle skillfully across the cableway—expressing once again the idea of how the castle is often the guardian of secret plots and hideout for the Mighty Wicked. The film references are countless and show the immediacy of the message: even Indiana Jones (*Indiana Jones and the Last Crusade*) must confront the Nazis perched in a castle to free his father held captive. Some castles represent so well the mysterious and romantic imaginary works to become the sites of many films: the castle in which the film *Ladyhawke* was set is the Rocca di Calascio in Abruzzo (Italy). Actually, since the 1980s the

Rocca has been used as the setting of various films. *Ladyhawke* was the first, followed by *The Name of the Rose* with Sean Connery based on the novel of the Italian author Umberto Eco, several films for the Italian television and *The American* with George Clooney. The reference is directed, citing the film adaptation of Bram Stoker's last great Gothic novel in 1897, *Dracula*, inspired by the figure of Vlad III Prince of Wallachia, the film of 1992, produced and directed by Francis Ford Coppola, animates the gloomy and mephitic atmospheres of the dark character that embodies the evil master of the castle par excellence.

The collective imagination, linked to these stories rich in emotions and imagination, art and poetry, restores to the castles the possibility to develop a revitalisation process thanks to the constant attractiveness they possess towards the cultural and tourist world. It is no coincidence that, very often, the castle protagonists of literary or cinematographic works, have been the object of valorisation, like the Castle of Elsinore (Helsingør) in Denmark, which hosts interactive exhibitions, theatrical performances and playful-cultural initiatives of great attraction, that in 2000 the monument has even become part of the UNESCO World Heritage.

The list of references to Castles is an inexhaustible source of quotations related to culture and tradition: from the Robin Hood of the fourteenth century English ballads to the masterpiece of John Ronald Reuel Tolkien, which tells of fortresses surrounded by countless walls, glittering cities perched and inaccessible and of invincible and gloomy towers (Tolkien 2004: 927).

The fascination process aroused by the castles also involves contemporary and perhaps unexpected forms and languages: the theme of the castle has inspired the production of a video game that has become "historical" or vintage as Super Mario, considered one of the most popular, long-lasting and best series of video games in history. Here the castles are extremely difficult to overcome and are the levels in which there are more lavas (fatal obstacles) as well as countless enemies, stunts and pitfalls. An interesting aspect of the video game is that "the attack on the castle" would seem to be the only way to cross these patterns. In fact, as in every video game, there are *shortcuts* that make the castle visitable without any trick or try to overcome: the castle becomes accessible. The idea of making these architectural complexes accessible can be interpreted as the creation of a *shortcut*, a combination of initiatives and programmatic choices that make it possible to transform the process of knowledge and the discovery of castles into an inclusive path that is part of the understanding of the "spirit" of the place. The analysis of the sustainability and the relative feasibility of the processes necessary for the realisation of a path accessible within a castle can be compared to the cognitive path necessary to the overcoming of a diagram of a video game: with one particularly complex scheme correspond to more attempts and reasonings, failures, patience and wit. In this perspective, the *shortcut* allows you to evade certain passages that may appear insurmountable and that prevent the player from continuing the adventure in this fantasy world or, in some cases, allow to discover hidden portions, new stories, unexplored places that narrate even better the history of that particular place and its spirit. "The Spirit of the Place—as we read in the International Council on Monuments and Sites (ICOMOS) Declaration—offers a more complete understanding of the living character and, at the same time, permanent monuments, of cultural sites and landscapes. It provides a richer, more dynamic and inclusive view of cultural heritage. The spirit of the place exists, in one form or another, practically in all the cultures of the world and is built by human beings in response to their social needs." Christian Norberg-Schulz, in a more specific sense of the relationship between man, built landscape and architecture of "things", states that the Genius loci of a place consists of the meanings gathered in it (Norberg-Schulz 2011). The castles and fortified structures in general are therefore proposed simultaneously as a huge management commitment and an opportunity for economic and social revival of a city or an entire territory. Some significant examples make it possible to understand how the contemporary era has the possibility, and the responsibility, of modifying the key of interpretation towards castles: accessibility and new destination of use are the bases of a correct process of re-appropriation of the place that, while assigning a new role, keeps alive and authentic its "spirit" (Federici 2017).

But how to do it in the right way? Academic studies and opportunities for in-depth study within universities are certainly privileged fields for sharing and deepening methodologies and their consequent sharing: the creation of an interdisciplinary and multicultural method is the first step in understanding what is the path to take.

27

The International Summer School (ISS) "Universal Design and Sustainable Tourism: Cidneo Hill and Its Castle in Brescia"

The ISS held at the University of Brescia, Italy, is the starting point to show how it is possible to theorise and experiment design solutions through international student cooperation. The International Summer School for Advanced Studies focused on the theme of accessibility to architectural heritage, the medieval fortress of the city, and its enhancement with an interdisciplinary and holistic approach in the perspective of Universal Design through application of the concept and practise of preservation and restoration. The elaboration of the different projects involved specialisations such as architecture, engineering, linguistics, sociology, communication and marketing. The Summer School refers to skills that at the University of Brescia, have been developed over the last 20 years and have seen the birth of the Brixia Accessibility Lab. The project is also connected to the new network Italian Accessibility Labs which involves, in addition to the University of Brescia, the Polytechnic University of Turin, the Ca'Foscari University of Venice, the University of Trieste, the University of Florence, the University of Naples Federico II and the Mediterranean University of Reggio Calabria. This synergy is related to an educational offer where the concept of accessibility read through architectural solutions and in a holistic form, as well as being an enhancement tool for people.

The aim is to go beyond the concept of accessibility as a physical value. Accessibility is also something tangible, made up of senses, perception and communication.

The experiment took place in Brescia: the history of the city as an organised urban centre begins with the occupation and then the Roman alliance in 27 BC. The role of the Cidneo Hill is fundamental since the first urban development according to the Castrum model (Treccani Degli Alfieri 1961). The castle, called *Falcone d'Italia* (Bertelli and Bertelli 1629) is one of the largest fortified complexes of the Italian peninsula (Villari 1986). The medieval fortress dominates the political and war events of the city until the end of the 800s when it lost its military function but remained the protagonist of bloody events until the end of the Second World War. Now the castle of Brescia is a place that for

28

too many years nobody had found a solution to the problem of visibility and usability by tourists and citizens themselves (Figure 1).

Figure 1   Brescia: Aerial view of the Cidneo Hill and the castle with the Arce in the
centre (photo taken from Berlucchi 2013: 82)

From this point of view, in an attempt to find a solution, after the 2017 edition (1st attack), this year the University of Brescia has proposed the 2nd attack on the castle.

ISS for advanced studies has focused, once again, on the issue of accessibility to cultural heritage and its empowerment (Treccani 2012). Inspired by the principles of sustainable development goals, workshops are conducted with a multidisciplinary approach under the perspective of Universal Design (Mace 1985). The universities and the skills involved came from all over the world: Norway, Russia, Mexico, Switzerland, Portugal, United States, Italy. After a first analysis regarding the relationship between the city and the Cidneo Hill (ISS 2017), the projects face three particular hotspots within the castle (Figure 2):

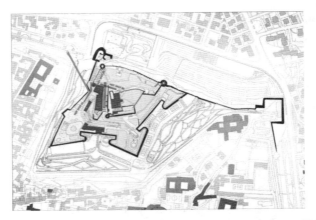

Figure 2   General plan of the castle. This image highlights the *Hotspots* on which the teams' projects are focused (designed by Mariachiara Bonetti)

- Hotspot 01: the design of a new *bistrot* in the Piazzale della Locomotiva (Fossa della Bissa). This space, built at the intersection of the optical cones overlooking the city, aims to create a contemporary construction, "ephemeral" and sculptural, whose design and construction are remanufactured every three to five years by architects who interpret the place as happens at the Serpentine Pavilion in London. The project proposed by the students, *culturAbility for all*, is inspired by the sculptures of Richard Serra producing an internal/external and mysterious effect that accompanies and guides the path. His perception from the entrance of the castle is that of a curvy plastic sculpture in corten; towards the city it offers two levels connected with a *stramp* that acts both as a staircase and as an accessible link with the bistro cover and, in the end, having generated new privileged points of view both on the city and on the castle.

- Hotspot 02: the "musealization" of the Piccolo and Grande Miglio. This project has a motto in his title, *MeeToo*, which recalls both the translation of *me to* as well as the acronym MEE which stands for "Musealization Enhances Experiences". The leitmotif of the project is the experiential aspect (made with a tactile technique

30

to be read with the hands), which, leaving the building unchanged, proposes the creation of an environment that reproduces, through a path accessible to all, the caves and prisons in the bowels of Cidneo reachable only with the guide of the Speleological Association of Brescia. The other two floors of the Grande Miglio include the installation of an interactive museum of urban-architectural development of the city and the castle, which is then reflected outside through the panorama of the city itself. In the Piccolo Miglio are housed the museum services of the complex and, on the upper floors, spaces for temporary exhibitions.

- Hotspot 03: the design of a new connection among the levels of Piccolo Miglio, Fossa Viscontea, Fossa dei Martiri and the drawbridge (Figure 3).

Figure 3 This image shows the Fossa Viscontea and the inaccessibility of this portion of the castle. The project must connect four different levels in a very compressed space (photo by Rapuzzi)

The connection between four levels that make accessibility within the Castle difficult has been the theme addressed by the third team, through a structure with a strong aesthetic impact justified by flexibility in use. A "Siege Tower", a stage machine composed of a thin and modular framed structure in which there is a lift that connects the levels of the Piccolo Miglio, the Fossa Viscontea, the viewpoint on the Fossa dei Martiri and the drawbridge. In the meshes it is possible to compose and decompose through prefabricated cubes (wooden boxes that recall the materials of the mobile towers in a contemporary reinterpretation of the Shakespearean Globe Theater) different scenographies depending on the use that make the backdrop of the Fossa Viscontea always different: from a transparent scenic backdrop, when there are no performances, to a completely blind scene, when used as a screen and all possible intermediate combinations (Figure 4).

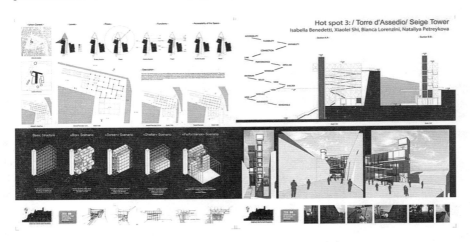

Figure 4   Hotspot 03: the design of a new connection among the levels of Piccolo Miglio, Fossa Viscontea, Fossa dei Martiri and the drawbridge (Summer School 2018: project designed by I. Benedetti, B. Lorenzini, N. Petreykova and X. Shi)

All these projects have been developed according to the concept of accessibility, in a holistic way, referring to the principles of Universal Design. The aim of these studies is to share the results of the research through international cooperation in search of a specific and declinable method in relation to the instances of each individual place. These concepts can become a collective resource that can elevate the social capital of a community, and expand individual freedoms, social opportunities and knowledges; moreover, they can also encourage each person to participate in community life and contribute to the growth of the society (Arenghi, Garofolo and Sørmoen 2016).

"Segni di Luce" (Signs of Light). Exhibition at Palazzo Pitti. Cemmo, Capo di Ponte (Brescia-Italy)[2]

This example deals with the practical realisation of accessible museum solutions, in the holistic sense of the term, within a historical structure, listed by the Archeology, Fine Arts and Landscape Superintendency and therefore what are the possible solutions makes a contemporary and multisensory musealisation completely usable without affecting architectural heritage.

Casa Zitti is located in Cemmo, Capo di Ponte (the first UNESCO site of Italy) and is a classic example of the *signorile* architecture of Val Camonica between the 14th and 15th centuries (Bonfadini and Marazzani 2004). This building, which has become a convent and then a school, looks like a typical enclosed architecture, inaccessible from the outside and very austere. The position, in times past, required a complex path to reach this place: in fact, this site can be compared to a castle that dominates the Val Camonica, the valley below (Figure 5).

Figure 5   Palazzo Pitti. Cemmo, Capo di Ponte (Fondazione Annunciata Cocchetti 2019)

The exterior appearance is rustic, with white walls and portals of varying workmanship (round or pointed arches, rough or well-worked stones) and made in various periods. To describe the palace, we can resume what Lucio Serino (the architect who worked on the restoration of the palace in 2010) says in the description of the valley architecture of the time: "Valleys around a cobblestone courtyard, which is the centre of the composition of the buildings, accessible from the entrance hall with the portal. The factory bodies, whose ground floors are reserved for service rooms and porches, are frequently on three sides. The wooden staircase is placed externally and acts as access to the loggia of the upper floor which is the distributive element of all the neighbouring compartments, otherwise among them passersby. It is to this plan that are the representation rooms also used for the family life: the largest environment is generally the most decorated both on the walls and the ceilings." (Serino 2004) The installation is placed in a stable way in the evocative setting of the "work" of the convent overlooking the Brolo (Fondazione Cocchetti 2012).

The philosophical author Mario Neva introduces to the exhibition with these words: "The set-up is placed in a stable position in the evocative setting of the *work* of the convent in front of the orchard. The proposal is of great emotional and spiritual impact: the encounter between history, the vitality of a congregation that has gone through the century of life, expressive and modern technology, based on the convergent game of light, sound, image and word. The exhibition is perfectly and deliberately inserted in the natural environment, which dominates the four elements of the Greek tradition stated by Empedocles, earth, water, air and fire. The tones are deliberately suggestive, evocative and not educational, and the intention is to propose an incentive high, a young, open to new generations, with a sort of dazzling immediatism."

Signs of Light is an exhibition with a stated objective: to draw attention to a practical and strong spirituality very rooted in its territory, using those languages that distinguish a simple, interactive and participatory communication, fascinating in the widest sense of the word. The project has set as its goal the creation of a path, a walk through the places, the life, the history of a prolific legacy which, over time, has sent a message to evolve and communicate through new ways, touching new territories, maintaining the primordial idea but knowing translate charism in a language appropriate to the historical moment and to new instances of the contemporary world, communicating through the principles of Universal Design (Lang 2001).

The exhibition is then defined as an "evocative journey" through the various levels of communication and, above all, designed to be able to accompany the person through a process of comprehension and a consequent deepening. The main node of the exhibition develops inside the built spaces: the architectural peculiarity of the building lends itself to an internal path, a discovery of the places, of the daily life, of the glances and of the glimpses that is possible to inhabite these sites and live beside who interprets a concrete spiritual inheritance (Figure 6).

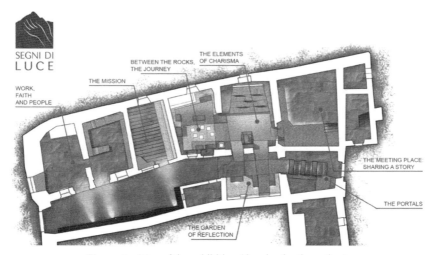

Figure 6 Map of the exhibition (drawing by the author)

The "evocative journey" is identified by a walkway characterised by generating a landscape that refers directly to paths in the surrounding landscape—climbs, jumps, the glimpses that climb on the slopes—thanks to a process of abstraction and the use of raw materials and reflected lights. The project proposes new constructive references through alienation, the loss of the architectural present: rough boards of the platform/trail are detached from the floor. The path crosses the various environments keeping visible the historical and architectural reality and, at the same time, allowing an in-depth understanding of the theme that varies according to the spaces you are visiting.

The path runs along a main axis creating a double filtering space to let the visitor estrange from the surrounding architectural environment and abstract the physical approach immersing themselves in the environments and themes proposed. The disposition and the fruition of the themes provide a consequentiality of concepts that enables a harmonious location with the context in which the exhibition is inserted. This ensures, according to the access envisaged, a continuity of meanings and experiences: the spaces physically close to the chapel thus assume an abstract, profound, meditative, metaphorical language. The spaces close to the garden, the place of work, the *incipit* of the path that allows a projection to the outside and to assume a participatory and empirical character, with the possibility to experiment in first person through workshops organised *ad hoc*.

The walkways, the volumes, and the ramps are made from raw materials, planks in wooden sheets. This poor material, with a typical warm and enveloping colour, masks hidden light sources, and conceptually reproposes the stones, the paths, the mule tracks, and translucent walls that turn into lamps, all to produce a continuum that makes the route you are currently taking recognisable (Figure 7).

The practical implication of this choice is to have created a guide accompanying the visitor and showing which is the direction to take, the contents of the exhibition, the activities to be performed, the places to stop. The communicative level becomes multisensorial so as to be much more inclusive (Baracco 2016). "Improving the usability conditions for all is one of the basic concepts underlying the enhancement of cultural heritage. Usability must be declined both in terms of physical accessibility and sensory-perceptive of the places of cultural interest, both as accessibility of contents of which they are witnesses. [...] The content (information and communication) to be transmitted may not be the same for a child or for an expert in the field; just like the means of communication

Figure 7 The image shows the structures that protect the pre-existing materials and that can house the electrical system for lighting and the touch screens. These elements constitute the paths and the creation of ramps solves the differences in height (photo by the author)

with the blind and deaf should be different. Universal design must be declined by seeking maximum flexibility in order to adapt the solutions to the greatest number of possible needs such that they can be customised for user profiles." (Arenghi and Agostiano 2017)

The entrance environments produce a filter that creates a physical and temporal pause compared with what was accomplished before reaching the exhibition. From here the showpiece is composed of a spatial sequence that is identified in specific themes that possess a strong communicative connotation:

- The Portals. During the journey a sequence of sentences takes a three-dimensional form. This installation assumes a particular meaning as it communicates a series of concepts and information that are "fixed" in the person who makes its entrance to the exhibition, embarking on the path that turns from evocative to spiritual.

However, the portals create a new and concentrated environment, allowing the enjoyment of the historical space in its entirety and unveiling new glimpses for observation.

- The Garden of Reflection. This space with dim lights indicates the path to be undertaken and allows, at the same time, the resting, the reflection. The seats and the walkways accompany the view towards infinity, thanks to the use of two inclined reflecting surfaces that multiply the vanishing perspective and anticipate the unfolding of the new spaces, reflecting lights and colours in an imperfect way and not fully declared, as yet enveloped in the morning haze.

- The Elements of Charisma. The passage from the Garden of Reflection to this new room foresees a rise of altitude, an ascent: it is a sensory approach not well identifiable along a ramp with a very slight inclination, but that allows to understand the beginning and the obtaining of something else. In this room the process of abstraction is at a maximum level. The architectural solutions accompanied by the continuous pouring of the water guide the visitor towards this complex and simple reality: the reality of the presence of a charism, narrated through the four elements, earth, air, water and fire. A "perspective box" in front of which some transparent diaphragms refer to these meanings and, at the same time, to the sensations of the places so characteristic around Cemmo: the Conca Rena (backlit), the woods, the dirt streets, the clouds, the sky and the inspiration that these places have instilled in M. A. Cocchetti and its presence at the same time. It is the incipit of the spiritual path, the first significant step towards a new understanding. The perspective box breaks down the architectural boundary and projects the view into a much broader space (Figure 8).

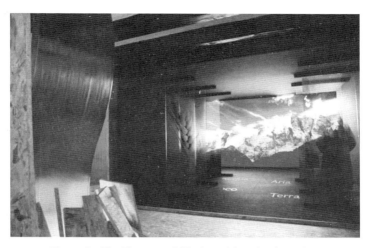

Figure 8   The Elements of Charisma (photo by the author)

- The Meeting Place: Sharing a Story. The strong architectural connotation of this room creates a very welcoming and multifunctional environment where visitors, looking the vision of a video clip, expressive synthesis of the whole exhibition, are transported to the discovery. We are not dealing with a didactic narrative, but with an emotional representation that stimulates the spectator. A few words, associated with images and enthralling music (Galuppi 2011), are enough to tell a complex story. Outside the projection, in the room, the wooden tables are transformed from a catwalk to a comfortable seat for sharing, meeting, and quiet enjoyment. This *escamotage* masks and solves the inaccessible elevation jump: it's a trick, a real *shortcut*. The truth is that these rooms were piggeries where they also stored meat and cheese, and therefore the floor level was very low in order to take advantage of the humidity and the temperature of the basement walls. The sobriety of the environment, deliberately kept naked, allows the spectator a total immersion in the landscapes, in the sky, in the streets that have been travelled to reach places and people (Figure 9).

Figure 9   The Meeting Place: Sharing a Story. The path becomes an object to sit on and
see the videos, meet and access a room that could not accommodate
people on wheelchairs (photo by the author)

- Between the Rocks, the Journey. From the hall dedicated to the *Charism*, a ramp
connects you to earn even more as the degree of deepening is greater, the level
of understanding increases. Accessibility is total: in this final room all the senses
are involved. Water and wind can be heard and touched or perceived through the
skin, the scent of wood, the sound of walking on wooden planks, rough surfaces,
alternating hot to cold and smooth stones and the lights that guide the way.
Advancing through historical, backlit, walkable photographs, here you can see the
screens that enable the use of images, characters, events, places that have made
the story of M. A. Cocchetti and the Sisters of Santa Dorotea di Cemmo. Here, the
touch-screen interface enables you to enter historical reality, to understand today
and to turn your gaze to future projects. Along the sides, the walkway bends create
a real orography and support some comfortable seats in the same material, as if
they were rocks on which to rest during the walk. The diffused lighting makes the
platform floating and permits images on the screens to emerge and thus attract
attention at first glance (Figure 10).

Figure 10   From the space of "the Elements of Charisma" to "Between the Rocks, the Journey":
the light and the images guide the visitors, also involving the hearing and the touch
through the pouring of water and breath of wind (photo by the author)

The view then goes out to the courtyard.

- The Mission. This place looks bare: the use of materials refers to the hull of a ship. The wooden planks, belonging to the historic building, are presented as crude boards on which the visitor can enjoy the vision of a video dedicated to the missionary.

- Work, Faith and People. These two chambers are presented simultaneously because the times are inseparable: the exposition of the ancient objects used for the work and the possibility of using them to work thanks to the creation of workshops dedicated to the traditional production of this place. The strong connotation of the working environments and the richness of the conserved objects allows unitarian and interconnected fruition. Room 06 is characterised by a long display element realised in the same material as the footboards and with the same orographical concept: multiple plans that make it possible to display objects with very different dimensions and to enable anyone to see and touch (excluding the oldest pieces), to understand the materials, use, and weight. The last room has a domestic setting, a snapshot of the time when these objects were used daily and the room is aimed at people because it allows to carry out some laboratory projects and fully understand the use of certain tools.

The journey then continues towards the garden of S. Maria where it is possible to carry out the activities of sharing, play, laboratory and work in spring and summer months. The garden represents a reality and a very important experience for the "evocative path"; there the contact with nature and the impact on the landscape are fundamental elements for understanding the history of this place from an inclusive point of view.

Exhibition spaces as well as the Garden have a very strong connotation, such as to inspire a profound reflection on different levels: some concepts are clearly proposed in order to deepen the themes, other inputs regarding involvement and an evocative and sensory perception not always declared but that constantly accompanies those who approach this content. The communication plans are the key to ensuring the involvement of different ages and cater to different ways of life exhibition and to different cultures. The concept of inclusive museum display must be communicated and transmitted without hindrance and language barriers because of its universality and simplicity (Mordi 2015).

Conclusions

The accessibility to cultural heritage today represents the possibility of contributing personally and directly to the growth of society in terms of enrichment and inclusion. It is now a shared concept that "physical access in itself does not mean a lot if one does not have access to the message, the values, or the meaning thereof. Heritage is very much the access to the values, since the reason for designating heritage is so much about preserving the values that are defined in the object or site. With values, I include the message, the story, the core of the heritage site or object. The challenge is how to get access to these values, without destroying the message they are embedded in" (Sørmoen 2016: 43).

With reference to the re-use, to the valorisation, of inheritance linked to certain places and to the shaping of their cultures and traditions, the examples shown reveal how this is sought in the *spirit of the place*. These sites, in fact, tell the story, the urban evolution and the meaning of the territories or cities, arriving today through a journey that needs to be reinterpreted to understand what decisions to make in order to create a sustainable future.

The reflection must also deal with the difficult balance between preservation and enhancement of cultural heritage, trying to find a correct language that can lead to the creation of a shareable method. In this context, and with these premises, the reflection on the concept of accessibility should not exclusively refer to regulatory aspects or regulations that indicate certain prohibitions or which wish to respect certain warnings: inclusion and accessibility to cultural heritage must be interpreted as an access to life.

Notes

1. EYCH 2018. Commission proposes 2018 as the European Year of Cultural Heritage, stating some fundamental concepts: "From archaeological sites to architecture, from medieval castles to folklore traditions and arts, Europe's cultural heritage is at the very heart of the collective memory and identity of European citizens." (European Commission 2016)

2. Segni di Luce—Signs of Light, dedicated to Beata Annunciata Cocchetti (2012). [Exhibition]. Istituto Suore di Santa Dorotea di Cemmo, Palazzo Zitti, XIV-XV sec Cemmo, Capo di Ponte (Brescia-Italy). Curator and designer: Architect Mariachiara Bonetti. Graphics: Akomi, Angelo Maragna.

◻ Disclosure Statement

No potential conflict of interest was reported by the author.

◻ Note on Contributor

Mariachiara Bonetti is an expert in accessibility, Design for All, Capability Approach and sustainable architecture in Italy, Africa and China. Since 2018 she is a researcher at the University of Brescia (Italy) for accessibility to cultural heritage and since 2019 at the RUCU (Iringa, Tanzania, Africa). Since 2019 she is an Adjunct Professor of Interior and Urban Design at SantaGiulia Academy of Fine Arts of Brescia. She was also an Adjunct Professor in the course of Architecture at Politecnico di Milano (2011–2017), since 2017 she participates in international workshops for architecture and museographic innovation and conferences at the UAUIM (Bucharest, Romania) and at the University of Brescia as Lecturer, Visiting Professor and member of Scientific Committees. In 2017 she was invited to the Zhejiang University Museum of Art and Archaeology (Hangzhou, China) to develop the subject of accessibility and participates as a jury member at Piranesi Prix de Rome 2017 (Villa Adriana, Rome, Italy). Since 2011 she realises exhibitions and accessible installations within the Lombard historical heritage and for the UNESCO sites (Brescia, Italy). Since 2010 she realises accessible and inclusive structures, built with local technologies, in Benin, Tanzania and Cameroon.

□ References

Arenghi, Alberto, Ilaria Garofolo, and Oddbjørn Sørmoen. 2016. *Accessibility as a Key Enabling Knowledge for Enhancement of Cultural Heritage*. Milano: Franco Angeli.

Arenghi, Alberto, and Maria Agostiano. 2017. Cultural Heritage and Disability: Can ICT Be the "Missing Piece" to Face Cultural Heritage Accessibility Problems? In *Smart Objects and Technologies for Social Good*, edited by Ombretta Gaggi, Pietro Manzoni, Claudio Palazzi, Armir Bujari, and Johann M. Marquez-Barja, 70-77. GOODTECHS 2016. Cham: Springer.

Arenghi, Alberto, and Mariachaira Bonetti. 2018. Attacco Al Castello: Accessibilità Alle Strutture Fortificate. Il Caso Del Colle Cidneo E Il Castello Di Brescia. *Archistor* 10: 162-207.

Baracco, Lucia. 2016. *Barriere Percettive e Progettazione Inclusiva*. Trento: Centro Studi Erickson.

Berlucchi, Nicola (ed.). 2013. *Una fortezza per la città. La valorizzazione del colle Cidneo e del suo Castello*. Brescia: Grafo.

Bertelli, Pietro, and Francesco Bertelli. 1629. *Theatro delle città d'Italia (di P. Bertelli), con nova aggiunta (di F. Bertelli)*. Padova: F. Bertelli.

Bonfadini, Paola, and Sara Marazzani. 2004. *Echi del Rinascimento in Valle Camonica*. Milano: ITL.

CoE (Council of Europe). 2005. Council of Europe Framework Convention on the Value of Cultural Heritage for Society. Accessed May 15, 2019. https://www.coe.int/en/web/ conventions/full-list/-/conventions/rms/0900001680083746.

European Commission. 2016. Commission Proposes 2018 as the European Year of Cultural Heritage. Accessed May 15, 2019. http://europa.eu/rapid/press-release_IP-16-2905_ en.htm.

Federici, Fabrizio. 2017. Spunti per un'autentica valorizzazione. December 23, 2017. Accessed May 15, 2019. https://www.artribune.com/arti-visive/2017/12/valorizzazione-cultura/.

Fondazione Annunciata Cocchetti. 2012. *Nata dal Niente. Studi su casa Madre*. Milano: ITL spa.

Fondazione Annunciata Cocchetti. 2019. Palazzo Zitti. Cemmo, Capo di Ponte. Accessed May 17, 2019. http://www.fondazionecocchetti.bs.it/gallery.php.

Galuppi, Baldassarre. 2011. Sacred Music. [CD] Milano: Sony Music Entertainment Italy s.p.a. Giulio Prandi (Orchestre, Chef d'orchestre), Ghislieri Choir & Consort (Interprète).

ICOM (International Council of Museums). 2018. Culture and Local Development: Maximising the Impact. Guide for Local Governments, Communities and Museum. Accessed May 15, 2019. https://icom.museum/wp-content/uploads/2018/12/OECD-ICOM-GUIDE-MUSEUMS-AND-CITIES.pdf.

ICOMS (International Council on Monuments and Sites). 2008. Québec City Declaration on the Preservation of the Spirit of Place. Accessed May 15, 2019. https://whc.unesco.org/uploads/activities/documents/activity-646-2.pdf.

Lang, Caroline. 2001. *The Disability Directory for Museums & Galleries*. London: The Council for Museums, Archives and Libraries. Accessed May 15, 2019. https://www.accessibletourism.org/resources/uk_museumsand-galleries_disability_directory_pdf_6877.pdf.

Mace, Ron. 1985. *Universal Design, Barrier Free Environments for Everyone*. Los Angeles: Designers West.

Mordi, Loretta. 2015. Why Museums Need to Embrace a Culture of Accessibility. September 9, 2015. Accessed May 15, 2019. https://rereeti.wordpress.com/2015/09/09/why-museums-need-to-embrace-a-culture-of-accessibility/.

Norberg-Schulz, Christian. 2011. *Genius loci*. Milano: Mondadori Electa.

Serino, Lucio. 2004. Un'architettura vernacolare del Rinascimento. In *Echi del rinascimento in Valle Camonica: studi su Casa Zitti a Cemmo di Capo di Ponte*, 60-87. Milano: Fondazione Annunciata Cocchetti.

Sørmoen, Oddbjørn. 2016. Access to the Message. An Aceessibility Rethink. In *Accessibility as a Key Enabling Knowledge for Enhancement of Cultural Heritage*, edited by Alberto

Arenghi, Ilaria Garofolo, and Oddbjørn Sørmoen, 43-58. Milano: Franco Angeli.

Tolkien, John Ronald Reuel. 2004. *Il Signore Degli Anelli*. Milano: Bompiani.

Treccani, Gian Paolo. 2012. Il Colle Restaurato. In *Castello di Brescia. Il Falcone d'Italia*, 80-83. Roccafranca, Brescia: La Compagnia della Stampa.

Treccani Degli Alfieri, Giovanni. 1961. *Storia di Brescia*, Vol. 5. Brescia: Morcelliana Ed.

UE (United Europe). 2018. Report on structural and financial barriers in the access to culture. Accessed May 22, 2019. http://www.europarl.europa.eu/doceo/document/A-8-2018-0169_EN.html?redirect.

UN (United Nations). 2006. United Nations Convention on the Rights of Persons with Disabilities. December 6, 2006. Accessed May 22, 2019. http://www.un.org/disabilities/documents/convention/convention_accessible_pdf.pdf.

UN (United Nations). 2015. Agenda 2030 for Sustainable Development, Goal 11. Accessed May 15, 2019. https://sustainabledevelopment.un.org/post2015/transformingourworld/publication.

UNESCO (United Nations Educational, Scientific and Cultural Organization). 2016. Culture: Urban Future. Global Report on Culture for Sustainable Urban Development. Accessed May 22, 2019. https://unesdoc.unesco.org/ark:/48223/pf0000245999.

Villari, Giusi. 1986. *La fortezza veneta a Brescia*. Brescia: CAB.

Walpole, Horace, Ann Ward Radcliffe, and Jane Austen. 1963. *The Castel of Otranto*. New York: Holt, Rinehart and Winston, Inc.

Agroecological Heritage: Elucidating the Place of Cycads in Indigenous Mesoamerican Epistemologies

Joshua D. Englehardt[1], Angélica Cibrián Jaramillo[2],
Michael D. Carrasco[3]

1. Centro de Estudios Arqueológicos, El Colegio de Michoacán, A.C., Cerro de Nahuatzen 85, La Piedad, Michoacán, México, 59379. CONTACT Joshua D. Englehardt: jenglehardt@ colmich.edu.mx

2. Laboratorio Nacional de Genómica para la Biodiversidad, Centro de Investigaciones y Estudios Avanzados del Instituto Politécnico Nacional, Libramiento Norte, Carretera León, Km 9.6, Irapuato, Guanajuato, México, 36821

3. Department of Art History, Florida State University, 1019 William Johnston Building, 143 Honors Way, Tallahassee, FL, USA, 32306 ~

Abstract: Cycads (*Cycadales*) are an ancient order of gymnosperms, one family of which is endemic to Mexico. Historically, although never domesticated, in ancient Mesoamerica and modern Mexico they have played a significant role in regional agroecology, as well as indigenous foodways, cultural practices, and beliefs. As a botanical resource that occurs in tropical and subtropical regions, cycads in Mesoamerica are used in a variety of ways and figure prominently in regional cultural traditions, in which they often possess a close relationship with maize. This contribution speaks to this underappreciated, now often critically endangered plant. A critical heritage perspective that considers the rhizomatic networks and indigenous epistemologies within which these plants are imbricated allows for the fuller consideration of a series of key issues that span multiple disciplines, including archaeology, ethnography, human geography, and art history. Preliminary results of an on-going interdisciplinary research project are shared with the aim to stimulate further discussion on the significance of cycads in Mesoamerican beliefs, foodways, and ecology. We suggest that a closer examination of cycad-human relationships has the potential to motivate conservation of these endangered plants in ways that engage in local communities and work to highlight the environmental and cultural role of cycads, as well as the significance of ancient and modern cultural practices that incorporate this natural-cultural hybrid.

Keywords: cycads, agroecology, ethnoecology, biocultural heritage, Mesoamerican epistemologies

Introduction

In this article, we explore the role of cycads in ancient Mesoamerican and modern Mexican agroecological systems and indigenous epistemologies from an interdisciplinary perspective, focusing particularly on the conceptual relationships between cycads and maize. Cycads (*Cycadales*) are an ancient order of gymnosperms, one family (*Zamiaceae*) of which is endemic to Mexico. Throughout their range in the Americas, these plants are threatened or critically endangered, and are currently protected under the Convention on International Trade in Endangered Species.[1] Historically, although never domesticated, in ancient Mesoamerica and modern Mexico they have played, and continue to play, a significant though often underappreciated role in regional agroecology, as well as indigenous foodways, cultural practices, and beliefs, just as they did in the Caribbean, Africa, Australia, and Asia (Beck 1992; Bonta and Bamigboye 2018; Bradley 2005; Hayward and Kuwahara 2012; Khuraijam and Singh 2012; Kira and Miyoshi 2000;

Mickleburgh and Pagán-Jiménez 2012; Pagán-Jiménez et al. 2015; Patiño 1989; Radha and Singh 2008; Smith 1982; Thieret 1958; Veloz Maggiolo 1992). The lack of scholarly focus on those in Mesoamerica appears to stem from their toxicity, which, while requiring similar processing to that of manioc (*Manihot esculenta* Crantz; Cox and Sacks 2002; Whiting 1963, 1989), seemingly diverted attention away from cycads, despite considerable evidence indicating their utilitarian and symbolic use from the Pleistocene–Holocene transition to the present (Bonta et al. 2019). As a botanical resource that occurs in diverse ecosystems, cycads are used in a variety of ways (Alcorn 1984; Bonta 2010a; Bonta et al. 2019; Pérez-Farrera and Vovides 2006; Sifuentes de Ortiz 1983; Tristán 2012; Valdez 2009; Vite Reyes et al. 2010) and figure prominently in regional mythologies and foodways in which they often possess a close relationship with maize (Bonta 2010b; Carrasco 2012, 2015; Diego-Vargas 2017).

This contribution speaks to this underappreciated and critically endangered plant. A heritage perspective that considers the place of cycads within indigenous epistemologies allows for the fuller consideration of a series of key issues that span multiple disciplines, including archaeology, ethnography, human geography, and art history. These issues include their cultural significance as evidenced in the archaeological and art historical records and the culinary and symbolic uses of cycads among indigenous populations. This chapter examines these issues by exploring the role of cycads in Mesoamerican agroecological systems, particularly their enduring relationship to maize, through a range of data, from genomic, archaeological, linguistic, art historical, to contemporary ethnographic and human geographical evidence. Preliminary results of an on-going interdisciplinary research project are shared with the aim to present new data and stimulate further discussion on the significance of cycads in Mesoamerican beliefs, foodways, and ecology. We suggest that a closer examination of cycad-human relationships has the potential to motivate conservation of these endangered plants in ways that engage in local communities and work to highlight the environmental and cultural role of cycads (see Ruiz-Mallén et al. 2015; Vovides 1989; Vovides and Iglesias 1994; Vovides et al. 2010), as well as the significance of ancient and modern cultural practices that incorporate this natural-cultural hybrid (see Descola 2013).

Cycads: A Very Brief Introduction

Cycads belong to an ancient order of gymnosperms related to conifers, araucaria, and ginkgos (Figure 1). There are approximately 300 species of cycads in the world,[2] native to tropical and subtropical regions throughout the world, but sadly many are critically threatened or endangered (see Donaldson 2003). Cycads are dioecious, meaning that there are both male and female plants. They reproduce through cones, or strobili, which bear either seeds or pollen. Their coralloid roots form facultative symbioses with cyanobacteria to fix nitrogen in the soil. Cycads are extremely resistant plants, thriving in a variety of ecosystems (Chamberlain 1919; McVaugh 1992; Norstog and Nicholls 1997; Whitelock 2002). Throughout their range, cycads have served a variety of cultural uses, ranging from food, to poison, and to important symbolic roles.

a.   b.   c.   d.

Figure 1   Three species of Mexican cycads, illustrating distinctive leaves and female strobili: a. and b. *Ceratozamia fuscoviridis*, Hidalgo; c. *Dioon edule*, Veracruz; d. *Zamia furfuracea*, Veracruz (a. and b. photos by Michael Calonje; c. photo by Chip Jones; d. photo by Angélica Cibrián; all used under CC BY-NC-SA 4.0 license)

Cycads in Mexico

In Mexico, three genera and 73 species of cycads have been documented (Calonje et al. 2019; Gutiérrez-Ortega et al. 2018; Nicolalde-Morejón et al. 2013; Vázquez Torres 1990). In fact, Mexico is second in the world in terms of cycad biodiversity. Cycads have played— and continue to play—a vital role in the region, in indigenous agroecology, foodways, beliefs, and diverse cultural practices. Despite their ample distribution within Mexico, as well as considerable evidence that suggests the utilitarian and symbolic use of this botanical resource since at least the Pleistocene-Holocene transition through the present, there has been precious little scholarly attention devoted to cycads in the region.

The Place of Cycads in Ancient Mesoamerica and Modern Mexico: An Interdisciplinary Approach

To combat this situation, the authors have undertaken a multi-disciplinary research project that seeks to elucidate the finely reticulated networks within which these plants are enmeshed from a critical heritage perspective. We have focused particularly on the relationships between cycads, humans, and maize in both past and present, as well as their place within regional mythologies and foodways, considering five primary lines of evidence: ethnographic, archaeological, linguistic, ideological, and genomic. Below, we summarise previous work and briefly detail some of the preliminary results of this research.

Ethnography

Ethnographic research has revealed many uses of cycads in the present, from ornamental (as houseplants or in landscaping) to ritual-religious (for example, cycads are often used to decorate altars during religious festivities). Further uses include as a pesticide, as medicine and an entheogen in some communities, and even as a poison (derived from the cyanobacteria in cycad roots) (Bonta 2010a; Bonta et al. 2019; Sifuentes de Ortiz 1983; Tristán 2012; Valdez 2009; Vite Reyes 2012; Vite Reyes et al. 2010).

Cycads in Mexico are also used as a foodstuff (see Bonta et al. 2019: Figure 8;

Carbajal-Esquivel et al. 2012), as they are in other areas of the world (Beck 1992; Bradley 2005; Hayward and Kuwahara 2012; Khuraijam and Singh 2012). They are consumed as basic subsistence food or starchy staple, as famine food, and as ritual food. Their seeds are ground to produce flour, from which a variety of preparations arise, including tortillas and tamales (Figure 2; see also Bonta et al. 2019: Figures 10, 11). The processing of cycad seeds involves nixtamalization with ash or lime to remove toxins derived from cycad roots. This is similar to the preparation of maize, as well as manioc, another important and already ancient starchy resource (Brown et al. 2013; Isendahl 2011) consumed in large quantities that, like cycads, requires either boiling or multiple leachings to render it edible. Given cycads' antiquity, the use of nixtamalization in its processing, as well as the presence of preparations "traditionally" associated with maize, it appears possible that key components of the maize complex were developed prior to the domestication of that plant, originally for the processing and consumption of cycads (see Bonta et al. 2019).

Figure 2   Preparation of cycads for consumption in San Luis Potosí, Mexico
(photos by Angélica Cibrián and Francisco Barona-Gómez)

Ethnographic evidence also reflects the symbolic and ritual-religious use of cycads. In many communities, cycad leaves are incorporated in ceremonial decorations, often combined with maize cobs and leaves (see Bonta et al. 2019: Figures 19, 25, 26, 30, 35). Cycad cones and leaves also figure prominently in the decoration of church facades in some regions (Bonta et al. 2019: Figures 2, 7). Pérez-Farrera and Vovides (2006; Valdez 2009) have documented a ritual pilgrimage in the community of Suchiapa, Chiapas. Villagers make a 140 km ritual procession, replete with ceremonial rites and music along the route, to harvest the leaves of *Dioon merolae* on the slopes of Mt. Nambiyugua. On their return, the leaves are used to decorate altars and churches during the festival of the Holy Cross. Finally, residents of some communities in the northern sierra of Hidalgo venerate the Aztec deity Chicomexóchitl (see Bonta et al. 2019; Diego-Vargas 2017; Vite Reyes 2012). Although most often associated with flowers and maize, some representations of her appear to reference cycads, and ethnographic data bear out this convergent association. Ethnographic evidence thus exposes multiple parallels and overlaps between cycads and maize, as well as similar patterns of human use, interaction with, and conceptualisation of these plants. The syncretism evidenced by these associations suggests that cycads played a significant role in pre-Hispanic ideological systems.

Archaeological Data

Archaeological evidence supports such temporal depth, indicating that cycads have been used persistently in Mesoamerica for at least the last 7500 years. Richard MacNeish's (1954a, 1954b, 1958) excavations of dry cave sites and rock shelters in the Tehuacán valley and Sierra Madre de Tamaulipas revealed a rich inventory of wild, managed, and cultivated foods, which by volume greatly surpassed the domesticated crops, such as corns, beans, and squash central to later Mesoamerican foodways (Table 1; see also Hanselka 2011, 2017; Kelley 1954; Smith 2005; Smith 1967).

Although the archaeological data are limited, in this case it demonstrates the alimentary importance of cycads as early as 6000 BP. It is clear that at these cave sites, cycad seeds played a significant dietary role and were the dominant plant remains, particularly in the earliest occupational phases. The critical point is that by the Archaic Era (to 4000 BP), at a time before or synchronous with the development of modern maize (Matsuoka et al. 2002; Rosenswig et al. 2015; Terrell et al. 2003), cycads were consumed in quantities surpassing or similar to other plant resources, such as maguey and various palms, forming a major component of Mesoamerican dietary strategies in these regions. Moreover, as data from more recent occupational phases demonstrate, cycads continued to be exploited in significant quantities even after the domestication of maize.

Table 1   Key elements in the diet of the hunter-gatherers in the Sierra de Tamaulipas cave sites, showing significance of cycads in early subsistence strategies (data from MacNeish 1958)

Phase	Radiocarbon dates	% of total volume of wild plants en diet	Total of all food/L	Dioon/L and % of total food	Domest. Plants/L	Maize/L and % of total food
La Perra	4500 BP–4000 BP	76%	19.77	8.10 (41%)	1.84	0.85 (4%)
Laguna	2000 BP	51%	23.72	3.09 (13%)	9.28	5.91 (28%)
Los Angeles	500 BP–200 BP	42%	15.57	3.44 (22%)	6.17	5.42 (35%)

Linguistics and Ideology

A convergent association between cycads and maize is supported by a variety of linguistic evidence from indigenous languages throughout Mexico (Bonta and Osborne 2007). Although cycads are known by many vernacular names according to ethnic regions, it is striking that many indigenous terms for cycads reveal a conceptual linkage with maize (Table 2)—a relationship often conceived in terms of kinship (see also Bonta et al. 2019: Table S1).

It is also striking that in many regions the Nahuatl term "teosinte" is used to refer to cycad species, and not to *Zea mays parviglumis*, the wild grass ancestral to maize (Bonta et al. 2006; Wilkes 1967). This detail becomes more significant when considered in conjunction with Aztec cosmology. In this ideological system, cosmic history unfolds through a series of cosmic ages, each of which possesses its own presiding deity, people, food, etc. (Table 3; Berdan 2014: Table 7.3). In this scenario, wild and managed foods transitioned to the precursors of domestication, and finally the sequence ends with maize (Carrasco 2012, 2015; Staller and Carrasco 2010: 6). It has generally been assumed that teosinte unambiguously names *Zea mays parviglumis*; however, Bonta (2010b, 2012; Bonta et al. 2019) has shown that the term and its cognates also frequently refer to various cycad species, possibly in reference to regionally specific taxa that serve similar conceptual and dietary roles. It is thus possible that the term references cycads as foundational in a remote past, within a classificatory system in which myth, history, agriculture, and ecology are interwoven. Thus, terms that may at first seem to have a clear meaning actually function within a more complex system of botanical and ecological reference that remains largely opaque.

Table 2 A selection of indigenous terms for cycads in Mexican languages, showing convergences with maize terms (see also Bonta et al. 2019: Table S1)

Species	Location	Term	Translation	Language
C. latifolia	Huasteca (SLP)	*ahaatik a eem*	Lord of maize	Téenek
C. latifolia	Aquismón (SLP)	*bo'jor*	Olote (green maize)	Téenek
C. latifolia	Aquismón (SLP)	*ejatalem*	The life of maize	Téenek
C. latifolia	Aquismón (SLP)	*la carne del maíz*	Meat of maize	Spanish
C. latifolia	Huasteca (SLP)	*tsubal*	Life of maize	Téenek
C. fuscoviridis, Z. fischeri, Z. loddigessii	(Hgo)	*alma del maíz, alma de cintli*	Soul of maize/maize cob	Spanish +Nahautl
C. fuscoviridis, Z. fischeri, Z. loddigessii	(Hgo)	*cintli (i nana)*	Maize (mother of)	Nahautl
C. fuscoviridis, Z. fischeri, Z. loddigessii	(Hgo)	*cuacintli elote de monte*	Forest maize/cob	Nahautl
C. fuscoviridis, Z. fischeri, Z. loddigessii	(Hgo)	*madre del elote/ maíz*	Mother of maize/ cob	Spanish
C. fuscoviridis, Z. fischeri, Z. loddigessii	(Hgo)	*padre del elote, tatatlcintli*	Father of maize/cob	Spanish +Nahautl

Continued

Species	Location	Term	Translation	Language
C. fuscoviridis, Z. fischeri, Z. loddigessii	(Hgo, SLP)	*teocintle*	Sacred cob	Nahautl
Z. loddigessii	Papantla (Vz)	*amigo del maíz*	Friend of maize	Spanish
Z. loddigessii	(S Vz)	*maíz de coshca*	"Coshca" maize	Spanish+ Popoluca
D. edule	Pameria (SLP)	*maíz del monte, maíz gordo*	Mountain maize/fat maize	Spanish
D. merolae	Sierra Madre del Sur (Oax)	*maízviejo*	Old maize	Spanish
C. morettii, C. "mexicana"	Huayacocotla, Vz; Sierra Norte, Pue	*Tepetmaizte, tepezintle*	Mountain maize	Nahuatl+ Spanish

Table 3   Tenochtitlan sequence of the five ages (after Berdan 2014: Table 7.3)

Name of sun	Presiding deity	Human / Food	Fate of humanity	Type of destruction
NauiOcelotl (Four Jaguar)	Tezcatlipoca	Giantsroots/ wild foods	Eaten by jaguars	Jaguars
HauiEhecatl (Four Wind)	Quetzalcoatl	Humans pine nuts/acorns (*acocentli*)	Transformed into monkeys	Hurricanes
NauiQuizhuitl (Four Rain)	Tlaloc	Humans aquatic seed (*acecentli*)	Transformed into dogs, turkeys, butterflies	Fiery rain
NauiAtl (Four Water)	Chalchiuhtlicue	Humans wild seeds (*teocentli*)	Transformed into fish	Great flood
NauiOllin (Four Movement)	Tonatiuh	Humans maize	To be devoured by tzitzimeme (celestialmonsters)	Earthquakes

The Téenek, a group of Mayan language speaking peoples in San Luis Potosí and northern Veracruz, offer a particularly compelling example of such conceptual overlap in language and larger symbolic thought. The Téenek's major cultural hero is the child deity Thipaak, who brings maize to people. He is said to be the *ehatal*, "soul", the *tzitziin*, "spirit", and *ichiich*, "heart" of maize (Ochoa 2010: 542; see also Alcorn 1984; Alcorn et al. 2006).

The Téenek nomenclature for cycads (Table 4) reveals their conceptual convergence with maize, either through the deity Thipaak or through the incorporation of a maize term such as *way'* or *eem*. Further, certain zamias are known among the Téenek as the "spirit of maize" and "Maize Lord".

Table 4 Téenek linguistic terms for cycads

Téenek cycad term	Gloss
Tsalam Thipaak	Thipaak shade
Tsakam way'	Small ear/cob
Tsakam Thipaak	Small Thipaak
Ahaatik a eem	Lord of Maize
Ts'eenthipaak	Sierra Thipaak

Significantly, such conceptual conflation between plants, animals, and abstract concepts (such as sacrifice, fertility, etc.) is relatively common in Mesoamerican epistemologies and symbolic systems (Carrasco 2012, 2015; Stross 2006). Elements of this symbolic web may also occur in pre-Hispanic art and iconography. For example, although previous interpretations of Formative Period phytomorphic deities often look to maize as a source for such imagery (see Taube 1996, 2000), the formal attributes of many representations of ancient Mesoamerican deities more closely resemble the physical characteristics and the growth habits of cycads. In Figure 3, the cone like element in the headdress of the figure on the left and in the right hand of the seated figure in the centre brings to mind the strobili of a *Dioon* cycad, rather than the patterns of grains on a maize cob. If this is the case then it would align with the ethnographic and linguistic data that demonstrate the conceptual convergence of maize and cycads in Mesoamerican ethnoecological systems. Although complex and at times ambiguous, the string of metonymic connections reflected in Mesoamerican art suggests that cycads were also integrated in this symbolic web, one that was likely formed in the Archaic and Early Formative Period (ca. 4500 BP–3000 BP), concurrent with the extensive exploitation of cycads indicated by the archaeological data, as well as the diversification of modern domesticated maize.

Figure 3   (L-R) Drawing of Olmec "Maize God", stone sculpture, Harvard Peabody Museum (after Taube 2004: Figure 13); Seated greenstone figure, Cleveland Art Museum (after original by Linda Schele); Dioon purpusii strobilus, Oaxaca (drawings by Michael Carrasco; photo by Chip Jones, used under CC BY-NC-SA 4.0 license)

Genomics

Genetic research on Mexican cycad species, focusing specifically on *Dioon* spp., shows many aspects of the historical relationships between populations, which complements other lines of evidence (cf. Zeder et al. 2006). Climates for *Dioon* localities vary significantly: *Dioon* covers seven of the 19 biogeographic provinces in Mexico and can be found growing in beaches (sea level) and in high mountains, also from dry climates to very humid sites (Gutiérrez-Ortega et al. 2018). Population-level genetic markers were used to measure how populations are genetically connected across these provinces with the goal of reconstructing their recent dispersal, in sites that include a large part of Mexico, and a single site in the north of Honduras. Leaf tissues from the *Dioon* genus were sampled from 31 different locations and stored in liquid nitrogen, herborized, or transported fresh to the laboratory and stored at −80°C for posterior DNA extraction. DNA was used to estimate population-level parameters using microsatellites or SSRs (simple sequence repeats in a tract of repetitive

DNA; see Prado et al. 2016) as genetic markers that allow the reconstruction of family-level relationships and genealogies.

To explore the genetic variation among locations, and measure how they relate to one another, we used a principal component analysis (PCA) approach that transforms multivariate genotype data and allows us to identify genetic groups. We employed the R package gstudio[3] to perform the PCA of the raw genotypes of all the individuals (Dyer 2014).

We also estimated the divergence among populations and migration events that took place after population splits, using TREEMIX (Pickrell and Pritchard 2012) and SumTrees[4]. Populations with a small number of samples (n ≤ 10) and loci with large quantities of missing data were excluded, resulting in a total of 9 loci. 100000 independent topologies were generated using TREEMIX and a consensus tree topology was obtained using SumTrees in the dendropy.org package. Once the consensus topology was obtained, we ran TREEMIX again using the consensus topology, and migration edges were added one by one to generate jackknife estimates and standard errors of the migration weight.

We found extensive genetic flow between cycad populations, despite large distances and geographic barriers. The PCA (Figure 4) revealed that genetic differentiation of *Dioon* populations is first divided into two main groups, one with *Dioon merolae* and *D. caputoi* genetically close, and a second gradient with the rest of the species. We see two main subgroups within the gradient that follow an isolation by distance pattern, that is, populations that are close to other populations are more genetically closer than populations that are far away. *Dioon holmgrenii* and *D. mejiae* form one of the subgroups, while *D. sonorense*, *D. tomaselli*, and *D. stevensonii* group in the other. The *spinulosum* clade—most closely related to the common ancestor of all *Dioon* cycads—is in the middle, suggesting that Mexican *Dioon* species may have originated in the east and south groups concentrated along the Sierra Madre Oriental. *Dioon edule* from the sand dunes is also separated from the rest. Population level patterns in *Dioon* in some regions, such as Honduras and North Eastern Mexico, suggest few large-distance dispersal events and open the possibility that these plants were actively dispersed by humans as part of the Mexican culture, at least for those sites but probably for others as well.

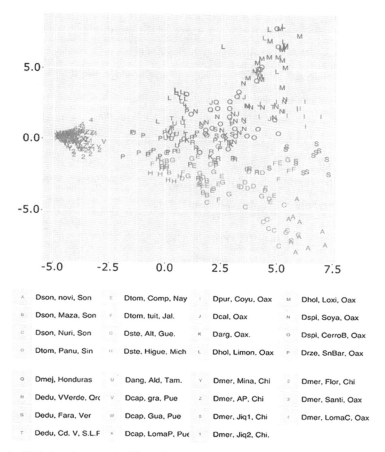

	Dson, novi, Son	E	Dtom, Comp, Nay	I	Dpur, Coyu, Oax	M	Dhol, Loxi, Oax
B	Dson, Maza, Son	F	Dtom, tuit, Jal.	J	Dcal, Oax	N	Dspi, Soya, Oax
C	Dson, Nuri, Son	G	Dste, Alt, Gue.	K	Darg, Oax.	O	Dspi, CerroB, Oax
D	Dtom, Panu, Sin	H	Dste, Higue, Mich	L	Dhol, Limon, Oax	P	Drze, SnBar, Oax
Q	Dmej, Honduras	U	Dang, Ald, Tam.	Y	Dmer, Mina, Chi	2	Dmer, Flor, Chi
R	Dedu, VVerde, Qrc	V	Dcap, gra, Pue	Z	Dmer, AP, Chi	3	Dmer, Santi, Oax
S	Dedu, Fara, Ver	W	Dcap, Gua, Pue	0	Dmer, Jiq1, Chi	4	Dmer, LomaC, Oax
T	Dedu, Cd. V, S.L.F	X	Dcap, LomaP, Pue	1	Dmer, Jiq2, Chi.		

Figure 4 PCA showing genetic differentiation among the *Dioon* genus, each letter represents a single individual of a population

The population tree we constructed (Figure 5) shows a topology similar to previously published phylogenies (González et al. 2008; Gutiérrez-Ortega et al. 2018; Calonje et al. 2019), confirming the clades proposed previously, but with new insights in patterns of expansion and migration after populations separated that cannot be detected with a phylogeny. The high standard error of the tree branches is due to the nature of the SSRs loci mutation model, and the addition of more edges does not increase variance significantly, hence the fitted tree with six migration events explains most of the variance in ancestry between populations. We note migrations to both sides between *D. mejiae* and populations from the *edule* clade and migration between *tomasellii* clade and the *purpusii* clade in both directions, after these populations split due to ancestral dispersal or vicariance events such as orographic and major climatic barriers. In all, both the PCA and the TREEMIX suggest that there is a recent establishment of most modern populations in the Mexican landscape, with a few recent migration events across major geographic distances that could be explained by human dispersal. This adds to, and is congruent with, evidence that speaks to ample and ancient use of cycads in Mexican culture.

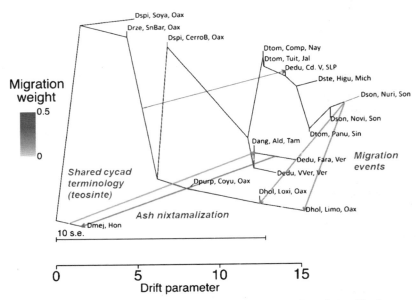

Figure 5 Best-fitted maximum-likelihood population tree displaying relationships between populations. Migration events are shown in edges coloured according to the migration weight of the source population. Notice that the migration edges have directionality

Discussion

Considering the discrete lines of evidence together, we detect a corridor extending from Oaxaca in the south to Tamaulipas in the north that runs along the Sierra Madre Oriental. In this corridor, archaeological, ethnographic, and linguistic data indicate the significance of cycads in indigenous belief systems and practices for thousands of years, up to the present. Genomic analysis of *Dioon* spp. indicates very close genetic relationships among the various species of the east and south groups in the Sierra Madre Oriental corridor and extending into Oaxaca and Chiapas. Further, the epicentre of cycad diversification appears to be located within this geographic corridor, precisely in the area in which archaeological, ethnographic, and linguistic data regarding the use and cultural significance of cycads is most densely concentrated. The data also suggest correlations between dispersal and population split events in cycad evolution and cultural processes, such as the development of specific cultural practices (e.g. nixtamalisation), and episodes of demographic migration, as well as the promulgation of shared linguistic terms—such as teosinte—that refer to cycads. Finally, many lines of evidence suggest a conceptual convergence between maize and cycads in indigenous Mesoamerican thought.

Given the overlaps detailed above, as well as the documented similarities in cycad and maize preparation complexes, and the antiquity of cycadales in general, it is possible that cycads may have formed a sort of "mental template" for the domestication of maize itself. Cycad cones formally resemble maize cobs, and the data reveal a deep-rooted conceptual relationship between cycads and maize—a relationship conceived in terms of kinship (Table 2) and reflected in complex convergences within larger ideological systems (Bonta 2010b, 2012). This hypothesis is speculative, and further research is underway to clarify this possibility.

Beyond their symbolic significance, however, it is also clear that cycads have great potential economic value. For example, coralloid cycad roots fix N_2, thereby improving soil economy. Inter-cropping with cycads is therefore beneficial to companion plants. It is thus possible that cycads factored in to agricultural production strategies before the domestication of "traditional" Mesoamerican cultigens, such as maize or other N_2-fixing legumes, facilitating sustainable crop management practices. Although this idea is also speculative, it does invite a theoretical reconsideration of current models of domestication and the origins of agriculture in ancient Mesoamerica, and elsewhere (see Freeman et al. 2015; Gremilliona et al. 2014; Terrell et al. 2003).

Concluding Thoughts

In conclusion, the data derived from this multidisciplinary investigation have revealed significant utilitarian, symbolic, and ritual roles for cycads in the ethnoecological systems of ancient Mesoamerica and modern Mexico. It is abundantly clear that various cultures in this geographic area recognize cycads as a key resource. Cycads also figure prominently in regional mythologies and epistemologies, in which they often possess a close conceptual relationship with maize, and they continue to be a part of Mesoamerican foodways among various groups. The environmental and cultural role of cycads reveals multiple convergences, as well as the significance of ancient and modern cultural practices that incorporated this natural-cultural hybrid to preserve alimentary history and encode ecological knowledge in higher order mythologies, ideological systems, and epistemologies. In sum, the data reveal the existence of long and complex cycad-human relationships.

This brief glimpse reveals the potential richness of the subject. We suggest that a closer examination of cycad-human relationships has the potential to stimulate further discussion on the significance of cycads in Mesoamerican beliefs, foodways, and ecology, as well as the dynamic cultural processes—such as domestication—in which cycads may have been involved. Further study of this hybrid, natural-cultural heritage will advance our understanding of this plant, the complex indigenous ecologies in which it is imbricated, and the communities that valued—continue to value—cycads.

Notes

1. Accessed May 2, 2019; see also Donaldson 2003. https://cites.org/sites/default/files/eng/cop/17/WorkingDocs/E-CoP17-58.pdf.

2. Accessed May 2, 2019. http://www. cycadlist.org.

3. Accessed May 2, 2019. http://dyerlab.github.io/gstudio/.

4. Accessed May 2, 2019. https://dendropy.org/programs/sumtrees.html.

□ Acknowledgements

The authors thank Mark Bonta, Michael Calonje, Andrew Vovides, Roberto Lunagómez, Maura Ordoñez, Sara Ladrón de Guevara, Flip Arnold, Amber VanDerwarker, Francisco Barona Gómez, Francisco Pérez Zavala, José SaídGutíerrez Ortega, Leandro Matthews Cascon, and Marcia Bezerra.

□ Disclosure Statement

No potential conflict of interest was reported by the authors.

□ Funding

This work was supported by the National Endowment for the Humanities under Grant #HD-51921-14 and Fellowship #FA–233454–16; and the Consejo Nacional de Ciencia y Tecnología under Grant #2015-02-901.

□ Notes on Contributors

Joshua D. Englehardt is a Research Professor at the Centro de Estudios Arqueológicos de El Colegio de Michoacán, Mexico, and a Level I National Investigator of the Consejo Nacional de Ciencia y Tecnología. He specialises in Mesoamerican archaeology and visual culture, with a research focus on the development of Mesoamerican writing systems in the Formative Period. He is the codirector of the Mesoamerican Corpus of Formative Period Art and Writing, an interdisciplinary project that is developing digital tools for the investigation and presentation of early Mesoamerican visual cultures. Developing out of this work, he has a growing interest in the application of digital technologies in the humanities and the impact of new media on archaeological, art historical, and heritage studies. He is also currently a member of a multidisciplinary team currently exploring the cultural uses and significance of cycads and maize. Recent publications include *Archaeological Paleography* (Archaeopress, 2016), and the edited volumes *Agency in Ancient Writing* (University Press of Colorado, 2012) and *Interregional Interaction in Ancient Mesoamerica* (University Press of Colorado, 2017), as well as over twenty articles and book chapters that stem from his fieldwork throughout Mexico and over twenty years of living, working, or studying in the Global South.

Angélica Cibrián Jaramillo is an expert in plant genetics and genomics. She graduated with honours in biology at UNAM. As a Fulbright scholar, she did a Master and PhD in Ecology, Evolutionary and Environmental Biology, and obtained certificate in Environmental Policy at Columbia University, New York. She spent time in Bioversity International in Rome and worked for other UN organisations focused on issues of policy on plant genetic resources. After her PhD she was a postdoc and Research Assistant between 2007 and 2011 at the New York Botanical Garden, the American Museum of Natural History, at Harvard University, and at New York University on plant genetics. Since 2012 she is the head of the Ecological and Evolutionary Genomics Lab at LANGEBIO, CINVESTAV, a leading institution on the use of genomic tools to understand plant biodiversity. Her lab aims to explore the genomic basis of plant diversity, in particular of the wild relatives of Mesoamerican crops. Her scientific contributions lie in emerging fields such as: genomics of plants of economic importance; functional phylogenomics and plant evolution; and comparative metagenomic and genomic analysis of plant-associated microbiomes. Her works have been published in prestigious international journals including PNAS, PLOS Genetics, Plant Cell, BMC Genetics, Molecular Ecology and Genome Biology and Evolution.

Michael D. Carrasco serves as an Associate Professor of visual cultures of the Americas and cultural heritage studies in the Department of Art History. Drawing on a broad range

67

of subjects—including poetics, iconography, image theory, and ecology—his principal areas of research include the origins of writing and indigenous aesthetics, theology, and epistemologies in Mesoamerica. The other main area of his scholarship lies in cultural heritage, particularly in digital humanities and the juncture between folk traditions and global art systems. His recent work has been supported by internal funding from FSU, an NEH Digital Humanities Level II Start-up Grant; an NEH Fellowship; the Consejo Nacional de Ciencia y Tecnología; and a Japan Council of Local Authorities for International Relations (CLAIR) Furusato Vision Project. His publications include the edited volumes *Parallel Worlds: Genre, Discourse, and Poetics in Contemporary, Colonial, and Classic Maya Literature* (University Press of Colorado, 2012) and *Pre-Columbian Foodways: Interdisciplinary Approaches to Food, Culture, and Markets in Ancient Mesoamerica* (Springer, 2010), and the exhibition catalogue *Decolonizing Refinement: Contemporary Pursuits in the Art of Edouard Duval-Carrié*. His articles have appeared in the Cambridge Archaeological Journal, Mexicon, and the World Religious Cultures, among others.

□ References

Alcorn, Janice B. 1984. *Huastec Mayan Ethnobotany*. Austin: University of Texas Press.

Alcorn, Janice B., Barbara Edmondson, and Cándido Hernández Vidales. 2006. Thipaak and the Origins of Maize in Northern Mesoamerica. In *Histories of Maize: Multidisciplinary Approaches to the Prehistory, Linguistics, Biogeography, Domestication, and Evolution of Maize*, edited by John E. Staller, Robert H. Tykot, and Bruce F. Benz, 600-611. New York: Academic Press.

Beck, Wendy. 1992. Aboriginal Preparation of Cycas Seeds in Australia. *Economic Botany* 46 (2): 133-147.

Berdan, Frances F. 2014. *Aztec Archaeology and Ethnohistory*. Cambridge: Cambridge University Press.

Bonta, Mark A. 2010a. Human Geography and Ethnobotany of Cycads in Xi'ui, Teenek, and Nahuatl communities of northeastern Mexico, Final Report. May 27, 2010. Accessed May 2, 2019. http://www.cycad.org/grants/2009/Bonta-TCS-2009-Grant-Final-Report.pdf.

Bonta, Mark A. 2010b. Maize and Cycads: In Search of Sacred Ancestors. *The Cycad Newsletter* 33 (4): 4-7.

Bonta, Mark A. 2012. Cycads and Human Life Cycles: Outline of a Symbology. In *Proceedings of Cycad 2008: The 8th International Congress on Cycad Biology*, 13-15 January 2008, Panama City, Panama, edited by Dennis W. Stevenson, Roy Osborne, and Alberto Sidney Taylor Blake, 133-150. Memoirs of the New York Botanical Garden Vol. 106. New York: New York Botanical Garden Press.

Bonta, Mark A., María Teresa Pulido-Silva, Teresa Diego-Vargas, Aurelia Vite-Reyes, Andrew P. Vovides, and Angélica Cibrián-Jaramillo. 2019. Ethnobotany of Mexican and Northern Central American Cycads (Zamiaceae). *Journal of Ethnobiology and Ethnomedicine* 15 (4): 1-34.

Bonta, Mark A., Oscar Flores Pinot, Daniel Graham, Jody Haynes, and Germán

Sandoval. 2006. Ethnobotany and Conservation of Tiusinte (Dioon Mejiae Standl & L. O. Williams, Zamiaceae) in Northeastern Honduras. *Journal of Ethnobiology* 26 (2): 228-257.

Bonta, Mark A., and Roy Osborne. 2007. Cycads in the Vernacular: A Compendium of Local Names. In *Proceedings of the seventh international conference on cycad biology* (Xalapa, Mexico, 2005), edited by Andrew P. Vovides, Dennis W. Stevenson, and Roy Osborne, 143-175. New York: New York Botanical Garden Press.

Bonta, Mark A., and Samuel O. Bamigboye. 2018. Use of Cycads as Ritual and Recreational Narcotics. *South African Journal of Botany* 115: 280-281.

Bradley, John J. 2005. "Same Time Poison, Same Time Good Tucker": The Cycad Palm in the South West Gulf of Carpentaria. *Journal of Australian Studies* 29: 119-133.

Brown, Cecil H. 2010. Development of Agriculture in Prehistoric Mesoamerica: The Linguistic Evidence. In *Pre-Columbian Foodways: Interdisciplinary approaches to Food, Culture, and Markets in ancient Mesoamerica*, edited by John E. Staller, and Michael D. Carrasco, 71-107. New York: Springer.

Brown, Cecil H., Charles R. Clement, Patience Epps, Eike Luedeling, and Søren Wichmann. 2013. The Paleobiolinguistics of Domesticated Manioc (Manihot esculenta). *Ethnobiology Letters* 4: 61-70.

Calonje, Michael, Alan W. Meerow, M. Patrick Griffith, Dayana Salas-Leiva, Andrew P. Vovides, Mario Coiro, and Javier Francisco-Ortega. 2019. A Time-Calibrated Species Tree Phylogeny of the New World Cycad Genus *Zamia* L. (Zamiaceae, Cycadales). *International Journal of Plant Sciences* 180 (4): 286-314.

Carbajal-Esquivel, Haydeé, Javier Fortanelli Martínez, José García-Pérez, Juan A. Reyes-Agüero, Laura Yáñez-Espinosa, and Mark Bonta. 2012. Use Value of Food Plants in the Xi'iuy Indigenous Community of Las Guapas, Rayon, San Luis Potosi, Mexico. *Ethnobiology Letters* 3: 39-55.

Carrasco, Michael D. 2012. Mayan Agrarian Mythologies: The Lifecycle of Maize and Humans. Wenbin Li (trans.). *The Religious Cultures in the World* 76 (4): 18-24. [卡拉

斯科，迈克尔·D. 2012. 玛雅农业神话：玉米和人的生命轮回. 李文彬，译. 世界宗教文化 76 (4): 18-24.]

Carrasco, Michael D. 2015. Cycads, Maize, and Garfish: The Representation of Ethnoecological Systems in Olmec Iconography. In *Schedule and Abstracts of the 10th International Conference on cycad biology (CYCAD 2015)*. Coral Gables: Cycad 2015 organizing committee, Montgomery Botanical Center.

Chamberlain, Charles J. 1919. *The Living Cycads*. Chicago: University of Chicago Press.

Cox Paul A., and Oliver W. Sacks. 2002. Cycad Neurotoxins, Consumption of Flying Foxes, and ALS-PDC Disease in Guam. *Neurology* 58: 956-959.

Descola, Philippe. 2013. *Beyond Nature and Culture*. J. Lloyd (trans.). Chicago: The University of Chicago Press.

Diego-Vargas, Teresa. 2017. Relaciones culturales entre las cícadas y el maíz en localidades nahuas y teenek de la Huasteca. Master's Thesis, Universidad Autónoma del Estado de Hidalgo, Pachuca.

Donaldson, John S. (ed.). 2003. *Cycads: Status Survey and Conservation Action Plan*. Gland: World Conservation Union.

Dyer, Rodney J. 2014. GStudio: A Package for the Spatial Analysis of Population Genetic Marker Data. December 17, 2014. Accessed May 3, 2019. https://mran.microsoft.com/snapshot/2014-11-17/ web/packages/gstudio/vignettes/gstudio.pdf.

Freeman, Jacob, Matthew Peeples, and John M. Anderies. 2015. Toward a Theory of Non-linear Transitions from Foraging to Farming. *Journal of Anthropological Archaeology* 40: 109-122.

González, Dolores, Andrew P. Vovides, and Cristina Bárcenas. 2008. Phylogenetic Relationships of the Neotropical Genus Dioon (Cycadales, Zamiaceae) Based on Nuclear and Chloroplast DNA Sequence Data. *Systematic Botany* 33 (2): 229-236.

Gremilliona, Kristen J., Loukas Barton, and Dolores R. Piperno. 2014. Particularism and the Retreat from Theory in the Archaeology of Agricultural Origins. *PNAS* 111 (17): 6171-6177.

Gutiérrez-Ortega, José Said, María Magdalena Salinas-Rodríguez, José F. Martínez,

Francisco Molina-Freaner, Miguel Angel Pérez-Farrera, Andrew P. Vovides, Yu Matsuki, Yoshihisa Suyama, Takeshi A. Ohsawa, YasuyukiWatano, and Tadashi Kajita. 2018. The Phylogeography of the Cycad Genus Dioon (Zamiaceae) Clarifies its Cenozoic Expansion and Diversification in the Mexican Transition Zone. *Annals of Botany* 121: 535-548.

Hanselka, Kevin. 2011. Prehistoric Plant Procurement, Food Production, and Land Use in Southwestern Tamaulipas, Mexico. Doctoral Dissertation, Washington University, St. Louis.

Hanselka, Kevin. 2017. Revisiting the Archaeobotanical Record of Romero's Cave in the Ocampo Region of Tamaulipas, Mexico. *Journal of Ethnobiology* 37 (1): 37-59.

Hayward, Philip, and Sueo Kuwahara. 2012. Sotetsu Heritage: Cycads, Sustenance and Cultural Landscapes in the Amami Islands. *Locale: The Australasian-Pacific Journal of Regional Food Studies* 2: 26-46.

Isendahl, Christian. 2011. The Domestication and Early Spread of Manioc (Manihot Esculenta Crantz): A Brief Synthesis. *Latin American Antiquity* 22 (4): 452-468.

Kelley David H. 1954. *Valenzuela's Cave (Tmc 248): Report.* Andover, MA: Peabody Museum of Archaeology, Phillips Academy.

Khuraijam, J. S., and Rita Singh. 2012. The Ethnobotany of Cycas in the States of Assam and Meghalaya, India. In *Proceedings of Cycad 2008: The 8th International Congress on Cycad Biology,* 13-15 January 2008, Panama City, Panama, edited by Dennis W. Stevenson, Roy Osborne, Alberto Sidney Taylor Blake, 151-164. Memoirs of the New York Botanical Garden Vol. 106. New York: New York Botanical Garden Press.

Kira, Kesayoshi, and Aki Miyoshi. 2000. Utilization of SOTETSU (Cycas revoluta) in the Amami Islands. *Kagoshima University Forests Research Bulletin* 22: 31-37.

MacNeish, Richard S. 1954a. *Ojo de Agua Cave (Tmc 274): Report and catalog of excavated material.* Andover, MA: Peabody Museum of Archaeology, Phillips Academy.

MacNeish, Richard S. 1954b. *Romero's cave (Tmc 247): Report.* Andover, MA: Peabody Museum of Archaeology, Phillips Academy.

MacNeish, Richard S. 1958. Preliminary Archaeological Investigations in the Sierra de Tamaulipas, Mexico. *Transactions of the American Philosophical Society, New Series*

48 (6): 1-210.

Matsuoka, Yoshihiro, Yves Vigouroux, Major M. Goodman, Jesus Sanchez G., Edward Buckler, and John Doebley. 2002. A Single Domestication for Maize Shown by Multilocus Microsatellite Genotyping. *PNAS* 99 (9): 6080-6084.

McVaugh, Rogers. 1992. *Flora Novo-Galiciana: Gymnosperms and Pteridophytes*. Ann Arbor: University of Michigan Herbarium.

Mickleburgh, Hayley L., and Jaime R. Pagán-Jiménez. 2012. New Insights into the Consumption of Maize and Other Food Plants in the Pre-Columbian Caribbean from Starch Grains Trapped in Human Dental Calculus. *Journal of Archaeological Science* 39: 2468-2478.

Nicolalde-Morejón, Fernando, Jorge González-Astorga, Francisco Vergara-Silva, and Dennis W. Stevenson. 2013. Biodiversidad de Zamiaceae en México. *Revista Mexicana de Biodiversidad* 85: 114-125.

Norstog, Knut J., and Trevor J. Nicholls. 1997. *The Biology of the Cycads*. Ithaca: Cornell University Press.

Ochoa, Lorenzo. 2010. Topophilia: A Tool for the Demarcation of Cultural Microregions: The Case of the Huaxteca. In *Pre-Columbian foodways: Interdisciplinary approaches to food, culture, and markets in ancient Mesoamerica*, edited by John E. Staller, and Michael D. Carrasco, 535-552. New York: Springer.

Pagán-Jiménez, Jaime R., Reniel Rodríguez-Ramos, Basil A. Reid, Martijn van den Bel, and Corinne L. Hofman. 2015. Early Dispersals of Maize and Other Food Plants into the Southern Caribbean and Northeastern South America. *Quaternary Science Reviews* 123: 231-246.

Patiño, Víctor Manuel. 1989. Notas preliminares sobre el uso de las Zamiaceas por los pueblos primitivos y aculturados del intertrópico americano. *Perez-Arbelaezia* 2 (8): 429-442.

Pérez-Farrera, Miguel Angel, and Andrew P. Vovides. 2006. The Ceremonial Use of the Threatened "espadaña" Cycad (Dioon merolae, Zamiaceae) by a Community of the Central Depression of Chiapas. *Boletín de la Sociedad Botánica de México* 78: 107-113.

Pickrell, Joseph K., and Jonathan K. Pritchard. 2012. Inference of Population Splits and Mixtures from Genome-Wide Allele Frequency Data. *PLOS Genetics* 8 (11): e1002967.

Prado, Alberto, Fret Cervantes-Díaz, Francisco G. Perez-Zavala, Jorge González-Astorga, Jacqueline C. Bede, Angélica Cibrián-Jaramillo. 2016. Transcriptome-Derived Microsatellite Markers for Dioon (Zamiaceae) Cycad Species. *Applications in Plant Sciences* 4 (2):1500087.

Radha, P., and Rita Singh. 2008. Ethnobotany and Conservation Status of Indian Cycas Species. *Encephalartos* 93: 15-21.

Rosenswig, Robert M., Amber M. VanDerwarker, Brendan J. Culleton, and Douglas J. Kennett. 2015. Is It Agriculture Yet? Intensified Maize-Use at 1, 000 cal BC in the Soconusco and Mesoamerica. *Journal of Anthropological Archaeology* 40: 89-108.

Ruiz-Mallén, Isabel, Christoph Schunko, Esteve Corbera, Matthias Rös, and Victoria Reyes-García. 2015. Meanings, Drivers, and Motivations for Community-Based Conservation in Latin America. *Ecology and Society* 20 (3): 33-47.

Sifuentes de Ortiz, María S. 1983. *Importancia económica del chamal Dioon edule Lindl. (Cycadaceae) en el estado de Nuevo Leon, México.* Monterrey: Facultad de Ciencias Biológicas, Universidad Autónoma de Nuevo León.

Smith, Bruce D., 2005. Reassessing Coxcatlan Cave and the Early History of Domesticated Plants in Mesoamerica. *PNAS* 102 (27): 9438-9445.

Smith, C. Earle. 1967. Plant Remains. In *Prehistory of the Tehuacan Valley: Environment and Subsistence*, edited by Richard S. MacNeish, 220-255. Austin: University of Texas Press.

Smith, Moya. 1982. Late Pleistocene Zamia Exploitation in Southern Western Australia. *Archaeology in Oceania* 17 (3): 117-121.

Staller, John E., and Michael D. Carrasco. 2010. Pre-Columbian Foodways in Mesoamerica. In *Pre-Columbian Foodways: Interdisciplinary Approaches to Food, Culture, and Markets in Ancient Mesoamerica*, edited by John E. Staller, and Michael D. Carrasco, 1-21. New York: Springer.

Stross, Brian. 2006. Maize in Word and Image in Southeastern Mesoamerica. In *Histories of Maize: Multidisciplinary Approaches to the Prehistory, Linguistics, Biogeography, Domestication, and Evolution of Maize*, edited by John E. Staller, Robert H. Tykot, and Bruce F. Benz, 577-598. London: Academic Press.

Taube, Karl A. 1996. The Olmec Maize God: The Face of Corn in Formative Mesoamerica. *Res* 29/30: 39-81.

Taube, Karl A. 2000. Lightning Celts and Corn Fetishes: The Formative Olmec and the Development of Maize Symbolism in Mesoamerica and the American Southwest. In *Olmec Art and Archaeology in Mesoamerica*, edited by John E. Clark, and Mary E. Pye, 297-331. Washington, D. C.: National Gallery of Art and New Haven: Yale University Press.

Taube, Karl A. 2004. *Olmec Art at Dumbarton Oaks*. Washington, D. C.: Dumbarton Oaks Research Library & Collection.

Terrell, John Edward, John P. Hart, Sibel Barut, Nicoletta Cellinese, L. Antonio Curet, Tim Denham, Chapurukha M. Kusimba, Kyle Latinis, Rahul Oka, Joel Palka, Mary E. D. Pohl, Kevin O. Pope, Patrick Ryan Williams, Helen Haines, and John E. Staller. 2003. Domesticated Landscapes: The Subsistence Ecology of Plant and Animal Domestication. *Journal of Archaeological Method and Theory* 10 (4): 323-368.

Thieret, John. 1958. Economic Botany of the Cycads. *EconomicBotany* 12 (1): 3-41.

Tristán, Elvia. 2012. Aprovechamiento alimentario de Dioon edule Lindl. (Chamal) en comunidades de la región Xi'iuy del estado de San Luis Potosí. Undergraduate Thesis, Universidad Autónoma de San Luis Potosí.

Valdez, Ulises. 2009. *La flor de espadaña en Terán: Ofrenda de los hojeros a la Santa Cruz*. Suchiapa: Universidad Politécnica de Chiapas.

Vázquez Torres, Mario. 1990. Algunos datos etnobotánicos de las cícadas en México. *Memoirs of the New York Botanical Garden* 57: 144-147.

Veloz Maggiolo, Marcio. 1992. Notas sobre la Zamia en la Prehistoria del Caribe. *Revista de Arqueología Americana* 6: 125-138.

Vite Reyes, Aurelia. 2012. Etnobotánica de cícadas en comunidades nahuas y mestizas de Tlanchinol, Hidalgo. Master's Thesis, Universidad Autónoma del Estado de

Hidalgo, Pachuca.

Vite Reyes, Aurelia, Ma. Teresa Pulido Silva, and Juan Carlos Flores. 2010. Aspectos etnobotánicos de las cícadas en algunas zonas de Hidalgo, México. In *Sistemas biocognitivos tradicionales: paradigmas en la conservación biológica y el fortalecimiento cultural*, edited by Ángel Moreno, María Teresa Pulido, Ramón Mariaca, Raúl Valadéz Azúa, Paulina Mejía Correa, and Tania V. Gutiérrez Santillán, 481-486. Mexico City: Asociación Etnobiológica Mexicana.

Vovides, Andrew P. 1989. Problems of Endangered Species Conservation in Mexico: Cycadsanexample. *Encephalartos* 20: 35-49.

Vovides, Andrew P., and Carlos G. Iglesias. 1994. An Integrated Conservation Strategy for the Cycad Dioon edule Lindl. *Biodiversity and Conservation* 3 (2): 137-141.

Vovides, Andrew P., Miguel Angel Pérez-Farrera, and Carlos Iglesias. 2010. Cycad Propagation by Rural Nurseries in Mexico as an Alternative Conservation Strategy: 20 Years on. *Kew Bulletin* 65 (4): 603-611.

Whitelock, Loran. 2002. *The Cycads*. Portland: Timber Press.

Whiting, Marjorie G. 1963. Toxicity of Cycads. *Economic Botany* 17 (4): 270-302.

Whiting, Marjorie G. 1964. Food Practices in ALS Foci in Japan, the Marianas, and New Guinea. *Fed Proc* 23: 1343-1345.

Whiting, Marjorie G. 1989. Neurotoxicity of Cycads: An Annotated Bibliography for the Years 1829–1989. *Lyonia—Occasional Papers of the Harold L. Lyon Arboretum* 2 (5): 201-270.

Wilkes, H. Garrison. 1967. *Teosinte: The Closest Relative of Maize*. Cambridge: Bussey Institution of Harvard University.

Wright, Sewall. 1950. Genetical Structure of Populations. *Nature* 166 (4215): 247-249.

Wright, Sewall. 1965. The Interpretation of Population Structure by F-Statistics with Special Regard to Systems of Mating. *Evolution* 19 (3): 395-420.

Zeder, Melinda A., Eve Emshwille, Bruce D. Smith, and Daniel G. Bradley. 2006. Documenting Domestication: The Intersection of Genetics and Archaeology. *Trends in Genetics* 22 (3): 139-155.

Relationships Between Urban Anthropology and Cultural Heritage in São Paulo, Brazil [1]

Heitor Frúgoli Jr.

University of São Paulo, Address: Av. Prof. Luciano Gualberto, 315, Cidade Universitária, São Paulo, SP, Brazil, CEP 05508-010, Caixa Postal 72042.
CONTACT Heitor Frúgoli Jr.: hfrugoli@uol.com.br

Abstract: The intention is to approach my experience as an anthropologist and member of the São Paulo State Council for the Defense of the Historical, Archeological, Artistic and Touristic Heritage (CONDEPHAAT)—which examines, debates and deliberates over requests on cultural heritage management or registers nonmaterial heritage, demanded by citizens or suggested by the Heritage Preservation Unit.

Since CONDEPHAAT has participants from several areas of study, which confers a heterogeneity on views of cultural heritage, I will emphasize the specificities related to the contributions of Brazilian Anthropology (of the City).

On the one hand, I will analyze aspects of my training as an urban anthropologist and the way in which theories of heritage have been approached in this field, considering a debate that occurs mostly inside national borders, given broader characteristics of Brazilian Anthropology. On the other hand, I will emphasize the dynamics by which certain heritage demands marked by relevant sociocultural aspects can be analyzed and approved.

For that, a selected number of cases will be presented (all of which I was a reporting commissioner). The main question has been how to highlight anthropologically relevant sociocultural dimensions, where participants tend to have different perceptions and goals regarding the subject.

Keywords: heritage-making, urban anthropology, São Paulo, Brazil

Introduction

I will deal here with aspects of my experience as an anthropologist and member of the collegial body of the São Paulo State Council for the Defense of the Historical, Archeological, Artistic and Touristic Heritage (CONDEPHAAT) that examines, debates and deliberates collectively over requests on cultural heritage management or registering nonmaterial heritage, solicitated by any citizen or suggested by the Unit for the Preservation of Historical Heritage (UPPH).[2] Given that CONDEPHAAT counts among its participants who are trained in various disciplines, an aspect which confers a heterogeneity of views on the concept of heritage, I will try here to highlight specificities related to anthropology of the city, as much as the scope and the reach of these same specificities.

As already indicated, this does not purport to be an exhaustive analysis, rather it represents a selective focus on my own experience of more than five years as an advisor. For this purpose, I will attempt to go through, in an abridged manner, how cultural heritage emerged as a subject of intervention and research in the field of Brazilian urban anthropology via referential authors (authors of reference) such as Antônio Arantes, Gilberto Velho e José Guilherme Magnani.[3] In the last section, I will broach recent requests of cultural heritage management and registration of CONDEPHAAT, of which I participated as a rapporteur, for a brief assessment of its significance in the sphere of cultural heritage.

Urban Anthropology and Cultural Heritage

Aspects of Antônio Arantes's academic and institutional trajectory permit us a crosswise cutting, beginning with his definition of cultural heritage, as it does not deal with a theoretic instrument for explaining the social, rather with ideological constructions or representations that require further explication, which brings us to the context of the (long-standing) cultural dynamics explored by anthropology over a long time, as well as the role of heritage in the construction of contemporary urban experience (Arantes 2009: 11). He also maintains that heritage is a sociocultural construct that results from myriad negotiations and conflicts involving actors, objects and administrative practices. The reconstitution of such a field allows for important perspectives on our recent past, as for the mobilizations of civil society against the military regime of the 1970s and 1980s, when the role of anthropologists gained increasing visibility, as well as the more recent context, marked by the increase in the reconstruction of collective identities and the demands for social recognition and cultural rights, a sphere in which the dimension of nonmaterial heritage came to find considerable expression (Arantes and Motta 2013: 72-75).

At the end of the 1970s, Arantes advanced a study on popular culture in Brazil, with a focus on the relationship between artistic production and political participation among workers in the Zona Leste of São Paulo[4], in a milieu noted for the robust role of social movements. During this period, he was invited to develop a revitalization program for the Chapel of São Miguel Archangel, "with the participation of local musicians, poets, actors and plastic artists" whose chapel space would be "a catalyzing element for the popular, local art production" (Arantes 2008: 9).[5]

Arantes's experience with the Brazilian National Institute of Historical and Artistic Heritage (IPHAN), over which he presided between 2004 and 2006, distinguished itself by the implementation by the Department of Nonmaterial Heritage and the National Program for Nonmaterial Heritage, with a renewed approach on popular culture. If the theme of preservation had its origins in the 1933 Athens Charter promulgated by Le Corbusier and CIAM and later in the 1964 Venice Charter, which expanded the notion of heritage for contextual uses and aspects (as much architectural as historical and social), the field of nonmaterial heritage retains a relationship with the UNESCO Conventions of 1972 (Protection of World Cultural and Natural Heritage) and 2003 (Safeguarding of Intangible Cultural Heritage) (Arantes 2009: 12-13). In this sense, according to the author, such an enlargement leads to the necessity of overcoming the polarization between tangible and intangible assets, as well as opens up the field of heritage to questions of ethical, juridical, political and humanitarian nature, especially in relation to the rights and lifestyles of indigenous and traditional populations (2009: 15), beyond obviously the working classes previously mentioned. In this sense, "difference, diversity and conflict are completely dissociable from it" (Arantes 2009: 16).[6]

This presents an opportune moment to bring another author, Gilberto Velho (2006), into the discussion. Specifically I will address his participation in the Consultative Council of the National Historical and Artistic Heritage Service (SPHAN) in the case of the Casa Branca do Engenho Velho *terreiro*[7] of Candomblé in Salvador, Bahia in 1984, of which he served as rapporteur. Such a process was controversial at the time, as the normative way until then, had been to designate religious, military and civic buildings from the Luso-Brazilian tradition as culture heritage sites (2006: 237). The *terreiro*, or sacred ground, in question covered a modest farmstead, with a grove of trees and stones associated with the cult of Afro-Brazilian *Orixás*, being the most important ritual sacrality. The anthropologist's condition leads him to interrogate the concept of culture, the religious system from the African tradition and its reach in Brazilian society, as well as its role in the realm of sociability and identity in a city such as Salvador. In an affair noted for the opposition of the political and ecclesiastical authorities as well as sectors of the mainstream press to this registration—facing the belief that a religion "could not be recognized as a cultural heritage site"—there were, in counterpoint, supports coming from "artists, intellectuals, journalists, politicians and religious leaders who diligently dedicated efforts to the campaign for the recognition of Afro-Bahian heritage" (2006: 239).[8] Such a registration constituted, for Velho (2006), a long-awaited recognition of the multiethnicity and sociocultural pluralism of Brazilian society, as well as a kind of reparation for the centuries-old intolerance of elites towards Afro-Brazilian beliefs and rituals, to say nothing of the confrontation with the real estate sector,[9] highly interested at the time in the land on which the *terreiro* is found, and which exerts a predominant role, as we know, in the construction and destruction of the urban landscape of our cities. The aforementioned article, however, called attention to the sociocultural heterogeneity making up contemporary metropoles, in which conflict is inherent, aimed at discrete situations of its manifestations, aspects which must be taken into account in practices of heritage preservation (Velho 2006).

Let us turn finally to an important writing by José Guilherme Magnani (2013) on the topic of heritage, in which recent or older cases of cultural heritage recognition are analyzed, notably two in particular: the first, related to Santana de Parnaíba, a city and municipality in the São Paulo metropolitan region, whose historic center was registered by CONDEPHAAT in 1982, and whose previous conflicts between functionaries from official bodies and inhabitants over the politics of the preservation of historic heritage was such that CONDEPHAAT hired Magnani as a consultant. Having emerged in 1580 and transformed into a colonial town in 1620, Santana de Parnaíba was an important transit point for settler expeditions heading towards Mato Grosso and Goiás in the Brazilian hinterland, counting, among others, the house of the *paulista* (i.e. from the state of São Paulo) trailblazer Anhanguera from the second half of the seventeenth century. An ethnographic survey conducted in 1984 permitted the reconstitution of a certain heterogeneity in the local, its sociocultural composition, leading to the classification between inhabitants from "inside" and "outside", and among the latter, a division arose between "foreigners", "artists", "functionaries", each of whom had distinct visions of what would constitute local heritage. A significant confluence meanwhile, appeared during the festival of Corpus Christi and the procession on the "carpet" produced by the community, this same festival which combines the religious cycle and the profanity of the local. Such an event precipitated the direct observation of agents, its relationships with public and private space, and the degrees of belonging to local families, facilitating a better understanding of their engagement with the topic of heritage (Magnani 2013).

Another case discussed in the same article (Magnani 2013) relates to the Parque do Povo [People's Park], granted status by CONDEPHAAT in 1984, that relied on a multidisciplinary team which included the guidance of Magnani and members of the Urban Anthropology Nucleus to carry out a research study that reinforced the argumentation for registration (Magnani and Morgado 1996). According to the author, in the mid-1980s, "the registration of spaces like Candomblé *terreiros*, vestigial sites of *quilombos*[10], workers' village towns, edifications typical of migrants and others of this sort, in other words, bound to the lifestyle (dwelling, work, religion) of social groups or ethnically differentiated was no longer causing surprise" (2013: para. 13).[11] In an area of 150000 square meters, considerably valued, there were pitches for different amateur soccer teams, as well as a circus and a theater. If the initial argument for registering a cultural heritage site was related to its considerable green space, the presence for decades of the said teams justified the need to preserve the park. This was because it was a popular leisure area, in a non-peripheral area of the city. Political initiatives spearheaded by park users, journalists, councilors and university students led to the decree being issued in 1995 (seven years after the opening of the process). However, as Magnani shows, such cultural heritage protection did not guarantee the subsequent presence of such football teams, due to alleged illegal practices practiced by the soccer associations, but that in fact, according to the author, the interests of the residents and users of the Itaim-Bibi region, tied to the most privileged social classes, on such space (2013: para. 23).

This became effective, as Simone Scifoni's 2013 article shows, beginning with an urban renewal plan in the area and led by the municipality in 2006, which according to the author, resulted in the elimination of the football pitches, demolition of the installation mounted by the social clubs and the transfer of the circus school (with the exception of the Vento Forte, through the intervention of the Ministry of Culture), and the installation of "extensive lawns, hiking trails, fitness equipment, playgrounds and new saplings of trees" (Scifoni 2013: 138).[12]

In the words of Magnani, "currently the concept of a nonmaterial asset is put into action in order to be able to reflect on the specificity of these cases; even still, when the asset in dispute involves as interests of another type that is not 'merely' cultural, it is difficult to ensure adequate protection, which entails the need to resort to other instruments for characterizing an asset as worthy of protection, and implement other means, beyond those presently anticipated in legislation" (2013: para. 25).[13]

Experiences in the CONDEPHAAT

Let us turn our attention finally to the CONDEPHAAT, as already explained, in light of the cross section of my own experience as an adviser and anthropologist, seeking a dialogue with the issues raised herein. This experience has revealed particular syntheses of the cases already discussed, with latitude given to other rulings in its purview. In this article, I will analyze four requests in which I participated as an adviser and rapporteur.[14]

Emerging in 1968, the CONDEPHAAT underwent a reorganization of its administrative structure in 2006, with the creation of the aforementioned Unit of Preservation of Historical Heritage (known by its Portuguese acronym UPPH). In this sense, it basically fulfills the same mandate as that of the CONDEPHAAT in terms of technical analysis, administrative procedures and deliberations. As already stated, its advisers come with multitudinous and varied backgrounds, are nominated by public institutions and are recognized by dint of their knowledge and diversified commitments. The actions of the CONDEPHAAT have been aimed not only at monumental assets but to relative constructions and varied social, economic and political contexts, and more recently to the registration of intangible assets.

It is important to point out that two cases analyzed in this article engage with a specific period of the CONDEPHAAT, corresponding to that of the presidency of Ana Lúcia Duarte Lanna, a professor in the School of Architecture and Urbanism at the University of São Paulo. In a subsequent balance sheet of her administration (2013–2015), Lanna (2016) assumes the cultural heritage as an eminently political field, based on multiple interests, mediations and conflicts, involving social actors and institutional plans of various orders whose configurations vary over time. Given the critical role of the CONDEPHAAT in responding to social demands in the sphere of heritage, as well as proposing policies and interfering positively in the same sphere, we can mention the more systematic attention in the period in paid to the topic of nonmaterial heritage, as well as cases located at the border between the recognition of material heritage and the registration of intangible heritage (Lanna 2016), that, as already discussed in this article, constitutes a special sphere for action by anthropologists.

Within the existing modalities in the aforementioned border, one can highlight, going back in time, the designation of the cultural heritage site Axé Ilê Obá by CONDEPHAAT in 1990, a Candomblé *terreiro* of the Ketu branch of Candomblé,[15] situated in Vila Facchini, São Paulo, according to an article by the anthropologist Rita Amaral (1991) that figured into the dossier required by CONDEPHAAT for the preservation of the locale, whose recognition was initially sought by "Mother"[16] Sylvia de Oxalá in 1986. It concerned a building, only twelve years old at the time, in an area measuring four thousand square meters, with a shed (*barracão*) for the settlement of longhouses (*ongás*) in honor of deities such as Oxalá, Ogum, Oxum e Xangô, for the religious obligations of the *terreiro* and residents. This resulted in a dossier with hundreds of pages worth of "information, photos, genealogies, explanations, architectural blueprints, bibliographies, letters, telegrams (and requests from the *orixás*, says 'Mother' Sylvia)" (Amaral 1991: para. 13).[17]

As already witnessed in the case of SPHAN's 1984 decision in Salvador, related by Velho (2006), there can often be, through a material recognition of culture heritage sites, the intention of protection mainly focused on nonmaterial practices. It was possible to engage with these thematics during the request's opening on the impending registration of black social clubs in the state of São Paulo, which are tied to leisure practices, entertainment and communitarian support of the [Afro-Brazilian] community of African descent beginning in the end of the 19th century, encompassing the Charitable Cultural and Recreation Club September 28 (Jundiaí), Charitable Society May 13 (Piracicaba) and Mayflower Recreational Family Guild (São Carlos).[18] The dossier in question, systematically produced by the UPPH, basically argued that:

The clubs are an expression of black associativism, representing forms of thinking, resisting and acting from the end of the 19th century to the first half of the 20th century, that deals with the topic of paulista history still permeated with lacunae, whose opening of the study of cultural heritage preservation sites could contribute to advancements in understanding such a reality; that the study in conjunction with such clubs could signal a more adequate proposal for the cultural heritage that they represent; that there still lacks greater recognition for the contributions of black culture on the part of the cultural politics of preservation of heritage.[19]

In the conclusion of my favorable assessment of the opening of the cultural heritage management study (dated February 9, 2014 and approved unanimously), I argued that:

The detailed investigation truly pinpoints a form of knowledge about historical dimensions relevant to the black population and culture, besides signaling the possibility of recognizing cultural heritage sites that could come to strengthen such clubs in the present, principally with regards to the possibility of gathering younger generations into the collective struggles of Afro-Brazilians by the expansion of their rights in contemporary reality.[20]

Let us look at the second case, also situated at the border between the material and nonmaterial, but linked to the preservation of places of painful/troubling memory, such as those tied to policies of political violence during authoritarian periods. In the CONDEPHAAT, this happened during the granting of cultural heritage site status, by a unanimous vote in January 2014, to the Department of Information Operations-Center for Internal Defense Operations (DOI-CODI) building. While it is banal in terms of architectural significance, it housed an organ of state repression of the Brazilian military dictatorship,[21] on Tutoia Street in São Paulo, where a military police station still operates today.[22] As Renato Cymbalista (2017: 232) affirms, "Tutoia is certainly the most emblematic locale that harkens back to the memory of the dictatorship", and even though the debate over places of painful and distressing memories has been growing in Brazil, the country is still well behind vis-à-vis comparable experiences that have already taken place in Germany, South Africa, Chile and Argentina.[23]

At the end of 2017,[24] I had the opportunity to be an adviser and rapporteur on what could has been defined as a locale of painful memory, but which unfortunately did not occur. It concerned the call for the designation of the Fazenda Cruzeiro do Sul, also known as Nazi Farm, given that its former owners, the Miranda Rocha family, via its political ties to the Brazilian Integralism movement,[25] used child slave labor in the locale, aligned with Nazi and xenophobic ideology.[26] According to the doctoral thesis of Sidney Aguilar Filho (2011), fifty orphaned and destitute children—primarily black and multiracial—were brought from the Romão Duarte orphanage in Rio de Janeiro to this farm in 1933. There, their names were traded for numbers and they were forced into slave labor for the next ten years, only to be freed without any remuneration or any rights, details were corroborated by accounts of elders who had suffered this grave injustice. While concrete connections between the Miranda Rocha family to Nazism have not been established with absolute certainty, bricks bearing the Nazi swastika were discovered years later by a rancher at this same site.[27]

Sadly, during the course of the studies and inspections related to the process, the current owners carried out intentional and criminal demolitions that partially disfigured the locale, which nonetheless did not prevent the recognition of this cultural heritage site. In my position writings, I defended the same locale as a "place of painful social memory" given that just as grievous as the Nazi ideology that inspired such a practice was the articulation of a kind of doubling down or perpetuation of African slavery in Brazil.[28] This can clearly be seen as this harrowing practice mostly targeted children of African descent, and being that slave labor was in fact a topic of enormous currency in the country, as evinced by

86

numerous reports, denunciations, documentaries and reports. Unfortunately, the proceedings did not reach a vote, essentially because the case involved the train station by which these children were transported and some advisers understood that this would necessitate two separate proceedings. It is hoped that in the near future, with the changes needed, this will once again be analyzed by the CONDEPHAAT.

Let us now proceed to the third case. Following the publication of the 57439/2011 decree, related to the Registration of Nonmaterial Cultural Assets that constitutes the Cultural Heritage of the State of São Paulo, processes of registering nonmaterial heritage were initiated, aside from other practices already enumerated while waiting for the finalization of the studies. Although such a sphere is proceeding at a slow pace—given the need to move forward in acknowledging the demands of a number of communities (e.g. *caipiras, quilombolas, caiçaras*, Afro-Brazilians)[29], one can cite the process in which I had the chance to be an advisor-rapporteur concerning the registration of nonmaterial heritage of rural *samba* from São Paulo.[30]

An important cultural practice scattered throughout different cities in the state of São Paulo, this regional musical genre and dance style bears multiple names (*samba de bumbo, jongo, batuque de umbigada or samba de vela*), though it is generally known as São Paulo-style *samba* (*samba paulista*). If we get past a certain dichotomy between rural and urban, or black São Paulo-style *samba*, and if we emphasize its historical origins which are linked to slavery, whose associative model differs in a certain manner from the cultural and economic model that predominates in Brazil, which is derived from the *samba* parades performed by Rio de Janeiro's *samba* schools (*escolas de samba*). Consequently, these are communitarian practices that do not resemble the economical organization present in those samba schools.

In my favorable opinion dated Delember 2, 2015, approved unanimously and whose audience included the presence of practitioners of certain modalities of São Paulo-style *samba*, I agreed with the orientation proposal suggested by the UPPH, recalling, in the words of Ana Lanna (2016: 7) that "the finalization of this hearing was made possible by the adaptation of the rule that instituted the registration of intangible assets in São Paulo"[31] with the necessity in hindsight of establishing adequate actions for safeguarding heritage. At this juncture, I think an evaluation of the favorable achievements of this registration, would be propitious, bearing in mind arrangements between initiatives of cultural agents and public authority, notably in this case, the state government, as well as possible partners like the IPHAN.[32]

To conclude, it is important to shed light on a controversial case related to the creation of the Pinacoteca Museum in the city of Mogi das Cruzes in 2016, in the former administrative building and jail Antiga Casa de Câmara e Cadeia (itself designated a cultural heritage site one month prior, in the same year, by the CONDEPHAAT). The implantation of the aforementioned museum gave rise to a denunciation of the artistic interventions that had already been achieved, especially certain graffiti artwork, which led to the opening of the proceedings of which I was the rapporteur.[33] In short, the graffiti installation—coloring the façade of the designated site's base and on part of the closing wall from the outside to the side street—was construed as an unacceptable intervention in a designated cultural heritage site due to physical damage and its impact on the landscape. The local Office of Culture, however, countered that such an intervention had passed through various forums, academic conferences, meetings and cycle of dialogue with groups of youth from Mogi das Cruzes, with the goal of creating and inculcating communal cultural policies in the city— in direct dialogue with those tied to the local hip hop culture, something that is, as a matter of fact, quite common already in the São Paulo metropolitan region.[34] We had, as the above account demonstrates, a paradox deriving from greater visibility and increased prominence of the building due to this graffiti, even if the visual dimensions of this artistic intervention caused unease among diverse visitors.

Briefly, the UPPH had suggested a conciliatory proposal, contingent upon the acceptance of the artistic intervention that had already made over the period of two years, after which it would return to the color scheme matching the rest of the building. From my perspective, this formed a kind of satisfactory agreement, between those schooled in this urban art and those who defend a more traditional use of a designated cultural heritage site. There is nothing to prevent new dialogues from being established in the future between the Pinacoteca Museum and local street artists, provided that more appropriate frameworks for its reversibility are considered.[35] The existent controversy itself could transcend the current, contentious plan through meetings where different artistic conceptions could be displayed and debated, deepening the rich dialogue already established by the local public power with the dwellers of Mogi das Cruzes.[36]

The approval of this opinion was obviously not unanimous and I fully comprehended the positions of advisers opposed to the writing of graffiti on a designated heritage site. However, I tried to take into consideration efforts to deepen relations with the public for whom graffiti constituted a powerful reference, despite the fact that such a fleeting art could not become something permanent.

Brief Conclusions (and Recent Challenges)

In short, myriads are the challenges facing the CONDEPHAAT, while noting that I understand to be playing a relevant role within its attributions and limitations. It is necessary to advance in the dimensions related to the cultural heritage, especially in the complex articulations between the material and nonmaterial spheres. I also think the role of anthropology, besides other areas of human sciences, is on this horizon of activity. In the field of anthropology focused on urban contexts, we have seen how research studies already carried out, accumulated reflections and dialogues with the public power make up a rich substrate from which new practices can occur, such as those that were briefly discussed in this article.

Of the four proceedings analyzed in this article, three directly relate to dimensions tied to policies, either historical or made present by those of African descent, which would require a much deeper reflection than what was put forth up to now.

For now, it behooves us to remember that such an all-inclusive body of topics has been significantly addressed in Brazilian urban contexts with a strong colonial history, such as the historic city of Salvador, Bahia. In the words of the anthropologist John Collins,[37] speaking of this city, "if we take into account its role in the non-aligned movement of the second half of the twentieth century, or if we count the number of Africans sent to this Brazilian city in the eighteenth century or any other American *entrepôt,*[38] the city of [Jorge] Amado[39] could very well serve or did serve as a certain kind of African capital" (Collins 2017: 26).[40]

Along these lines, we can also think in the context of Rio de Janeiro, especially starting in 2011 when in the course of implementing large-scale urban reforms and public works in the port city, archeological records of stone slabs from the former Valongo Wharf (*Cais do Valongo*) were found. The Wharf received hundreds of thousands of African slaves between the mid-18th century and the 19th century,[41] after which it was remodeled and transformed into the Empress's Wharf (*Cais da Imperatriz*). In 2017, the Valongo Wharf obtained the title of UNESCO World Heritage Site, which spurred a panoply of institutional actions associated with the African diaspora in the region, in the direction, also, of its patrimonialization (Guimarães 2013).

Beyond the possible contributions of urban anthropology to the realm of cultural heritage, until now discussed through my own practice as a member of the CONDEPHAAT (2013–2017),[42] it is fitting to end this article with some brief considerations of the relationships between knowledge and action in the field of cultural heritage production, a topic of the present conference's session.

Even without having participated directly in research on cultural heritage (as seen in the trajectories of Arantes e Magnani) nor explicit formulations of cultural policies (as highlighted in the case of Arantes), my participation as an adviser of the CONDEPHAAT (in certain dialogue with Velho's considerations, 2006) evokes questions tied to the public sphere. This is the case not only when we develop certain arguments based on scientific knowledge, in debates during CONDEPHAAT sessions, that are explained in our position articles—in the fulfillment of a social role that in fact falls to those affiliated with public universities—but also when we publicly defend certain points of view. It is worth highlighting a specific occasion when various advisers opposed the possible reduction, by a decision from the State Secretariat of Culture to which the Council is subordinate, of the university representation in the CONDEPHAAT (at the end of 2016),[43] whose obtainment was still counterposed by an increase in representatives affiliated with the government and institutions lacking an established tradition of patrimonial practice, a fact which ended up weakening the critical role of the university (and by consequence, that of anthropology as well) in the decisions of the CONDEPHAAT from then on. It is not by chance then that an open letter from the Institute of Brazilian Architects—São Paulo,[44] published at the end of 2017, pointed to a series of decisions contrary to the designated heritage assets in the city of São Paulo, putting demands and agendas regarding heritage status on the backburner—while simultaneously privileging private interests—on the part of the CONDEPHAAT and the Municipal Council for the Preservation of Historical, Cultural and Environmental Heritage of the City of São Paulo (CONPRESP). In a dossier published some days later entitled "Quem tem medo dos antropólogos (as). Dilemas e desafios para a produção e práticas científicas" ["Who's afraid of the anthropologists? Dilemmas and challenges for scientific production and practices"] (Machado, Motta, and Facchini 2018)—which aimed to face the present, difficult Brazilian political scenario, marked by the suppression of a series of rights to plurality—an article by Izabel Tamaso (2018) rightly addresses the relationship between knowledge and scientific practices in its public dimensions within the realm of heritage. She draws attention to the reflexiveness inherent in the various possibilities of being an anthropologist, such as how we act "as members of advisory councils on heritage" (2018: 66),[45] with questions that were discussed in the present article. According to Tamaso (2018: 67), we need a more collective and shared coalescence of our production of knowledge and practices, which ought to be aimed at improving the policies related to patrimonial assets (material and nonmaterial), as well as the strengthening of vulnerable populations who are carriers of cultural assets.

The present article, that began with an overview of the diversified contributions by

Brazilian urban anthropology's foremost authors to the field of cultural heritage, has tried to show the challenges encountered during my task as an anthropologist and university professor in the heritage council with singular characteristics, via the analysis of the production dynamics in specific opinions later submitted to vote, with varying results and in dialogue with sets of circumstances (internal to the council), which were also variable. Throughout the studied period, obstacles have increased exponentially, principally if we take into account the wider national political conjuncture,[46] with inevitable repercussions on the deliberative powers of CONDEPHAAT itself. This has created, beyond the attention to the specificities related to exercise of anthropology in a multidisciplinary field, the need for political confrontation in institutional terms, particularly in the current national context marked by strong conservatism and the curtailment of rights.

Notes

1. Article translated by Cheryl Leung (doctoral candidate in the Department of Middle East, South Asia and African Studies [Mesaas], Columbia University) for Session 1—"Blurred borders of knowledge and action: Dilemmas of practice and research in the heritage-making field"—of the 2018 Association of Critical Heritage Studies (ACHS) Conference, Hangzhou, China, September 1–6, 2018. Topic partially presented at the Federal University of Bahia (Salvador, Brazil, 2017), at the State Institute of Historical and Artistic Heritage of Minas Gerais (Belo Horizonte, Brazil, 2016) and at the Center for Research and Education SESC-São Paulo (São Paulo, Brazil, 2014).

2. Both affiliated with Secretariat of Culture for the State of São Paulo.

3. Arantes is one of the founding instructors of the University of Campinas and ex-president of CONDEPHAAT and the IPHAN; Velho (deceased in 2012) was a full professor of the National Museum and the Council of SPHAN—which predated IPHAN; Magnani is a full professor in the Department of Anthropology at the University of São Paulo and previously was a member of CONDEPHAAT. See Agier (2015) for a global work that talks with subjects tackled by such authors.

4. Translator's note: "Western Zone" refers to the area in the municipality of São Paulo situated to the west of Tamanduateí River, with a large contingent of poor residents.

5. Our translation of "com a participação de músicos, poetas, atores e artistas plásticos locais" and "elemento catalisador da produção artística popular local".

6. Our translation of "diferença, diversidade e conflito lhes são totalmente inescapáveis".

7. Translator's note: terreiro refers to the sacred house/yard or grounds where the syncretic Afro-Brazilian Candomblé religion is practiced.

8. Our translation of "artistas, intelectuais, jornalistas, políticos e lideranças religiosas que se empenharam a fundo na campanha pelo reconhecimento do patrimônio afro-baiano".

9. This question resurfaced in the public arena at the end of 2016, when the then-Minister of Culture Marcelo Calero resigned, for not ceding to the political pressure of Secretary of Government Geddel Vieira Lima—both tied to the administration of Michel Temer, who assumed power with significant controversy following the impeachment of Dilma Rousseff—so that IPHAN (linked to the Ministry of Culture) would approve the construction of a 30-story building (overturning a previous ruling) on the seafront of Salvador, comprising the area encompassing other historical heritage sites in the vicinity. Geddel was the owner of an apartment in the aforementioned building and renounced his ownership following the episode. See Amora, Dimmi. 2016. "IPHAN diz que veto a prédio de Geddel tem 'respaldo na legislação'" ["IPHAN says that veto to Geddel's building has 'backing of legislation'"]. Folha de S. Paulo, November 20, 2016. Accessed May 16, 2018. http://www1.folha.uol.com.br/poder/2016/11/1833932-iphan-diz-que-veto-a-predio-de-geddel-tem-respaldo-na-legislacao.shtml.

10. Translator's note: maroon societies or runaway African slave communities.

11. Our translation of "o tombamento de espaços como terreiros de candomblé, sítios remanescentes de quilombos, vilas operárias, edificações típicas de migrantes e outros dessa ordem, isto é, ligados ao modo de vida (moradia, trabalho, religião) de grupos social e/ou etnicamente diferenciados – já não causava muita estranheza".

12. Our translation of "extensos gramados, pistas de caminhada, aparelhos de ginástica,

playground e novas mudas de árvores".

13. Our translation of "Atualmente o conceito de bem imaterial é acionado para poder contemplar a especificidade desses casos; mesmo assim, quando o bem em disputa envolve interesses de outro tipo que não o 'meramente' cultural, dificilmente se consegue assegurar a devida proteção. O que implica a necessidade de recorrer a outros instrumentos para caracterizar um bem como digno de proteção, e implementar outras medidas, além das atualmente previstas na legislação".

14. Out of a total of 26 requests.

15. Translator's note: Candomblé Ketu is the largest branch (nation) of Candomblé, a religion practiced in Brazil, Argentina, and Uruguay. The word Candomblé means "ritual dancing or gather in honor of gods" and Ketu is the name of the Ketu (Benin) region in Nigeria. Its liturgical language, known as Iorubá or Nagô, is a dialect of Yoruba. Candomblé Ketu developed in the early 19th century and gained great importance to Brazilian heritage in the 20th century.

16. Translator's note: mãe-de-santo literally means Mother of (the) Saint or Candomblé priestess.

17. Our translation of "informações, fotos, genealogias, explicações, plantas arquitetônicas, bibliografias, cartas, telegramas (e pedidos dos orixás, diz 'mãe' Sylvia)".

18. Our translation of "Clube Beneficente Cultural e Recreativo 28 de Setembro (Jundiaí), Sociedade Beneficente 13 de Maio (Piracicaba) e Grêmio Recreativo Familiar Flor de Maio (São Carlos)". See case n. 01097/2011 (of January 2, 2012), whose author for the preliminary dossier was the sociologist Augusto Medeiros da Silva (case voted during the managerial oversight of Ana Lanna).

19. This passage, of my authorship, synthesizes the final part of the aforementioned UPPH dossier. The original in Portuguese states that "os clubes são expressão do associativismo negro, representando formas de pensar, resistir e agir do final do sec. XIX à primeira metade do séc. XX; que se trata de um tema da história paulista ainda

permeado por lacunas, cuja abertura do estudo de tombamento poderá contribuir para avanços no conhecimento de tal realidade; que o estudo em conjunto de tais clubes poderá sinalizar uma proposta mais adequada para o patrimônio cultural que representam; que ainda falta maior reconhecimento das contribuições da cultura negra por parte da política cultural de preservação do patrimônio".

20. The original in Portuguese reads "a investigação detalhada realmente aponta uma forma de conhecimento sobre dimensões históricas relevantes da população e cultura negra, além de sinalizar para a possibilidade de tombamentos que podem vir a fortalecer tais clubes no presente, principalmente quanto à possibilidade de aglutinar gerações mais jovens, nas lutas coletivas dos afrodescendentes pela expansão de seus direitos na realidade contemporânea". On CONDEPHAAT's decision, see Marques, Jairo. 2014. "Clubes sociais negros do final do século XX entram em processo de tombamento" ["Black social clubs from the end of the twentieth century enter into the process of cultural heritage recognition"]. Folha de S. Paulo, May 25. Accessed May 5, 2018. http://www1.folha.uol.com.br/cotidiano/2014/05/1459707-clubes-negros-do-final-do-seculo-xix-entram-em-processo-de-tombamento.shtml.

21. The DOI-CODI was a body subordinate to the Army, responsible for intelligence and repression of the Brazilian government during the military regime that carried out military coup of 1964.

22. The report was authored the anthropologist Silvana Rubino, and the historian responsible for the technical report was Deborah Neves; such a body was created in 1969, and extinguished in 1985; journalist Wladimir Herzog (1975) is the victims of imprisonment, torture and murder.

23. Among the studies cited, see Aguilera (2017).

24. Already under the presidency of architect, Carlos Augusto Faggin, lecturer at FAU-USP.

25. Translator's note: a fascist political movement in Brazil created in October 1932 whose principal ideologues were Plínio Salgado, Gustavo Barroso and Miguel Reale.

26. Whose final technical position article was written by the historian Deborah R. Leal Neves and the architect José A. Chinelato Zagato.

27. See Revista Galileu. 2014. "O segredo nazista brasileiro" ["The Brazilian Nazi secret"]. March 10, 2014. Accessed May 16, 2018. https://revistagalileu.globo.com/ Revista/noticia/2014/03/o-segredo-nazista-brasileiro.html.

28. Translator's note: the Lei Áurea (Golden Law in English), adopted on May 13, 1888, officially abolished slavery, ostensibly putting an end to five hundred years of African chattel slavery and making Brazil the last country in the Western Hemisphere to abolish this reprehensible institution.

29. Translator's note: caipiras denote inhabitants of rural areas in the interior of south-central Brazil whose racial origins and traditional culture are similar to those of the caiçaras who inhabit the coastal regions of southern Brazil; caiçaras descend from indigenous people, Europeans and Africans, who historically inhabited the coastal regions of the southeastern and southern Brazil; quilombolas are former residents of runaway slave communities (quilombos).

30. See the proceedings n. 69504/2013 (from June 13, 2013), whose technical position article was authored by Mário Augusto M. da Silva (hearing voted during the tenure of Ana Lanna).

31. Our translation of "a finalização desse processo foi possível pela adequação do regramento que instituiu o registro do patrimônio imaterial em São Paulo".

32. The question of the communities assuming the steering of nonmaterial records is fundamental; I was also the adviser to the opening of studies concerning the designation of Virado à Paulista (the traditional São Paulo platter consisting of beans, pork, manioc flour, fried plantain, eggs, kale, rice and torresmo, that dates back to the first Portuguese settlers of the state) as nonmaterial heritage (process n. 01087/2011, approved on December 15, 2014), a classic if humble dish indisputably inscribed in São Paulo's alimentary habits (akin to the "full English" breakfast), whose challenge, however, lay in a clearer mapping which would be the main stakeholders involved. In

any case, such a registration was made at the beginning of 2018 (when I was no longer on the Council), with a certain social repercussion. See Seto, and Guilherme. 2018. "Virado à Paulista é tombado e se torna 'patrimônio imaterial'" ["Virado à Paulista is overturned and becomes 'nonmaterial heritage'"]. Folha de S. Paulo, February 6, 2018. Accessed February 8, 2018. https://www1. folha.uol.com.br/cotidiano/2018/02/ virado-a-paulista-e-tombado-e-se-torna-patrim onio-imaterial.shtml.

33. Refer to proccedings n. 77397/2016 (from Dctober 7, 2016), whose registration was led by the historian Elisabete Mitiko Watanabe and the architect Elizeu Marcos Franco (these proceedings were voted on under the auspices of Carlos Faggin's tenure).

34. On hip-hop in São Paulo, see Macedo (2016).

35. The same Pinacoteca do Estado Museum in São Paulo bears graffiti on its sides but on removable pillars.

36. Excerpt from the ruling August 8, 2017. Our translation of "entre os adeptos dessa arte urbana e aqueles que defendem um uso mais tradicional de um bem tombado. Nada impede que, futuramente, novos diálogos possam ser estabelecidos entre a Pinacoteca e a street art local, desde que pensados em suportes mais apropriados quanto à sua reversibilidade. A própria controvérsia existente poderia transcender o atual plano conflitivo, através de encontros onde as distintas concepções pudessem ser expostas e debatidas, aprofundando-se o rico diálogo já estabelecido pelo poder público local com a população mogiana".

37. He has researched in depth the relationship between the policies of cultural heritage and vulnerability of the black population in the district of Pelourinho (Collins 2015).

38. Translator's note: transshipment port city.

39. A famous writer from Bahia (1912–2001) of the Brazilian modernist school who authored many books about Salvador and Bahia.

40 Our translation of "se tomarmos em conta seu papel no movimento não alinhado da segunda parte do século XX, ou se contamos o número de africanos mandados a essa cidade brasileira que recebeu mais escravos no século XVIII que qualquer outro

entrepôt americano, a cidade de [Jorge] Amado poderia bem servir, ou servia, como certo tipo de capital da África".

41. Built in 1811, it was the site of landing and trading of African slaves until 1831, when the ban on the transatlantic slave trade was enacted (though clandestine trade continued until 1888). During the 20 years of its operation, between 500 thousand and one million slaves landed at Valongo. Brazil received about 4.9 million slaves through the Atlantic trade.

42. I did not, in this article, address an earlier experience in the CONDEPHAAT between 2002–2003.

43. See "Manifestação ao CONDEPHAAT" ["Protest at CONDEPHAAT"] (Undersigned document, December 12, 2016); see, on the same subject, "Note of Repudiation", Brazilian Association of Anthropology, January 13, 2017. Accessed May 16, 2018. http://www.portal.abant.org.br/images/Noticias/79_Nota_de_ Rep%C3%BAdio_%C3%A0_redu%C3%A7%C3%A3o_das_representa%C3%A7% C3%B5es_das_universidades_no_CONDEPHAAT_1.pdf.

44. See "Carta Aberta: São Paulo, patrimônio cultural em risco, Instituto de Arquitetos do Brasil" ["Open Letter: São Paulo, cultural heritage at risk, Institute of Architects of Brazil"], Vitruvius, November 14, 2017. Accessed May 16, 2018. http://www. vitruvius.com.br/jornal/news/read/2809.

45. Our translation of "como membros dos conselhos consultivos de patrimônios".

46. By the way, on September 2, 2018, during the 2018 ACHS conference, the Brazil's National Museum (Rio de Janeiro) was totally destroyed by fire, with irreparable losses. This was certainly related to the lack of public investments to its proper protection. See "UNESCO in Brazil regrets fire at the National Museum", UNESCO Office in Brazil, September 3, 2018. Accessed February 26, 2019. http://www. unesco. org/new/en/brasilia/about-this-office/single-view/news/unesco_in_brazil_ regrets_ fire_on_the_national _museum/.

Acknowledgements

Sincere thanks to the technicians of UPPH (Secretariat of Culture for the State of São Paulo) for preparing the dossiers analyzed in this article.

Disclosure Statement

No potential conflict of interest was reported by the author.

Funding

This work and participation in the 2018 ACHS World Congress of Cultural Heritage were supported by myself.

Note on Contributor

Heitor Frúgoli Jr. is an Associate Professor at the Department of Anthropology of the University of São Paulo (USP) and a coordinator of Anthropology of the City Study Group (GEAC-USP). He was a Visiting Professor at University of Leiden (2010) and directeur d'études at École des Hautes Études en Sciences Sociales (Paris, 2013). He is CNPq (National Council for Scientific and Technological Development) researcher since 2005. Educational background: Visiting Scholar, University Institute of Lisbon (ISCTE-IUL) (2011); PhD, University of São Paulo, USP (Sociology) (1998); Visiting Scholar, University of California, San Diego (1995–1996); MA, University of São Paulo, USP (Anthropology) (1990).

References

Agier, Michel. 2015. *Anthropologie de la Ville*. Paris: PUF.

Aguilar Filho, Sidney. 2011. Educação, Autoritarismo e Eugenia: Exploração do Trabalho e Violência à Infância no Brasil (1930–1945). Doctoral Dissertation, University of Campinas, São Paulo.

Aguilera, Carolina. 2017. Santiago de Chile a Través de Espejos Negros: la Memoria Pública Sobre la Violencia Política del Período 1970–1991 en una Ciudad Fragmentada. In *Patrimônio Cultural: Memória e Intervenções Urbanas*, edited by Renato Cymbalista, Sarah Feldman, and Beatriz M. Kühl, 89-112. São Paulo: Annablume.

Amaral, Rita. 1991. O Tombamento de um Terreiro de Candomblé em São Paulo. *Comunicações do ISER* 41: 8-11.

Arantes, Antônio A. 2008. Entrevista. *Ponto Urbe* 3: 1-17.

Arantes, Antônio A. 2009. Patrimônio Cultural e Cidade. In *Plural de Cidade: Novos Léxicos Urbanos*, edited by Carlos Fortuna, and Rogerio C. Leite, 11-24. Coimbra: Almedina.

Arantes, Antônio A., and Antonio Motta. 2013. Dossier: Cultural Heritage and Museums (Foreword). *Vibrant* 10 (1): 71-75.

Collins, John F. 2015. *Revolt of the Saints: Memory and Redemption in the Twilight of Brazilian Racial Democracy*. Durham and London: Duke University Press.

Collins, John F. 2017. Prefácio. In *Disputas em Torno do Espaço Urbano: Processos de [Re]Produção/Construção e Apropriação da Cidade*, edited by John Gledhill, Maria G. Hita, and Mariano Perelman, 25-29. Salvador: Edufba.

Cymbalista, Renato. 2017. Lugares de Memória Difícil: as Medidas da Lembrança e do Esquecimento. In *Patrimônio Cultural: Memória e Intervenções Urbanas*, edited by Renato Cymbalista, Sarah Feldman, and Beatriz M. Kühl, 231-236. São Paulo: Annablume.

Ferro, Lígia. 2011. Da Rua para o Mundo: Configurações do Graffiti e do Parkour e Campos de Possibilidades Urbanas. Doctoral Dissertation, University Institute of Lisbon.

Guimarães, Roberta S. 2013. O Encontro Mítico de Pereira Passos com a Pequena África: Narrativas de Passado e Formas de Habitar na Zona Portuária Carioca. In *A Alma das Coisas: Patrimônio, Materialidade e Ressonância*, edited by José R. Gonçalves, Nina P. Bitar, and Roberta S. Guimarães, 47-78. Rio de Janeiro: Mauad X/Faperj.

Lanna, Ana L. D. 2016. Patrimônio Cultural: Políticas e Práticas—Relatório da Gestão 2013/2015 da Presidente do CONDEPHAAT. *Arquitextos* 189: 1-10.

Macedo, Márcio. 2016. Hip-Hop SP: Transformações entre uma Cultura de Rua, Negra e Periférica. In *Pluralidade Urbana em São Paulo: Vulnerabilidade, Marginalidade, Ativismos*, edited by Lúcio Kowarick, and Heitor Frúgoli Jr., 23-53. São Paulo: Editora 34/FAPESP.

Machado, Lia Z., Antônio Motta, and Regina Facchini (eds.). 2018. Quem tem Medo dos Antropólogos (as)? Práticas Científicas em Novos Cenários Políticos. *Revista de Antropologia* 61 (1): 9-32.

Magnani, José G. 2013. A Antropologia, entre Patrimônio e Museus. *Ponto Urbe* 13: 1-17.

Magnani, José G., and Naira Morgado. 1996. Tombamento do Parque do Povo: Futebol de Várzea Também é Patrimônio. *Revista do Patrimônio Histórico e Artístico Nacional* 24: 175-184.

Motta, Antônio. 2014. Patrimônio. In *Dicionário Crítico das Ciências Sociais dos Países de Fala Oficial Portuguesa*, edited by Lívio Sansone, and Cláudio A. Furtado, 379-391. Salvador: Edufba/ABA.

Scifoni, Simone. 2013. Parque do Povo: um Patrimônio do Futebol de Várzea em São Paulo. *Anais do Museu Paulista* 21 (2): 125-151.

Snyder, Gregory J. 2009. *Grafitti Lives: Beyond the Tag in New York's Urban Underground.* New York and London: New York University Press.

Tamaso, Izabela. 2018. Quando o Campo São os Patrimônios: Conhecimento e Práticas Científicas na Esfera Pública. *Revista de Antropologia* 61 (1): 60-70.

Velho, Gilberto. 2006. Patrimônio, Negociação e Conflito. *Mana* 12 (1): 237-247.

Mosques and Modernism in the Three Phases of the Turkish Republic

Klas Grinell

Gothenburg University. CONTACT Klas Grinell: klas.grinell@lir.gu.se

Abstract: This article builds on interviews with eight Turkish modern architects that were born in the 1930s, conducted in a research project called "Modernity retired". The main focus of the interviews was the ageing architects' views on modernism and modernity. Here I focus on how those views relate to the Muslim heritage of Turkish architecture, and more specifically on mosque architecture. The article traces the historical relations between modernist architecture and mosque architecture, with a special focus on the founding fathers of modernism, and on Turkish architecture. The key question is how the modernist concept of "function" can be understood in relation to religious practice and architecture. The conclusion is that the modern Turkish history shows more constructive meetings between modernism and Islamic tradition than the current dichotomy between government endorsed neo-Ottomanism and oppositional secular modernism.

Keywords: Turkish architecture, modernism, mosque, function, neo-Ottomanism

Modernism vs. Mosques

Modernism is often seen as a total break from tradition. Everything should be new. But as William Curtis states in his history of modern architecture "the most profound architects of the past hundred years were steeped in tradition" (Curtis 1996: 13). But what does Curtis mean by "tradition"? Tradition for him seems to be shorthand for "Western architectural tradition"; a quite narrow group of architectural references, buildings and writings. Such a conception of a singular architectural tradition risks cementing cultural borders and Western supremacy. There are in fact many different and differing traditions, as well as different strands within traditions.

The secularization thesis, which was an important aspect of modernization theory, said that the removal of religious authority from the political sphere was connected to a rationalization of society that would also turn people away from religion toward rationalism/ modernism. The opposite of modernism is traditionalism, and in its strongest version, religious traditionalism. "Tradition" has several meanings. I would propose a definition of tradition as a discourse where the boundaries of tradition are set by the furthest references that can still be forwarded in communication. In European tradition we can refer to Thales or Vitruvius, but not to Nagarjuna or Miskawayh. This is not the same "tradition" as the modern binary of traditionalism, though. There tradition is rather to be tied to inherited practices, and in the gravest form, to religious superstition.

The Turkish village programs of the 1930s (*köycülük*) built on a totally rational and civilizing perspective. In the words of the architect Aptullah Ziya, who proposed a mosque-free ideal village: "the worst thing about a village mosque, which has been the only cultural and social centre for the village, is that within its four walls it offers a bastion for the reactionaries who are the organizers of oppression and ignorance." (quoted in Bozdogan and Akcan 2012: 38) Instead of a mosque, the republican ideal village included a *halkevi* (people's house) for the organization of enlightenment. The Republic should create a brand new Turkish culture and citizenry (one can only wonder how Aptullah [meaning servant of God] felt about his name). The mosque seems to be an anathema to Turkish modernism, even if mosques are the most important architectural monuments in Turkish tradition. But is the mosque maybe an anathema mainly to early modernism?

Mosques and Modernist Architecture

In 1957, when Walter Gropius was 75 years old, he got the commission to design the new University of Baghdad, at a time when the Iraqi regime had also hired other modernist icons like Frank Lloyd Wright to design an opera house, Le Corbusier a sports hall, and Alvar Aalto an art museum (Marefat 2008: 5). None of these projects was fully realized; Wright's and Aalto's designs were dropped altogether because General Qasim's regime, which took over in 1958, deemed Aalto's museum and Wright's opera house too grandiose; Le Corbusier's arena was partly altered and finished belatedly in 1982, long after his death. Gropius was the only one who saw most of his ideas realized (Al-Sayegh 2013). According to US policy planner William Polk, who went with him to Baghdad, Gropius was particularly engaged in the mosque that was to be the centerpiece of the new campus. According to Polk, Gropius also asked, "What, really, was a mosque?" He thus started studying mosque architecture. According to Seyyed Hossein Nasr, whom he contacted for these studies, Gropius said that, "I can never build a building without knowing what its function is. What do you do in a mosque?" (Nasr and Jahanbegloo 2010: 158) They had long discussions on that question. Nasr is not very happy about simple modernist glass boxes, but says that "Gropius was truly aware of the shortcomings of such buildings for sacred use, and when it came to the creation of an Islamic sacred place he said 'I cannot do it because I do not belong to that tradition' " (Nasr and Jahanbegloo 2010: 159). Gropius must have changed his mind, or maybe Nasr has mistaken memories, as Gropius actually did design a university mosque. According to Polk, Gropius came to the idea that a mosque is consisted of three fundamental elements. The first was the *mihrab*, or prayer niche, which according to Polk didn't interest Gropius much. The second and most important element was the minaret. The third was the space of assembly. Gropius designed a tent-like, concrete dome with supporting corners set in pools of water that should reflect the light inward on the ceiling of the prayer hall (Polk 2004: 40). Gropius' Baghdad designs have been interpreted as part of a late regionalist and vernacular turn, together with his 1961 US embassy in Athens (Lefaivre and Tzonis 2012: 148). In the end the mosque was not built on the chosen location and the design and the materials used were also altered and made more traditionally Islamic and Arab.

There are important earlier engagements with mosques from modernist architects. One of the iconic writers and builders in the modernist architectural tradition is Le Corbusier, most probably included in Curtis' quoted reference to the "most profound architects": a man who took great inspiration from religious architecture, and even built a church as one of his most iconic buildings. As a young man Le Corbusier traveled in the Ottoman Empire, to Istanbul. The title for this chapter is taken from his description of Istanbul mosques. For some reason he did not want this travel diary to be published until the very last months of his life, in 1965. The modern young Turkish architects who started working in the 1950s thus did not know these words, even if his travels and "oriental" inspiration were known.

Mosques and Modern Turkish Architects

Turkish modernists did not only attached to modernism; an inherent part of the modernization program was nationalism. The historic master architect Sinan was a great source of national pride, builder during the great days of Sultan Suleiman the Law Maker, Caliph of the Muslims, known in the West as Suleiman Magnificent. In the republican construction of a national history one important aspect was to prove the Turkish qualities of art and architecture produced in the Ottoman Empire. The art historian Celal Esad Arseven, who taught architectural history at the Academy of Fine Arts in Ankara between 1920 and 1941, was the first to argue for the eastern Turkic origins of the architecture of Turkey, with Sinan as the most masterful expression of this Turkish tradition. Arseven also stressed that Sinan's buildings showed a purer Turkish style than the hybrid of Seljuk architecture burdened with excessive decorations. True Turkish tradition was argued to be in tune with modernism (Necipoglu 2007).

An interesting topic is thus how our interlocutors view the religious aspect of Turkish (architectural) tradition. There is quite a range of stances among them. At one end of the spectrum is the strong modernism of Neset Arolat, who identifies himself as "a son of Atatürk". Modernism for them means looking to the West, adapting a Western lifestyle and taste. That had already been the choice of his father, who read French modern poetry and belonged to the Young Turk modernists in the late Ottoman era. For Arolat the star architect was Ludwig Mies van der Rohe, maybe the most austerity of the founding fathers of modern architecture. With Neset Arolat there is no talk of mosques or the religious tradition of Turkey (even if he proudly mentioned that his son, the famous postmodern architect Emre Arolat, designed the Sancaklar Mosque, which was later proclaimed the world's best religious building of the year at the World Architecture Festival in Singapore in 2013). Dogan Tekeli speaks nothing of Islam. In an article for the journal *Architectural Design*'s special issue on Islam, Tekeli wrote a presentation of "Contemporary architecture in Turkey" where he states that among the most important Modern architects in Turkey "not one has sought a direct relationship with the Ottoman architecture of the past or deployed the grammar of Islamic architecture per se. All have made use of modern international technology, and employed a rational Western architectural language that reflects the ideology of the Turkish Republic" (Tekeli 2004: 95).

Another position is represented by Sevinc Hadi (who studied with Neset Arolat in Stuttgart in the early 1960s), who speaks about learning from Sinan. She shows a great interest in space and volume and talked about how they studied this in the old mosques of Istanbul, especially those by Sinan. From him she learnt to work with the interplay between different heights and volumes, visible for example in the self-designed summer house where we talked to her. She claims the mosques by Sinan were the main influence for this modernist architecture, putting the Sokullu Mehmet Pasha mosque in Azapkapi at the top of her list of the most perfect example of the combination of spaces. This is an interesting choice. Many speak about the Süleymaniye complex in Istanbul and the Selimiye in Edirne as Sinan's masterpieces. The mosque in Azapkapi is smaller, a late work of Sinan's, built in

1577–1578. It is said to be "one of Sinan's most successful interpretations of the eight-pierced, centrally-domed mosque form" (Sözen 1988: 295). The prayer hall is almost quadratic, with a continuous balcony along three sides. Six of the eight piers supporting the arches around the central dome are free standing, and thus the prayer hall dome flows into four smaller and lower semi-domes, that along with the balcony makes the room more open-ended than many other Ottoman mosques (Goodwin 1971: 285-287). For Hadi, the mosque is not so much a room with a function but an organization of space and volume, except also for its flowing light coming from masterly placed windows spanning from floor to roof. There is nothing in what she says that relates this to the functionality of the building as a mosque.

For Cengiz Bektas on the other hand it sometimes seems as if Islam and modernism are, at the bottom, the same thing. They are all about producing goods for the people in an ethical way. His father the Pilgrim installed the first street light in his Anatolian home town of Denizli, under which the children gathered to do their homework in the evenings. This was done out of a religious conviction that you should do good for others. Later his father was the first individual to donate a school to the government. Cengiz designed it with the main focus that there should be nothing intimidating in the school, as a contrast to the heavy and imposing school building he had gone to.

We were born modern, Bektas says, not as a tendency, but as a condition. Turkish modernism was, and should be, vernacular, which means that it has to work with local materials and techniques and work with nature rather than against it. The dictum of "Form Follows Function" is nothing new to Turkey, nothing that departs from tradition. On the contrary, this can be learned from both Sinan and the traditional countryside houses that Hakki Eldem studied. Turkish modernism came under too much influence from German and Italian trends and became nationalist, aimed at making an impression rather than function. With later US influence the international style entered Turkey.

For Bektas the modern ethos takes form in relation to Islam. In Turkish "mosque" is *cami*, which Bektas's traces to its Arabic etymological meaning of "bringing together". Modernism is also about bringing together, about understanding the functions in tradition.

This is more precise than Hadi's use of volumes. Bektas has written a whole book about Seljuk caravan lodges. When you study and learn the interplay between surface and content you can adapt traditional solutions and techniques to contemporary needs. If you understand tradition you are modern. If you only superficially use it as an inspiration you become a traditionalist, a simple copycat, out of touch with contemporary needs.

The Form and Function of Mosques

Bektas designed the first modern mosque in Turkey (Figure 1). The aim was still to bring people together. Sinan had to construct domes in order to build a space that was functional. Techniques have changed, and in 1962 there was no functional need for a dome or a minaret. Those functions could be met with a flat modern roof and loud speakers, Bektas says, mirroring the words of the late 1920s Turkish modernists. In order to keep the vital contact with nature Bektas, used a Seljuk solution taken, but transformed, from the caravan lodge architecture to let daylight enter the prayer hall in such a way that you could tell time according to the flow of light. The Seljuk tradition is present as a function, not in order to make the mosque look old. On the contrary, it is there to fill a function according to a modernist ethos.

Figure 1 Etimesgut Cami (photo from Cengiz Bektas archive SALT CC 3.0)

Bektas talks about his inside-out approach to architecture. The outside should show the function of the building. He is close to quoting Le Corbusier's *Towards an Architecture* without mentioning him: "The Plan proceeds from within to without; the exterior is the result of the interior." (Le Corbusier 1946: 11)

This view of architecture is almost contrary to how the architecture of the Islamic tradition is usually described, where the interior is to be concealed from the outside view. Mosques are mostly often surrounded by high, plain walls, and only the more elaborate portal, and the rising minaret and dome mark the importance and function of the buildings (Frishman 1994: 41). It is interesting that Bektas adapts his findings from a study of Seljuk caravan lodges to his mosque instead of building on Seljuk or Ottoman mosque architecture.

Who decides what is functional? The only other interlocutors to design a mosque are Aksüt and Marulyali, who came in second in the international competition for the mosque of London in the late 1960s. Their mosque too follows the modern paradigm and resists symbolic forms like the dome. Neither Aksüt, Marulyali nor Bektas seems to make any personal use of mosques. Especially Bektas argued that Turkish modern architects should take greater interest in mosque design in order to produce alternatives "to the technically and architecturally inadequate vernacular mosques spreading across small towns and villages". As Bozdogan and Akcan note, the unconventional mosque design was received with enthusiasm only by secular architects. Those actually using the mosques were not impressed by any improved or adapted functionality (Bozdogan and Akcan 2012: 197). Even with all the concern for doing good for the people, there is still a paternalistic architectural confidence in knowing what is good for the people. The feeling that the traditional and conventional symbols and methods of creating sacred space were still functional was not met with much respect.

Mohammed Hamdouni Alami argues that architecture cannot merely be judged from its physical functions, rather architecture functions in a poetical mode. This does not mean that other functions such as usage are unimportant, but that the poetic function is the dominant one. From this he argues that the minaret, which was not present in the earliest developments of mosque architecture, never had any significant function except from the symbolic one. It was there to be a visible landmark. That a mosque's basic functions are met just as well without a minaret is not due to modern technical achievements for the dissemination of the call to prayer. Denying the minaret a place in modernism would rather require an argument about the superfluous nature of landmarks and symbols (Hamdouni Alami 2010: 63-128). From Hamdouni Alami's perspective the modernist departure from traditional mosque architecture rests on a shallow and misinformed understanding of the aesthetics that informed the traditional mosques in the central Islamo-Arabic lands.

Is there any way to talk about an intersubjective sacred architectural functionality? Thomas Barrie (2012: 82) argues that "architecture built to serve ritual, as sacred architecture nearly always is, needs those individual and communal rituals to complete them—they depend on humans to animate their spaces and articulate their meaning". The functionality of sacred architecture, as Barrie calls it, would thus have to be judged by those that try to animate it. The idea of sacred architecture seems to differ from the modernist discourse of our interlocutors most when it comes to symbols. According to Barrie, "we still need symbols to materialize the unknown and structure our (often inadequate) understandings" (Barrie 2012: 93). In our conversations this is seldom addressed, and the impression is that symbolism often is connected with ornamentation and dishonest replication of tradition. Religion is partly an experience of being integrated in a continuous tradition and religious spaces, therefore they need to function as reminders of this continuity. This kind of symbolic and ritual functionality seems hard to reconcile with the modernist concept of "function" as we have met it. For me this is a point where the difference between Mies van der Rohe and Corbusier becomes most visible and important.

Le Corbusier (2007: 100) describes what a mosque is:

It must be a silent place facing towards Mecca. It needs to be spacious so that the heart may feel at ease, and high so that prayers may breathe there. There must be ample diffused light so as to have no shadows; the whole should be perfectly simple; and a kind of immensity must be encompassed by the forms. The floor must be more spacious than a public square, not to contain great crowds but so that the few who come to pray may feel joy and reverence within this great house.

The poetic note of the young Corbusier is very much attuned to the spiritual function of the mosque, even if he also highlights some aspects that are more often attached to modernism, such as the "coat of whitewash" and the "elementary geometry [that] orders these masses: the square, the cube, the sphere" (Le Corbusier 2007: 102, 104), and he also loathes the "repugnant and revolting painted ornamentation" (Le Corbusier 2007: 103) that he claims the Young Turks have added to the simplicity that he admires.

For all our interlocutors, the flat roof is emphasized in a way that makes it into something like a symbol for modernism and the modern era. Designing a mosque with anything but a flat roof seems unthinkable for the few who ever considered building a mosque. Is the dome merely a technique that Sinan had to use and that progress has made redundant? Not necessarily. For Le Corbusier (2007: 100), "the half-sphere has the unique charm of eluding measurement".

Only two years after Bektas's modern mosque, in 1964, a modernist mosque was designed on Kinali Island, the closest of the Prince Islands outside of Istanbul, by architects Turhan Uyaroglu and Basar Acarli. This mosque has a vault-like roof made from concrete plates, and a very prominent minaret, even if neither of them follows traditional designs. The minaret is free-standing and is more of a sculpture than part of the building. There are no stairs inside of the minaret; instead the muezzin provides a room at the bottom of the minaret from where to announce the call to prayer via loudspeakers (even if the loudspeakers were not integrated in the original design but are attached in much the same way as they are on most traditional minarets). The vaulted roof of the prayer hall reminds more of a pyramid than a classical Ottoman mosque, and the walls of the prayer hall and the traditional enclosed courtyard are in rough cut stone (Ürey 2010: 69-85). The Kinali mosque could thus be said to be a more balanced fusion of tradition and modernism than Bektas's stricter modernism.

The Modernity of Neo-Ottoman Mosques

All our Turkish interlocutors are very critical of the current neo-Ottomanist architecture promoted by the Justice and Development Party (AKP) government. Tradition is only present as surface, ornament and style. This is speculative, dishonest and a bad traditionalism. Buildings like the big Kocatepe Mosque (Figure 2) in Ankara are dismissed as mere replicas. There are multiple explanations for this stance. One is of course political and has to do with a redistribution of power from the old Republican elites of Turkey, to which the modern architects belong materially and ideologically. Another aspect of this involves the possible role of religion in the Turkish public sphere. This pairs with the fact that architectural history up until the 1980s "routinely portrayed the history of Western Architecture as history of architecture *par excellence*" making other architectural forms seem "sedated, static and unevolving" (Rabbat 2004: 18). This resonates with the stance of our Turkish interviewees.

Reproducing the sublime spaces and volumes of Sinan's mosques is out of touch with the contemporary situation, it is argued. The nuanced historians Bozdogan and Akcan also call the Kocatepe Mosque "a direct replica" that "replicates the Ottoman tradition to the minutest detail" even if it is up-scaled in size and contains a whole different technical machinery. In contrast to the feelings of repulsion this type of neo-Ottoman architecture seems to produce in our interlocutors, Bozdogan and Aksüt can still conclude that by housing a supermarket and parking garage in its lower level "this distinctly postmodern juxtaposition of a consumer society with renewed religiosity can be viewed as an appropriate symbol of the culturally conservative and economically liberal turn that Turkey took in this period [the late 1980s]" (Bozdogan and Akcan 2010: 219-220). Michael Meeker goes further and argues that the representatives of the mosque should not simply be understood as revivalist conservatives. They stress the modernity of Kocatepe and thus republican Islam, which is demonstrated in the technical sophistication of the mosque with its centrally heated floor, its elevators and intercom system. It is thus not only a postmodern juxtaposition but a conscious association and fusing of architectural "motifs from classical mosque architecture" with "techno-scientific artifacts of mass society" (Meeker 1997: 181). The Kocatepe Mosque is as modern a national symbol as the Anit Kabir with which it competes as a landmark of Ankara and complements in order to show the two foundations of contemporary neo-Ottoman Kemalist Turkish modernity.

Figure 2   Kocatepe Mosque (photo by Asim Bharwani CC BY-NC-ND 2.0)

There are still compelling arguments for viewing neo-Ottoman mosque architecture as represented also in the new grand Camlica Mosque by Bahar Mızrak and Hayriye Gül Totu replications of a frozen heritage. It should however be remembered that the Kocatepe mosque project as designed by Hüsrev Tayla and M. Fatin Uluengin was commenced already in 1967. Neo-Ottomanism is thus older than the third republican phase. What makes relevant to call it a superficial style would be its freezing of Ottoman architecture into a symbol of a golden age that does not acknowledge the living and evolving practice of Ottoman mosque architecture. There are also template drawings available for easy replication of this generic neo-Ottoman mosque to be ordered from the Department of Religious Affairs (Rizvi 2015). But contratry to what Suzy Hansen and Norman Behrendt argue in a *New York Times* Magazine piece from 2017, the mosques built under Erdogan's rule are actually more diverse in their styles than the concept of neo-Ottomanism that might imply. The Ahmet Hamdi Akseki Mosque (Figure 3) in the Cankaya district of Ankara completed in 2013 is actually an interesting and quite congenial mix of the original Kocatepe design, a classical one-domed Ottoman golden age mosque, and a more international Saudi-inspired contemporary style.

Figure 3   Ahmet Hamdi Akseki Mosque (photo by Osman Sözer, CC 3.0)

None of the old modernists seem to be able to find any opening for reconciling this Muslim modern social imaginary with their traditional laicist modern social imaginary.

Turgut Cansever was an exception, a truly modern architect and devout Muslim who articulated a self-image as a modernist indebted to Turkish-Islamic traditions with a great admiration for Sinan. Many of his buildings won acclaim from his fellow modernists, and international acclaim like the Aga Khan Award in 1992 for his Demir vacation houses in the luxurious tourist resort of Bodrum. According to Cansever this "site-specific architecture sensitive to locality, culture, crafts and tradition" was a result of his Islamic world view—something that Cengiz Bektas at a symposium at the time dismissed as religious propaganda. Interestingly Cansever also saw the monumental neo-Ottoman mosque designs as shallow imitations and replicas, even if he was also critical of modernist uses of the traditional typology (Bozdogan and Akcan 2012: 220), as in the first draft for a Kocatepe mosque done in 1957 where the dome was transformed into a shell dome resembling a blown up square tent where canvas stuck in the ground on its four corners by sharp poles, minarets that resemble spaceships.

As said above, Sinan was an important inspiration for Cansever, even if it should be mentioned that he was also a student and assistant of the acclaimed vernacular modernist Sedad Hakki Eldem. Trying to capture the qualities of Sinan, Cansever (2004: 66) writes:

> Nothing jarred, nothing was exaggerated; every part played its appropriate role, excluding all fetishising tendencies. Tawid (unity of existence) established unconditional submission to God's will, while setting the foundations for a feeling of security, and was reflected as polychromy, brightness, clarity and tranquility of movement; harmonising with attitudes of sublimity, respect, simplicity, responsibility. All these facets coalesced, contributing to the achievement of monumentality on a human scale, a harmonious realisation of the sublime unity.

Cansever's own less imposing interpretation of a contemporary mosque, with tile-covered domes and local Seljuk-inspired brick walls can be seen in the Karakas Mosque (Figure 4) in Antalya, completed in 1998. The two different generations of Kocatepe designs contrast with the Cansever's Karakas Mosque in their monumental character. The design of either of them can hardly be said to follow from their functionality as spaces for prayer and reflection. They are not places where my heart feels at ease.

Figure 4   Karakas Mosque (photo by Bernard Gagnon, Wikimedia.org)

The modernist and the un-built Kocatepe Mosque might be well-proportioned and innovative. The use of classical morphology is very different from Bektas's digested and transformed traditional elements. Still, both of them develop their reshaped form in an intellectual and abstract theorization that is totally detached from the wants and ideas of the local users of the facility. It is modernism from above. This might be the case with Cansever's work too. The difference is that he himself has a deep-rooted personal relation to the functionality of a mosque.

Even if most new mosques in Turkey follow similar lines of the neo-Ottoman design to the Kocatepe, there are a number of more or less modernist mosques in the country. The most celebrated is the mosque for the Grand National Assembly, which received the Aga Khan award in 1995, designed by Behruz and Can Cinici in 1989. The mosque is only for the use of the parliamentarians, and like Bektas's military mosque it is thus not accessible to the public. The mosque has the form of a heavily grounded, low pyramid where the steps are organized similarly to the semi-domes of Ottoman mosques. The overall impression is heavy, even if there are also parts like the prayer wall that are more transparent by way of glass walls. The minaret is replaced by a Cypress tree (Ürey 2010: 99-111; Al-Asad 1995, 1999).

There are at least a dozen other more contemporary examples. In more contact with our period of interest is one of the most outlandish mosques in Turkey, the 1971 mosque in Derinkuyu, Cappadocia, designed by the sculptor and former mayor of the city Hakkı Atamulu. The Derinkuyu Mosque has connotations of Le Corbusier's 1954 Notre Dame du Haut in Ronchamp. Atamulu's mosque is designed as a single mass of concrete where the minaret rises in the narrow end of a triangular shape in a style that we in the Nordic countries decode as a ski jump ramp (Ürey 2010: 135-145).

There are also Turkish-designed modern mosques in other parts of the world, like Dorük Pamir's and Ercüment Gümrük's 1986 design for the mosque at the Islamic Center for Technical and Vocational Training and Research in Bangladesh, in red brick with a flat roof and very strict geometric arches and squares. It is an example that combines modernist and Islamic elements, even if more attuned to Turkish and primarily Seljuk traditions than Bengali ones. Vedat Ali Dalokay's Shah Faisal Mosque (Figure 5) in Islamabad, Pakistan

(1970–1986) is more Ottoman inspired and reuses his design for the first Kocatepe mosque project, with slender minarets and a concrete tent-like roof (Khan 1994).

Figure 5   Shah Faisal Mosque (photo from Wikimedia.org)

Conclusions

Neo-Ottoman architecture affects more than mosques. Like Menderes in the 1950s, Recep Tayyip Erdogan has taken a strong personal interest in the refurbishment of Istanbul, his home town, where he rose to fame as a mayor in the 1990s. One of the first and most controversial proposals back then was the construction of a big mosque at Takism Square, across the secular icon of the now dismantled Atatürk Cultural Center. Even if this proposal was abandoned in the late 1990s, it still lingered as a threatening and mobilizing symbol of the change that AKP is implementing in Turkey. This is one of the genealogies vibrating in the Gezi Park protests of 2013. In 2017 construction work on a typically neo-Ottoman replica mosque was commenced at Taksim.

Among our interlocutors the resistance towards the efforts to reclaim a Muslim and

Ottoman heritage in the official symbolism and everyday life of the Turkish republic ran very deep. The critique should not be read only as a staunch modernist laicist who is aversion to everything Islamic. There are of course also many different Muslim positions, many of which are also critical of the AKP's aesthetic as well as the increasingly authoritarian and self-opinionated rule of Erdogan.

There is a fixation on the new and clean in 'urban transformation' projects such as those in Ayazma, Fener/Balat, Süleymaniye, Sulukule and Tarlabasi, or the current cleaning spree in Gezi Park [—] This obsession with the clean, tidy, new appearance seems like what rulers who lived in rural areas one or two generations ago understand to be modernity. (Aktar 2013)

The social engineering of the contemporary Turkish rulers shows similarities with the ambitions of the late 19th century Young Turk positivist modernists. It is anti-cosmopolitan, strives for a national unity, and also has a generic clean and shiny unitary aesthetic that is very modern, and partly inherent in Kemalism. According to such a view the problem with the neo-Ottoman refurbishment is less its Islamic side than its belated positivist understanding of uniform modernization, maybe even its kinship with the brutally modern Corbusian city planning ideas (Le Corbusier 1987).

It thus seems as if the relation between mosques and modernity does not constitute such a neat dichotomy as the modernization paradigm might suggest; that religious buildings challenge the modern concept of functionality in interesting ways; and that the iconic modern architects were more positively interested in mosques than their legacy suggests.

⊡ Disclosure Statement

No potential conflict of interest was reported by the author.

⊡ Funding

This work was supported by the Swedish Research Council Under Grant 2010-1673.

⊡ Note on Contributor

Klas Grinell, an Associate Professor in the History of Ideas, Gothenburg University, Director of Center for European Research, Gothenburg University (CERGU) and Culture Strategist at the Cultural Affairs Administration, City of Gothenburg. He was former curator and research coordinator at the National Museums of World Culture. From 2015 to 2018, he was a project leader for "Museological framings of Islam in Europe". He is now working in the project "Reconciliatory heritage: Reconstructing heritage in a time of violent fragmentations (2017–2021)". His research interests are situated within the triangle of Islamic studies, Heritage studies and European studies.

□ References

Aktar, Cengiz. 2013. Clean and Tidy. Today's Zaman, June 17, 2013.

Al-Asad, Mohammad. 1995. *Technical Review Summary: Mosque of the Grand National Assembly, Ankara, Turkey*. Geneva: The Aga Khan Award for Architecture.

Al-Asad, Mohammad. 1999. The Mosque of the Turkish Grand National Assembly in Ankara: Breaking with Tradition. *Muqarnas* 16 (1): 155-168.

Al-Sayegh, Hadeel. 2013. A Conflict of Visions: Contesting the Legacy of Old Dreams of a Modern Baghdad. May 16, 2013. Accessed March 10, 2019. https://www.thenational. ae/arts-culture/a-conflict-of-visions-contesting-the-legacy-of-old-dreams-of-a-modern-baghdad-1.455330.

Barrie, Thomas. 2012. Sacred Space and the Mediating Roles of Architecture. *European Review* 20 (1): 79-94.

Bozdogan, Sibel, and Esra Akcan. 2012. *Turkey: Modern Architectures in History*. London: Reaktion books.

Cansever, Turgut. 2004. The Architecture of Mimar Sinan. *Architectural Design* 74 (6): 64-70.

Curtis, William J. 1996. *Modern architecture since 1900*. New York: Phaidon.

Frishman, Martin. 1994. Islam and the Form of the Mosque. In *The Mosque: History, Architectural Development and Regional Diversity*, edited by Martin Frishman, and Hasan-uddin Khan, 17-42. London: Thames & Hudson.

Goodwin, Godfrey. 1971. *A History of Ottoman Architecture*. London: Thames and Hudson.

Hamdouni Alami, Mohammed. 2010. *Art and Architecture in the Islamic Tradition: Aesthetics, Politics and Desire in Early Islam*. London: Tauris.

Khan, Hasan-uddin, 1994. An Overview of Contemporary Mosques. In *The Mosque: History, Architectural Development and Regional Diversity,* edited by Martin Frishman, and Hasan-uddin Khan, 246-267. London: Thames & Hudson.

Le Corbusier. 1946. *Towards an Architecture*. New York: Praeger.

Le Corbusier. 1987. *The City of Tomorrow and its Planning*. New York: Dover Publications.

Le Corbuiser. 2007. *Journey to the East.* Cambridge MA: MIT Press.

Lefaivre, Liane, and Alexander Tzonis. 2012. *Architecture of Regionalism in the Age of Globalization: Peaks and Valleys in the Flat World.* New York: Routledge.

Marefat, Mina. 2008. From Bauhaus to Baghdad: The Politics of Building the Total University. *TAARII Newsletter* 3 (2): 1-12.

Meeker, Michael. 1997. Once There Was, Once There Wasn't: National Monuments and Interpersonal Exchange. In *Rethinking Modernity and National Identity in Turkey,* edited by Sibel Bozdogan, and Resat Kasaba, 157-191. Seattle: University of Washington Press.

Nasr, Seyyed Hossein, and Jahanbegloo Ramin. 2010. *In Search of the Sacred: A Conversation with Seyyed Hossein Nasr on His Life and Thought.* Santa Barbara, CA: Praeger.

Necipoglu, Gülrü. 2007. Creation of a National Genius: Sinan and Historiography of "Classical" Ottoman Architecture. *Muqarnas*no 24: 141-184.

Polk, William R. 2004. Gropius and Fathy Remembered. *Architectural Design* 74 (6): 38-45.

Rabbat, Nasser. 2004. Islamic Architecture as a Field of Historical Enquiry. *Architectural Design* 74 (6):18-23.

Rizvi, Kishwar. 2015. *The Transnational Mosque: Architecture and Historical Memory in the Contemporary Middle East.* Chapel Hill: University of North Carolina Press.

Sözen, Metin. 1988. *Sinan: Architect of the Ages.* Istanbul: Turkish Ministry of Culture and Tourism.

Tekeli, Dogan. 2004. Contemporary Architecture in Turkey: An Evaluation. *Architectural Design* 74 (6): 90-97.

Ürey, Özgür. 2010. *Use of Traditional Elements in Contemporary Mosque Architecture in Turkey.* Master Thesis, Middle East Technical University, Ankara .

The Grey Area of Gender in Intangible Cultural Heritage: Analysis of Japan's Inscribed Elements on the Representative List of the Intangible Cultural Heritage of Humanity

Helga Janse

University of Tsukuba, World Heritage Studies, Tennodai 1-1-1, Tsukuba, Ibaraki 305-8571, Japan. CONTACT Helga Janse: d17_helga@heritage.tsukuba.ac.jp

Abstract: Matters of gender equality within intangible cultural heritage (ICH) are often seen as sensitive or complex, making them easier to avoid than to address. The difficulties become apparent in the handling of gender within UNESCO's Convention for the Safeguarding of the Intangible Cultural Heritage (ICHC). In this study, the author seeks to shed some light on this grey area by analysing elements inscribed on the Representative List (RL) of the Intangible Cultural Heritage of Humanity. Available data on gender found in the official documents (nomination files and periodic reports) pertaining to all elements from a single country (Japan) are extracted, categorised, aggregated and analysed with the objective of identifying patterns at the national level. Japan has the second highest number of elements inscribed on the list, as well as legal instruments for safeguarding intangible cultural heritage dating back to the 1950s. By approaching the elements on a collective level, this study identifies existing gender imbalances in the examined elements, with a male dominance in access, participation and representation. The study also finds indications that gender equal representation was not a prioritised factor in the national nomination selection process.

Keywords: intangible cultural heritage, gender, UNESCO, Japan

Introduction

There is a connection between intangible cultural heritage (ICH) and gender. A case in point is the occurrence of gender coded traditions where participation is linked to the participants' assigned gender. However, matters of gender within ICH are often seen as sensitive or complex, making them easier to avoid than to address. The underlying debate of universalism versus cultural relativism is a factor, as well as differing attitudes towards gender equality, and conflicting ideological views. The intersection of gender equality and the safeguarding of traditional practices is thus laden with potential conflict, and gender equality considerations within ICH are often treated as a grey area.

The difficulties become apparent within the context of UNESCO's 2003 Convention for the Safeguarding of the Intangible Cultural Heritage (ICHC). A 2013 evaluation of the convention conducted by UNESCO's Internal Oversight Service found that it had proven problematic to integrate UNESCO's Global Priority Gender Equality into the mechanisms of the convention. The evaluation referred to this issue as "the elephant in the room", and pointed out that it was "a very sensitive issue given the apparent lack of consonance between the human rights values of gender equality and non-discrimination and the fear that a high proportion of ICH would be excluded if these tests were applied more strictly to defining/identifying ICH" (UNESCO Internal Oversight Service 2013: para. 72). The evaluation also found a lack of in-depth debate about gender equality and ICH and appropriate guidance, causing the mechanisms of the convention to be gender-blind (UNESCO Internal Oversight Service 2013: para. 78).

In this study, the author seeks to shed some light on this grey area of gender within

ICH by, concentrating on the ICHC, looking at tendencies through aggregated data from all elements from an individual country. This is done by analysing the information available on gender in the official documents (within the mechanisms of the convention) pertaining to the elements listed on the Representative List (RL) of the Intangible Cultural Heritage of Humanity by the State Party of Japan.

Japan stands out among the state parties to the ICHC in a number of ways. Japan played an influential role in the creation of the convention[1] (Hafstein 2004), and currently (October 2018) has the second largest number of inscribed elements. Furthermore, national heritage legislation protecting both tangible and intangible heritage properties existed in Japan before the creation of the ICHC. This also means that the already existing registries of the legislative system were available as a basis when composing the national inventory.

The Japanese elements inscribed on the RL exist in two safeguarding systems—the national heritage legislation and the convention.[2] By inscription on the RL, the properties/ elements protected by the national heritage legislation are being displayed on an international arena, where the goals and ideals may differ from the local contexts. The two systems form different contexts, and both of them are separated from the local circumstances within which the practice takes place. As Hafstein notes, the use of lists itemises culture, and the lists of ICH "artifactualise cultural practices and expressions, decontextualising them from the social relations in which they take place in order to recontextualise them in national inventories with reference to other practices and expressions under the same national government and in international lists with reference to other 'masterpieces' of humanity", rendering the practices transferable (Hafstein 2009: 105).

In the intersection between these two systems, UN ideals meet local and national heritage management. The 2003 convention, and arguably the Representative List of the Intangible Cultural Heritage of Humanity in particular, is an arena where the state parties are faced with navigating through the set goals and ideals of this international arena, and finding strategies for meeting the criteria when nominating elements. On this arena, the elements and/or their descriptions can be expected to be adjusted to some extent.

This study presents an analysis of the gender situation presented on this representative and international arena. The study uses quantitative and thematic analysis. Available data on gender in the official documents pertaining to the Japanese elements were extracted, categorised, aggregated, and analysed, with the objective of identifying patterns and tendencies on the national level. Thematic analysis was used to examine the discourse surrounding gender and how roles and rules are portrayed. Both analyses were used to examine the handling of gender within Japan's implementation of the ICHC. Additionally, since the choice of the nominated and later inscribed elements are a result of a national selection process, an examination of these elements could also give indications of whether gender was a factor in that selection process. The study is part of a research project on the interaction between ICH and gender in Japan.

The Grey Area of Gender in the ICHC

The ICHC sets out to safeguard ICH, while at the same time adhering to human rights instruments. The 2003 convention is formulated in a way that, at least in theory, makes human rights considerations an indismissible part of its implementation. The definition of ICH in the convention text contains criteria stipulating that only such ICH as is compatible with human rights instruments (as well as with requirements of mutual respect among communities, groups and individuals, as well as of sustainable development) are to be considered by the convention (Convention for the Safeguarding of the Intangible Cultural Heritage, article 2.1). The author chooses to refer to this as the "goodness criteria". In theory, if strictly applied, this would mean that practices which are not up to par with human rights standards should not be recognised for the purposes of the convention, and should consequently not be inscribed on any of the Lists of Intangible Cultural Heritage.

However, for the purposes of implementing the ICHC, it is difficult to find a clearly defined line which separates acceptable practices from unacceptable practices, in terms of adhering to human rights instruments (Blake 2015). Moghadam and Bagheritari (2007) has written about the ICHC in a 2007 article where they express criticism and concern that the convention risks failing to protect the human rights of women, due to its gender-neutral language and its lack of reference to Convention on the Elimination of All Forms of Discrimination Against Women (CEDAW) and other instruments pertaining to women. They argue that "there must be agreement that 'culture' is not a valid justification for gender inequality" and that when drafting culture conventions due "attention must be directed to all human rights instruments, and especially those pertaining to women" (Moghadam and Bagheritari 2007: 11).

The 2013 evaluation conducted by UNESCO's Internal Oversight Service identified a number of problems pertaining to the handling of gender considerations within the convention, and a list of recommendations was presented (UNESCO Internal Oversight Service 2013). It was also pointed out that the lack of requests for sex-disaggregated data in the periodic reporting was a lost opportunity (UNESCO Internal Oversight Service 2013: para. 79). The evaluation prompted several changes in the following years (2014–2016), such as revisions of all relevant documents and forms (nomination forms, forms for periodic reporting, and the operational directives) to include gender-specific guidance and questions, the creation of two training units on gender in the capacity-building program, as well as the creation of a brochure on gender and ICH (UNESCO 2015, 2018).

Blake (2015: 286) (who is also listed as one of the authors of the above-mentioned evaluation) discusses gender dynamics within the ICHC in *International Cultural Heritage Law* (2015) and points out that it is sometimes difficult to determine whether a cultural practice falls within the standards of human rights instruments or not.

A large number of traditional cultural practices can be viewed in this light [reference to the conflict between universal human rights standards and cultural relativism] and it is not always easy to decide on which side of the "human rights line" a cultural manifestation falls. Of course, such practices as female infanticide or cannibalism are clear human rights violations but others that involve, for example, sexually segregated rituals or secret knowledge held by a highly privileged elite are difficult to judge. Furthermore, such cases also raise the very sensitive question as to who should be given the power to decide this—is it only the cultural community itself that perpetuates such practices or some outside agency?

In noting the lack of practical definitions and guidelines for determining what constitutes gender discrimination within the framework of the convention, Blake (2015: 182) detects a nervousness among the state parties and other stakeholders.

The, as yet unresolved, question of how to address the gender dynamics of ICH and its safeguarding within the framework of the 2003 Convention is a recently acknowledged issue. Up until recently, there has been little proper debate about gender equality and ICH and most of the Convention's mechanisms and the related documents, forms, and assessments have been "gender blind". This may well reflect a nervousness on the part of State Parties, the ICH Committee of the Convention, and UNESCO itself of entering into an arena where it is necessary to deal with ICH elements—some of which may already be inscribed on the RL—that may pose a challenge to the principles of non-discrimination and equality.

A point in question is how to handle discriminatory practices. Blake writes that one way could be to encourage the communities themselves to engage in dialogue to find ways of removing discriminatory practices if they want the element to be recognised as ICH by the convention, and that such an approach "would recognize the fact that traditional cultural practices are inherently flexible and have a great capacity to evolve to meet current needs, of which gender equality is one" (Blake 2015: 182-183). Interesting to note is that this might mean altering the practice to fit the convention. Blake has earlier posed this question, writing that in cases where there is a clear conflict between gender-based discrimination and ICH elements, "creative approaches will need to be found for this. In such cases, is it appropriate for parties and the Intergovernmental Conference (IGC) (or the subsidiary body) to encourage transformations in an ICH element that sanitize it while keeping its core value?" (Blake 2014: 301) A UNESCO brochure on ICH and gender, part of the basic information kit of the 2003 convention, suggests a difference in approach depending on the category of the element.

> Traditional crafts […] often rely on particular divisions of labour with complementary and gendered roles. Social practices, festive events and performing arts, on the other hand, can be occasions to stage the problems and social prejudices of the community concerned, including issues related to gender roles and/or inequalities. (UNESCO 2015: 4)

The brochure also points out the dynamic nature of gender, and states that gender roles, like ICH, are "constantly changing and adapting to new circumstances" (UNESCO 2015: 4). Furthermore, it notes that many traditions that were once open only to one gender group, have since been opened up by the community (UNESCO 2015: 4).

About the Japanese Elements

The state parties of the convention are obliged to create national inventories over ICH. Japan's inventory (The Inventory of ICH in Japan as of March 2015) consists of over 400 elements[3] and largely coincides with national registries over heritage properties protected by the Japanese law. Legal protection of intangible heritage was established with the introduction of the Law for the Protection of Cultural Properties in 1950. The law has been amended a number of times through the years and new categories have been added. In the current version of the law, there are mainly three categories pertaining to intangible heritage: intangible cultural properties, intangible folk cultural properties, and conservation techniques for cultural properties (Law for the Protection of Cultural Property [Japan]. Law No. 214, 1950.).

From the inventory, elements can then be nominated for inscription on one of the two international lists.[4] Japan currently (October 2018) has 21 elements inscribed on the RL and no inscriptions on the List of Intangible Cultural Heritage in Need of Urgent Safeguarding. Three elements which were originally inscribed individually have been revised into group elements. The element *Sekishu-Banshi: papermaking in the Iwami region of Shimane Prefecture* was inscribed in 2009, but the inscription was later replaced when the group element *Washi, craftmanship of traditional Japanese hand-made paper* was inscribed in 2014, since the former element forms a part of the latter. Similarly, the inscriptions of the two elements *Hitachi Furyumono* (2009) and *Yamahoko, the Float Ceremony of the Kyoto Gion Festival* (2009) were replaced with the inscription of the group element *Yama, Hoko, Yatai, float festivals in Japan* in 2016. See Table 1 for a list of all elements and their year of inscription.

Materials and Methods

The official UNESCO documents pertaining to the 21 elements inscribed on the RL by Japan form the basis of the materials used in this study. These documents consist of the nomination files of the Japanese elements listed on the RL, and the two submitted periodic reports from the State Party of Japan (Report on the implementation of the convention and on the status of elements inscribed on the Representative List of the Intangible Cultural Heritage of Humanity 2010, 2016). The periodic reports contain status reports on the individual elements. It should be noted that the three elements *Kabuki theatre, Ningyo Johruri Bunraku puppet theatre, and Nôgaku theatre* lack nomination files since they were already proclaimed Masterpieces of the Oral and Intangible Heritage of Humanity, and therefore directly incorporated in the RL in 2008. A summary of the data sources is shown in Table 1.

Table 1   Year of inscription and available data sources (all elements)

Basic information	Available data sources (o = available, x = not available)		
Name of element	Year of inscription	Nomination file	Periodic report 2010	Periodic report 2016
Kabuki theatre	2008	x	o	o
Ningyo Johruri Bunraku puppet theatre	2008	x	o	o
Nôgaku theatre	2008	x	o	o
Akiu no Taue Odori	2009	o	o	o
Chakkirako	2009	o	o	o
Daimokutate	2009	o	o	o
Dainichido Bugaku	2009	o	o	o
Gagaku	2009	o	o	o
Hayachine Kagura	2009	o	o	o
Koshikijima no Toshidon	2009	o	o	o
Ojiya-chijimi, Echigo-jofu: techniques of making ramie fabric in Uonuma region, Niigata Prefecture	2009	o	o	o
Oku-noto no Aenokoto	2009	o	o	o
Traditional Ainu dance	2009	o	o	o
Kumiodori, traditional Okinawan musical theatre	2010	o	x	o
Yuki-tsumugi, silk fabric production technique	2010	o	x	o
Mibu no Hana Taue, ritual of transplanting rice in Mibu, Hiroshima	2011	o	x	o
Sada Shin Noh, sacred dancing at Sada shrine, Shimane	2011	o	x	o
Nachi no Dengaku	2012	o	x	o
Washoku, traditional dietary cultures of the Japanese, notably for the celebration of New Year	2013	o	x	o
Washi, craftmanship of traditional Japanese hand-made paper	2014	o	x	o
Yama, Hoko, Yatai, float festivals in Japan	2016	o	x	x

The available data on gender in these documents were extracted, and after analysing what type of information was available and common among the elements, the author could isolate a range of questions to pose to the material. The questions are the following:

- Concerning gender restrictions: Are there any gender restrictions? If so: Are there any gender restrictions for women? Are there any gender restrictions for men? What is the restriction?
- Concerning the practitioners: Are all practitioners women? Are all practitioners men?
- Concerning the preservation association members[5]: Are all members women? Are all members men?

Following that analysis, the resulting data were sorted into the categories of gender restrictions, participation as a practitioner, and participation as a preservation association member, and then aggregated and analysed. Based on the combined results of these three categories, the overall character of the element (here called character index) was determined. The character index can be either "female", "male", or "mixed". "Mixed" in this case means that both the practitioners and the preservation association members are mixed and that gender restrictions are *either* non-existing *or* affecting both women and men. In other words, both elements that are free of gender restrictions, and elements that have separate roles for women and men, can count as mixed according to this classification.

The information on gender in the documents was also analysed thematically, focusing on the descriptions of gender roles and rules. Other international as well as national official documents, such as committee meeting summary records and designation decisions, were examined by the author to provide further information and context. It should be noted that the information available in the nomination files and periodic reports is inconsistent in scope and detail in gender matters, since the files and reports have been compiled in different years and presumably by various authors. The forms for the nomination files and the periodic reports have been revised a number of times since the start of the convention. The revisions reflect an increased focus on gender, and information regarding gender is requested to a greater extent and in more detail in more recent versions than in the previous forms. Since the inscriptions of the elements examined in this study range from year 2008 to 2016, a variance between the forms is visible in the examined material.

Concerning the scope of the article, the study is focused on the official information provided by the State Party to UNESCO. While the information provided in the official descriptions cannot be expected to give an exhaustive picture of the actual situation of the individual elements[6], it can reflect the characteristics of the selection of elements and give a picture of how gender matters are handled in the nomination process. Furthermore, the study focuses only on the elements inscribed on the RL, and their descriptions in the nomination files and periodic reports. In other words, the national inventory and the national registries are not examined in this study.

It should also be noted that while intersectionality is an important perspective in analysing gender structures, the scope of this study is limited to gender. Sex and gender are two highly complex terms which are often used interchangeably. Furthermore, they are often used in a binary way. The gender categories used in this article are based on and reflect the categories used in the data. It is noted that a majority of Japan's listed elements are (described as) "gendered". Gender restrictions and tendencies of gender role divisions are frequent in the descriptions of the examined elements. Also, it is noted that the gender codes used in the descriptions in the official documents are strictly binary. There are no descriptions of more than two genders.

Notes on Data Interpretation

Since the information provided on gender is not in all cases explicit, the information has been subjected to interpretation and approximation in the data extraction process. For example, concerning the existence of gender restrictions, the elements have been examined based upon the description of roles and the participants, and whether role divisions are described as free and voluntary or not. A distinction is made between restrictions and tendencies. For example, the nomination file for *Mibu no Hana Taue* describes how some roles are performed by men and other roles performed by women. This is interpreted as that gender restrictions do exist, and that they exist for both women and men, and that the restrictions consist of separate roles for women and men. In comparison, the element *Yuki-tsumugi, silk fabric production technique* is also described as having something akin to a role division between women and men, but with an important difference. The 2016 periodic report describes that two of the three production processes are carried out by mostly women, while most members involved in the third process are men. The keyword is most/mostly. This indicates that the role division is not a rule but rather a tendency, and that exceptions likely exist. Similarly, the information on the element *Traditional Ainu dance* describes that "the songs are sung by mostly women while both men and women dance" (Periodic report 2016). This is interpreted as the description of a tendency rather than a rule. Also, because of the in many cases non-explicit information on gender and sex, the results were divided into different levels of certainty. For example, regarding whether gender restrictions for women exist or not, the possible answers are Yes, Indicated Yes, No, Indicated No, and Information missing. A summary of the interpretation of extracted data from all elements is shown in Table 2, which also contains a summary of the character indexes of all elements.

Table 2 Summary of interpretation of data regarding restrictions and participation and assessment of character indexes (all elements)

Basic information	Interpretation of data								Assessment
	Restrictions				Participation				
					Practitioners		Association members		
Name of element	Gender restrictions existing	Gender restrictions existing for women	Gender restrictions existing for men	Type of restriction	Are all practitioners women?	Are all practitioners men?	Are all association members women?	Are all association members men?	Character index
Kabuki theatre	Yes	Yes	No	Women barred from being actors	No	Yes and No	No	No	Male
Ningyo Johruri Bunraku puppet theatre	Information missing	Information missing	Information missing	Information missing	Indicated No	Information missing	No	Yes	Male
Nôgaku theatre	No	No	No	-	No	No	No	No	Mixed
Akiu no Taue Odori	Yes	Yes	Yes	Separate roles for women and men	No	No	No	No	Mixed
Chakkirako	Yes	No	Yes	Men barred from participation in performing the ritual	Yes	No	No	No	Female
Daimokutate	Yes	Yes	No	Women barred from participating	No	Yes	No	Yes	Male

Continued

Basic information	Interpretation of data								Assessment
	Restrictions				Participation				
					Practitioners		Association members		
Name of element	Gender restrictions existing	Gender restrictions existing for women	Gender restrictions existing for men	Type of restriction	Are all practitioners women?	Are all practitioners men?	Are all association members women?	Are all association members men?	Character index
Dainichido Bugaku	Yes	Yes	No	Women barred from participating in at least some dances	No	Indicated Yes	No	Yes	Male
Gagaku	Information missing	Information missing	Information missing	Information missing	Information missing	Information missing	Information missing	Information missing	Information missing
Hayachine Kagura	Information missing	Information missing	Information missing	Information missing	Indicated No	Indicated Yes	No	Yes	Male
Koshikijima no Toshidon	Yes	Yes	No	Women barred from participation in performing the ritual	No	Yes	No	Yes	Male
Ojiya-chijimi, Echigo-jofu: techniques of making ramie fabric in Uonuma region, Niigata Prefecture	Indicated No	Indicated No	Indicated No	-	No	No	Information missing	Information missing	Mixed

136

Continued

Basic information	Interpretation of data								Assessment
	Restrictions				Participation				
					Practitioners		Association members		
Name of element	Gender restrictions existing	Gender restrictions existing for women	Gender restrictions existing for men	Type of restriction	Are all practitioners women?	Are all practitioners men?	Are all association members women?	Are all association members men?	Character index
Oku-noto no Aenokoto	Information missing	Information missing	No	Information missing	No	Indicated Yes	No	Yes	Male
Traditional Ainu dance	Indicated No	No	Indicated No	-	No	No	No	No	Mixed
Kumiodori, traditional Okinawan musical theatre	Yes	Yes	No	Women barred from being actors	No	Yes and No	No	No	Male
Yuki-tsumugi, silk fabric production technique	Indicated No	Indicated No	Indicated No	-	No	No	No	No	Mixed
Mibu no Hana Taue, ritual of transplanting rice in Mibu, Hiroshima	Yes	Yes	Yes	Separate roles for women and men	No	No	Indicated No	Indicated No	Mixed
Sada Shin Noh, sacred dancing at Sada shrine, Shimane	Information missing	Information missing	Information missing	Information missing	Information missing	Information missing	Information missing	Information missing	Information missing

Continued

Basic information	Interpretation of data								Assessment
	Restrictions				Participation				
					Practitioners		Association members		
Name of element	Gender restrictions existing	Gender restrictions existing for women	Gender restrictions existing for men	Type of restriction	Are all practitioners women?	Are all practitioners men?	Are all association members women?	Are all association members men?	Character index
Nachi no Dengaku	Indicated Yes	Indicated Yes	No	Women probably barred from participation in performing the ritual	No	Indicated Yes	No	Yes	Male
Washoku, traditional dietary cultures of the Japanese, notably for the celebration of New Year	No	No	No	-	No	No	Information missing	Information missing	Mixed
Washi, craftmanship of traditional Japanese hand-made paper	No	No	No	-	No	No	No	No	Mixed
Yama, Hoko, Yatai, float festivals in Japan	Information missing	Information missing	Information missing	Information missing	Information missing	Information missing	Information missing	Information missing	Information missing

Results

The results of the quantitative analysis are presented below, followed by the findings of the thematic analysis. The results of the quantitative analysis are presented in the following order: participation as a practitioner, participation as an association member, restrictions on participation and roles, and character indexes (Table 2). The overall results are discussed in the observations and discussion section.

Regarding the practitioners, all-male elements are more common than all-female elements. One of the 21 examined elements was performed by only women, while six of the elements were performed by only men (two "Yes", four "Indicated Yes"). In the two elements *Kabuki theatre* and *Kumiodori, traditional Okinawan musical theatre*, women are barred from performing as actors but are allowed in other roles, for example as musicians. If these two elements are also interpreted as performed by only men, the total number of elements performed by only men rises to eight.

Regarding the association members, all-male preservation associations are significantly more common than all-female preservation associations. None of the examined associations had all-female members, while seven of the examined associations had all-male members.

Regarding restrictions on participation and roles, gender restrictions are common within the examined elements. Nine of the 21 examined elements were described as containing restrictions regarding gender (eight "Yes", one "Indicated Yes"). These restrictions are affecting women and men to a varying degree. Eight of the 21 examined elements were described as containing restrictions affecting women (seven "Yes", one "Indicated Yes"), while men were affected by restrictions in three of the 21 elements.

Among the nine cases of existing gender restrictions, two referred to separate roles for men and women within the element, one referred to the barring of men, and six referred to the barring of women. Stereotypical role divisions between men and women were not counted as restrictions if being described as tendencies rather than rules (as in the cases of the three elements *Traditional Ainu dance, Yuki-tsumugi, silk fabric production technique* and *Ojiya-chijimi, Echigo-jofu: techniques of making ramie fabric in Uonuma region, Niigata Prefecture*).

The character index indicates whether an element is mostly "male", "female", or "mixed" in the overall results. To qualify as mixed, the element must fulfill the following requirements: 1) practitioners are mixed, 2) association members are mixed, and 3) gender restrictions are either non-existing or affecting both women and men. This means that elements such as *Nôgaku theatre* where approximately 96% of the association members are men (Periodic report 2010) still qualify as mixed. Out of the 21 elements examined, one classifies as female, nine as male, eight as mixed, and in three elements the provided information is not sufficient enough to determine the character. As mentioned earlier, the mixed group contains both elements without gender restrictions (mixed and gender neutral/inclusive) and those with restricted gender roles (mixed and gender specific), and a distinction can be made between these two. For example, the element *Washi, craftmanship of traditional Japanese hand-made paper* is categorised as mixed and gender neutral/inclusive while the element *Akiu no Taue Odori* is categorised as mixed and gender specific.

Thematic Analysis

Below follow the findings of the thematic analysis. Concerning the professional performing arts (belonging to the category Important Intangible Cultural Property as per the classification in the national heritage legislation system), the official documents of two of the elements describe an outspoken female exclusion. The 2010 periodic report's mention on the element *Kabuki theatre* describes an art form originally performed by women, where women were later excluded.

Kabuki Theatre originated in the early seventeenth century as dances and skits played by women. The then administrative authority banned women, and boys successively appeared on stage. As a result, *Kabuki Theatre* developed into a full-blown theatrical art performed only by adult male actors. Female roles are performed by male actors who are called "Onnagata" and equipped with special performance skills. (Periodic report 2010: 14)

As a side note, within the mechanisms of the Japanese heritage legislation, Kabuki is associated with a designation requirement stating the role of Onnagata as one of the requirements for designation (Agency for Cultural Affairs 2005).

Regarding the element *Kumiodori, traditional Okinawan musical theatre*, the nomination file states that "Male actors perform all the female roles" (Nomination file of Kumiodori, traditional Okinawan musical theatre 2010: 4) and that "In 1972, when Okinawa was returned to Japan from the U.S., Kumiodori was designated [...] as Important Intangible Cultural Property [...] To avoid unruly changes in the performing art, the following requirements were set upon its designation. [...] c. Actors must play all female roles [...]" (Nomination file of Kumiodori, traditional Okinawan musical theatre 2010: 4-5). This designation requirement is similar to the case of Kabuki theatre above (Agency for Cultural Affairs 2008). Interesting to note is that the nomination includes the statement that "Kumiodori does not include any features leading to sexual or racial discrimination, and it has no fear of provoking intolerance or exclusion of specific religious or ethnic groups" (Nomination file of Kumiodori, traditional Okinawan musical theatre 2010: 5).

The description of the element *Nôgaku theatre* also contains an account of exclusion of women but describes a change in this restriction.

Traditionally Noh has always been performed by male actors, and today's performances are also held in that way, but women were soon allowed to take lessons in singing, dancing or playing an instrument, as a hobby. Some women displayed outstanding talent, and as they became better and better, they were then allowed to become professional Noh actors after the Second World War. From among such professional actors, one third was chosen to form the Japan Noh Association, and over the last 10 years, around 20 of the Association's members have been female. (Periodic report 2010: 22)

The periodic report furthermore mentions how some roles can be difficult for women, describing that: "Some areas of Noh are easy for women, while others are not. Most female

Noh actors are Shite, and wear masks to act out different characters. The flute is also easy for women to play." (Periodic report 2010: 22-23)

Regarding the craft techniques, all of the three craft techniques inscribed qualify as "mixed" (subcategory: gender neutral/inclusive) in terms of the so-called character index applied in this study. While described as not having gender restrictions, two of the three elements are ascribed gender tendencies. The description of *Ojiya-chijimi, Echigo-jofu: techniques of making ramie fabric in Uonuma region, Niigata Prefecture* states that "Most people involved in production techniques are women; they have long supported their families with this work. It is mostly women who harvest the ramie plant and weave fabrics, and it is mostly men who create fabrics woven with dyed threads" (Periodic report 2016: 28). The description of *Yuki-tsumugi, silk fabric production technique* states that "Members working on the first process, *ito-tsumugi*, are mostly older women. Most members in the *kasuri-kukuri* group are men in their 50s to 60s. Members involved in *hata-ori* are mostly women who, similar to *kasuri-kukuri* members, are in their 50s to 60s" (Periodic report 2016: 75).

There are two taue type rice cultivation rituals on the list, *Akiu no Taue Odori* and *Mibu no Hana Taue, ritual of transplanting rice in Mibu, Hiroshima*, both qualifying as "mixed" (subcategory: gender specific) in terms of the character index applied in this study. Women's roles are frequently described in terms of visual appearance and attire. The nomination files describe how "Females are well dressed up with colorful and fashionable kimono and wear a headdress decorated with artificial flowers" (Nomination file of Akiu no Taue Odori 2009: 2), and "When most of the ploughing is completed, girls called Saotome begin to prepare for the transplantation. They wear colourful dresses, and hats called Suge-gasa" (Nomination file of Mibu no Hana Taue, ritual of transplanting rice in Mibu, Hiroshima 2011: 3). Men's roles in Mibu no Hana Taue are described in terms of skill and importance: "The man who manages the first cattle in line is called Omouji or Omouji-zukai. He skillfully controls the cattle to plough the rice field. This is an honourable role in 'Mibu no Hana Taue'." (Nomination file of Mibu no Hana Taue, ritual of transplanting rice in Mibu, Hiroshima 2011: 3)

A man called Omouji-tsukai skillfully maneuvers a cow and ploughs while singing a plowing song. The Omouji-tsukai maneuvers the cow in the front; this role is a great honor. Men plough the paddy. They move in beautiful, complex patterns and show their skills. The Sanbai leads the rice-planting song; he is an older man who is a good singer. The seedlings are prepared by women called Saotome who wear sedge hats. A woman called Onari-san gives the Saotome food during lunch. (Periodic report 2016: 79)

The description of women's roles in terms of visual appearance and attire is present also in the one element with exclusively female participants, *Chakkirako*. According to the description in the nomination file, "The girls are well dressed up with colourful kimonos, which are worn on the New Year's Day or other special celebration days" (Nomination file of Chakkirako 2009: 2), and "Because it is colourful and brilliant dances by girls, it has been also performed at the celebration of a new construction of houses or a bountiful catch of fish" (Nomination file of Chakkirako 2009: 3). While the participants are all women, the preservation association of this element has both female and male members. "Men and women in their fifties to sixties are the President, Deputy President, accountants, secretary generals, administrators, and governors. The dancers are girls who are teenagers or the younger, while women in their forties to seventies are the leading singers in charge of songs and dances. Mothers in their thirties to forties are also responsible for looking after and helping the dancers." (Periodic report 2010: 30)

The element *Traditional Ainu dance* stands out among the other elements. It is described in the official documents as an element where some roles are performed by both women and men, and some roles have a gender tendency of female participation. "In every organization, the songs are sung by mostly women while both men and women dance." (Periodic report 2016: 66)

The element *Washoku, traditional dietary cultures of the Japanese, notably for the celebration of New Year* is an exception in several ways. It is the only element which is not protected by the Japanese heritage legislation. All the other elements on the list, as well as all the other elements on the national inventory, are protected cultural properties under the Law for the Protection of Cultural Properties. *Washoku* was included on the national inventory by a decision of the Council for Cultural Affairs (The Inventory of ICH in Japan as of March 2015). It also stands out in terms of scale, since it is designed to represent the dietary culture of the whole population. The "taste of mother's cooking" is mentioned in both the nomination file (Nomination file of Washoku, traditional dietary cultures of the Japanese, notably for the celebration of New Year 2013: 4) and the 2016 period report, and the periodic report describes how "The flavors and the basic knowledge and skills of home cooking are known as the 'taste of mother's cooking'. They are transmitted from parents and grandparents to children, and sustained along with table manners, spiritual aspects, and health aspects" (Periodic report 2016: 91).

Among the 12 elements categorised as Important Intangible Folk Cultural Properties (as per the categorisation of the Japanese heritage legislation), one element qualifies as "female", three as "mixed", and six as "male" as per the character index applied in this study (in two elements the information is not enough to determine character index). Four of these are described in terms of exclusively male participation, and three of them also in terms of age restrictions or tendencies. The nomination file of *Daimokutate* describes that "From the seventeenth to the late nineteenth centuries, [...] The eldest son recognized as the heir of each family performed Daimokutate [...] at the age of seventeen. [...] Since the twentieth century, [...] If there is no young man exactly seventeen years of age in the community, these days a senior young man assumes the role instead" (Nomination file of Daimokutate 2009: 3). In *Dainichido Bugaku*, "Some dances must be performed by young boys. Therefore, young boys necessary for the dances have been added to the Association" (Periodic report 2016: 59). The nomination file of *Koshikijima no Toshidon* clearly states that "Men who live in the community are eligible to disguise themselves as Toshidon. The role of Toshidon is not open to anybody; it is limited to men living in each community" (Nomination file of Koshikijima no Toshidon 2009: 2). Regarding *Nachi no Dengaku*, the nomination file gives that "Originally the Association members were mainly groups of young men living in Nachisanku but as the number of young people in the area has recently decreased, OBs from the young men's groups, or Nachisanku natives who have moved to the neighbourhood have become members, and are helping to transmit the element. There are currently 60 members, men in their 30s to 70s" (Nomination file of Nachi no Dengaku 2012: 4).

The description of *Oku-noto no Aenokoto* is interesting since the official documents show a change in the way the element is described. Oku-noto no Aenokoto is an agricultural ritual, and in the nomination file this ritual is described as performed by the "housemaster" of each house, and this person is referred to as "he". The 2010 periodic report also uses the same type of language. In the 2016 periodic report the word "housemaster" has been changed to "household head" and is no longer referred to in terms of gender (Periodic reports 2010, 2016; Nomination file of Oku-noto no Aenokoto 2009).

Observations and Discussion

The results show that there is a noticeable difference in visibility between women and men in the examined elements. There are indications of imbalances regarding the sex-ratio of participants, the sex-ratio of association members, gender restrictions, and overall character indexes—all indicating a male dominance. Elements with only male participants are more common than elements with only female participants. The material contains no descriptions of all-female preservation associations, while all-male preservation associations are described in a third of the elements. In the elements where there are gender restrictions, women are more often affected than men. The character index used in this study shows that "male" elements are significantly more common than "female" elements.

Since the choices of elements to nominate are the results of a national selection process, the results of this study indicate that gender equal representation was not a factor given priority in that selection process. The selection process has thus far resulted in, in terms of the character index, nine "male", one "female" and eight "mixed" elements (three elements are missing sufficient information to determine the character). If gender equal representation had been a factor given priority, a different result, with a more even balance between male and female elements and possibly more mixed elements, could have been expected. By inscription on the RL, the elements are being displayed on an international and representative arena. The image currently displayed by Japan on this arena is one where ICH is presented as a male dominated domain. The frequency of preservation associations with only male members adds to the image of officially recognised ICH in Japan as an arena where predominantly men's voices are being heard.

Another observation is that in the descriptions of existing gender restrictions, the restrictions are treated as non-problematic, and the existing gender restrictions are described as facts. There are also no descriptions (with the possible exception of *Nôgaku theatre*) of practices where gender roles or restrictions are being challenged, re-evaluated, or discussed in the present day. Regarding how gender is handled in the descriptions, a variance in approach is discernible. While gender has been omitted in some descriptions, others give more detailed accounts of roles and ratios, while some hints at a cautiousness in how to approach gender. It should be noted that the nomination files and periodic reports have been compiled in different years and presumably by various authors, which can be a factor in the explanation to the variance in approach.

Are the above identified gender imbalances in the Japanese elements a result of a "gender blindness" in the national implementation process which has benefitted men? How come men are significantly more visible in the descriptions of the listed elements than women? There could be several explanations for the above indicated imbalances, and a point in question is how well the patterns identified in this study reflect the gender circumstances of the national registry. One plausible scenario is that the Japanese registry is male dominated, and so therefore the nominations naturally reflect that imbalance. This would raise the question as to why the registry is male dominated. Possible explanations could be that women are more often banned from participation than men, for example because of religious reasons, or that male traditions have, for some reason or other, more often been identified as valuable intangible heritage and consequently registered. Another possible scenario is that the Japanese registry is not male dominated, but that male elements have been prioritised, consciously or unconsciously, when selecting elements for nomination. This would raise the question as to why male elements have been prioritised. The gender circumstances of and the relationship between the national registry, the national inventory, and the elements inscribed on the RL will be explored by the author in future research.

Lastly, this study finds that while the data provided on gender in the official documents were inconsistent in detail and scope, by aggregating the available data from individual cases to the national level it was possible to assess the overall situation and identify gender imbalances. Concerning the ICHC, while the gender situation on the individual case level may be complex, the structures of gender representation on the collective level can be rendered visible utilising the tools available in the mechanisms of the convention.

Notes

1. See also Aikawa's (2004 and 2009) descriptions of the process of the development of the convention.

2. The element Washoku, traditional dietary cultures of the Japanese, notably for the celebration of New Year is an exception.

3. It should be noted that some elements are registered multiple times since the Japanese heritage legislation recognises individual practitioners as well as groups.

4. Aside from the lists, there is also a Register of Good Safeguarding Practices.

5. In general, the Japanese elements are associated with preservation organisations involved with the continuation of the practice in question.

6. In 2014, the Consultative Body responsible for evaluating the nominations for the Urgent Safeguarding List reported frustration that its evaluations must entirely be based on the dossier, with no possibility of on-site observations. (UNESCO 2014: para. 36)

◻ Disclosure Statement

No conflict of interest was reported by the author.

◻ Funding

The research was made possible by the author receiving the Japanese government (Monbukagakusho: MEXT) scholarship.

◻ Note on Contributor

Helga Janse is a PhD student at the University of Tsukuba, Japan, and doing research on Intangible Cultural Heritage. She has worked for the Swedish National Heritage Board and was the agency's representative in the national working group tasked with developing a master plan for the implementation of the 2003 convention in Sweden. She has served as the Secretary of International Council on Monuments and Sites (ICOMOS) Sweden, and has worked in Japan, China and Georgia.

References

Agency for Cultural Affairs. 2005. Proceedings of the 48th meeting of the Subcommittee on Cultural Properties at the Council for Cultural Affairs. Report (Designation decision concerning Kabuki). July 15, 2005. Accessed November 22, 2018. http://www.bunka. go.jp/seisaku/bunkashingikai/bunkazai/kako/gijiyoshi_48.html.

Agency for Cultural Affairs. 2008. Proceedings of the 84th meeting of the Subcommittee on Cultural Properties at the Council for Cultural Affairs. Report (Designation decision concerning Kumiodori). July 18, 2008. Accessed November 22, 2018. http://www. bunka.go.jp/seisaku/bunkashingikai/bunkazai/kako/gijiyoshi_84.html.

Aikawa, Noriko. 2004. An Historical Overview of the Preparation of the UNESCO International Convention for the Safeguarding of the Intangible Cultural Heritage. *Museum International* 56 (1–2): 137-149.

Aikawa-Faure, Noriko. 2009. From the Proclamation of Masterpieces to the Convention for the Safeguarding of Intangible Cultural Heritage. In *Intangible Heritage*, edited by Laurajane Smith, and Natsuko Akagawa, 13-44. London: Routledge.

Blake, Janet. 2014. Seven Years of Implementing UNESCO's 2003 Intangible Heritage Convention—Honeymoon Period or the "Seven-Year Itch"? *International Journal of Cultural Property* 21: 291-304.

Blake, Janet. 2015. *International Cultural Heritage Law*. Oxford: Oxford University Press.

Hafstein, Valdimar Tr. 2004. The Making of Intangible Cultural Heritage: Tradition and Authenticity, Community and Humanity. Doctoral Dissertation, University of California.

Hafstein, Valdimar. Tr. 2009. Intangible Heritage as a List: From Masterpieces to Representation. In *Intangible Heritage*, edited by Laurajane Smith, and Natsuko Akagawa, 93-111. London: Routledge.

Moghadam, Valentine, and Manilee Bagheritari. 2007. Cultures, Conventions, and the Human Rights of Women: Examining the Convention for Safeguarding Intangible Cultural Heritage, and the Declaration on Cultural Diversity. *Museum International* 59 (4): 9-18.

Nomination files for inscription on the Representative List. Accessible through the UNESCO ICH website: https://ich.unesco.org/en/lists.

2009, Akiu no Taue Odori, File No. 00273.

2009, Chakkirako, File No. 00274.

2009, Daimokutate, File No. 00276.

2009, Dainichido Bugaku, File No. 00275.

2009, Gagaku, File No. 00265.

2009, Hayachine Kagura, File No. 00272.

2009, Koshikijima no Toshidon, File No. 00270.

2009, Ojiya-chijimi, Echigo-jofu: techniques of making ramie fabric in Uonuma region, Niigata Prefecture, File No. 00266.

2009, Oku-noto no Aenokoto, File No. 00271.

2009, Traditional Ainu dance, File No. 00278.

2010, Kumiodori, traditional Okinawan musical theatre, File No. 00405.

2010, Yuki-tsumugi, silk fabric production technique, File No. 00406.

2011, Mibu no Hana Taue, ritual of transplanting rice in Mibu, Hiroshima, File No. 00411

2011, Sada Shin Noh, sacred dancing at Sada shrine, Shimane, File No. 00412

2012, Nachi no Dengaku, File No. 00413.

2013, Washoku, traditional dietary cultures of the Japanese, notably for the celebration of New Year, File No. 00869.

2014, Washi, craftmanship of traditional Japanese hand-made paper, File No. 01001.

2016, Yama, Hoko, Yatai, float festivals in Japan, File No. 01059.

Periodic report, Japan. 2010. Report on the Implementation of the Convention and on the Status of Elements Inscribed on the Representative List of the Intangible Cultural Heritage of Humanity. Accessed November 20, 2018. https://ich.unesco.org/doc/src/ICH-10-2010-EN-ver-01.doc.

Periodic report, Japan. 2016. Report on the Implementation of the Convention and on the Status of Elements Inscribed on the Representative List of the Intangible Cultural Heritage of Humanity. Accessed November 20, 2018. https://ich.unesco.org/doc/src/ICH-10-2016-instructions-EN.doc.

UNESCO. 2003. *Convention for the Safeguarding of the Intangible Cultural Heritage.* Paris: UNESCO.

UNESCO. 2013. Evaluation of UNESCO's Standard-setting Work of the Culture Sector: Part I—2003 Convention for the Safeguarding of the Intangible Cultural Heritage. Accessed November 22, 2018. https://ich.unesco.org/doc/src/IOS-EVS-PI-129_REV.-EN.pdf.

UNESCO. 2014. Item 9 of the Provisional Agenda: Report of the Consultative Body on its work in 2014. Accessed November 22, 2018. https://ich.unesco.org/doc/src/ITH-14-9.COM-9-EN.doc.

UNESCO. 2015. Intangible Cultural Heritage and Gender. Accessed November 22, 2018. https://ich.unesco.org/doc/src/34300-EN.pdf.

UNESCO. 2018. Operational Directives for the Implementation of the Convention for the Safeguarding of the Intangible Cultural Heritage. Amended in 2018. Accessed November 22, 2018. https://ich.unesco.org/doc/src/ICH-Operational_Directives-7.GA-PDF-EN.pdf.

The Crafting of a New Act on the Protection of Cultural Property—The German Case

Julia Weiler-Esser

Lawyer with HerA – Heritage Advisors, Germany.
CONTACT Julia Weiler-Esser: j.weiler-esser@heritage-advisors.de

Abstract: In 2007 Germany finally decided to become a state party to the UNESCO 1970 Convention and to transfer it into the German law. This decision was the starting point of long and heated discussions amongst all stakeholders involved, wrestling for the perfect Act. An evaluation in 2013, however, proved the Act to be a drastic failure and gave way to yet more discussions and debates. In 2016 a new Act, designed to improve upon the original, came into force. This article will examine the different expectations that a modern Act on the Protection of Cultural Property (KGSG in German) has to meet. It will give an overview of most German stakeholders' perceptions and claims. Against this background, the decisions which were the basis of the 2007 legislation will be examined, focusing on the mistakes that were made and their outcomes. Subsequently, the new Act and its changed focus and prioritisation will be presented, analysing the already-known outcomes and additional expected outcomes. Germany, being a contemporary example of changes in the cultural policy and law, will be presented as a case study, illustrating just how poorly good intentions can be translated into law, but hopefully also what can be learned from experience and which mistakes could be avoided in other countries.

Keywords: UNESCO 1970 Convention, German Act on the Protection of Cultural Property, cultural heritage

Germany was amongst a number of countries that took the longest time in ratifying the UNESCO treaty of 1970, which was an important starting point for the creation of international standards for the protection and restitution of illegally-exported cultural goods. Only in 2007—and after a hasty debate—was the German Act on the Protection of Cultural Property (KGSG in German) instituted. Those in the art market, as well as collectors and museums, especially feared the difficulties in buying and importing cultural goods. Meanwhile, sceptic archaeologists found the new regulations to not be strict enough, and therefore useless.

A 2013 report by the federal government on the protection of cultural property in Germany proved the sceptics right. The implementation of international law to the German law had been an overly-generous interpretation of the UNESCO treaty, especially regarding the interests of the market and its many collectors. Not one piece of art had been restituted on the grounds of the Act, though several requests had been made. Worse, Germany became known for its lax legal regulations and became a market for cultural goods of doubtful provenance, causing further pressure on a diplomatic level internationally. Preparations preceding the necessary amendments were again followed by unusually-high public attention and interest groups were fearful: private collectors—of losing the value and fungibility of their objects, and museums—for if the new regulations were too strict the legal barriers would increase for international loans, as well as endangering their prettiest pieces to claims of restitution.

Scientific experts, on the other hand, found the new measures not strict enough in effectively stopping the trade in illegally-excavated and imported goods, and therefore argued that in this way Germany would essentially be condoning the continued digging and looting of the most culturally-rich regions of the earth, putting our common cultural heritage at risk.

This article will give an overview of the many legal and ethical aspects a modern KGSG needs to consider in order to be effective as well as practicable. It will examine the area of conflict between international, national and regional law in Germany, together with national and international interests. It will not only consider the economic interests of (private) owners of cultural goods—as well as the scientific perspectives of museums and archaeologists in academia—but also the art market, which is now facing much stricter regulations in Germany.

The German case, being a contemporary example of changes in cultural policy and law, will be examined regarding the weaknesses of the old Act and the practical problems they caused. Finally, this article will focus on the learnings and alterations of the new law, discussing some known results and venturing an outlook on additional future effects.

Legal and Ethical Aspects of Creating a Modern Act for the Protection of Cultural Property

Cultural objects are the precious treasures of every nation. For the people of their countries of origin they carry a meaning and offer the opportunity to delve into the history of their ancient ancestors. The artefacts can form an identity and be a source of national pride. The opportunity to study history and culture from these objects is of great importance, and worth far more than just their commercial value.[1] This perception of cultural goods has been growing in many countries around the globe. Their illegal excavation and exportation is increasingly regarded as a major crime to the population, as well as future generations.[2] In China, a number of laws and regulations relating to the protection of cultural heritage have been in place for decades.[3] There is a growing interest in the restitution of looted art works, and this interest can also be seen elsewhere.[4]

The knowledge that can be retrieved from these objects, however, arises only partly from the item itself—most of the information that can be learned from archaeological objects is due to their context in the surrounding area, by analysing their function and significance through the association of items found in the earth around them. It is, therefore, not enough to simply restore looted cultural property to their countries of origin, but of greater importance to prevent cultural objects from being illegally-excavated, without any competent documentation or publication of their historical or cultural context, thus depriving humanity of the story that they could tell.

Potentially all the countries in the world therefore have a law protecting their cultural goods that prevent cultural loss due to illegal excavations and unlawful exportation, as well as regulations for restitution and repatriation. One hundred and thirty-one countries base their laws upon the UNESCO treaty of 1970,[5] although the way each country has chosen to implement this treaty into national law may differ. Deciding the exact wording of the national law requires legal as well as ethical choices.

Many interest groups are involved in the cultural sector: dealers, collectors, artists, museums, researchers and even members of the public that are interested in their culture and history. Most of them have different opinions of how and to what extent—different cultural goods need to be protected. At the same time, practicability and effectiveness of a law is essential. The ideal law would therefore need to be known to all stakeholders involved, easy to access, and be easily-understood by everybody. In order to create this ideal law, the following problems need to be addressed.

1. The easiest way to prevent cultural loss—the prohibition of sales and exports of cultural goods—would obviously cause an enormous outcry on the side of dealers and collectors. Cultural goods have always been articles of trade. Regulations on specific goods or different types of cultural goods have to be well-chosen in order not to disrupt an entire industry. But whose needs come first—the interests of the art business sector, or the interests of museums, researchers and the public, who, in order to learn more about cultural objects, which would not be for sale, would keep them in public institutions? How can regulations balance the interests

between the market and academia, and the proportion of the public that are interested in their past?

2. How should illegally-imported cultural goods be treated? To whom do they belong and how can restitution be managed in a just and fair way? Most countries are not only source countries or buyers, but also suffer from illegal excavations, and are platforms for the trade of unlawfully-imported goods. A balanced solution for a safe and well-monitored export and import is therefore as necessary as a fair and transparent process to restitute foreign treasures.

3. Laws should provide legal security. The less a law takes to interpret the wording, the easier and clearer it is to fathom for ordinary people. At the same time, however, a too-specifically drafted law can never be adapted for a multitude of cases, and takes the risk of leaving too many questions unsolved. The text needs to be flexible so that it can apply to the multifarious world of art and culture, but also needs to provide clarity and security to those who search for reliable answers. Especially regarding that in art and cultural law there are many people who have no legal background. Nevertheless, in many cases the value of objects, and the (not only monetary) risk, if the law is not observed, can be very high.

Finding a law that manages to bring all these aspects together and finding a way to actually regulate and facilitate all the livelihood of the parties involved, would be a masterstroke, and very likely impossible to achieve. Nevertheless, it must be attempted. After two different laws, both of which were closely followed by the public and discussed with enormous interests by all involved,[6] Germany is working its way to a better—yet still not perfect—legal solution. The following will therefore examine the German way, the discussion and the massive shortcomings and mistakes which have been made in the process, and hopefully help to learn from the past. It will include the evaluation by the Federal Government, focusing on all the problems and clearly naming mistakes which have been made.[7] Many questions regarding legal security, ethical priorities, effectiveness and accessibility have been discussed. All these aspects—and many more—have been brought to a solution, to a text, to a "new" law. This law has been forged with good intentions and many expectations about how it will work and which outcomes it will have. For now, about two and a half years after the Act's coming into force, some results can already be described. Before this article comes to that point, a short overview of German art and cultural law will help to elucidate the forthcoming examinations of revisions and amendments.

The Co-Existence of International, National and Regional Law Together with International and National Interests

Germany is part of the European Union and of international coalitions such as the UN. It therefore includes the European law in its national regulations, as well as international treaties such as the UNESCO 1970 Convention.[8] In addition, the German law consists of federal law—applicable in the whole country—and of regional law—applicable only in a specific region (Germany consists of 16 regions in total). The law of monument protection is given on a regional level (based on the European law, however).[9] On a federal level Germany legislates on the export, import and trading of cultural goods, the restitution of foreign art works, but also on the protection of national treasures against export to foreign countries. A new Act on the protection of cultural goods through the regulation of trade and eventual restitution accordingly had to be decided on a federal level, being therefore also universally-applicable in the whole of Germany, expediting the process, since only one legislator was involved in crafting of it, not 16. However—and although Germany likes to see itself as a "nation of culture" (Kulturnation)[10]—the decision to finally become part of the UNESCO 1970 Convention took 37 years.[11] In 2007 the Act on the Return of Cultural Property, was also implemented into the national German law.[12] Before this step was done, Germany had faced criticism on an international level, and reminded of its shortcomings regarding its cultural law—especially regarding the restitution of foreign cultural goods, looted and illegally exported to Germany, yet hardly ever restituted.[13] Eventually it was international politics that made the German Government change its mind and try to find a satisfying solution.

Only a few years later, international pressure again, together with national critics and a devastating evaluation of the law, gave way to important amendments, which changes the whole character of the Act, pushed also by the fact that the illegal trade of cultural goods had been estimated by several international institutions[14] to be one of the most important black markets in the world.[15] According to statistics, the trade is valued at six billion euros.[16]

The Perspective of Different Stakeholders

Besides the different political and diplomatic levels which were involved in the process, drafting a good KGSG was very difficult for Germany, because many national stakeholders had very specific opinions regarding the law. The following will briefly present some points of view that must be included in the new and ideally perfect law.

Collectors

The first group discussed at this point is the inhomogeneous group of the private collectors. It consists of "hobby archaeologists", or pot hunters, as well as educated enthusiastic connoisseurs and wealthy investors, seeking the unique.[17] All of them are anxious to curtail their rights in dealing antiques—in one way or another.

Generally drying out the market is regarded as an effective method in ceasing illegal excavation and exportation from source countries to Germany.[18] That means, collectors are regarded as part of the problem, or—even worse—the root. Obviously, collectors are none too pleased about this opinion. They feel misunderstood, since they often see themselves as private archaeologists, or as art lovers with historical and cultural knowledge, caring for cultural objects, both finding and protecting them.[19] Not only do they fear financial loss if their rights to buy and sell artefacts are impacted, but would also feel villainised or criminalised. From their point of view, a perfect Act for Cultural Protection would be as generous as possible, with low requirements regarding documentation, a strong focus on personal ownership and very clear and specific regulations regarding objects which are out of trade.[20]

Museums

Museums are not only places of collections and presentations, but also of research and preservation. Usually they have a great interest in keeping their artworks together, in accumulating further objects and research as well as publishing them. Sadly, although all of these activities have the side effect of supporting the illegal trade of cultural goods,[21] are obviously the essence of a museum's purpose. They therefore wish for specific regulations regarding the acquisition of artworks (including the handling of donations of uncertain provenance, for example) as well as the restitution of unlawfully-acquired objects—ideally combined with funding for their provenance research. Usually they are not determined to buy or accept artworks at any cost,[22] but wish for a regulated market for well-documented and correctly-excavated and imported cultural goods. For international loans and temporary exports/imports, they hope for little and comprehensive bureaucracy.

Archaeologists in Academia

Professional archaeologists, especially those who have already had the pleasure of visiting the origins of the most important objects and their excavations, have a great interest not only in the objects themselves, but also in their provenance and the entire situation of their finding. They feel profoundly sad, when confronted with pictures of plundered areas, destroyed temples or robbed museums in regions of war, for example. Many archaeologists therefore would want a perfect KGSG to stop the trade of those goods completely and to do much more research on the provenance of previously-identified cultural artefacts.[23] They ask for strict and precise provisions on the import and export of antiquities and for respect regarding the legal requirements of the countries of origin.[24]

The Art Market

A very different view on that topic can obviously found with professional art dealers, who for centuries have made their living with the import and export of cultural goods as well as the national and international art market. They see themselves as scapegoats of the momentary debate, and emphasise that until recently many countries of origin did not pay much attention to their cultural goods leaving the country, even allowing national treasures to be exported without specific documentation. After a long time of great indifference on the side of countries that now claim vehemently for the restitution of their national treasures, they do not feel responsible for the vending of illegally-excavated cultural objects.[25] They are therefore strictly against a documented provenance, including export and import licenses, as a mandatory requirement for the vending of antiquities. Furthermore, they feel overstrained by further requirements for documentation and the preservation of these documents.[26]

Obviously, there are more professions who have to apply provisions regarding cultural objects which have not been analysed at this point. There are policemen and customs officers, who decide which object to seize, which kind of paperwork to ask for, how to identify the objects and above all how to apply German and international laws correctly. An aspect of the law, which is very often not considered, is still one of Germany's biggest problems.[27] These professionals do not necessarily have a specific opinion regarding the protection of cultural goods, but for the sake of the precision and efficiency of their work, they wish for clear, easily accessible regulations and information—the more precise, the better.

Decisions and Mistakes, Crafting the Act on the Return of Cultural Property

Having these perspectives in mind and the very different expectations the new Act was facing, the following will now examine the decisions that were taken for the Act on the Return of Cultural Property in 2007 and the mistakes that were made, moving on to the outcome of these mistakes and the lessons learned in crafting a new—and hopefully better—Act in 2016.

Since 2016 that what has been adapted to one single Act was previously regulated in three different Acts: the Act to Prevent the Exodus of German Cultural Property[28]—in force since 1955[29]—should preserve German cultural property, whose removal abroad would mean a significant loss to Germany's cultural heritage. The restitution of cultural objects was regulated by two Acts: the Act Implementing Directives of the European Communities on the Return of Cultural Objects Unlawfully Removed from the Territory of a Member State and Amending the Act to Prevent the Exodus of German Cultural Property of 15th October 1998[30] and the Act on the Return of Cultural Property of 18th May 2007.[31] Regarding the treatment of cultural property, the legislation was described as the following: states of origin had a right to request the return of illegally-exported objects (Act on the Return of Cultural Property 2007: sec. 6). Each object needed a permit for the import (Act on the Return of Cultural Property 2007: sec. 14) and dealers had the obligation to produce records of their sales (Act on the Return of Cultural Property 2007: sec. 18). Those violating the law faced the risk of punishment (Act on the Return of Cultural Property 2007: secs. 20, 21).

The right to request the return of looted cultural goods had the following conditions: regarding an object removed[32] from the territory of another member state of the EU, sec. 6 (1) of the Act on the Return of Cultural Property 2007 required that the object was "publicly classified" as a "national treasure possessing artistic, historic or archaeological value". In case of objects that were unknown prior to their removal (such as looted antiques), the state requesting the object had to register it within one year after it could get knowledge of it. The object also had to belong to one of the categories listed in the Annex to the Council Directive 93/7/EEC, or to be listed as part of a public collection or an equivalent.[33] Similar requirements applied to objects which had been unlawfully removed[34] from the territory of another state party: the object had to be "specifically designated by the requesting state party as being of importance for archaeology, pre-history, history, literature, art or science" (or designated as such within a year after the state was able to get knowledge of the object)—and the object had to belong to one of the categories specified in Article 1 of the UNESCO 1970 Convention (Act on the Return of Cultural Property 2007: sec. 6 [2]).

For those importing cultural objects into Germany, the importer had to provide a licence proving its legal export (Act on the Return of Cultural Property 2007: sec. 14). This licence was obligatory for all objects, entered in a list, kept by the state of origin, published in, and accessible from Germany. Registration in a list of protected national property was also a requirement for the punishment of violations of this Act (Act on the Return of Cultural Property 2007: sec. 20 [1] No. 3).

These regulations clearly supported the decision to make the new Act as easy to access and apply as possible. Everybody simply had to check a list of national cultural treasures for the object in their hands in order to know whether the export or import was legal. This list was supposed to provide legal security to dealers and collectors—as well as to German tourists, importing "souvenirs".[35] It refers to Article 5 of the UNESCO 1970 Convention, which obliged the party states to list their protected national property.[36]

The possibility to classify cultural goods after their exportation as national treasures was meant to help to prevent illegal digging, since newly- and illegally-excavated cultural goods could obviously never be part of any national or international list. This regulation was supposed to curb the dealing of looted art works and dry out the market, while the deadline of one year after the state of origin could get knowledge of the object was meant again to provide legal security for dealers, collectors and museums who were thinking of a new acquisition.

Unfortunately, these decisions seem to be a fair balance of all the interests of the stakeholders involved, but even though the laws allowed for the restitution of unlawfully-imported cultural goods, not one restitution took place.[37] Although it was the legislator's intention to live up to the international responsibility of protecting cultural heritage when implementing the UNESCO 1970 Convention into the German law,[38] the final version of this Act proved to have two impossibly-high requirements: firstly, an entitlement to return only for cultural objects which have been entered on to a public list of the country of origin that is accessible for inspection in Germany, and secondly, the possibility for a subsequent addition to such a public list which proved to be of no help.[39]

First of all, there are few countries that keep lists of their cultural heritage.[40] Most states generally define all their archaeological findings as national treasures, and *res extra commercium*, to the effect, that no further listing of single objects is needed.[41] The requirement of a list therefore made any request for the return of a stolen object impossible.

The same is true concerning the provisions on import licences for cultural property, which had been listed by their states of origin. Although this provision was meant to prevent looted cultural objects from entering German territory in the first place, with the corollary that no restitution would then be necessary,[42] this provision did not measure up to former expectations. The states who did not keep a listing of single items they regarded as national treasures, neither produced a record of objects they wanted a licence for when exporting to Germany.[43] Given that the punishment for unlawful import into Germany depended on the listing of smuggled cultural goods, the Act was not able to achieve its purpose and proved to be not a balance of interests, but instead overly favourable regarding the interests of dealers and collectors.

Learnings and Alterations of the New Law

Since the ramifications of the 2007 Act had not been easy to foresee—some thought that the Act would not do enough to effectively protect cultural heritage, others feared the imminent collapse of the German art market—an evaluation of the effects of the Act was scheduled five years after it came into force.[44] The report, published in April 2013, came to a devastating conclusion that made further amendments to the Act inevitable—as well as the need to implement the new EU law, Directive 2014/60/EU of May 2014,[45] and the new Operational Guidelines for the implementation of the UNESCO 1970 Convention adopted in Paris in July 2014.[46] After a heated debate in the German parliament (*Bundestag*), and an even more heated debate in public, the new KGSG entered into law on August 6, 2016, after being adopted by the *Bundestag* without any dissenting votes, and with the broad support of the Federal Council (*Bundesrat*) in early July of 2016.[47] The new Act brings together the key areas of cultural property protection (imports, claims for return, protection against removal and due diligence requirements) in one single Act.

One of its main goals is to ensure that antiquity dealers refrain from dealing with unprovenanced or looted cultural property.[48] The means by which this will be achieved are stricter import and export provisions, amendments regarding the provisions for the return of cultural property, due diligence provisions in dealing with cultural property and penal sanctions. This certifies that cultural goods can only be imported legally to Germany if they have been exported legally from their country of origin (KGSG 2016: secs. 28-32). Anyone importing cultural property, in particular archaeological goods, to Germany will be required to obtain **a valid export license** issued by the country of origin. The important detail of this regulation is that the object needs to have an export license of its country of **origin**, not the country from which it entered German territory.[49] Most state parties of the UNESCO 1970 Convention have laws regulating the export of their cultural goods. Germany is now establishing a homepage, where all those Acts can be checked.

The requirements for the **claim to return** a cultural object have been adapted to the reality of most state parties: objects do not need to be listed individually prior to their export, or within one year after the country of their origin could get knowledge of their existence—but they have to be regarded as protected national property according to the national law of their country of origin. For cultural goods imported from a member of the EU, the right for return requires, therefore, that they were unlawfully exported from their country of origin after December 31, 1992.[50] For cultural goods imported from another state party of the UNESCO 1970 Convention the requirements are the following: (1) if it belongs to the categories of Article 1 of the aforesaid Convention,[51] (2) it left the country's territory unlawfully after April 26, 2007,[52] (3) it had been designated before the export by national law as being of importance or inalienable[53], and (4) it can be related to the state party making the request.[54] Since requesting state parties are often unable to prove when the cultural property in question was unlawfully exported from its territory (due to the unlawful nature of the trafficking), the new Act provides that cultural property is presumed to have been unlawfully-exported from the respective state party after April 26, 2007, if the possessor of the cultural property in Germany does not present evidence proving that

164

(s)he has already possessed the cultural property prior to this date. Bilateral agreements between Germany and the requesting state party are not required.[55]

Not only will the importation of cultural objects be submitted to stricter provisions, selling a stolen, unlawfully-excavated or illicitly-imported cultural object is also forbidden (KGSG 2016: sec. 40). **Due diligence provisions** require the sellers (professional dealers as well as private individuals) to make sure that the object they are dealing with has not been stolen, illegally exported, or illegally-excavated.[56] For archaeological goods and cultural goods worth more than €2500, professional dealers also have to check and record further information, such as the names and addresses of all persons involved in the deal (the seller, supplier, purchaser and the client), the documents for export and import and the provenance of the cultural goods, etc.[57] The records have to be kept for 30 years.

To ensure abidance by the law, the KGSG also includes stricter **penal sanctions** (KGSG 2016: secs. 83-88) than the former Act, including up to five years' imprisonment.

Although not everybody is aware of that fact, Germany has not only been a market country for looted cultural goods, but also a country of origin.[58] Providing for the protection of cultural heritage in general, regulations regarding German cultural goods can therefore be seen as "the other side of the coin". The legal situation mirrors the requirements regarding the legal provisions in other member or party states: in order to export cultural property, the new Act requires an export license not only for the export outside the Single European Market (the EU law) but also—consistent with the EU law (Article 36 TFEU)[59]— for export outside of Germany, but within the Single European Market.[60] Coins that are exempt from this requirement, if they exist in high quantity, are not of particular relevance for archaeological research and not a national treasure of a member state.

The export license will be granted if the object to be exported is not in the process of being registered to the list of protected cultural property,[61] or has previously been unlawfully-imported to Germany. If archaeological objects are "national cultural property"[62]—either because they are part of a public collection, or because they have been listed as protected cultural property,[63] a license for their temporary, as well as permanent export outside Germany might not be granted if, judged by a single case, the interests of German cultural heritage preservation prevail (KGSG 2016: secs. 22, 23). If cultural objects are listed as national cultural property, claims for the return of such property are now also subject to longer limitation periods (75 years) under EU law; if they are not, the limitation period is 30 years.[64]

These regulations show the legislator's will to move the focus from the dealers' and collectors' interests, to the interests of archaeologists, museums and—important to mention—foreign countries claiming their national treasures. Since everybody wants to check if an object is protected by its country of origin, they need to check the national law of the country—sometimes even several laws, if the country cannot be exactly determined. The new Act offers more flexibility regarding foreign law and covers many more objects than its predecessor, and at the same time is much harder to deal with. For complete certainty, in many cases, an expert has to decide about where an object might have come from, if it is authentic and so on, in order to determine whether it falls under the new law or not. A better protection of cultural goods through a much broader definition of what should be protected and returned to its country of origin (or stay in Germany) comes now—at the cost of legal security and simplicity of application.

Another highly disputed point is the decision to include a deadline into the new Act. Since before April 26, 2007[65]/December 31, 1992[66], it was not illegal to import cultural goods without proper paperwork, objects which entered Germany before these deadlines, can still be traded without the otherwise necessary documentation. This helps collectors and other owners of cultural goods, who would otherwise lose the possibility to sell their property, but dealers now have to provide sufficient paperwork, or prove that the objects were imported before the corresponding date, since sec. 52 (2) of KGSG 2016 contains a reversal of evidence: if there is no proof that an object entered Germany before 2007, it is supposed to have been imported after this deadline.[67]

However, the outcome of this Act is still uncertain. Many people feared for the immediate collapse of the German art market.[68] Others believed that the new Act washed all looted and smuggled art works clean, since now people just have to present fake paperwork, proving an earlier import to Germany.[69] For now, about two years after the entry into force of the new Act, the following can be stated that for the art market it can be said that an enormous swell of discontent is taking place.[70] Apparently some antiquity dealers have already closed down their businesses because they did not have the necessary documents for the goods they planned to sell.[71] Others have had to withdraw objects from their auctions for which they did not possess the corresponding paperwork.[72] However, most cultural objects will come with some kind of documentation—or at least a former possessor, able to declare their provenance in lieu of oath. If that is not the case for objects currently in the antiquities shops, it will probably become so very soon—making any unprovenanced cultural goods unsellable and drying out the seemingly-endless supply of new and unknown antiquities, in quantities that could not have possibly been circulating in Germany for decades already.[73] It is hoped that the new Act will also curb the looting and unlawful excavations of goods in their countries of origin, many of which are at crisis-point and are unable to stop it themselves, as even restitution—if it can be realised under the new Act—can only bring back the object, not its historical significance when found *in situ*.

If these hopes are to be realised, it is to be evaluated five years after its coming into force (KGSG 2016: sec. 89)—then we will know, if the new priorities and decisions of the KGSG lead to a different outcome, and still take all stakeholders' interests into account.

Notes

1. Wantuch-Tohle 2015: 20-21.
2. Lee 2012: 8-11. Especially in cases like China, where, for example, an estimated 90%–95% of all tombs of major significance have already been illegally-excavated. Meyer/ Blair Brysac 2015: 11.
3. Lee 2012: 13.
4. Several African countries, for example, are asking with increasing emphasis for the restitution of cultural goods looted during times of colonialism.

5. See the UNESCO database of national cultural heritage laws: http://www.unesco.org/ new/en/culture/themes/illicit-trafficking-of-cultural-property/unesco-database-of-national-cultural-heritage-laws/.

6. Winands 2016: 199; Stürmer 2016; Walser 2016; Schließ 2016; Peitz 2015.

7. https://www.bundesregierung.de/Content/DE/StatischeSeiten/Breg/BKM/ Kulturgutschutz-neu/%C3%9Cberblick%20gesetzliche%20Grundlagen/Externe%20 Links/2013-04-24-bericht-kulturgutschutz.pdf?__blob=publicationFile&v=1 (English summary: https://www.bundesregierung.de/Content/DE/_Anlagen/BKM/2013-07-11-bericht-kulturgutschutz-englisch.pdf?__blob=publicationFile&v=2).

8. Convention on the Means of Prohibiting and Preventing the Illicit Import, Export and Transfer of Ownership of Cultural Property, referred to as the UNESCO 1970 Convention.

9. Weiler-Esser 2018: 12.

10. Grütters (Minister of State for Culture) 2016: 35.

11. Germany was the 115th of the now 131 countries. In comparison, China signed the treaty in 1989.

12. On May 18, 2007.

13. See note 7.

14. Those are the United Nations Educational, Scientific and Cultural Organization (UNESCO), and the United Nations Office on Drugs and Crime (UNODC).

15. In fact, the United Nations Global Report estimated the annual trade in illicit antiquities to be the third most profitable black market behind drugs and arms (Calvani 2009: 29; Schack 2009: 69).

16. Brochure of the UNESCO, CLT/2011/CONF. 207/6: 2. http://unesdoc.unesco.org/ images/0019/001916/191606E.pdf. See also Schack 2009: 69.

17. Especially after the financial crisis in 2008, prices for artworks, including antiquities, rose to new highs, making them one of the best investment categories of these times (Wessel 2015: 74-75).

18. Zimmermann 2016: 27.

19. Like in China, where some private collectors bought national treasures at international auctions to bring them back to China, in Germany some collectors invest private money to buy art works from private collections and leave them to public museums, in order to make them accessible to everyone (Wessel 2015: 82-83).

20. Sturm 2016: 73.

21. See the booklet of Renfrew 2000.

22. After a long time of indifference and several scandals in Germany (e.g. at the Badisches Landesmuseum, Karlsruhe) and abroad (e.g. at the Metropolitan Museum, New York), awareness for the provenance and legitimacy of ownership rose over time (Wessel 2015: 97-100).

23. The strongest protagonist for the cessation of any kind of trade is Dr. Michael Müller-Karpe, who states that all objects currently on the market are either robbed or fakes (Müller-Karpe 2010: 93).

24. Marcus Hilgert, Secretary General & CEO, Cultural Foundation of the German Federal States, in an interview with Schließ 2016.

25. Ursula Kampmann, speaker of the IADAA (International Association of Dealers in Ancient Art), in Wessel 2015: 112. For smaller things such as coins, proper documentation is even now not necessarily given in every country (Ulrich Künker, Association of German Coin Dealers).

26. Astrid Müller-Katzenburg for the IADAA, the Association of German Art Dealers and the Association of Antiquarians, Protocol for the hearing of specialists and interest groups, see note 8: 83-84.

27. In Germany there are less than 20 police officers specialised and trained in art law, Allonge 2014: 17. Only a small group of policemen have basic training in identifying and dealing with cultural goods.

28. (Gesetz zum Schutz deutschen Kultur gutes gegen Abwanderung—KultgSchG) in the version published on July 8, 1999, Federal Law Gazette, Part I, 1754, as most recently amended by Article 2 of the Act of May 18, 2007, Federal Law Gazette, Part I: 757.

29. As far as the period before re-unification is concerned, this article focuses on the legislation of West-Germany.

30. (Kulturgutsicherungsgesetz—KultgutSiG), Federal Law Gazette, Part I: 3162.

31. (Kulturgüterrückgabegesetz—KultGüRückG) Act Implementing the UNESCO Convention of 14 November 1970 on the Means of Prohibiting and Preventing the Illicit Import, Export and Transfer of Ownership of CulturalProperty and Implementing Council Directive 93/7/EEC of 15 March 1993 on the Return of Cultural Objects Unlawfully Removed from the Territory of a Member State, Federal Law Gazette, Part I: 757.

32. After December 31, 1992, the deadline referring to the *Council Directive 93/7/EEC of 15th March 1993 on the Return of Cultural Objects Unlawfully Removed from the Territory of a Member State.*

33. For further specifications of these collections, see sec. 6 (1) Act implementing the Cultural Property Convention.

34. After April 26, 2007, the day of the implementation of the UNESCO 1970 Convention into German law.

35. Weiler-Esser 2016: 136.

36. "Article 5: To ensure the protection of their cultural property against illicit import, export and transfer of ownership, the States Parties to this Convention undertake, as appropriate for each country, to set up within their territories one or more national services, where such services do not already exist, for the protection of the cultural heritage, with a qualified staff sufficient in number for the effective carrying out of the following functions:

[…]

(b) establishing and keeping up to date, on the basis of a national inventory of protected property, a list of important public and private cultural property whose export would constitute an appreciable impoverishment of the national cultural heritage; […]."

The Convention did not make the listing a necessary requirement for the restitution of such cultural objects, however.

37. The evaluation of the Act on the Return of Cultural Property was very clear: "Despite several requests for return submitted by foreign states since 2008, in not one single case has the Act on the Return of Cultural Property actually led to a return of cultural property. The Act's relatively high conditions for return could not be met by any state seeking a return. Existing difficulties associated with application of the Act could not be remedied by jurisprudence. The simplification of the process of returning illicitly exported cultural objects to their countries of origin envisioned by legislators in 2007 has failed to materialise in practice."

38. Parliamentary documents (*Bundestags Drucksache*) 16/1371.

39. German courts of law did not help make the Act a success: either they saw no proof that an object had been unknown to the country of origin before (Higher Administrative Court Münster, GRUR 2013, 964)—admittedly though, this could not be easily proven—or provide any kind of auction catalogues or exhibition through which a state was able to attain knowledge of an object's existence, and thus were denied the claim for return, since the state had not added the object to a public list within one year of the publication of such a catalogue (Administrative Court Osnabrück, 1 A 187/10 of 17 May 2011; Administrative Court Köln, 10 K 3537/11 of April 25, 2012 [quoted from Krischok 2016: 55].

40. Krischok 2016: 55.

41. Weidner 2013: 34.

42. Winands/List 2016: 199.

43. Krischok 2016: 57.

44. See the explanatory memorandum to the Act on the Return of Cultural Property, Bundestag Printed Paper 16/1371 of May 4, 2006, general part, 13 (in German).

45. Directive 2014/60/EU of the European Parliament and of the Council of 15 May 2014 on the Return of Cultural Objects Unlawfully Removed from the Territory of a Member

State and Amending Regulation. These amendments were due to the new EU law that required the extension of the limitation period for claims for return (three years instead of one year), the new provisions on the compensation for the return, and due diligence requirements related to the acquisition of cultural property. Under the new German Act, these EU standards also apply to the State Parties of the UNESCO 1970 Convention.

46. www.unesco.org/new/fileadmin/MULTIMEDIA/HQ/CLT/pdf/OPERATIONAL_ GUIDELINES_EN_FINAL.pdf .

47. An English translation has not yet been published.

48. Grütters 2016: 35.

49. Many art dealers thought the legal export from a transit country should be sufficient for a legal import to Germany. The stronger requirement for a legal export from the country of origin was internationally welcomed though, for example at the Fourth Session of the Subsidiary Committee of the Meeting of States Parties to the UNESCO 1970 Convention, Paris, 26-28 September 2016. Winands/List 2016: 204.

50. Regardless of when this state became a member of the EU. Winands/List 2016: 204.

51. "Article 1: For the purposes of this Convention, the term 'cultural property' means property which, on religious or secular grounds, is specifically designated by each State as being of importance for archaeology, prehistory, history, literature, art or science and which belongs to the following categories:

(a) rare collections and specimens of fauna, flora, minerals and anatomy, and objects of palaeontological interest;

(b) property relating to history, including the history of science and technology and military and social history, to the life of national leaders, thinkers, scientists and artist and to events of national importance;

(c) products of archaeological excavations (including regular and clandestine) or of archaeological discoveries;

(d) elements of artistic or historical monuments or archaeological sites which have been dismembered;

(e) antiquities more than one hundred years old, such as inscriptions, coins and engraved seals;

(f) objects of ethnological interest;

(g) property of artistic interest, such as:

(I) pictures, paintings and drawings produced entirely by hand on any support and in any material (excluding industrial designs and manufactured articles decorated by hand);

(II) original works of statuary art and sculpture in any material;

(III) original engravings, prints and lithographs;

(IV) original artistic assemblages and montages in any material;

(h) rare manuscripts and incunabula, old books, documents and publications of special interest (historical, artistic, scientific, literary, etc.) singly or in collections;

(i) postage, revenue and similar stamps, singly or in collections;

(j) archives, including sound, photographic and cinematographic archives;

(k) articles of furniture more than one hundred years old and old musical instruments."

52. After the date of both the requesting State's and Germany's ratification of the UNESCO 1970 Convention (Germany ratified this on April 26, 2007).

53. "Article 13: The States Parties to this Convention also undertake, consistent with the laws of each State:

[...]

(d) to recognize the indefeasible right of each State Party to this Convention to classify and declare certain cultural property as inalienable which should therefore *ipso facto* not be exported, and to facilitate recovery of such property by the State concerned in cases where it has been exported."

54. As before, claims for return according to the UNESCO 1970 Convention and for Member States of the EU are further completed by claims according to The Hague Convention or directly applicable European Acts.

55. In contrast to the situation in the US, for example, where only bilateral treaties based

on the UNESCO 1970 Convention render a right for return possible. Siehr 2009: 80.

56.   The new legal due diligence requirements are based on the codes of conduct of the national and international art trade associations. Winands/List 2016: 205.

57.   See KGSG 2016: sec. 42.

58.   Sandage 2009: 8.

59.   Treaty on the Functioning of the European Union.

60.   Sec. 24 of KGSG 2016 referring to Article. 1, 2 and Annex 1 of Council Regulation (EC) No 116/2009 of December 18, 2008 on the export of cultural goods.

61.   Cultural objects should be registered as "national cultural property", if they are of high importance for the cultural heritage of Germany, its "Länder" (Federal Lands) or historic regions and it would therefore be a severe loss losing them through export from Germany (KGSG 2016: sec. 7). This list has been established in 1955 and features only about 2,700 entries so far. The new Act newly regulates and further specifies the process for registering objects to the list.

62.   According to sec. 6 of KGSG 2016.

63.   As described in note 61.

64.   Winands/List 2016: 201.

65.   For other party states of the UNESCO 1970 Convention.

66.   For other member states of the EU.

67.   Any kind of documentation will be accepted as proof. If there is none, a declaration in lieu of an oath, according to sec. 27 of the administrative procedures law of the Länders. Winands/List 2016: 206.

68.   Manigold 2017.

69.   Heinken/Müller-Karpe 2016.

70.   Manigold 2017.

71.   Manigold 2017.

72.   Manigold 2017.

73.   See also Renfrew 2000: 36.

☐ Disclosure Statement

No potential conflict of interest was reported by the author.

☐ Funding

The author received no specific funding for this work.

☐ Note on Contributor

Julia Weiler-Esser is a German lawyer and art historian with a Doctor's Degree in Art History at the University of Bochum and legal advisor at HerA–Heritage Advisors. She studies in Art History and Law (Universities of Bonn, Florence and Cologne), Magistra Artium at the University of Bonn; First Legal State exam at the Higher Regional Court of Cologne, Second Legal State exam at the Higher Regional Court of Berlin. Her former positions include Friedrich Ebert Foundation Shanghai and judicial clerkship (with placements amongst others at the German Ministry of State for Culture and the EU Commission, Directorate-General for Culture).

◻ References

Allonge, René. 2014. Die Bekämpfung der Kunstkriminalität aus Sicht deutscher Ermittlungsbehörden. In *Kunst & Recht*, edited by Peter Mosimann, and Beat Schönenberger, 15-41. Bern: Stämpfli Verlag.

Calvani, Sandro. 2009. Frequency and Figures of Organized Crime in Art and Antiquities. In *Organised Crime in Art and Antiquities*, edited by Stefano Manacorda, 29-40. Milan: International Scientific and Professional Advisory Council (ISPAC).

Grütters, Monika. 2016. Kulturgut verpflichtet! Die Gesetzesnovelle zum Kulturgutschutz läutet einen längst fälligen Paradigmenwechsel ein. In *Altes Zeug: Beiträge zur Diskussion zum nachhaltigen Kulturgutschutz*, Aus Politik & Kultur 14, 34-36. Berlin: Deutscher Kulturrat.

Krischok, Heike. 2016. *Der rechtliche Schutz des Wertes archäologischer Kulturgüter.* Göttingen: V&R unipress.

Lee, Keun-Gwan. 2012. An Overview of the Implementation of the 1970 Convention in Asia. Accessed March 10, 2019. http://www.unesco.org/new/fileadmin/MULTIMEDIA/HQ/CLT/pdf/Lee_en.pdf.

Manigold, Anke. 2017. Aufgeheizte Situation. Die Debatte um den Kulturgutschutz hat auch dieses Jahr den deutschen Kunstmarkt dominiert. Das Gesetz gilt seit August – eine erste Bilanz. December 1, 2017. Accessed March 9, 2019. http://www.zeit.de/2017/01/kulturgutschutzgesetz-bilanz-kunstmarkt-kunsthandel-kulturgutschutz/komplettansicht?print.

Meyer, Karl, and Shareen Blair Brysac. 2015. *The China Collectors. America's century-long hunt for Asian art treasures.* New York: Palgrave Macmillan.

Müller-Karpe, Michael. 2010. Antikenhandel ./. Kulturgüterschutz. *Kunst und Recht* (3/4): 91-94.

Peitz, Christiane. 2015. Die Sammler verdrehen die Fakten. August 3, 2015. Accessed March 9, 2019. http://www.tagesspiegel.de/kultur/kulturgutschutzgesetz-die-sammler-verdrehen-die-fakten/12136430.html.

Renfrew, Colin. 2000. *Loot, Legitimacy and Ownership: The Ethical Crisis in Archaeology.* London: Duckworth.

Sandage, John. 2009. Introductory Chapter. In *Organised Crime in Art and Antiquities,* edited by Stefano Manacorda, 8-12. Milan: International Scientific and Professional Advisory Council (ISPAC).

Schack, Haimo. 2009. *Kunst und Recht.* Tübingen: Mohr Siebeck

Schließ, Gero. 2016. Wie das Kulturgutschutzgesetz den illegalen Raubkunst-Handel eindämmen soll. Interview with Markus Hilgert, Deutsche Welle online, September 21, 2016. Accessed March 9, 2019. http://www.dw.com/de/wie-das-kulturgutschutzgesetz-den-illegalen-raubkunst-handel-eind%C3%A4mmen-soll/a-19563190.

Siehr, Kurt. 2009. Die Umsetzung des UNESCO-Übereinkommens von 1970 in Deutschland aus der Sicht der Wissenschaft. In *Kulturgüterschutz – Künstlerschutz,* edited by Matthias Weller, Nicolai Kemle, and Peter M. Lynen, 79-96. Baden-Baden: Nomos.

Sturm, Birgit Maria. 2016. Aspekte der Novellierung des Kulturgutschutzes aus der Sicht des Kunsthandels und der Sammler. *Kunst und Recht* (3/4): 73-79.

Stürmer, Michael. 2016. Schützen wir die Kunst vor diesen Schützern! June 17, 2016. Accessed March 9, 2019. https://www.welt.de/debatte/kommentare/article156318986/Schuetzen-wir-die-Kunst-vor-diesen-Schuetzern.html.

Walser, Joachim. 2016. Gesetz zur Neuregelung des Kulturgutschutzrechts—kein Kunstwerk. *Kunst und Recht* 18 (5): 142-149.

Wantuch-Thole, Mara. 2015. *Cultural Property in Cross-Border Litigation: Turning Rights into Claims.* Berlin: De Gruyter.

Weidner, Amalie. 2013. *Kulturgüter als res extra commercium im internationalen Sachenrecht.* Berlin: De Gruyter.

Weiler-Esser, Julia. 2016. Die Auswirkungen des neuen Kulturgutschutzgesetzes auf den Handel mit Antiken. *Kunst und Recht* 18 (5): 133-141.

Weiler-Esser, Julia. 2018. 25 Jahre Vertrag von Valletta – ein Meilenstein im DenkmalschutzR? *Kunstrechtsspiegel* 1: 11-19.

Wessels, Günther. 2015. *Das schmutzige Geschäft mit der Antike*. Berlin: Ch. Links Verlag.

Winands, Günter, and Melanie List. 2016. Das neue Kulturgutschutzgesetz. *Kunst und Recht* 18 (6): 198-206.

Zimmermann, Olaf. 2016. Die Zerstörung, der Raub und der illegale Handel mit Kulturgut. Besitz von Raubkunst muss Gesellschaftlich und Rechtlich Geächtet Werden. In *Altes Zeug: Beiträge zur Diskussion zum nachhaltigen Kulturgutschutz*, Aus Politik & Kultur 14, 27-29. Berlin: Deutscher Kulturrat.

Advertisement: Construction and Communication of Memory (A Study on Media Advertisement in Malayalam—An Indian Language)

Sajitha K. V.

Thunchath Ezhuthachan Malayalam University, Tirur, Kerala, India.
CONTACT Sajitha K. V.: sajitharamakrishnantrithala@gmail.com

Abstract: Heritage is a cultural capital of society. Memory, literally nostalgia is what sustains and communicates. Precisely concepts which are widely shared and communicated as collective memories, prototypes and linked to objective manifestations are called cultural heritage. Memory or nostalgia shapes the present and sculpts the future "trends" socially and culturally. Memory is an intense subjective stimulus, and hence an indefatigable link between the cultural and biological milieus of society. "Memory is an indispensable condition of effective human life." (Tony Bennet 2005: 214) Market strategies and advertisement media continually target collective memories for conceptualisation and communication according to contemporary likes and dislikes. This market strategy of microphysics is memory. The end products are methodified at micro-levels within the space of media advertising. Multicultural identities involving castes, religion, women and environment are constructed and reconstructed. In this article I would like to explain advertising is a subject to an analytical study as to the mechanics of social discourse which is being constructed and communicated through memories.

Keywords: heritage, memory, advertisement, communication

Introduction

Heritage[1] is the cultural capital of society. It sustains and communicates as memories. Precisely concepts which are widely shared and communicated as collective memories, prototypes and linked to objective manifestations are called cultural heritage. Memory or nostalgia constructs the past and imagines the future by living in the present. In that sense memory is a social, cultural and political process. "Memory is an indispensable condition of effective human life." (Bennet 2005: 214) Market strategies and advertisement media continually target collective memories for conceptualisation and communication according to contemporary taste. This market strategy of microphysics is memory. Advertisement is a social discourse constructing and communicating different identities. In this article I would like to explain advertising is a subject to an analytical study as to the mechanics of social discourse which is constructed and communicated through memories.

Communication—Basic Principles and Social Praxis

Interaction, interchange, transaction, dialogue, sharing, communion are ideas that crop up in any attempt to define the term "communication". According to the modern understanding, communication can simply be defined as the exchange of a thought or experience. Hence communication is the interaction between two people or among a group, where a message or idea is clearly passed from the sender and is correctly interpreted by the receiver. The communication process has three main steps: the source (sender, speaker, transmitter, etc.), the message (words, symbols, signs, images, etc.), the receiver (listener, reader, viewer, etc.). Harold Lasswell understood the broader role of the mass media in the society, he described the process of communication in the media as follows "Who (Sender)—Says what (Message)—In which channel? (Medium)—To whom (Recipient)—With what effect (Effect)" (Hodkinson 2011: 8). Earlier the term communication, in linear terms, was defined as the transaction of existing ideas or information. But communication is not the mere sending or receiving of information in whatever form; rather, it is a whole situation and an experience a human relationship in sum. It is only through communication that a thought gains meaning and hence it becomes relevant only in that particular instant.

Today many structural changes have happened in the field of communication. Among these the most important one is the split in the concept of symbolic communication, i.e. language. Language embodies and expresses a community's culture. The evolution of communication from non-verbal gestures to verbal and then to the written and printed word has progressed to sounds, motions, visuals, colours, etc., thereby changing the forms and languages of communication. The importance and impact of the communication field has increased markedly today and so it demands a new approach. The basis for this change in the structure of communication is evolution of society based on the democratic approach. This resulted in destroying the compartmentalisation based on religion and other forms of restriction in existing in the society, and unifying the people. The most amazing thing about this is that, this change is taking place in a world in which we are also an integral part. This is made possible because of the new technological advances. Technological development and society are interlinked in an ever evolving process. Any technological advance, at any given time, inadvertently impacts the society of that time, affecting a change to its structure. According to Marshall McLuhan all media are extensions of some human faculties—psychic or physical, "During the mechanical ages we had extended our bodies in space. Today, after more than a century of electric technology, we have extended our central nervous system itself in a global embrace, abolishing both space and time as far as our planet is concerned. Rapidly, we approach the final phase of the extensions of men that is the technological simulation of consciousness, when the creative process of knowing will be collectively and corporately extended to the whole of human society" (McLuhan 1964: 1). Development of technology is the direct effect of advancement in the human ability. The discovery of different means of communication, starting with the print media, has brought in a major impact in the public sphere and culture in general. This has lead to a consumerist attitude in society which is largely due to encouraging influence of media. This in turn can be termed as the result of the evolution of communication. As a discourse this change can easily be identified through advertisement. In that sense, advertisement is a communicative power. So an advertisement is essentially a precise documentation of the representation of human relations and their interactions in society.

An Overview: The History of Advertisement

Since its infancy, advertisement has borne the purpose of propagation of worthy ideas. The initial stages of advertising in Greece and China involved the use of papyrus scrolls. As it is in the modern era, in ancient times, the art of advertisement was employed primarily in the field of commerce. Rocks, walls and even mud pots were assigned as the designated abodes of ancient advertisements.

A historical milestone in the evolution of advertising was reached in the 18th century when paper became the primary bearers of advertisement. It was as a part of this evolutionary process that newspapers began finding a place in the daily life of human beings from all over the world. Advertisements printed in early newspapers dealt with share market movements and it also helped source employees to various companies. It was much later, in 1836 that an advertisement related to commerce was printed for the very first time in the newspaper—"La Presse", French daily. In 1841 America ever got its first advertisement agency and by 1900 advertisement had metamorphosed into a viable career option for many people. The birth of the modern advertising characterised by its technical perfection can be attributed to the 1920s work by tobacco companies. From the 1920s through the early 1950s, cigarette ads dominated the advertising market. However, it was the advent of globalisation in America that ultimately triggered an unprecedented growth spurt in the field of advertising. America's trade allies who had newly launched their products into the American market were in desperate need of advertisers for their products and the advertising industry undoubtedly reaped great profits as a result.

To someone analysing the several facets of advertising, its evolutionary stages are critical. The metamorphosis of advertisement from being print only and its subsequent and rapid expansion into the new age media is one of the most important stages of its growth. New age advertisement bears in its essence and reflects the thought process of a generation that is no longer bound by the chains of social economic and religious divisions, one could even interpret this in reverse and state that new age advertisements had successfully punctured the illusionary walls of human separation based on caste, creed, colour and sex. "New age media successfully overcame the various segregation practices that had previously put man into different classes and finds itself in a sphere that resonates the modern ideology of classlessness. This marks the dawn of a new beginning in the history of mankind." (Rajeevan 2013: 190) In the postmodern era, the view of the world has evolved to encompass a convivial and educational give and take between the producers and consumers of print media, and the basis of all informational transactions as being speech centricity. The above stated evolution has taken men to a stage where his sensory receptors are completely dependent on the visual input of an object to be able to completely understand it. Assimilation can thus occur only through symbolic, visual representations. Visual imagery exercises greater influence on the audience over hearing and reading.

The advent of television channels happened after the 1950s. These channels gained the fees needed to televise programmes from the advertisements that sponsored the shows. Sponsored programmes started being telecasted on India televisions by January 1, 1976 with the aim of testing the market. Later on, spot advertising tactics were formulated. The arrival of cable networks by the 1980s and Internet in the 1990s transformed advertising into a grand business.

Advertisement: Social Relation Discourse

Advertising is the communication of social relations and is constructed within a specific cultural zone. It is a discourse, dealing with the memory of the people who are tied to each other. This construction and communication is happening in the cultural discourse of "Kerala/Malayali[2]". The West is based on logic but imagination was important to the East. In the mindset of Malayali imagination is still more important than logic. So we can regard Malayali as a characteristic imagined relation. Communication of advertisement is possible in these relations. The basic concept of the advertisement process is construction of consent, not a forceful action. The concept of a Malayali was greatly shaped within the bounds of colonial administrative control. The ideas linked to such a concept were created during the era of print media but consolidated during the transformation from a speech centric era to a visual age. By compressing all men into a single visual frame the caste distinctions amongst them were slowly washed away. This was also the need of the commercial markets at the time. It became an integral part of creating consumers for products. "Feuerbach (Theses on Feuerbach-VI) resolves the religious essence into the human essence. But the human essence is no abstraction inherent in each single individual. In its reality it is the ensemble of the social relations." (Max 2002: 14) In this sense, advertisement is a special process that creates human relations.

The consolidation of what encompasses the idea of a stereotypical Malayali was greatly achieved through Malayalam movies. However, it was the advertising industry that applied this concept to reap its benefits. The market at all times, demands that the members of society be bound by certain societal structures within specified cultural platforms. "The cycle of Representation, Identity, Production, Consumption, Regulation"[3] (Curtin and Gaither 2006: 37-38) happens within specially designed cultural circuits. Cultural circuits are formed by creating a conscious interference within the cultural process of Kerala. This process is done and sustained by creating an appetite for new, unique and different fields of experience in Keralites. What is included and not included within the concept of a "Malayali" is still debatable, yet the advent of advertising has promoted a certain extent of uniformity by exploiting and highlighting the key undisputable factors with the culture of Kerala. One might conclude that advertisements communicate and portray human relations in a completely different, new light.

Memory as a Communication Discourse of Advertisement

Memory is an indispensable part as well as a determinant of human life. Tony Bennet (2005: 214) has rightly called it "an essential part of human thought", and John Locke on the other hand refers to memory as "the necessary adjunct to reason" and "the storehouse of our ideas". Paul Connerton (2006: 35) puts forth a valid argument when he states "Memories' new position as a keyword is signaled by a cluster of symptoms, some closely connected other related more tenuously". Memory is that faculty of imagination which facilitates the creation of new things. It is memory and memory alone that gifts human beings the unique ability of imagination. In that sense one can go as far as to claim that memory is what makes a human being humane. The creation and subsequent communication of memory transpires within a distinctive space. Recognising the fact that memories ultimately stem from human necessities, Walter Benjamin (1969: 255) states that, "To articulate the past historically does not mean to recognize it the way it really was, it means to seize hold of a memory as it flashes up at a moment of danger". Memory essentially manipulates and uses the stagnant subconscious sphere of the human mind. "Memory seems so personal, at the same time it is shaped by collective experience and public representation." (Samuel 1996: VII) Memory is a sacred human experience that sustains human bonds. It is at the level of human perception that human values are created, sustained and shared amongst one another. Memory is the faculty that manufactures human experiences. In the first stage, these experiences are purely sensuous. It is these experiences that then transform into ideas and imagination to become a part of the human consciousness, thus becoming conscious human experiences. It thus changes from an involuntary process into a consciously stimulated human response. Memory is the process of coding and decoding that yields conscious human responses. Memory is that element which distinguishes a man from an animal. The emotional state and responses aroused within a man who stares at the sky on a moonlit night aren't the same as the responses triggered within an animal undergoing a similar experience. The man is consciously aware of that he objects to perceive. It is this unique faculty of the human mind that distinguishes him from other organisms. The conscious awareness of what a moon is has been embedded in the human mind within a discursive terrain. When we stare at the moon, certain key indicators help to resurrect the memories related to it. Memory is not pre-determined. During certain situations, specific key signifiers trigger an unexpected resurrection of human memories. "The art of memory, as it was practiced in the ancient world, was a pictorial art, focusing not on the words but images. It treated sight as the primary source. It put the visual first. Outward signs were needed if memory where to be retained and retrieved, something which (that) is not secured through hearing, is made firm by seeing." (Samuel 1996: VII) All humans exist within the theatres of memories. Memories exist in the mind's conscious domain only during active conversations. Memories are created within specific cultural landscapes. Cultural landscape thus becomes a key resource in the interpretation and articulation of heritage. Heritage is the process of weaving the present from a selective past. Human memories and recollections are the primary pillars of heritage formation. Sara McDowell (2008: 42) as quoted in Walker 1996, "Remembering and commemorating the past is an essential part of the present and is important for a number of reasons. Not only is it tied inexorably to our sense of identity, but also an inherent part of the heritage processes we remember the past in the light of our (present) needs and aspirations". "Without memory, a sense of self, identity, culture and heritage is lost." (McDowell 2008: 42) In a sense, cultural heritage is simply memories created as a byproduct of various cultural processes. "There are multiple types of memory: official; unofficial; public; private; collective; communal; local; national; societal; historical; emotional; postmemory; literal; and exemplary." (McDowell 2008: 40) Memory is part of the cultural process that extends much beyond the above mentioned classifications. The creation and recreation of memory happen within the restraints of these cultural processes.

Heritage is communicated through memories. It is always a network of various signifiers that ultimately weaves memories. Signifiers have the power to evoke similar emotional responses across time, space and cultures. Sara McDowell (2008: 39) quoted Turner's words (1967) in her essay: "Symbols thus act as a kind of shorthand, conveying and condensing complicated values or sentiments." Advertisement can thus be defined as the highly specialised process of creation of memories in accordance with the desires and vision of the present age, at a subtle, metaphysical level and its subsequent communication. Memories can be defined as a discursive form of communication in advertisements.

Advertisements as Construction of Memories

A human being, in essence derives his nourishment from memories. Imagination is the creative faculty of memory. Degeneration of memory and imagination essentially marks the end of a human being and his interpersonal relations. In such a scenario, all that remains is his body alone. This state can be evaluated as being equivalent to that of death. A human being has in fact a galaxy of memories. It is the interplay of memories that classifies human beings as a specialised class of beings that are capable of social interaction and logical thinking. Human beings can thus be defined as a compendium of the various experiences from which memory and imagination sprout. The social or imaginary relationships, termed as "Imaginary communities" by Benedict Anderson and as "Ensembles of social relation" by Karl Marx (1845: VI) are the invisible beads that act as cohesive forces in the social relationships of human beings. Such an act of amalgamation is termed as cultural heritage. The cultural heritage of society thus essentially becomes its cultural capital. The cultural capital becomes the determinant of human's social relationships through generations. Thus cultural heritage becomes a critical determinant and facilitator of interpersonal relationships. Cultural heritage is constructed and exchanged through memories and imagination. Thus it is the related social emotions that ultimately determine cultural heritage. Selection and construction are two critical elements of cultural heritage. On the one hand, it celebrates some aspects of the past, while consciously omitting some on the other. It is the unique logical inclinations of the present that ultimately determines cultural heritage. One must not mistake memory as a simple process of retrieving past events and experiences rather, it is complex and multifaceted. Memory cannot be defined as an innocent reunion with the past.

Memory is the experiential state where the expectations, fears and hopes of the present exist in amalgamation. The process of self evaluation, imagination, dreaming and interpersonal relationships of human beings exists within the interwoven framework of memories. Even the love that one human feels for another and his ability to convey the same exists in them as memories. The catharsis of the emotions, consternations and crises of the present is only possible through a synthesis of memories. Thus memory becomes the essential capital for the future.

The heritage industry is one of the areas of application of the faculty of memory, wherein memories are created and exchanged from a commercial standpoint. One of the fields of application of the process of creation and exchange of memories for the sake of marketing based on commercial inclinations is that of advertising. Both the need for the product and the product itself are manufactured by the commercial market. The process that ensures that these products reach their customer is knows as advertising. Cultural heritage is the communication tool or marketing tool used in advertisements for effective communication. Heritage can be defined as a form of communication. Since the exchange of heritage takes place through the medium of culture, it is termed as cultural heritage. The circumstance within which the exchange takes place, ultimately determines what meaning is assigned to it. The process of coding and decoding such signifiers is known as advertising. Advertising communicates heritage in the form of emotional, nostalgic and desirable memories. Thus, heritage itself can be termed as memory. Heritage or memory is not the past; rather it is characterised by interplay of the various logical inclinations of the present. One might hence be compelled to call memory a political act. The creation of memories is not a natural act; rather it is a highly specialised ideological act. Regional advertisements recurrently make use of highly personal, cultural, emotional, nostalgic, customary, and congenial or aesthetically pleasing signifiers. The process of creating such advertisements makes use of the sanitisation logic. What takes place is essentially a process of sanitisation of culture itself.

Whilst analysing the case study of a video advertisement (Figures 1–5 show screenshots taken from the video) for Vieda hair oil (a traditional blend trusted by generations), one is faced with the revelation that the conception of beauty as it prevails in the mind of a Keralite, is essentially the sum total of previous memories and its derivative imagination.

Figure 1   The Vieda hair oil and hairdo of the model looking "Aranmula Kannadi"

One such advertisement that was created, keeping in mind the unique socio-cultural identity of Kerala through the process of sanitising certain selected extracts of its multifaceted cultural dimensions, is Veida hair oil. Ideology is what determines how we perceive an object when we see it. Such ideological faculties have been included in this advertisement in a microphysical form. "Visual is central to the cultural construction of life." (Rose 2001: 6) Intrinsic to the visual image is the context in which they are placed and consider the wide "range of economic, social and political relations, institutions and practices that surround an image and through which it is seen and used" (Rose 2001: 17). It is through such visual signifiers that societies discover and identify one another. Perception is dependent on the various specialised inclinations (religion, castes, monetary, men, women, social hierarchy, political standpoints, cultures) of humans.

The concept of hair is thus closely linked with these prevalent beauty standards. The irony rests in the fact that a Keralite, who demonstrates his dissatisfaction in religious segregation by cutting his hair, and also invests in hair oil that nourish his hair. The idea that the hair oil has been carefully prepared by grandmothers, immediately links with the image of healthy and beautiful hair. This advertisement exploits the regional beauty standard that views thick, long hair as an indispensable part of female beauty. However, it goes against a woman's individual liberty. Long, thick hair becomes a critical element only within the confinements of the female standards of beauty as conceived in the society of Kerala. Yet, since the idea of beauty being associated with long, thick hair is critical to the survival of the hair oil industry, they continue preaching about the supposedly indispensable link between long hair and beauty. The social consensus within the society of Kerala, that hair is viewed as an essential sign of beauty was in fact, propagated and cultivated by such hair oil advertisements. Thus the key signifiers—thick, healthy black hair which is nourished by the oil blend handmade by grandmothers, become quiet critical. Figure 2, the image of a grandmother, while evoking the memories of the past, also brings into our awareness various micro fields of both scientific, environmental faculties and experiential and awareness fields of traditional knowledge, environmental awareness, a faith in one's past, the relation between human and his environment and the exemplary image of nourishing one's body with substances of an organic source. Though the advertisement is set against the backdrop of Kerala's very unique environmental, social and cultural framework, it can also be looked at as a glamorised rendition of the above mentioned signifiers.

Figure 2 Grandmother wearing mundum neriyathum (settu-mundu) is applying traditional handmade hair oil to her grandchild

The brand Veida cunningly uses the tag line "Ancient recipe for beautiful hair-oil handmade by grandmothers". The advertisement entails prominent placement of key indicators and employment of play of signifiers to evoke specific memories. The term "grandmother" used in the ad, thus turns into a key signifier that is coded and decoded throughout various stages of communicative exchange between the advertisement and the reader. An advertisement consists of several such signifiers that have been carefully beaded together. For any Keralite, the term "grandmother" evokes in him several memories of the past; the term has also become an indispensible part of Kerala's cultural heritage. In a sense, it is also a dream blended in imagination. The term "grandmother" metamorphoses into various forms of dream, love, trust, taste, imagination, affection and storytelling within a Keralite's field of experience, triggered by the resurrection of past experiences. These memories are what forms cultural heritage. Thus the idea of "grandmother" becomes a sacred discursive construction. The construction of the memory that is "grandmother" happens within a discursive terrain which is the culmination of myths, folklores, songs, literary works, movies and various fields of human experiences. Thus in this case, such key signifiers of memories have been manipulated to convey the idea that this brand of oil, carefully prepared using *indigo, hibiscus* and *tulasi* by someone who embodies the definitive memory or idea of a "grandmother" is the best choice for your hair. The advertisement for Vieda hair oil makes use of the wisdom, secrecy and affection associated with the idea of a "grandmother" within a Keralite's socio-cultural sphere. This is what ultimately constitutes the tactics involved in creating any advertisement. The idea of a "grandmother" is not limited to an individual sphere of experience; it extends to the experiential terrain of the society as a whole. As a result, advertisements are always created and communicated within the boundaries of societal relations.

This advertisement taps into the human view of the past as a golden period while projecting the memories of the grandmother to its audience. The term "grandmother" or the idea of heredity and tradition becomes critical at an emotional experiential level that encompasses man's bond to his past, his nostalgic reminiscences and inherent trust. It is not past itself that is important; rather it is human's bond to his past that is deemed critical. Heritage is essentially an interweavement of the past and present. "Heritage is a value-added industry." (Gimblett 1995: 369) This era of "Heritage Industry"[4] (Hewison 1987: 9) is characterised by sanitisation and commercialisation of the past in accordance with the interests of the present age. Thus advertising becomes a vital element in various applicatory spheres of the heritage industry. Emotional branding becomes very important in this field. Advertisements tap into the experiential sediments stored within the mind of a Keralite. The advertisement (Figure 3) uses key signifiers such as Aranmula mirror[5], Premier Padmini car[6], Tulsi Thara[7], Nalukettu[8], a grandmother in traditional Kerala wear (mundum neriyathum)[9], clock, radio, TV and camera of the ancient times. It is by presenting nostalgic memories of the past in the form of key signifiers that advertisements are closely associated with the cultural ethos of a Malayali and that of Kerala communicate the past sentiments carried within them effectively to the audience.

Figure 3   Premier Padmini Car, Tulsi Thara (Sacred Stone platform) and Nalukettu (House)

It is human nature to view the past as a golden era. One might refer to the past as a "golden country". This past then transforms into a distant land and its speech is a foreign language. This foreign language is constructed using prevalent market tactics. In simple terms, the creation of advertisements entails sanitisation and commercialisation of past memories in order to suit the demands of the present. In this case, "grandmother" is a past memory selected using various creational tactics employed in advertisements. The advertisement makes profits on the view that oil created by someone who embodies the traditional views of a grandmother is the ultimate, ancient secret to healthy hair. The advertisement also highlights the fact that Vieda hair oil bears within it, all the above mentioned desirable, traditional goodness.

Figure 4   Traditional handmade oil

Figure 5   Vieda hair oil

Conclusions

Heritage exists, only within the field of human memories. Signifiers aid in the exchange of these memories. Sara McDowell (2008: 43) as quoted by Whelan (2003), "Heritage is a highly politicized process that is subject to contestation and bound up in the construction, reconstruction and deconstruction of memory and identity". Advertisement can thus be defined as a specialised process which entails the construction of memories; it is a communicative power that manufactures different identities. The brand of Vieda aims at reintroducing the traditional homemade hair oil made by grandmothers into the market. Grandmother stands as the lone link which connects the past to the present. The advertisement successfully resurrects past memories in accordance with the desires of the present using signifiers like homemade oil, healthy hair, ancient secret, grandmother's affection, heritage, trust etc. Advertising is a discourse, and is the construction and communication of memories/cultural heritage in a subtle, metaphysical form.

The misconception that heritage is something old, is based on a conventional and objective point of view. Once heritage is viewed as the cultural capital as well as a process, we come to the understanding that it is the inclinations of the present that constructs heritage. This advertisement presents a sanitised version of the past or of the memory which is well within the grasp of the present imagination. Such a "pleasant past" presented through advertisements, interacts directly with the experiential plane of each individual. Such advertisements have helped to create a consumerist society within Kerala that devours the memories conveyed through them and seeks the reflections of their own identities in them. When advertisements are broadcasting within a public sphere using signifiers linked to middle class families, they construct the public opinion. Through a process of sanitisation and separation of certain elements within the dual natured cultural heritage of Kerala, advertisements trigger the process of singularising the various elements of heritage, and forgoing the spurious. As a result of this process of centralisation, the varied cultural heritage ethos of Kerala now belongs to its middle class. Advertisement is a discourse and thus characterised by a minuscule interplay of such power relations and argumentations.

Notes

1. Heritage is a cultural process or performance that is concerned with the production and negotiation of cultural identity, individual and collective memory and social and cultural values. Heritage is not a thing but rather a cultural practice that is ultimately about managing and negotiating cultural change (Smith 2007: 2). *Cultural Heritage: Critical Concepts in Media and Cultural Studies* vol. 1, edited by Lauranjane Smith. London: Routledge. Heritage as a value-loaded concept, meaning that in whatever form it appears, its very nature relates entirely to present circumstances. Tunbridge and Ashworth for instance note that the present elects an inheritance from an imagined past for current use and decides what should be passed on to an imagined future (David C. Harvey 2001: 6). Heritage pasts and heritage presents: Temporality, meaning and the scope of heritage studies. *International Journal of Heritage Studies* 7 (4): 319-338.

2. Malayali/Keralite—Relating to or characteristic of the south-western Indian state of Kerala or its inhabitants. A native or inhabitant of the south-western Indian state of Kerala. https://www.lexico.com/en/definition/keralite.

3. Circuit of culture: The circuit of culture consists of five moments in a process, regulation, production, consumption, representation, and identity—that work in concert to provide a shared cultural space in which meaning is created, shaped, modified, and recreated. There's no beginning or end on the circuit; the moments work synergistically to create meaning. However, each moment contributes a particular piece to the whole. Curtin, Patrica A, and T. kenn Gaither. 2006. Global public relation and the circuit of culture. December 15, 2006. Accessed July 3, 2019. https://www.sagepub.com/sites/default/files/upm-binaries/13710_Chapter3.pdf.

4. The impulse to preserve the past is part of the impulse to preserve the self. Without knowing where we have been, it is difficult to know where we are going. The past is the foundation of individual and collective identity; objects from the past are the source of significance as cultural symbols (Robert Hewison 1987: 47).

5. A unique metal alloy mirror, the Aranmula Kannadi made in Aranmula, a small town

in Pathanamthitta district, is the first product to get geographical indication in Kerala. A few households of the master craftsmen in Aranmula guard the secret behind its making. A unique blend of tin and lead in a fixed ratio results in this metallurgical miracle (https://www.keralatourism.org/kerala-article/sudhammal-aranmula/695). The Aranmula Kannadi is a front surface reflection mirror, which eliminates secondary reflections and aberrations typical of back surface mirrors, wherein image is reflected from the bottom layer where mercury is pasted. Thus one can say that a person sees his or her real image reflected only in the Aranmula Kannadi. Accessed July 3, 2019. https://www.kerala.gov.in/documents/10180/3bf4e2f9-d0d8-49b7-9529-5c4bc03125ce.

6. Inception of independent Indian automobile industry started off with two names: Hindustan Motors Ltd.'s Ambassador and Premier Auto Ltd.'s Padmini. Both are one of its kind cars plowing their roots deep into every individual born in India. If we notice, both the cars were of foreign origin, Ambassador being an evolved Morris Oxford III and Padmini being an indigenised version of Fiat 1100. We try to refresh the memories of Fiat that ruled millions of kilometres of Indian soil while ruling billion Indian souls. Premier Padmini started off as the Fiat 1100 Delight in 1964 on Indian roads. Yes, the car came to life in Italy under the roof of engineering marvel Fabbrica. Accessed July 3, 2019. https://www.motorbeam.com/history-fiat-premier-padmini/.

7. Tulsi Thara which is the sacred stone platform in front of traditional Kerala houses on which the Holy Basil (ocimum sanctum) commonly known as tulsi plant is grown. And every evening a lamp will be lighted at Tulsi Thara, which is usually done by a women member of the family. Tulsi is a sacred herb known as the Basil. It is believed that nothing can please the Lord Krishna more than Tulsi. According to vastu shastra Tulsi pot can be placed towards the North or East side with respect to the direction in which the House faces. Accessed July 3, 2019. https://www.kjasons.com/newsroom/112-stone-art/467-natural-stone-tulsi-thara.html.

8. An ancient form of architecture called "Nalukettu". This is one of the best architectural works of southernmost state of India-Kerala. The local translation of Nalukettu is

"nalu" (four) and "kettu" (built up side blocks). It is a house built up with four blocks and a central open courtyard. Nalukettu has four blocks known as Vadakkini (northern block), Padinjattini (western block), Kizhakkini (eastern block), and Thekkini (southern block). https://hubpages.com/education/Traditional-Architectural-Style-of-Kerala-Nalukettu. The Nalukettu was a typical feature of the Kerala tharavadu tradition, where joint families lived together for generations with a patriarch and matriarch overseeing all their affairs. At the centre of the house is a nadumuttam, which is an open courtyard that is served as the focal point of interactions between the family as well as various household activities and festivities. The larger and wealthier families had ettukettu or, the rarer, pathinaarukettu houses featured eight and 16 blocks with two and four courtyards respectively. All of these houses were built following the principles of ancient thachu shastra or the science of carpentry and developed during the 18th and 19th centuries, a time when the Nairs and Namboodiris (upper castes) dominated the society with their power and wealth. Accessed July 3, 2019. https://www.thehindu.com/real-estate/heritage-history-the-nalukettu-houses-of-kerala/article19239576.ece.

9. Mundum neriyathum (settu-mundu) is the traditional clothing of women in Kerala, south India. It is the oldest remnant of the ancient form of the saree which covered only the lower part of the body. In the mundum neriyathum, the most basic traditional piece is the *mundu* or lower garment which is the ancient form of the saree denoted in malayalam as "Thuni" (meaning cloth), while the *neriyathu* forms the upper garment the mundu. The mundum neriyathum consists of two pieces of cloth, and could be worn in either the traditional style with the *neriyathu* tucked inside the blouse, or in the modern style with the *neriyathu* worn over the left shoulder. Accessed July 3, 2019. https://wikimili.com/en/Mundum_Neriyathum.

☐ Acknowledgements

I would like to thank YANG Jianping (Elaine) for the accurate comments and suggestions for completing this article. I express my deep gratitude to my research supervisor, Dr. G. Sajina for her guidance, enthusiastic encouragement and useful critics of this article. I would also like to thank Dr. K. M. Bharathan, Dr. T. V. Sunitha, K. V. Sasi, Vipin Kumar, and Sachin for their advice and assistance in keeping my progress on schedule.

I would also like to extend my thanks to my colleagues Aswathy, Chinchu, Ramya, Ramisha, Sangeeth, Nidhin and Chandralekha.

Finally, I wish to thank my parents for their support and encouragement throughout my study.

☐ Disclosure Statement

No potential conflict of interest was reported by the author.

☐ Note on Contributor

Sajitha K. V. is a research student at Cultural Heritage Studies Department of Thunchath Ezhuthachan Malayalam University, Kerala. Her research work centres on how advertisements construct and communicate heritage and vice versa based on regional language advertisements. She has published four articles in research/academic journals in India.

References

Benjmin, Walter. 1969. *Illuminations: Essays and Reflection.* New York: Schocken Books.

Bennet, Tony, Lawrence Grossberg, and Meaghan Moriss (eds.). 2005. *New Keywords: A Revised Vocabulary of Culture and Society.* UK: Blackwell.

Connerton, Paul. 2006. Cultural Memory. In *Handbook of Material Culture*, edited by Chris Triley, Webb Keane, Susanne Kuchler, Mike Rowland, and Patrica Spyer, 315-324. London: Sage Publications.

Curtin, Patrica A., and T. Kenn Gaither. 2006. Global Public Relation and the Circuit of Culture. In *International Public Relations: Negotiating Culture, Identity, and Power,* 35-50. Thousand Oaks, CA: Sage Publications.

Gimblett, Barbara Kirshenblatt. 1995. Theorizing Heritage. *Ethnomusicology* 39 (3): 367-380.

Harvey, David C. 2001. Heritage Pasts and Heritage Presents: Temporality, Meaning and the Scope of Heritage Studies. *International Journal of Heritage Studies* 7 (4): 319-338.

Hewison, Robert. 1987. *The Heritage Industry: Britain in a Climate of Decline.* Methuen: paperback.

Hodkinson, Paul. 2011. *Media Culture and Society: An Introduction.* Olivers Yard: Sage Publications.

Keralatourism.org. 2007. Sudhammal—The Guardian Angel of Heritage. Accessed July 18, 2018. https://www.keralatourism.org/kerala-article/sudhammumal-aranla/695.

Kjasons.com. 2018. Natural Stone Tulsi Thara. Last modified on March 14, 2018. Accessed July 19, 2019. https://www.kjasons.com/newsroom/112-stone-art/467-natural-stone-tulsi-thara.html.

Marx, Karl. 1969. Theses on Feuerbach. In *Marx/Engels selected works* vol. 1, 13-15. Moscow: Progress Publishers.

McDowell, Sara. 2008. Heritage Memory and Identity. In *Ashgate Research Companion to Heritage and Identity*, edited by Brian Graham, and Peter Howard, 37-53. London: Routledge.

McLuhan, Marshall. 1964. The Medium is the Massage. In *Understanding Media: The Extensions of Man*, 1-18. New York: Signet Books.

Motorbeam. 2012. The Good Old Wine—Premier Padmini. Accessed July 19, 2019. https://www.motorbeam.com/history-fiat-premier-padmini/.

Oxford University press. n.d. Lexico Dictionary: Definition of Kerala in English. Accessed May 4, 2018. https://www.lexico.com/en/definition/kerala.

Rajeevan, B. 2013. *Vakkukalum Vasthukkalum: Words and Objects*. Kerala: D.C Books.

Rose, Gillian. 2001. *Visual Methodologies*. London: Sage Publications.

Samuel, Raphael. 1996. *Theatres of Memory: Past and Present in Contemporary Culture*. London: Verso.

Sanath, Nair. 2012. Traditional Architectural Style of Kerala—Nalukettu. March 31, 2012. Accessed July 19, 2019. https://hubpages.com/education/Traditional-Architectural-Style-of-Kerala-Nalukettu.

Smith, Lauranjane (ed.). 2007. *Cultural Heritage: Critical Concepts in Media and Cultural Studies*, vol. 1. London: Routledge.

The Hindu. 2017. Heritage history: The Nalukettu Houses of Kerala. Accessed July 19, 2019. https://www.thehindu.com/real-estate/heritage-history-the-nalukettu-houses-of-kerala/article19239576.ece.

Wikimili. n.d. Mundum Neriyathum. Accessed July 20, 2019. https://wikimili.com/en/Mundum_Neriyathum.

YouTube. 2017. ViedaKachiya Enna. Accessed July 18, 2018. https://youtu.be/9MA8X7O-kE.

Association Members with a Migration Background as "Unexpected" Heirs of Cultural Heritage in Allotment Garden Associations

Raimund Lazar

Leibniz University Hannover, Institute for Political Science Schneiderberg 50, 30167 Hannover. CONTACT Raimund Lazar: r.lazar@ipw.uni-hannover.de

Abstract: This article offers an attempt to employ the praxeological framework developed by Pierre Bourdieu to examine the role of social actors and the cultural heritage that they bring into play in the power relations involved in the reproduction of cultural heritage within various fields in society. The focus of the presented research project is on cultural heritage in associations in the form of association culture and in the cultural negotiation processes involved, which can be expected in allotment garden associations that have a rather heterogeneous composition of association members. Experts in the field often describe association members with a migration background as a homogenous group that tends to not participate in the association culture because of "cultural differences". The cases of voluntary engaged persons with a migration history introduced in this article indicate that the often prematurely feared changes to the association culture due to an increase of allochthonous members are inappropriate, as it is the similarities in habitus and therefore contribute to association members to engage in association culture. Furthermore, it is the labelling as being ethnically different that overshadows milieu-specific similarities and identifies the relatively new members as "others" not willing to participate.

Keywords: associations, allotment gardens, association culture, voluntary engagement, Bourdieu, habitus

Introduction

With almost one million members, the approximately 14000 allotment garden associations form a mass cultural phenomenon in German cities (BDG 2019). Parallel to the bourgeois high culture in the urbanisation processes of the 19th century, allotment associations—officially termed as "Kleingartenvereine" in German—developed as a part of a petty bourgeois folk culture, in which a healthy and self-sufficient diet was to counteract the health-endangering conditions in the cities. The reproduction of industrial labour, which was originally one of the primary social functions of these forms of associations, is a part of this association-specific cultural heritage, which, however, has lost much of its significance (Matthai 1989; Stein 2010), while the shared leisure interest in a garden remains until today. Gardening organised in associations has long been associated with petty bourgeois milieus which, due to a lack of private gardens and their taste preferences, chose these very associations for their leisure activities, thus forming voluntary electoral communities and consequently shaping the life of the associations. For social milieus that differentiate themselves from the petty bourgeois milieus and their taste, the entry into a allotment garden as a place of communitarisation was often out of the question (Jensen 2005; Tessin 1994).

In the course of constant or increasing demand for gardens in the city, allotment garden associations have undergone social diversification in recent decades. Due to their popularity, allotment gardens form a meeting place for actors from different milieus and strata, with their own traditional forms of practices, experiences and perspectives (Appel, Grebe and Spitthöver 2011). In addition to gardening, there can also be other traditional practices found in the associations, which can be traced back to the taste of tradition-oriented association members. For outsiders and new association members, the dominant taste represented in the associations is especially evident in the associations' social events and clubhouses.

The events and places oriented towards the community primarily not only serve socialising as such, but also for identification with the association and the commitment to the association, which may result out of it (Krüger 2012). Associations do not understand themselves primarily as service providers, but as solidarity communities. Its mission is to be open to all and to offer a place of social cohesion, and integration in the community of interests and to preserve traditions. However, association functionaries complain, that there is a declining interest among members in volunteering and taking part in the associations' sociable events (Appel, Grebe and Spitthöver 2011; LHH 2016; MUNLV 2009).

Materials and Methods

In the context of research on associations, different developments in allotment garden associations have been analysed, such as the diversification of the members of the association or the decreasing willingness to voluntary engagement (Appel, Grebe and Spitthöver 2011; Daglan and Wolf 2007; LHH 2016; MUNLV 2009). To what extent the socio-structural change in the composition of the association has an influence on the association culture and to what extent the association culture influences the participation in association life that is still largely unexplored.

Above all, the perspective of those who tend to participate less in traditional association life and less often take over a function in the association, such as people with a migrant background, needs to be further explored. Previous surveys on social and cultural diversity in allotment garden associations are often based on member statistics or on expert opinions. Neither analyse the complexity of the relationships between different members of the association, nor the social heterogeneity of the association members with a migration background sufficiently.

In the present research project the continuity and the change of association culture are examined more closely by interviewing association members who, at least at first sight, represent a deviation from the field traditionally dominated by *autochthonous* men. In particular, *voluntary* engaged women and persons with a history of migration represent "new" actors in the associations. The aim of the research project is therefore to investigate, among other things, whether the reproduction of the association-specific heritage is characterised more by a continuity of traditional practices or more by transformation and to what extent this is related to the association members' milieu-specific socialisation.

Under the conditions of an increasingly transforming and multicultural society, the following questions arise: In what ways are social actors, who do not fit in the traditional patterns of the autochthonous men of petty bourgeois milieus, bearers of the cultural heritage of these associations? Have they internalised the cultural heritage of the field as an obligation or do they break with traditions? Is it possible to discern patterns that point to the reproduction of traditional practices on the one hand and "modernised" practice patterns on the other, which can be explained by habitual dispositions and the relational positions of the actors in the respective field?

It can be assumed that irrespective of age, gender and ethnicity, there is a continuity of certain traditions and cultural heritage, due to inherited milieu-specific habitual dispositions, which are linked to a certain position in the social space. New association members may also adapt traditional forms of practice in the clubs on the basis of habitual similarities. At the same time, a dynamic of modernisation in the form of practices that distinguish themselves from the traditional patterns can be expected within the associations, which is due to the diversification of the association members. By looking at the dynamics of change in the associations, in addition to possible lines of conflict, the possibility of a transformation of cultural heritage is also focused.

Especially association members with a migration background are generally described as a relatively homogenous group, which hardly participates in life association. This description tends to neglect what claims, needs and wishes for participation is voiced by those who find themselves in an alleged outsider position and which lines of conflict may arise within the associations as a result. In order to close this gap in the research landscape, the research project primarily surveys members of the association who do not participate unconditionally in the dominant cultural practices or who are to be categorised as exceptions in the field due to personal characteristics. These are actors who, for reasons of age, gender, migration background or milieu, as contrasting cases represent or suggest a different logic of everyday practice and cultural heritage.

By looking at the members who volunteer in their association, conclusions can be drawn about their understanding and their fit with the dominant association culture. Which habitual dispositions characterise these persons and to what extent do they relate to the dominant association culture in the respective associations? The comparison with other voluntary engaged members should serve to elaborate a typical form, structure and logic of the practices of the actors involved. The project thus contributes to the exploration of engagement careers and, at the same time, to processes of change, which associations are subject to places of lived cultural heritage and social diversity.

The logic of the practice, the connections with the participation in the association life as well as the evaluation of the practices of the other association members are elaborated in qualitative interviews. On the basis of the transcribed interviews, the habitus-specific logic of action is reconstructed with the help of the habitus-hermeneutic method. With this method it is possible to interpret the action-orientated principle of habitus from the practice of social actors and at the same time to integrate the division principles of social space as well as the location and genesis of practice in this space into the analysis (Bremer and Teiwes-Kügler 2013; Lange-Vester and Teiwes-Kügler 2013). In addition, the methods of participant observation and document analysis are applied in order to understand the practice in its execution and materiality from the perspective of the researcher.

Praxeological Approach

Pierre Bourdieu's concepts of habitus, capital types, social fields and symbolic power

(Bourdieu 1984, 1992; Bourdieu and Wacquant 1996) are suitable to examine the association-specific practice of the different actors and the social relations in which they are integrated. With the help of Bourdieu's theory, the dynamics and conflictuality of the reproduction of the cultural heritage in the associations, which are connected with the field structure and the habitual dispositions, can be analysed. Such a praxeological research approach goes beyond the social statistical features of actors and rational choice explanatory approaches and instead holistically integrates social practice and the associated unequal opportunities and preferences.

In the research project presented in this article, the relational milieu concept developed by Vester et al. (2001) is applied, which builds on Pierre Bourdieu's concepts and thus also on the milieu conception of Emile Durkeim (1988) and the different principles of lifestyles identified by Max Weber (1980). The term milieu refers to a social group that develops a similar everyday culture based on family, professional or neighbourly relationships. Belonging to a milieu is therefore primarily dependent on internalised principles of lifestyle and the position in a social space (Vester et al. 2001; Vester 2004).

Similar to Bourdieu, Vester et al. (2001) developed a model of social space in which three social levels are distinguished, which vertically express an over- or sub-ordination of milieus. The uppermost level is above the line of distinction and characterised by the prevailing milieus. These milieus (about 20% of the population) are characterised by the accumulation of possessions, education and power and exert domination and distinction in relation to the milieus under them (Vester et al. 2001: 26-36). Below the line of distinction are the milieus of the middle (about 70% of the population). They are mainly made up of white-collar workers and small self-employed workers. Below the so-called line of respectability are the underprivileged milieus, who in turn are divided into low-skilled and precarious people (about 10% of the population) (Vester 2015).

The social space also includes a horizontal dimension, which further divides the vertical differentiation and illustrates milieu change and social mobility. The so-called horizontal pluralisation of class cultures is based above all on societal modernisation processes, which is reflected in the horizontal differentiation axis. Milieus on the left pole of the horizontal dimension are characterised by an avant-gardism and individual responsibility, on the right pole by values of duty and security as well as hierarchical attachment (Vester et al. 2001: 29). The identified social milieus in the social space are characterised by milieu-specific mentalities and action orientations that are "culturally inherited" through family socialisation over generations (Bourdieu 1984; Bourdieu and Passeron 1979). The category decisive for the determination of different milieus is habitus, as the "unifying, generative principle of all of practices" (Bourdieu 1984: 173).

Cultural Heritage Conceived as Habitus

Bourdieu has developed the central concept of habitus, in addition to the other key concepts of symbolic violence and social fields, in the course of his research to understand the practical meaning behind social practice. Habitus is an incorporated guiding principle for different practices and attitudes, thus forming a holistic context (Bourdieu 1987: 97-121). "How one speaks, dances, laughs, reads what he reads, what he likes, what acquaintances and friends he has, etc.—all this is closely linked."[1] (Bourdieu 1992: 32) The habitus dispositions of the actors, which are responsible for a largely unconscious practice, are mainly formed by socialisation in their environment of origin. Therefore, the habitus dispositions or social milieus do not change arbitrarily due to structural changes, but they are characterised by a relative constancy and inertia (Krais and Gebauer 2002: 61-64; Vester et al. 2001: 311-327).

Habitus can therefore also be regarded as a cultural heritage (Bonz and Wietschorke 2013; Bourdieu 2001: 193-199). Social actors inherit their cultural heritage through their socialisation, largely through cultural capital in their parents' home (Bourdieu 1983). This socialisation is at the same time bound to a place in the social space. Bourdieu illustrates this in his studies on the education system, in which he outlines the connections between the heirs and their habitus dispositions internalised in the parental home and success in the education system (Bourdieu and Passeron 1977, 1979).

Habitus not only unites the supposed contradictions between the objectivist approach of the structure of the social space and the subjectivist approach of the practice of the actors, but also represents the connection of the practice of the past and present. It represents collective history, as a historically evolved, milieu-specific product of the past, ways of thinking, seeing and acting (opus operatum) and is at the same time the generating principle of present mentalities and forms of practice (modus operandi). For an analysis of social practice, therefore, the genesis of the habitus as well as the actual conditions in which it becomes action-guiding must be included (Bourdieu 1987: 98-103). Thus, if in this research project the continuity and change of cultural heritage is to be examined, which is based primarily on action orientations, mentalities and a certain taste, the theoretical concept of habitus is particularly well suited, since it explains the reproduction of taste as well as the related social differences and symbolic order.

Cultural Heritage in Allotment Garden Associations: Association Culture and Voluntary Engagement

In this research project, cultural heritage is primarily understood and analysed as milieu-specific attitudes, habits and traditional everyday cultural practices. The shared beliefs and informal practices, e.g. sociability among the association members and identification with the association, can be described as association culture (Nagel and Conzelmann 2004), or in other words, as an association-specific cultural heritage. This cultural heritage manifests itself materially as a ritualised and traditional practice in the form of social capital-generating sociable events and the design of the association buildings and grounds. The feeling of community, belonging and social co-creation created by the association culture is an important prerequisite for another aspect of cultural heritage in associations, without which the association would not exist: the voluntary engagement of the association members (Braun 2011: 41).

The associations are social fields, with their own logics of practice, distributions of goods and hierarchical positions. In urban areas, associations are rooted in more or less constantly changing local contexts. The associations' cultural heritage in the form of a specific association culture is therefore not only to be determined by the fact that it has a certain age, and is cared for over generations and often described as endangered or in crisis (Braun 2011: 17). At the same time, it is well alive because it is based on the interaction and practices of the association members and thus offers potential for openness for updates and modifications.

Although attitudes, values and abilities are also recorded in writing, they are usually reproduced verbally or even tacitly in everyday practice and materially manifested in the bodies of the actors and in artifacts. Cultural heritage is thus inseparable from the social everyday life as well as the bodies of the actors. This perspective aligns itself with approaches that focus less on the separation of tangible and intangible aspects and more on the production, processuality, and the various appropriations of cultural heritage as well as the social hierarchies reproduced with them (Hall 2000; Harrison 2013; Kirshenblatt-Gimblett 2004).

Results

Gardening, the space for sociability as an important part of the association culture and the voluntary commitment to the association can be understood as formations of cultural heritage across associations. Gardening is practiced by almost all association members but it is less a practice that is done in cooperation with other association members. To counteract the isolation of the members and to further the social life in the association, the formal and official sociable events of the association should serve to move as many association members as possible to the care of the community and at the same time be open to guests and potential new association members (Matthäi 1989; Verk 1994).

There are associations that hold up to three official festivals a year. In addition to the "Laubenfest", which is the festive highlight in the summer, a spring festival, which opens the gardening season, and a season-ending harvest festival in the fall, is often hosted. In the field of investigation there are a few associations that do not celebrate the "Laubenfest" in the summer or any other festivities, often due to lack of demand. Most associations celebrate at least the summer festival, which is between one and three days long.

The festivals of the allotment garden associations are characterised by a popular taste of the milieus of the petty bourgeoisie, which, in contrast to the high-cultural and other more individualistic tastes, represents a traditional and conventional taste. Not the exclusive is celebrated, but rather the popular and down-to-earth. Among the association traditions maintained, is the conviviality, marching through the different paths of the association, flying the association flag, especially at the official openings and closures of the festival, and wearing the uniform of the allotment gardeners.

It is typical of the festivals that in addition to the public consumption of alcohol, the grilling of meat and the get-together in one or more marquees, an entertainment programme is organised. The entertainment programme also corresponds with a more traditional-conventional taste. Typically, a DJ is playing pop, oldies, folk and "Schlager" music. Comedians, brass and cover bands, entertainers and carny are often part of the festivities, which are often organised by the wives of the male board members. Children's parties and events, which exclusively are aimed at the conviviality of the female association members, are also typically integrated in the summer festival programme. The festival programme is open to all association members, although the majority of guests are autochthonous and about 50 years and older.

The interviewees in the field of investigation often reported that interest in the sociable events had declined overall. The festivals had lasted longer and would have been more crowded in the past. Despite decreasing interest, most associations endeavour to continue to hold the festivities, as board members generally consider the value of solidarity to be very important and the tradition of regular festivals should contribute to strengthening the sense of community and the resulting commitment to the association.

Many of the interviewed association members regret a decline in the interest in the association culture and cooperation in the association as a whole. This also manifests itself in the lack of willingness to work together and a reluctance to be a permanent member of the association board. Although it is often mentioned that especially people with a migration background cannot relate to the "German" festivals, there is however also a declining willingness to participate found among the autochthonous association members. Reasons for this are the aging process of many association members, and therefore an increasing individualisation and isolation, "modern" lifestyles, and other preferences as well as a diversified entertainment offer from other providers in the city.

The aging of the association members and the question of the heirs of the association culture is a specific aspect of allotment gardening. In the considered field of research, a generation change is imminent. In most associations allotment gardeners over 60 years old are the most strongly represented age group. Despite the lamented decline in interest in association life, the association culture in most associations is still characterised by an overall continuity. Apart from exceptions, the festivals continue to be held and association work is still carried out by the members. A fundamental transformation of the structures and the practices associated with the association culture cannot be recognised in the field of investigation.

"Unexpected" Heirs

However, there are exceptions in the field that at least at first glance represent an opening and suggest a transformation of association culture. Occasionally, women and persons with a migration background take over functions in the associations, which, at least because of their gender and ethnic difference, represent a change in the field dominated by autochthonous men. In the habitus-hermeneutic analysis that followed the interviews, however, habitual dispositions, taste preferences, and action orientations which are close to the dominant association culture examined and traditional, community-oriented practices, could frequently be identified.

Exemplary for this are Gülcan and Abdi[2], two association members who volunteer in different associations. They both immigrated with their parents from Turkey to Germany at a young age, both are in their mid-50s and have been members of an allotment garden association for about 15 years. Gülcan has been a chairwoman in her association for five years, an absolute exception as a woman with a migration history. In her association, however, women form more than the half of the board. Abdi is a "Wegewart" in his association, which means that he is the contact person for the garden neighbours in his part of the colony and he takes care of everybody that complies with the garden rules. Both Abdi and Gülcan have come to their position on the basis of being addressed by old-time association members and their recommendation, since they have already been noticed as being actively involved in association life.

Their voluntary work is relatively time consuming, as they spend one or two hours a day, several days a week to do their work in their association. Their distinctive work ethic and their sacrifice of leisure time for the association are associated with a pronounced ascetic habitus disposition. Gülcan and Abdi both belong to petty bourgeois milieus; they both work or worked as semi-skilled workers in the manual sector. Because of their habitus, they embody values, attitudes and a taste that are homologous to the cultural heritage of the petty bourgeois association culture, with its emphasis on community, the solidary commitment to the association and the idea of the allotment garden association as a place for "ordinary people".

Their involvement in the association also contributes to the respectability of their person, especially in contrast to other association members. Gülcan and Abdi already had "leading" roles in their occupations, for example as shift supervisors. In their associations, persons with a migration background make up about half of the members of the association and Abdi sees himself as a mediator between the autochthonous and allochthonous association members. He emphasises landlords with a migration background, in his colony, primarily Turkish-born association members, who do not always abide by the association rules and thus represents a problem for him that he has to take care of. As a consequence he has enforced that announcements and rules of the association were translated into Turkish.

The statement often made in the research field and literature is that people with a migration background tend to isolate themselves and have nothing left for the rather

"German" association culture stands in opposition to Gülcan's and Abdi's voluntary commitment and their emphasis on community in the association. Both continue this association-specific, petty bourgeois cultural heritage through their everyday practice and their taste, and at the same time symbolise a diversification of the field. The decisive factors are the shared values and the taste of the social actors, who fit in with the recognised and established forms of practice.

Cultural heritage, understood as caring for the community and working together in the association, in this case acts as a connecting force between social actors otherwise perceived differently because of their ethnic background. At the same time, Gülcan's and Abdi's commitment can be understood as social bridging by acting as a "cultural mediator" between the autochthonous and allochthonous association members. In addition to the already mentioned translation of the order of the garden in Abdi's association, both established a "Turkish" barbecue at their festivals. In questions of culinary taste and especially in the case of dishes, which are compatible with the food customs of the Muslim association members, boundaries or openings in the association culture often become evident.

The Ambivalent Effect of Cultural Heritage

In the field of investigation it has also been repeatedly reported that people with a migration background are confronted with resentment on the part of the autochthonous association members, because of racist prejudices. Another example from my own empirical work is to illustrate the simultaneity of the connecting and at the same time exclusionary power of cultural heritage.

In one case the association board lamented that tenants from the former Union of Soviet Socialist Republics (USSR) rather remained among themselves in one part of the garden colony and would not participate in association life. Last summer, the association board asked association members from the former USSR whether they wanted to perform with their choir, that they are a part of, as part of the programme of the summer festival. The choir, for the most part, is mostly made up of so-called Russian-Germans, all of whom are around 60 years old. They sing old German and Russian songs, which the singers mostly knew before they immigrated to Germany. Legally recognised as "German nationals", more than two million of these former Soviet citizens immigrated to Germany after the collapse of the USSR (Boutsko 2013). Following the invitation of the allotment garden association, the choir, who according to its official self-description wants to engage for the better coexistence in their city, decided to be part of the summer festival programme.

The choir represents a cultural heritage related to a migration history, including the singing of traditional songs and the language. Many of them speak German with a Russian accent or mainly Russian among themselves, which connects them to each other and distinguishes them from the autochthonous members of the association. The preservation of the cultural heritage of their—as they call it—old "homeland", in the form of singing old songs, which include the longing for a home and community, can be interpreted as more typical of petty bourgeois tradition-oriented milieus.

In terms of taste, the members of the choir, with their preferences for home cooked fare, relatively high public consumption of alcoholic drinks and traditional folk music, are close to what is established at the "Laubenfest" in their association by the same age group and a similar milieu. Both groups occupy approximately the same position in the social space, symbolically distinguishing themselves by their taste and related cultural heritage from more modern lifestyles. The appearance of the Russian-German choir therefore did not represent a break from the traditionally petty bourgeois festive culture of the association.

However, the choir showed up only for its appearance in the clubhouse and then it left the festival to eat and sing together in the allotment of a couple that is singing in the choir, and is also a member of the association. In the allotment they organised their own food and drink in preparation for the gathering. When I asked why they did not stay longer at the festival, one singer of the choir complained, that they were presented as "Russians"—a term they often hear in the everyday life of German society, in contrast to being insulted as "Germans" in the former USSR. The cultural heritage cultivated by the singing of the choir illustrates the unifying power it has for the group. For the strengthening of the perceived "we-group", it is the cultural "glue", the common practice of coming together and singing and the common experience of migration—the relatively young in the 1990s, but also the common history of migration, dating back to the 18th century.

In the face of a constantly transforming society, they often find their position in the social space as detached, due to a lack of recognised cultural capital and resentment on the part of the majority society due to their migration history. In the cultural heritage that they are familiar with, they find appreciation and security. The allotment garden association offers them the opportunity to cultivate their community in semi-private space and to share their cultural heritage with others in public space. Their appearance at the summer festival can be interpreted as a first step towards a joint production of the association culture.

In another point, the two groups previously described are similar: members from the choir and the allotment garden associations regret that their cultural heritage is being cultivated by fewer and fewer actors. This is not only due to the fact that the bearers of this cultural heritage are getting older and fewer. Even the younger generations do not make a purely arbitrary decision against the traditions and cultural heritage of their parents. For many of them, social opening processes and socialisation in the German education system have opened up new opportunities for social participation and the associated changes of place in the social space. With their more modern lifestyles they are increasingly symbolically distinguishing themselves from their parents' insistence on traditions and history.

Discussions

The aim of this article was to emphasise that cultural heritage is always tied to a milieu-specific taste and thus to a place in the social space. Social actors distinguish from one another by their everyday practice, for example through their leisure time behaviour. Taste and lifestyle, however, are not individually chosen without presupposition, but are due to the action orientations and preferences incorporated by socialisation—in other words, the habitus of social actors. Leisure behaviour is also dependent on associations of people based on lasting social ties, such as family, friends or neighbourhoods. In the case of association culture in allotment garden associations, it is a popular taste, which is particularly influenced and preferred by traditional petty bourgeois milieus. Therefore, these are "elective affinities" (Bourdieu 1984: 241) by social actors who, because of similar experiences and socialisation, have developed similar taste preferences and, in the case of association culture, cultivate a specific community in allotment garden associations. "Taste is what brings together things and people that go together." (Bourdieu 1984: 241)

The description of association members with a migration background in research literature is not sufficient, as they are usually described as a rather homogenous group that does not participate in association life due to "cultural" unfamiliarity. The presented cases exemplify how milieu-specific similarities of taste are decisive for the participation in the dominant association culture. Less than the attribution to a migration background, it is the habitus and related tastes that are crucial to the acquisition and reproduction of association-specific cultural heritage.

The cases Gülcan and Abdi as well as the "Russian-German" choir represent heterogenisation of the association culture, superficially due to their migration background. At the level of taste and everyday practice, however, they mainly symbolise a continuity of the dominant association culture. The often feared fundamental change in association culture brought on by "foreigners" cannot be verified by the examples presented. Rather, it is in their interest and to their liking to maintain the traditional celebrations and continues to cultivate them in the interests of the community—with the exception of the expansion of meals that are being served.

In the case of the choir, the common history of migration and the singing of the traditional songs, which can also be understood as a cultural heritage, represent a connecting element among the members of the choir. However, the similarities of taste with the autochthonous association members can be overshadowed by "unintentionally" emphasising the ethnic differences and thus reproducing old resentments. This indicates a necessary sensitivity, which should be demanded above all by the group, which is in the majority and thus in the dominant position in the associations—the autochthonous association members. There is a need to open up to those who are perceived as "new" or "different" in order to recognise similarities and facilitate cooperation. The examples presented here prove that there is willingness to participate in the association culture as well as a voluntary engagement in the association among the members with a migration background.

The cultural heritage of the allotment garden associations, understood as an association culture and voluntary engagement in the association, has the potential to unite association members of different ethnic backgrounds and to contribute to the creation of "social capital" (Bourdieu 1983). Thus, it can also contribute to social cohesion within associations, in the form of mutual recognition, identification and support. Using the example of communitarisation processes in allotment garden associations, it was shown how cultural heritage as a milieu-specific resource is intended to create the basis for the practical forms of sociability and engagement in the association and thereby reproduce itself.

Above all, the sociable events and the associated places make it clear that cultural heritage as resource and practice represents a milieu-specific taste, which results in association members feeling either attracted to or distanced from the dominant association culture due to their taste preferences. While the practice of gardening, which is done rather less in community, represents a connecting interest and potential for everyday exchange, association culture as an area of encounter between the different association members is ambivalent to evaluate. On the one hand, the dominant association culture serves to strengthen the community among like-minded association members. On the other hand, it can exert a segregating effect.

Thus, when speaking of association culture and groups of people who tend not to participate, there is a need for a theoretical approach that can relate both cultural practices and social actors to one another, to point out possible "elective affinities" as well as the finer distinctions along everyday practice. The solidary community aspect of the association-specific cultural heritage, however, is likely to continue to be maintained in the associations, when more attention is paid to the similarities in taste, instead of differences of gender and ethnic origin. Thus, the petty bourgeois and collectivist cultural heritage can continue to play a key role in allotment gardening, even if it is reproduced by actors who at first glance do not fit into the tried and tested pattern.

Notes

1. Author's translation.
2. The names have been anonymised.

☐ Disclosure Statement

No potential conflict of interest was reported by the author.

☐ Funding

The research project is a sub-project in the joint project "Cultural heritage as a resource? Competing constructions, strategic usages and multiple adoptions during the 21st century (CHER)". CHER is an interdisciplinary research project, funded by the Ministry for Science and Culture of Lower Saxony as well as the Volkswagen Donation.

☐ Note on Contributor

Raimund Lazar has a Degree in Social Sciences from the Leibniz University Hannover (Germany), where he is currently a research associate at the Institute for Political Science. In his research he examines the manifold formations of cultural heritage in football and allotment clubs and their influence on the participation of club members in club life. He specialises in social structure analysis, citizens' participation, and in urban studies. His most recent publication is titled "Urban social diversity—city districts subject to demand pressure" (Federal Institute for Research on Building, Urban Affairs and Spatial Development, 2019).

□ References

Appel, Ilka, Christian Grebe, and Maria Spitthöver. 2011. *Aktuelle Garteninitiativen.* Kassel: Kassel Univ. Press.

BDG (Bundesverband Deutscher Gartenfreunde e.V.). 2019. Zahlen und Fakten. Accessed February 29, 2019. https://www.kleingarten-bund.de/de/bundesverband/zahlen-und-fakten.

Bonz, Jochen, and Jens Wietschorke. 2013. Habitus und Kultur: Das Habituskonzept in den empirischen Kulturwissenschaften. Ethnologie—Volkskunde—Cultural Studies. In *Pierre Bourdieus Konzeption des Habitus. Grundlagen, Zugänge, Forschungsperspektiven,* edited by Alexander Lenger, Christian Schneickert, and Florian Schumacher, 285-306. Wiesbaden: Springer.

Bourdieu, Pierre. 1984. *Distinction: A Social Critique of the Judgment of Taste.* Cambridge: Harvard University Press.

Bourdieu, Pierre. 1987. *Sozialer Sinn. Kritik der theoretischen Vernunft.* Frankfurt am Main: Suhrkamp.

Bourdieu, Pierre. 1992. Die feinen Unterschiede. In *Die verborgenen Mechanismen der Macht,* edited by Pierre Bourdieu, 31-48. Hamburg: VSA.

Bourdieu, Pierre. 2001. *Meditationen: Zur Kritik der scholastischen Vernunft.* Frankfurt am Main: Suhrkamp.

Bourdieu, Pierre, and Jean-Claude Passeron. 1977. *Reproduction in Education, Society and Culture.* London: Sage Publications.

Bourdieu, Pierre, and Jean-Claude Passeron. 1979. *The Inheritors: French Students and their Relations to Culture.* Chicago: University of Chicago Press.

Bourdieu, Pierre, and Loïc Wacquant. 1996. *Reflexive Anthropologie.* Frankfurt am Main: Suhrkamp.

Boutsko, Anastassia. 2013. Catherine the Great and the "Russian-Germans". July 27, 2013. Accessed February 29, 2019. https://p.dw.com/p/19BOe.

Braun, Sebastian. 2011. *Ehrenamtliches und freiwilliges Engagement im Sport: Sportbezogene Sonderauswertung der Freiwilligensurveys von 1999, 2004 und 2009.*

Köln: Sport & Buch Strauß.

Bremer, Helmut, and Christel Teiwes-Kügler. 2013. Zur Theorie und Praxis der "Habitus-Hermeneutik". In *Empirisch Arbeiten mit Bourdieu: Theoretische und methodische Überlegungen, Konzeptionen und Erfahrungen*, edited by Anna Brake, Helmut Bremer, and Andrea Lange-Vester, 93-129. Weinheim: Juventa.

Daglan, Nilgün, and André Christian Wolf. 2007. Kleingärten als Orte für Bürgerengagement und Integration. *Stadt+Grün* 9: 39-42.

Durkheim, Emile. 1988. *Über soziale Arbeitsteilung*. Frankfurt am Main: Suhrkamp.

Hall, Stuart 2000. Whose Heritage?Un-settling "The Heritage", Re-imagining the Post-nation. *Third Text* 13 (49): 3-13.

Harrison, Rodney. 2013. *Heritage: Critical Approaches*. London: Routledge.

Jensen, Uffa. 2005. Der Kleingarten. In *Orte der Moderne: Erfahrungswelten des 19. und 20. Jahrhunderts*, edited by Alexa Geisthövel, and Habbo Knoch, 316-324. Frankfurt am Main: Campus Verlag.

Kirshenblatt-Gimblett, Barbara. 2004. Intangible Heritage as Metacultural Production. *Museum International* 56: 52-65.

Krais, Beate, and Gunter Gebauer. 2002. *Habitus*. Bielefeld: transcript.

Krüger, Timmo. 2012. Der Kleingarten als "Nische der Gemeinschaft": Eine Analyse des Diskurses um sozialen Wandel im ostdeutschen Kleingartenwesen. In *sinnprovinz. kultursoziologische working papers* 2, 36-42. Leipzig: Universität Leipzig.

Lange-Vester, Andrea, and Christel Teiwes-Kügler. 2013. Das Konzept der Habitushermeneutik in der Milieuforschung. In *Pierre Bourdieus Konzeption des Habitus*, edited by Alexander Lenger, Christian Schneickert, and Florian Schumacher F., 149-174. Wiesbaden: Springer VS.

LHH (Landeshauptstadt Hannover), Fachbereich Umwelt und Stadtgrün. 2016. Kleingartenkonzept 2016–2025. Accessed February 29, 2019. http://www.hannover.de/content/download/ 584989/13437736/file/Kleingartenkonzept+2016+-+2025.pdf.

Matthäi, Ingrid. 1989. *"Grüne Inseln" in der Großstadt: Eine kultursoziologische Studie über das organisierte Kleingartenwesen in Westberlin*. Marburg: Verl. Arbeiterbewegung u. Gesellschaftswiss.

MUNLV (Ministerium für Umwelt und Naturschutz, Landwirtschaft und Verbraucherchutz des Landes Nordrhein-Westfalen). 2009. Zukunft des Kleingartenwesens in NRW: Forschungsberichtzur Kleingartensituation in Nordrhein-Westfalen. Accessed February 29, 2019. http://docplayer.org/62230666-Studie-zukunft-des-kleingartenwesens-in-nordrhein-westfalen.html.

Nagel, Siegfried, and Achim Conzelmann. 2004. Was hält den Verein imInnerenzusammen? ZurOrganisationskultur in Sportvereinen. In *Sportvereine – Auslaufmodell oder Hoffnungsträger? Die WLSB-Vereinsstudie*, edited by Siegfried Nagel, Achim Conzelmann, and Hartmut Gabler, 151-165. Tübingen: Attempto.

Stein, Hartwig. 2010. Oasen in der Steinwüste-Der deutsche Kleingartenzwischenpädagogi scher Provinz, ökonomischer Nische und privatem Paradies. In *Gärten und Politik. Vom Kultivieren der Erde*, edited by Brita Reimers, 121-136. München: Oekom.

Tessin, Wulf. 1994. Der Traumvom Garten–einplanerischerAlptraum? Zur Rolle des Gartensimmodernen Städtebau. In *Europäische Hochschulschriften, Reihe 42, Ökologie, Umwelt und Landespflege*, 14-28. Frankfurt: Lang.

Verk, Sabine. 1994. *Laubenleben: Eine Untersuchung zum Gestaltungs-, Gemeinschafts- und Umweltverhalten von Kleingärtnern*. Münster: Waxmann.

Vester, Michael. 2004. Soziale Ungleichheit, Klassen und Kultur. In *Handbuch der Kulturwissenschaften*, edited by Friedrich Jaeger, and Jörn Rüsen, 318-340. Stuttgart: Metzler.

Vester, Michael. 2015. Die Grundmuster der alltäglichen Lebensführung und der Alltagskultur der sozialen Milieus. In *Handbuch Freizeitsoziologie*, edited by Renate Freericks, and Dieter Brinkmann, 143-187. Wiesbaden: Springer VS.

Vester, Michael, Peter v. Oertzen, Heiko Geiling, Thomas Hermann, and Dagmar Müller. 2001. *Soziale Milieus im gesellschaftlichen Strukturwandel. Zwischen Integration und Ausgrenzung*. Frankfurt am Main: Suhrkamp.

Weber, Max. 1980. *Wirtschaft und Gesellschaft*. Tübingen: Mohr.

Use the Impact of World Heritage Designation at Jiaohe Site in Xinjiang, China

LIU Yunxiao, Tim Williams

Institute of Archaeology, University College London, 31-34 Gordon Square, London, WC1H 0PY. CONTACT LIU Yunxiao: Yunxiao.liu@ucl.ac.uk

Abstract: Since the launch of the World Heritage Conventions in 1972, its concept and practice have been followed by countries that endeavour to preserve heritage at an international stage. Many more scholars are dedicated to reflections that a World Heritage (WH) title can bring impact not only to the heritage place itself, but also to local communities and regional development. Debates surrounding the relationship between WH designation and local community wellbeing (particularly local residents' resettlement), heritage tourism driven by the success of WH nomination, as well as the imbalance between conservation and reconstruction, have made great contributions towards sustainable heritage management. Particularly in China, politics has also been incorporated into the understanding of the WH nomination process.

Jiaohe (also named as Yar City) in Xinjiang along the Silk Road is an example to rethink what exactly the "WH" brand brings to the sites and locals. This article is trying to demonstrate that the WH programme is not only driven by government will, but also a practical approach for heritage sites in Xinjiang to enable them to be sustainable, which in turn can contribute to the locals' identity building and sense of place. Hopefully, a successful management of WH can improve the locals' living standards and enhance the relationship among locals, the government and archaeological sites in Xinjiang.

Keywords: World Heritage designation, the Silk Road, Jiaohe (Yar City), Xinjiang Uygur Autonomous Region

Introduction

The concept of World Heritage (WH) has been developed for more than four decades since it was first proposed in 1972. It aims to ensure the identification, protection, conservation, presentation and transmission to future generations of cultural and natural heritage of outstanding universal value (UNESCO 2017). In those four decades, UNESCO's World Heritage Centre (WHC) has incorporated new understandings of heritage in order to make the World Heritage List (WHL) more representatives of global heritage (Zhang 2016). This process has widened the diversity of heritage types, including cultural landscapes (Scazzosi 2004; Fowler 2003; Aplin 2007), industrial sites, modern architectures, and inhabited settlements, etc. (Labadi 2005; Askew 2010) Also, the key concept of "outstanding universal value" has evolved from "the best of the best" (unique sites) to the "representative of the best", the latter of which shows the comparison of the nominated sites with similar characters (Cameron 2005; Askew 2010: 30). Furthermore, some concepts of intangible heritage (Nas et al. 2002), cultural routes (Rössler 2006), and transnational nominations (Turtinen 2000; Reguant-Aleix et al. 2009) have been involved in WH designation in order to meet the global trend.

However, more and more scholars have started to rethink WH designation (Meskell 2013; Frey and Steiner 2011; Huang, Tsaur, and Yang 2012; Frey, Pamini, and Steiner 2013; Labadi 2005; D'Eramo 2014). Meskell (2013) argues that "political pacting" could influence the decision during the nomination process, which would ignore the global recognition. D' Eramo (2014) states that the WH programme is "urbicide", which could limit the development of the city or result in unsuitable development. In 2005, the local community decided to construct a bridge to encourage local development in the Dresden Elbe Valley, which was inscribed on the WHL in 2004. Most local residents deemed that Dresden can do without the UNESCO title (Connolly 2009). Finally, in 2017, UNESCO declared that one country can only nominate one World Heritage Site (WHS) per year. All the above indicate that WH designation has slowed down its pace and a reflection on what the WHL can exactly provide for both the sites and local communities.

Nevertheless, many developing countries including China are still obsessed with it. Becoming a WHS can lead to high international attention (Su and Lin 2014) and improve management and conservation (World Heritage Conventions 2008). Furthermore, a WHS could bring more economic benefits, as it easily becomes a tourism destination and thus can significantly contribute to the local revenue (Su and Wall 2012). Meanwhile, China is also pursuing WH designation as it can promote the "Chinese civilisation" both domestically and internationally.

"Silk Road: The Routes Network of Chang'an-Tianshan Corridor" was inscribed on the WHL in 2014, which best exemplifies the transformation of WH during the four decades as well as the benefits mentioned above. This programme is a transnational nomination inscription including China, Kazakhstan and Kyrgyzstan. Because even the individual sites are vital to the wholeness of the Silk Road concept, it would have not been a priority of the nomination process without the evolution of theory on cultural routes and corridor transboundary, etc.

In this cultural route, Xinjiang is in the vital position to connect with Kazakhstan and Kyrgyzstan. Due to the special geographic location of Xinjiang Uygur Autonomous Region, the Chinese government has pushed the cultural heritage sites in Xinjiang into the inscription process. Yet, not enough attention has been paid on what WH nomination could really bring to the local communities and the sites of Xinjiang.

This article focuses on Jiaohe (also named as Yar City), which is one of the most representative cultural heritage sites in Xinjiang. The site was inscribed on the WHL in 2014. Jiaohe comprises of the ruins of the fortress of Gaochang Ward of the Sixteen

Kingdoms during the Tang Dynasty (618 AD–907 AD). It was a strategic point of the ancient Silk Road and historically had an important position and influences on the history of Xinjiang, even on economic and cultural exchanges between the East and West.

Jiaohe: A Gem of Xinjiang's Cultural Heritage

Located 10 km west of Turfan city in Xinjiang (Figure 1), the ancient ruins of Jiaohe are the remains of a historical city which has existed for centuries from at least 2000 years ago (Liu 2004: 199) and has played a significant role during the development of the Silk Road. It is 1650 metres long from north to south, about 300 metres at its widest and is situated on a plateau approximately 100 metres wide which formed as a result of a river bifurcation. The Tang Dynasty ruled the Gaochang Kingdom in 640 AD and established Anxi Duhufu (official military agency) at Jiaohe in 640 AD. Moreover, Jiaohe was of great military significance in the western area of the kingdom (Meng 2001; Liu 2004). In the late 9th century, the Yar City became a part of the territory of Qocho Kingdom (ca. 848 AD–1283 AD) and was destroyed by the war in the 13th centurys (TCRB 2012: 22).

Most buildings were located in the southeast of the city, and there were two city gates, the South Gate and the East Gate. The layout of the city can be briefly divided into blocks of a temple complex, pagoda grove, official institution area, ancient tomb region and residential area. There have been five major excavations in total in Jiaohe since 1930. Archaeological surveys have revealed that a protective wall or parapet was constructed along the edges of the cliffs and along the edges of the plateau. Only about 50 metres of the parapet is in reasonably good condition now; the rest has collapsed and been buried in sand and earth. In terms of the quality of the architecture in Jiaohe, the streets and dwellings were created by unique digging skills. The long street was dug out from the top down, and then local dwellings were constructed. Meanwhile, timber was used in main fabrics (Sun et al. 2007; TCRB 2012: 22).

Figure 1   The overview of Jiaohe (photo from TCRB 2016)

Research Methods

In order to explore the impact of WH designation primarily at a local level in Xinjiang, the qualitative and quantitative methods would be combined to ensure that reliable results could be obtained. The preliminary survey was started in February 2017, mainly focusing on investigating how WH designation affected other regions and how the Xinjiang Uygur Autonomous Region Bureau of Cultural Heritage (XBCH) arranged their assignment of each site on the WHL. The survey's second data collection period occurred in June–July 2017 in Xinjiang, focusing on the relationship between the sites and their local people, examining their changes and how they influence each other.

To ensure that our results were as reliable as possible, we opted for several methods based on the triangulation rule, which generally refers to a process of cross-checking findings deriving from both quantitative (questionnaires) and qualitative (semi-structured interviews and observations) research (Bryman 2015; Deacon et al. 1998).

The Impacts of World Heritage Designation on Jiaohe

Management Strategies

In China, cultural heritage management currently falls into the remit of either the Division of Construction or the Division of Culture (Wang and Zhu 2006). Each division is represented at the national, regional, and municipal government levels (Tao 2012). At the municipal level, a range of bureaus are in charge of various aspects of heritage such as sustainable development planning, conservation and community involvement. On the other hand, different bureaus are also supervised by the people's government at the same level, which means each district should directly react to the people's government.

In the case of Jiaohe, the heritage management structure from the top to bottom consists of four major bureaus (Figure 2): the State Administration of Cultural Heritage (SACH), which oversees the general policy guidance, examination link and law enforcement supervision of the site's entire preservation work; XBCH, which is responsible for coordination with the relevant bureaus, management arrangements for each programme, overall funding plans and organising intensive training courses for the general staff; Turfan Cultural Relics Bureau (TCRB), which should ensure that each institute profitably carries out the relevant heritage preservation measures; and the Institute of Jiaohe Cultural Heritage Management (IJCHM), which takes care of the surrounding environment of Jiaohe and the site itself. Meanwhile, the administration at the higher level provides professional guidance. The nomination dossier of Jiaohe comprises of the Master Plan for Preservation and Restoration of the Ancient Ruins of Jiaohe (1999) and Management Plan for Site of Jiaohe City (2012). The Management Plan for Site of Jiaohe City (2012) was written by SACH and the Institute of Architectural History. Each cultural heritage division is supervised by local people's government at each level.

There is one unusual approach for Jiaohe management. The preservation work for Jiaohe is conducted by TCRB and Academia Turfanica, which is a research institute that aims

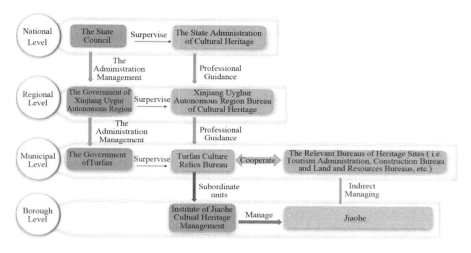

Figure 2   The hierarchical management system of Jiaohe

to explore the Turfanica studies. Many staff members work in TCRB, who are also employed by Academia Turfanica. It is effective for each institute to conduct management strategies as, in practice, the TCRB has the power to carry out further.

Regarding IJCHM, there are in total nine permanent staff members (including retired staff members), which consists of administrative staff, professional and technical staff and daily maintenance staff, etc. Although the Master Plan states that the staff must graduate from the faculty of law, economy or languages (Master Plan 2012: 22), in practice most of them graduated from middle school. In addition to this institutional setting, IJCHM innovatively set up a system in 2013 inviting a local tourism company to get involved in the Jiaohe management. Most employees from the local company come from Yahrguziler village, which is the nearest village of the site. Additionally, this company could help with IJCHM to deal with daily work, such as daily patrol. Meanwhile, the institute could also bring the job opportunities to locals.

In order to improve the preservation awareness of the site to the staff, TCRB provides the training courses to all staff members. Nonetheless, there is a gap between expectations and practical trainings according to interviews[1]. It is argued that some courses do not function for the site management. On the other hand, the subject limitation of staff employment is consciously strict, which means some changes on staff arrangement have been made after training courses.

Besides, during the nomination process, the central and local governments established a team to supervise a series of work arranged for WHL. It is undoubted that this team has made large contributions to making the nomination succeed, and then reflected on the site management, for example, understanding the relationship between the site and local residents by visiting locals. The staff affirmed the contribution from the team, as well as the positive influences on locals. It also reaffirms that success cannot be achieved without support from local communities.

In order to follow the WH principles of the Outstanding Universal Value (OUV), authenticity and integrity of Jiaohe, a buffer zone (Staneva 2006) was established in 1999, which was then further expanded from 68 to 3200 hectares in 2008 (Master Plan 2012: 26). The buffer zone comprises of a series of zones along the historical wall of Jiaohe, up to roughly 1–1.8 km from the wall. The space is then further fragmented by relocated local settlements, rivers, hills and IJCHM. As an important tool for conservation of properties inscribed on the WHL (Stovel 2009), the buffer zone affords the necessary protection for Jiaohe from urban development and specific natural hazards such as flooding. The zone was designed with detailed considerations. The village which was located close to the wall was relocated further from it, but still within the area of the proposed buffer zone so that daily farming would have little impact on the historical environment.

However, the execution of the buffer zone plan can be a challenge between the government and the local community. While the village has been relocated further from the wall, the original space occupied by the settlement was supposed to have a new covering of vegetation in order to protect the site from sandstorms. As part of the government's preservation policies, the local community is in charge of planting new trees. Yet, due to the management structure it would take a long time for the government to allocate sufficient budget, which has greatly delayed the planting process.

Conservation: A Top Priority of Jiaohe from 1999 to 2014

According to UNESCO's requirements, the site nominated by its state party must have a detailed management plan and a strong legal framework as part of their nomination dossier for a successful WH designation (Shackley 2009: 200). Smith (2002) and Jimura (2011) further state that the conservation of a WHS can be improved through the nomination process as the dossier itself serves as the conservation guideline. Even after being inscribed on the WHL, WHSs should still be required to keep improving their management and conservation (Bianchi 2002).

In the case of Jiaohe, conservation remains as a top priority from the preparation stage of the WH nomination since the 1990s to its everyday management after its successful inscription in 2014 (Table 1). As we can see from Table 1, Jiaohe is persistently conducting conservation projects. Besides these big projects, daily maintenance and safety checks are also part of conservation work in Jiaohe. From 2006 to 2012, heritage conservation was conducted with about 4 billion RMB invested in total. It is assumed that even the nomination process is not the initial reason for conservation in Jiaohe; it is a catalyst for further enhancing work.

At the beginning of 2006, this (conservation) project was not designed as the nomination project. After two years, it was combined with the Silk Road project and the government also provided extra money. (Local Manager)

Table 1   The Conservation Chronicles of Jiaohe

Year	Conservation development of Jiaohe
1957	Named as the first group of Xinjiang Uygur Autonomous Region's Priority Protected Cultural Heritage Sites
1961	Named as the first group of National Priority Protected Cultural Heritage Sites
1992–1995	UNESCO and Japanese government invested 1 million USD
1994	IJCHM was established
2003	SACH approved the Plan of Culture Heritage Preservation and Tourism in Turfan (2002–2020) and a conservation plan in detail (2002–2020)

Continued

Year	Conservation development of Jiaohe
2004	Turfan City's Regulations for the Conservation and Administration of the Site of Jiaohe and Xinjiang Uyghur Autonomous Region's Regulations for the Conservation and Administration of the Site of Jiaohe were issued
2006–2012	Rescue and Consolidation Project (the Silk Road [Xinjiang section] State Priority Cultural Heritage Conservation and Restoration Project)
2007–2008	Flood Prevention Projects
2013	Regulations for the Administration of the Site of Jiaohe

There were two important stages in Jiaohe conservation work. The first in the 1990s mainly focused on constructing roads (Figure 3) in site and reinforcing the Grand Buddhist Temple. The second stage was from 2006 to 2015, which emphasised reinforcing the fragile timbers construction and emergency conservation work for the structural wall of buildings. With four recommendations proposed by UNESCO (2014: 26) on the conservation of the Silk Road, at the end of 2015, a conservation report of the state (China) had been submitted to UNESCO, which illustrated the conservation work in response to the suggestions made by UNESCO.

Figure 3   Road construction (photo by LIU Yunxiao, July 2017). This shows that the path has been built in different conservation projects (1990s and 2006–2015) with different materials (bricks and wood)

Meanwhile, the local community was also actively engaged in the preservation of the site since they realised Jiaohe is their treasure. This phenomenon was contributed by WH designation, as the government educated local residents in order to preserve the integrity of the site. At the beginning, some local activities damaged the site (Gulibaikere 2013; Sun 2006). Local residents believed that the soils in Jiaohe could well support cultivation of crops and herbs, and then used them as ingredients for Chinese medicine. In addition, some residents consistently collected soils and structural materials from the site, which directly damaged the structure of the site.

After the publicity from the administrations, local community started to preserve it from other hazards. Whenever locals found tourists climbing the cliff to enter Jiaohe, they would stop their work and report to the administrative office (Gulibaikere 2013: 21). Due to the special geography of Jiaohe, flooding could occur in the river valley every summer. In order to protect their farmlands, farmers planted lots of trees in the river valley, which also effectively protected Jiaohe from flooding.

Indeed, local residents would be glad to do something with the government to contribute to Jiaohe, such as cooperating with the government to conduct conservation projects. In the past, there was no particular administrative institute near the site and to preserve, so that the efforts made by local residents were more important than those made by the government.

Tourism and Recognition of Sites

As Shackley (2009: 200) states, WH designation normally can bring more visitors, as it makes the site highly visible (Jimura 2011; Smith 2002), which may also promote its recognition in the public minds (Smith 2002; Bianchi 2002). Additionally, WH designation is a marker of "authenticity" and "quality" for both national and international tourists, which could boom the tourism industry (Wang et al. 2015).

Below is the number of visitors in Jiaohe after becoming a WHS (Figure 4). Local tourism companies have actively engaged with development strategies, such as designing new advertisements and videos. "Becoming a WHS highlights its significance in two aspects: promoting our preservation work for heritage sites, and then developing the cultural heritage tourism in Turfan." (Local Manager) A new visitor centre was built in 2016, and most of the staff members working at the visitor centre are hired by a local tourism company.

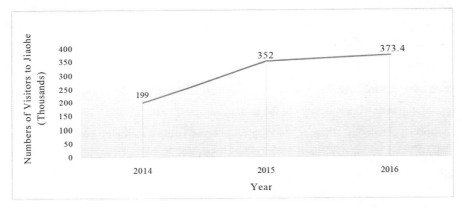

Figure 4   Numbers of visitors in recent years—data collected from Turfan United Tourism Company during field work (July 2017)

After the nomination, 76% of current Turfan residents think that local tourism infrastructure has been improved in these years and 15% of the locals agree that it has seen great improvement (Figure 5). According to local managers, revenue from the entrance fee has been reinvested into the preservation project and renovation of the local infrastructure; for example, new public toilets were built. Additionally, as part of the preparation working for WH designation, SACH funded the construction of paved paths in Jiaohe in the 1990s, which allowed easy access to the site. New air-conditioned shuttle buses are also provided from the new visitor centre to the site entrance, which affords better visiting experience during the summer and shortens the journey.

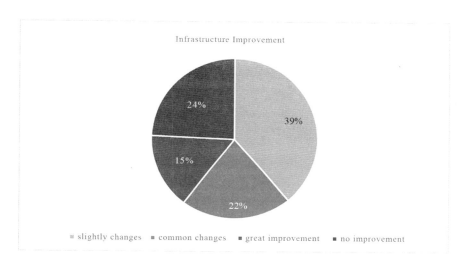

Figure 5   Questionnaire data—the degree of infrastructure improvement in the eyes of the locals

However, many residents complained to us that Jiaohe has more expensive entrance tickets since it became a WHS. The price is ridiculous in the eyes of some residents from Turfan city. A young woman told me that she has not been to Jiaohe since she moved to Turfan as the ticket is more expensive, and once she has a discount she might go. Therefore, for local tourism in Jiaohe, the primary conflict is between expensive tickets and the low average income.

Also, Jiaohe has built statues for its "WHS" brand close to the highway to attract visitors. The two statues—one near the highway and the other inlaid on the surface of the visitor centre—serve as the local landmarks which make the site visible for tourists from long distances. The one near the highway was built as an observation platform made by a tourism company. The company charges the entrance fee if visitors want to get in and take pictures. The other statue inlaid with Jiaohe title is to show Turfan people's confidence in their heritage sites and culture, as well as the reputation that Jiaohe enjoys at an international level.

Interpretation and Education

Before the 1990s, there were no approach for interpretations in Jiaohe, even panels. Since the Turfan Museum was established in 1990 and TCRB was set up three years later, interpretation and education in Turfan started. WH nomination has constructed Jiaohe into a better understood heritage site with publicity work carried out well. It is argued that WH designation brings new interpretation ideas to Jiaohe, which directly improves the recognition degree of the public.

The cultural heritage bureau in Turfan has collaborated closely with the media in order to disseminate the information of the site. Its efforts include releasing working information to the media and websites and then catching the eyes of the public, setting more collaborations with other famous associations and taking various videos with the mainstream media and playing on TV screens, specifically, establishing the counterpart with well-known media contact mechanisms, such as CCTV (China Central Television), Phoenix Satellite TV and Xinjiang TV. Turfan has cooperated with CCTV to create a series of documentaries on the Silk Road, as well as provided open access to the public. Moreover, taking advantage of website platform, Turfan has enlarged the scope of academic research and publicity. Until 2013, more than 50 articles had been used by the SACH official website (Li 2012).

There has also been encouragement for the Turfan Academia to host important meetings in Turfan. For example, the "Silk Road Transnational Joint Declaration of the World Cultural Heritage International Consultation" (2006), and "Tourism Development and Preservation of Cultural Heritage in Turfan Symposium". According to surveys, nearly 95% of the participants know that Jiaohe has been inscribed on the WHL.

The site interpretation of Jiaohe is divided into three sections: museum exhibitions (in Turfan Museum), site exhibition hall and in-site display. In terms of museum exhibitions, the museum was refurbished as an exhibition hall in 2010 only for the theme of the Silk Road which emprasises Jiaohe and Qocho City.

The site exhibition hall is situated in the visitor centre of Jiaohe that has been opened since 2016. The visitor centre is approximately 1000 m²; there is a long corridor behind the entrance with interpretation panels on both sides. The ticket centre is in the middle, where visitors can buy tickets for the site and shuttle buses, and it also supports payment online. This visitor centre also serves local managers, providing a better working environment with a rest area.

Because the visitor centre is in the periphery of Jiaohe for its preservation, most visitors choose shuttle buses to the site, especially in hot summer. Normally, shuttle buses run every 15 minutes and each bus can carry eight people. A 4D cinema has also been built at the visitor centre in order to give visitors a brief idea of what Jiaohe is, but it has not finished yet. Now there is a screen, which is a temporary one instead of a 4D screen, which regularly shows a short introduction film. All of the above could enhance the visitor experience and provide better understanding to visitors.

The in-site display relies much more on interpretation panels, which were designed in 2013 to meet the standard requirements of WH designation. This means all nominated sites have the same style panels. According to the managers from XBCH, it is because of the WH designation. Additionally, all the sites in Xinjiang have the similar interpretation schedules and approaches, and thus sometimes this would ignore the characters of the site itself, and then affect the impressions and values from visitors. Although this is the quickest method for authorities to meet the criteria of WHL, it ignores the special characteristics for sites themselves. Also, the site managers from both sites told us that they do not have any plan to change, at least for the next five to ten years.

In 2016, IJCHM and a local company initially designed a new interpretation programme—"travel in Jiaohe in the night". This activity was inspired from the Alhambra night tour, which is a WHS in Spain. Due to the higher temperature in Turfan during the tourism season (summer), it is an effective method to attract visitors. This programme is a result of combining international ideas and the local environment. The visiting route was designed delicately, starting from the southern gate of Jiaohe, leading to the Great Buddhism Temple with the candles. On the temple square, visitors can enjoy the local intangible heritage performances, such as Shattrath solo, hot wapusk and Mukam performances. Referring to Zhang (2016: 84), appropriate approaches could bring a renaissance of cultural and intangible culture of the site. All activities aim to express the Xinjiang culture. This is the first attempt to involve visitors in the evening in cultural heritage sites in Xinjiang, and it has been a great success (IJCHM 2017).

> The most important influence for Yahrguziler village is enhancing our identity for Jiaohe site and our culture. In the past, we only got to know the history of Jiaohe from our fathers and grandfathers but now we know something different from the interpretation work by interpreters. This is much more important for our future generations to recognise Jiaohe from other perspectives, indeed enhance their local pride and be proud of our culture, and finally put Jiaohe into the next development stage. (Local Manager)

Furthermore, Turfan Museum exhibitions have been entirely updated during the nomination process, as well as creating outreach educational programmes for the public. Since 2015, "the portable museum" project has started with the slogan "closer to the public and making a sustainable society" (IJCHM 2015). This project is in cooperation with IJCHM, where the staff and volunteers carry out different activities in local places, such as schools, poverty-stricken villages and nursing homes. They bring their brochures, panels and basic equipment to such places. Normally, after several days, some local people will go back to Jiaohe site and have a revisit. Also, some educational work is added to this project. The main aim is to instil in local communities the proper acknowledgement of cultural heritage sites and their history about Turfan. Interpreters will interweave the story of the Silk Road. Moreover, on a cultural heritage holiday, Jiaohe could provide free entrance for the public, usually once a month.

These approaches directly promote the positive image of Jiaohe, even the acknowledgement of the Silk Road in the public's minds. Nevertheless, according to interviews in Turfan, there are still many residents who have no idea about *opening museums*, and many residents did not visit Jiaohe. It is assumed that the publicity work has been neglected after listing compared with during the nomination. In recent years, how to improve the visitor experience and how to create economic benefits are becoming important sections in the daily work. Furthermore, how to express the value of the Silk Road related to Jiaohe is still a question that managers are concerned about.

Closing Relationship Between Jiaohe and Local Communities

UNESCO's WHC declares that seeking approaches to ensuring the active involvement of local communities will help with people's identification (WHC 2002). Shackley (2009: 203) also states that WHS could be a symbol for nationalism to enhance local identity. It is assumed that local residents are ideally responsible for recognising the values of the site and protecting their heritage. In Jiaohe (during the process), in order to strengthen the relationship between the site and the local residents, the local government held regular meetings and decided to have cooperation with local companies.

WH designation could strengthen the connections among various associations within a WHS (Jimura 2011; Smith 2002). Smith (2002) states that sites from WHL can receive various political supports from national, regional, and local levels. For local residents, a WH designation could also increasingly draw their attention to their living places, ultimately giving rise to an increase in their pride for their culture (Evans 2002; Shackley 2009). Encouraging involvement of residents with the site itself could improve the quality of their lives, thus fulfilling the community spirit and recommendations of UNESCO (Conforti et al. 2015). Finally, a WH designation should be more sustainable for the development of cultural heritage sites and practices once local communities would like to be given a voice and continue to get involved in the site management systems (Chirikure et al. 2008).

The approaches that could establish stable relationships between local residents and Jiaohe are spontaneous preservation behaviours from locals. In fact, the preservation work in Jiaohe was started by surrounding residents of the Yahrguziler village for generations. As they consider that Jiaohe is a precious treasure given by their ancestors, preserving Jiaohe is their tradition. Furthermore, folk beliefs have also contributed to the preservation of the site. The residents believe that there are ghosts in Jiaohe, so that they could not go there alone, especially in the evening. The imam (a hong) and the mullah (maola), who are highly respectable elderly people in Islamic communities, also forbid their people to go to Jiaohe alone.

Due to the fact that Yahrguziler residents are much more familiar with Jiaohe and have preserved the site for a long time, the first generation of site keepers hired by Turfan Heritage Bureau in 1978 were Yahrguziler residents, and most of the second generation of site keepers were also selected from the Yahrguziler village. Around the 1970s, the government suggested that site keepers start selling tickets at the price of one yuan per ticket. In 1980, the local Yahrguziler residents were highly engaged in the conservation project planned by the government. Also, the chief of Yahrguziler was encouraging residents to contribute to the site and actively looked for some adobes to help with this project. The government paid 1.6 yuan per person per day (local resident). Around the 2000s, the son of the first site keeper took over his position to become the second generation of this site keeper family. Compared to his father, he took notes for every site viewing and regularly reported to his leader (Gulibaikere 2013: 29). In that time, they used the donkey as the main means of transportation.

Orbasli (2002: 189) expresses concerns that international recognition and publicity of a WHS could make many historic sites become "products" with standard similar features, and may create further pressures on the environment, eventually affecting local people's lives. In the case of Jiaohe, some conflicts occurred during the WH designation, such as residents' resettlement and the installation of monitoring systems. The latter caused dissatisfaction among some residents as it could be a way of privacy invasion. However, they finally agreed with the installation as the system can also help keep their properties safe, specifically livestock. Another main problem was resettlement, and also referred to as land requisition. The Yahrguziler residents were not against the removal, as the government provided more benefits, such as new houses, extra money and job opportunities. At the beginning of the work, the Chinese government had a 40-million-yuan resettlement budget, and planned to move approximately 80 households (Sun 2005). The result was successful, and there was not one resident who complained about moving and resettling to any relevant departments.

Makuvaza (2014: 10) worries that in some cases, many communities that reside close to WHS would be marginalised as the result of the WH designation. In the case of Jiaohe, residents are generally satisfied with the resettlement as this is an effective method to improve their living standards. Also, they are the same group removed to Jiaohe in 1990s. However, some residents were nervous as they need to change their lifestyle. Some farmers lost their land and received money, and they had to consider seeking a job. Currently, some of them are working with the tourism companies, some of them are doing small businesses, and some of them stayed at home.

Nevertheless, the nomination caused a shift in local industry to some degree. In the past, some of them sold tea during tourist seasons, some sold fruits, and some provided transportation services—donkeys. After several years, museum souvenir shops have been built near the entrance, so some local residents also have begun to sell souvenirs. The participants of this small market have increased in several years, and some residents have started to let their stores in the market hall earn the money. The Yahrguziler village committee also introduced a company to manage the parking area and the income from the rent is divided among the local families.

About 37% of the residents (including Yahrguziler villagers and Turfan citizens) deem that Jiaohe could influence their lives (Figure 6). In these groups, the most affected from the site is the group which has lived here for more than six years, and then the groups living for three to six years. This result illustrates that the elder generation of residents of Jiaohe is much more concerned about the site.

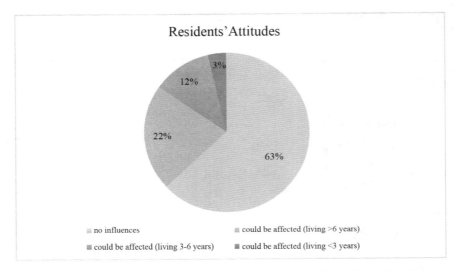

Residents' Attitudes

3%

12%

22%

63%

- no influences
- could be affected (living >6 years)
- could be affected (living 3-6 years)
- could be affected (living <3 years)

Figure 6   Questionnaire data—could the site influence the lives of its residents?

Furthermore, managers mentioned the local involvement in this listing process. They argued that the government had told the requirements of WHL to the residents if they want local residents to make contributions, such as resettlement, land acquisition and job opportunities. Local residents were not involved in any evaluation or decision-making process. It is because the government thought local residents cannot understand what WHL actually is and what international rules are.

Overall, Yahrguziler residents are important elements in the nomination process of Jiaohe, as this influenced their lifestyles and recognitions of Jiaohe. It is a fact that Yahrguziler residents maintain a close relationship with Jiaohe, and therefore they would like to make some changes for the site.

Conclusions

Jiaohe's heritage management has undergone several stages of dramatic changes of preservation and management since the 1990s. The success of WHL in 2014 marked the biggest development of heritage interpretation to the public. While cultural heritage bureaus and various stakeholders at both the national and local levels have actively engaged in the management of the site, local residents have begun to embrace its new role as both a WHS and heritage tourism destination, which has influence on the local understanding of the historical environment.

China has been engaged in WH nomination for three decades, with 52 WHSs on the list, and it is time to rethink what the WH status can actually bring to designated sites, and how local people can interact with and benefit from the designation. In this case study, it was impressive to learn from the interviews that both the government and local residents have been so keen on including Jiaohe onto the nomination of the Silk Road. The main influences have been analysed from tourism, heritage management, interpretation work, community involvement, and stakeholder relationship. Becoming a WHS provides a new start for Xinjiang's heritage management.

In the Chinese context, WH nomination is tightly entwined with the pursuit of tourism development in the past 20 years. The nomination practice has full support from each level of bureaucracy. As Jiaohe is situated in a complex geographical environment, conservation of the remains is still the most important aspect of the work. Regarding tourism, it has only been three years since the site was added to the WHL, but an increase in the number of visitors has already been shown. In addition, facilities such as toilets, restaurants, shuttle buses, parking lots and B&Bs, have been upgraded in order to attract more tourists. In terms of interpretation and presentation, curators have tried their best to improve the exhibition, and to create a better dialogue with visitors via digital screens and a more accessible audio guide system. Education and outreach schemes have been set out to involve not only tourists but also local communities. Achieving the WH designation directly improves the current condition of the site and its surroundings and encourages more scholars to conduct their research on the site. Local government's publicity also emphasises the greatness and values of the Silk Road, which has become a focus in regional media.

The local residents have actively engaged in everyday maintenance of the site. As a result of the success of WH nomination, the living condition of local residents has improved after resettlement in new accommodations. Furthermore, the application caused a shift in local industry, from farming industry to tourism industry (the local resident income comes mainly from house rent and food services), which shows that economic growth could be stimulated by providing job opportunities in the heritage industry realm. WH designation has introduced the concept of "preserve our heritage" for the local communities and has encouraged them to preserve their heritage spontaneously. It is possible that even without WHL in the future, heritage sites would also be preserved well.

However, the collision of understandings on heritage still existed in the nomination process of Jiaohe, which actually is a common phenomenon in China. The writing of the application dossier and management plan was assigned by the SACH to Beijing-based institution, which could help to make the site more "understandable" by international professional communities according to the WH OUV criteria. After becoming a WHS, the local government then would accommodate the WH criteria with Chinese characteristics. Furthermore, in practice the management and interpretation could not reach international standard. Another controversial topic is the impact on tourism; this conflict is primarily based on the tickets, with ticket prices doubling after being added to the WHL. This may directly lead to the loss of visitors, especially local visitors who cannot afford the tickets. In the cases of Jiaohe and other heritage sites along the Silk Road, WH nomination is indeed the very beginning of the journey towards a healthy and sound management and conservation, and how to protect both the safety of heritage and the benefit of local communities is the core after all.

Note

1. Due to privacy protection, all the interviewees are anonymous.

☐ Acknowledgements

Firstly, we would like to thank the interviewees who generously gave their time and help to our research. Also, we are grateful to Xinjiang Uygur Autonomous Region Bureau of Cultural Heritage, Turfan Cultural Relics Bureau, Academia Turfanica Institute of Jiaohe Cultural Heritage Management and Yahrguziler village, for allowing us access to their resources.

We would also deeply appreciate the amazing support from Pang Rui who devotes her time to refining this research as much as she can.

☐ Disclosure Statement

No potential conflict of interest was reported by the authors.

☐ Notes on Contributors

LIU Yunxiao had a Bachelor's degree in Conservation of cultural relics in Northwest University (China), and then a Master's in Managing Archaeological Site (UCL) and currently is a PhD in Heritage Management (UCL).

He has a background in Silk Road cultural heritage, with a focus on Xinjiang. Also work for the UCL as a Research Assistant, involved in "Central Asia Archaeology Landscapes".

Tim Williams has a background in urban archaeology, especially the Silk Road (with a focus on Islamic & Central Asia), approaches to complex stratigraphy, earthen architecture conservation, and archaeological site and heritage management.

He worked for the Museum of London as a Senior Archaeologist, and then was Head of Archaeology Commissions at English Heritage, before joining UCL in 2002. He currently works at UCL as a Reader and undertakes a five-year project named "Central Asia Archaeology Landscapes".

He is an International Council of Monuments and Sites (ICOMOS) expert member on advisory missions and panels, and member of the International Scientific Committee on Archaeological Heritage Management (ICAHM). He is also an expert member of UNESCO transnational Silk Road serial nomination project and undertook the ICOMOS Silk Roads thematic study.

References

Aplin, Graeme. 2007. World Heritage Cultural Landscapes. *International Journal of Heritage Studies* 13 (6): 427-446.

Askew, Marc. 2010. The Magic List of Global Status. In *Heritage and Globalisation*, edited by Sophia Labadi, and Colin Long. 19-44. London: Routledge.

Bianchi, Raoul V. 2002. The Contested Landscapes of World Heritage on a Tourist Island: The Case of Garajonay National Park, La Gomera. *International Journal of Heritage Studies* 8 (2): 81-97.

Bryman, Alan. 2015. *Social Research Methods*. Oxford : Oxford university press.

Cameron, Christina. 2005. Evolution of the Application of "Outstanding Universal Value" for Cultural and Natural Heritage. In *Special Expert Meeting of the World Heritage Convention: The concept of outstanding universal value Session reports: 29th Session*, 6-9. Paris: UNESCO World Heritage Centre.

Chirikure, Shadreck, Gilbert Pwiti, Charlotte Damm, C. A. Folorunso, David McDermott Hughes, Caroline Phillips, Pascall Taruvinga, Shadreck Chirikure, and Gilbert Pwiti. 2008. Community Involvement in Archaeology and Cultural Heritage Management: An Assessment from Case Studies in Southern Africa and Elsewhere. *Current Anthropology* 49 (3): 467-485.

Conforti, María Eugenia, J. Carlos Díez Fernández-Lomana, Mercedes Mariano, María Luz Endere, and Antonio J. Romero Alonso. 2015. World Heritage and the Local Community: The Case of Atapuerca (Burgos, Spain). *Conservation and Management of Archaeological Sites* 17 (4): 327-339.

Connolly, Kate. 2009. Bridge Takes Dresden off Unesco World Heritage List. June 25, 2009. Accessed March 3, 2019. https://www.theguardian.com/world/2009/jun/25/dresden-bridge-unesco-heritage-status.

Deacon, David, Alan Bryman, and Natalie Fenton. 1998. Collision or Collusion? A Discussion and Case Study of the Unplanned Triangulation of Quantitative and

Qualitative Research Methods. *International Journal of Social Research Methodology* 1 (1): 47-63.

D'Eramo, Marco. 2014. UNESCOcide. *New Left Review* 8: 47-53.

Evans, Graeme. 2002. Living in a World Heritage City: Stakeholders in the Dialectic of the Universal and Particular. *International Journal of Heritage Studies* 8 (2): 117-135.

Fowler, Peter. 2003. World Heritage Cultural Landscapes, 1992–2002. Accessed March 5, 2019. https://whc.unesco.org/en/documents/10.

Frey, Bruno S, and Lasse Steiner. 2011. World Heritage List: Does It Make Sense? *International Journal of Cultural Policy* 17 (5): 555-573.

Frey, Bruno S, Paolo Pamini, and Lasse Steiner. 2013. Explaining the World Heritage List: An Empirical Study. *International Review of Economics* 60 (1): 1-19.

Gulibaikere, Maiming. 2014. The Impact of Tourism for Yahrguziler Village. *Heilongjiang Shizhi* 000 (18): 46-47. [古丽拜克热·买明. 2014. 交河故城旅游开发对亚尔果勒村民的影响. 黑龙江史志 000 (18): 46-47.]

Huang, Chia-Hui, Jen-Ruey Tsaur, and Chih-Hai Yang. 2012. Does World Heritage List Really Induce More Tourists? Evidence from Macau. *Tourism Management* 33 (6): 1450-1457.

Institute of Architectural History in China. 2012. Management Plan for Site of Jiaohe City. [中国建筑设计研究院建筑历史研究所. 2012. 交河故城管理规划.]

Institute of Jiaohe Cultural Heritage Management. 2015. "The Movable Museum" in Turfan. Accessed March 3, 2019. http://wwj.tlf.gov.cn/info/854/70794.htm.

Institute of Jiaohe Cultural Heritage Management. 2017. A Success of "Travel Jiaohe in the Night". Accessed March 3, 2019. http://wwj.tlf.gov.cn/info/854/72847.htm.

Jimura, Takamitsu. 2011. The Impact of World Heritage Site Designation on Local Communities—A Case Study of Ogimachi, Shirakawa-Mura, Japan. *Tourism Management* 32 (2): 288-296.

Labadi, Sophia. 2005. A Review of the Global Strategy for a Balanced, Representative and Credible World Heritage List 1994–2004. *Conservation and Management of*

Archaeological Sites 7 (2): 89-102.

Li, Conghui. 2012. The Summarize of Turfan Cultural Relics Bureau in 2012. *Academia Turfanica Research* 1 (8): 4.

Liu, Xuetang. 2004. The Development of Jiaohe. *Research Center of Chinese Frontier Archaeology* 1: 198-214. [刘学堂. 2004. 论交河城的兴起、构筑特色、发展和废弃. 边疆考古研究 1: 198-214.]

Makuvaza, Simon. 2014. *The Management Of Cultural World Heritage Sites and Development in Africa: History, Nomination Processes and Representation on the World Heritage List*. London: Springer Science & Business Media.

Meng, Fanren. 2001. The Research of Layout of Jiaohe. *Acta Archaeologcia Sinica* 4: 483-508. [孟凡人. 2001. 交河故城形制布局特点研究. 考古学报 4: 483-508.]

Meskell, Lynn. 2013. UNESCO's World Heritage Convention at 40: Challenging the Economic and Political Order of International Heritage Conservation. *Current Anthropology* 54 (4): 483-494.

Nas, Peter J. M. 2002. Masterpieces of Oral and Intangible Culture: Reflections on the UNESCO World Heritage List. *Current Anthropology* 43 (1): 139-148.

Orbasli, Aylin. 2002. *Tourists in Historic Towns: Urban Conservation and Heritage Management*. London: Taylor & Francis.

Reguant-Aleix, Joan, M. Rosaria Arbore, Anna Bach-Faig, and Lluís Serra-Majem. 2009. Mediterranean Heritage: An Intangible Cultural Heritage. *Public Health Nutrition* 12 (9A): 1591-1594.

Rössler, Mechtild. 2006. World Heritage Cultural Landscapes: A UNESCO Flagship Programme 1992–2006. *Landscape Research* 31 (4): 333-353.

Scazzosi, Lionella. 2004. Reading and Assessing the Landscape as Cultural and Historical Heritage. *Landscape Research* 29 (4): 335-355.

Shackley, Myra. 2009. *Visitor Management*. London: Routledge.

Smith, Melanie. 2002. A Critical Evaluation of the Global Accolade: The Significance of World Heritage Site Status for Maritime Greenwich. *International Journal of Heritage*

Studies 8 (2): 137-151.

Staneva, Hristina. 2006. World Heritage Committee in 2006 and the Buffer Zone Issue. In *The World Heritage Convention and the Buffer Zone in Hiroshima. International Scientific Committee on Legal, Administrative and Financial Issues (ICLAFI) Conference*, Vol. 1, 39-41.

Stovel, Herb. 2009. ICOMOS Position Paper. In *World Heritage Papers 25—World Heritage and Buffer Zones Patrimoine Mondial et Zones Tampons,* 23-49. Paris: World Heritage Centre, UNESCO.

Su, Mingming, and Geoffrey Wall. 2012. Global–Local Relationships and Governance Issues at the Great Wall World Heritage Site, China. *Journal of Sustainable Tourism* 20 (8): 1-20.

Su, Yuwen, and Huilin Lin. 2014. Analysis of International Tourist Arrivals Worldwide: The Role of World Heritage Sites. *Tourism Management* 40: 46-58.

Sun, Chunhua. 2005. Working for Nomination process. Turfan Daily Newspaper, January 10, 2005. [孙春华. 2005. 合力"申遗"保护故城. 吐鲁番日报，2005-01-10(4).]

Sun, Manli. 2006. A Study of the Protection and Reinforcement about the Ruins of Jiaohe in Turfan. Doctoral Dissertation, Lanzhou University.

Sun, Manli, Xudong Wang, Zuixiong Li, Shouyun Liang, and Lu Zhang. 2007. Technology of Protection and Reinforcement for Observation Platform in Ruins of Jiaohe. *Rock and Soil Mechanics* 28 (1): 163-168. [孙满利，王旭东，李最雄，梁收运，张鲁. 2007. 交河故城瞭望台保护加固技术. 岩土力学 28 (1): 163-168.]

Tao, Yingwen. 2012. Analyzing Urban Living Heritage in China—The Case of the Sijie Historic Quarter in Nantong. Thesis, University of Cambridge.

Turtinen, Jan. 2000. *Globalising Heritage: On UNESCO and the Transnational Construction of a World Heritage.* Stockholm: Center for Organizational Research Stockholm.

UNESCO. 1999. Operational Guidelines for the Implementation of the World Heritage Convention. Accessed March 5, 2019. https://whc.unesco.org/archive/opguide99.pdf.

UNESCO. 2014. Convention Concerning the Protection of the World Cultural and Natural Heritage. Accessed March 5, 2019. https://whc.unesco.org/archive/convention-en.pdf.

UNESCO. 2017. World Heritage. Accessed March 5, 2019. http://whc.unesco.org/en/about/.

Wang, Xiaomei, and Haixia Zhu. 2006. A Study on Comparison and Analysis of Chinese and Foreign Cultural Heritage Management System. *Journal Of Xi'An Jiaotong University (Social Sciences)* 26 (3): 39-43. [王晓梅，朱海霞. 2006. 中外文化遗产资源管理体制的比较与启示. 西安交通大学学报（社会科学版）26 (3): 39-43.]

Wang, Zhaoguo, Zhaoping Yang, Geoffery Wall, Xiaoliang Xu, Fang Han, Xishihui Du, and Qun Liu. 2015. Is It Better for a Tourist Destination to Be a World Heritage Site? Visitors' Perspectives on the Inscription of Kanas on the World Heritage List in China. *Journal for Nature Conservation* 23: 19-26.

World Heritage Committee. 2002. The Budapest Declaration on World Heritage. Accessed March 5, 2019. http://whc.unesco.org/en/documents/1334.

Xinjiang Uygur Autonomous Region Bureau of Cultural Heritage. 2011. *The Third Archaeological Survey in Xinjiang*. Beijing: Science Press. [新疆维吾尔自治区文物局. 2011. 新疆维吾尔自治区第三次全国文物普查成果集成——吐鲁番卷. 北京：科学出版社.]

Zhang, Rouran. 2016. "Value in Change": What Do World Heritage Nominations Bring to Chinese World Heritage Sites?" Doctoral Dissertation, Australian National University, Cancerra.https://openresearch-repository.anu.edu.au/handle/1885/117265.

Producing "Cultural Heritage" and Framing "Expertise": Berlin's Pergamon Museum

Annette Loeseke

New York University Berlin. CONTACT Annette Loeseke: annette.loeseke@nyu.edu

Abstract: Taking Berlin's Pergamon Museum as a case study, the article explores how the museum has appropriated cultural heritage from the (so-called) Ancient Near East and produced what has become known as the Pergamon Altar or Ishtar Gate, for example. Apart from the acquisition, the article addresses the reproduction of the ancient monuments in Berlin in the early 20th century, and the museum's historical as well as current curatorial approaches to present the reproduced monuments. By exploring the strategies that museum professionals have developed to transform ancient remains from the Near East into iconic museum exhibits on display in Berlin's Museum of the Ancient Near East (Vorderasiatisches Museum) in the Pergamon Museum, the article discusses how the various ways, the fragments-turned-exhibits have crossed borders, have contributed to the production of cultural heritage. By examining the practices of presenting objects and setting up displays through a multi-modal analysis of the architectural reproductions, modern reconstructions, wall paintings, decorations, wall panels, labels, photographic images, and printed information, the article explores how museum professionals have framed the museum's role in the production of "cultural heritage" and addressed these transformational practices of appropriation and re-interpretation.

Keywords: museums, cultural heritage, display, framing, research framework

Introduction

Berlin's Pergamon Museum, located on Museum Island in Berlin's historic centre, was built to house the reproduced ancient monuments from (so-called) Asia Minor and the Near East—today Iraq, Syria and Turkey—the remains of which were excavated, brought to Berlin and pieced together in the late 19th and early 20th centuries (Gaehtgens 1996: 64-74; Website Museum of the Ancient Near East/About the collection). These architectural exhibits include the (so-called) Pergamon Altar from Ancient Greece (2nd century BCE) and the Roman Market Gate of Miletus (2nd century CE) in the galleries of the Antiquities Collection, and the Babylonian Ishtar Gate and Processional Way (6th century BCE) in the galleries of the Museum of the Ancient Near East (Vorderasiatisches Museum), located on the ground floor of the south wing of the Pergamon Museum. On its website, the museum identifies the "world-renowned reconstructions of the magnificent, giant, brilliantly coloured architectural structures of Babylon" as "its most famous treasures", on display "along the central axis of the museum",[1] and further: "In the Vorderasiatisches Museum (Museum of the Ancient Near East) a lost wonder of the world can still be marvelled at today: the walls of the ancient city of Babylon."[2] It's more than that: "Here the visitor can actually walk through the Ishtar Gate, down the Processional Way and along the facade of the Throne Room of King Nebuchadnezzar II, dating back to the 6th century BCE."[3] While claiming that the museum represents ancient cultures by building up "a picture of 6000 years of art and culture in Mesopotamia, Syria and Anatolia", the museum website also highlights its displays, labelled as a set-up of authentic ancient monuments[4] that visitors can immerse themselves into.

The historical presentation of monumental reproductions has only slightly been altered since the museum opened in 1930 (Bakkor 2013: 89-90; Haffner 2019: n.p.). Large wall paintings, which had been planned since the late 1920s, have decorated the walls in selected galleries since the 1930s. The acquisition history and the role of various stakeholders in leading excavations and setting up the museum displays are well documented and published. However, while the museum has addressed the history of the acquisition, reproduction, and reconstruction of its exhibits, and while it claims, on its website, to build "on current approaches to [...] post-colonial theory" and investigate "the research history, provenance, and cultural-political significance of the objects in its collection",[5] it has not, to this day, critically and transparently challenged its role in this long and ongoing process of appropriation and re-interpretation.

Taking Berlin's Museum of the Ancient Near East in the Pergamon Museum as a case study, the article explores the complex ways the museum displays today which generate what the museum labels as ancient cultures.[6]

In his study *Antiquity on Display: Regimes of the Authentic in Berlin's Pergamon Museum*, Can Bilsel examines the history of the architectural displays in the Pergamon Museum and explores to what extent the reproductions from ancient fragments should be interpreted as modern imaginations that replace the ancient originals lost over time (Bilsel 2012). By tracing the excavations in the Near East, the shipping of the fragments to Berlin and the various stages of modern reproduction, he critically reflects the historiographical and cultural-political discourses of the early 20th century among museum professionals in Berlin. It is the modern German lens from the 19th and early 20th centuries, Bilsel argues, which reflects the German politics behind the excavations in the Near East as well as the erection of the museum in Berlin.

In his article "The Undoing of a Monument: Preservation as Critical Engagement with Pergamon's Heritage", Can Bilsel further looks at how this German lens is complemented by a contemporary Turkish perspective (Bilsel 2005). By tracing the history of the reproduction of the Pergamon Altar in Berlin and examining the context and various motivations behind the recent Turkish claims for restituti on, the article explores how the perception of the German framing of the reconstructed monument's authenticity keeps informing current debates about restitution. It is Bilsel's suggestion to interpret the staged monuments in the Pergamon Museum as both reproductions of lost ancient artefacts and modern imaginations of an ancient past that this study draws on.

In his publication, *Zur Repräsentation von Geschichte und Kultur des Alten Orients in großen europäischen Museen*, Hussein Bakkor discusses in depth how cultural-historical perspectives, and historicising, contextualising approaches conflicted with art-historical concepts of exhibits as masterpieces (Bakkor 2013). While he thoroughly describes the ambiguous curatorial concepts, the focus of the analysis primarily remains on the exhibits as opposed to an integrating, more nuanced understanding of display that this study suggests.

In her recent article, "Babylonische Löwen: Rezeption und Wanderungen", Dorothee Haffner expands the perspective and explores the history of the Babylonian reproductions in the Pergamon Museum (Haffner 2019). She examines both earlier drafts of wall decorations and popular decorations in the Berlin subway inspired by the museum displays, and traces how some of the Berlin reproductions were traded by the museum and became objects of exchange in museums across Europe.

While these recent publications study the museum's activities, exhibits, displays, and interpretive contexts, research on how museum curators have addressed the museum's role in the (re-)production of cultural heritage, both in the past and the present, has been limited. While drawing on the discussed literature, this study examines more specifically how the museum display (re-)produces "cultural heritage", generates research frameworks and frames the museum's institutional image.

Suggesting a multi-modal analysis of the museum display, this article explores how the Museum of the Ancient Near East in the Pergamon Museum addresses the transformational strategies of material and scholarly appropriation. I seek to particularly integrate into my research components of museum displays, such as wall paintings, decorations, photographic images, and printed informational material on labels and wall panels provided in the galleries, that have so far been marginalised. By drawing on such an integrative, multi-layered notion of display, the article aims to assess the museum's framing of its role in producing and promoting "cultural heritage" and identify potential biases and blind spots in its presentation. By examining the visual narratives that museum curators have developed to transform ancient fragments into reconstructed monuments that serve as iconic museum exhibits and major tourist attractions, the article seeks to shed light on how museum professionals frame their contribution to the production of cultural heritage, the generation of academic knowledge and the establishment of academic disciplines.

Berlin Context

Museum Island in Berlin's historic centre consists of five museum buildings that were built over the span of 100 years, and opened between 1830 and 1930, respectively (Gaehtgens 1996; Loeseke 2019a: 143-146). The Pergamon Museum was the last museum on Museum Island to open its doors to the public. In 1901, a first museum was opened on the spot of the current museum. However, due to unsolid ground as well as its insufficient size, the museum was pulled down shortly after the opening. Construction of the current monumental three-winged building started in 1910.[7] After delays, in part due to the First World War, the museum finally opened to the public in 1930.

The architectural exhibits are reproductions of ancient monuments that had been in ruins when German railroad engineers and scholars arrived on the spots in the Near East (Bilsel 2012: 89-124, 139-158). Various stakeholders, such as museum conservators, university scholars, engineers, businessmen and others, collaborated in the multi-layered process of excavation, appropriation and re-interpretation (Gaehtgens 1996: 67-72; Bilsel 2012: 89-100). The fragments of the Pergamon Altar and friezes, for example, were found by German engineer Carl Humann. While museum director Theodor Wiegand oversaw the excavations at Milet, his father-in-law, director of the Deutsche Bank, Georg von Siemens, had intersecting interests in building and operating railroads in the Near East. The German Archaeological Institute (Deutsches Archäologisches Institut, DAI) in Athens, following the foundation of the DAI in Rome, was founded by archaeologist Ernst Curtius who had previously led the excavations at Olympia. Similar institutions were subsequently founded in Cairo, Damascus and Baghdad (Bilsel 2012: 197-207). While, through these excavations, the museums in Berlin were successful in establishing their international reputation, academia benefited as well, not least from the formation of academic disciplines, the foundation of institutes and the publication of scholarly articles (Gaehtgens 1996: 73-74). Other influential supporters of excavations were associations such as the German Oriental Association (Deutsche Orient-Gesellschaft, DOG), founded in 1898 (Bilsel 2012: 18). Museum managers such as the influential director-general of the Royal Museums in Berlin, Wilhelm Bode, relied on these associations to establish close relationships with private funders, entrepreneurs and businessmen such as Ernst von Siemens and James Simon, co-founder of the DOG (Gaehtgens 1996: 73). Scholars, museum conservators, private donors, and the state—in the constitution of the German Empire and the Weimar Republic, in particular—collaborated not only in regards to the excavation of the fragments, but also the formation of the collections and the installation of the displays in the museums (Gaehtgens 1996: 72-74; Loeseke 2019b; Paul 1995: 11-12, 15-23; Bilsel 2012: 145-147). The generation of expertise can thus be described as a collaborative enterprise.

Display

After the excavated fragments from the excavation sites in the Near East had been brought to Berlin, the reproduction began. Yet, only parts of the ancient monuments could be rebuilt inside the Pergamon Museum, despite the museum's monumental size and the fact that it had replaced a former, smaller museum building that had been considered too small to house the finds from the excavations. In fact, the exhibits represent specific "Berlin" versions of the ancient monuments that fit into the galleries of the 20th century Pergamon Museum building (Bilsel 2012: 9, 14, 17). They consist of ancient fragments and modern replacements that generate a display that hypothetically imagines portions of the façades of the ancient monuments (Bilsel 2012: 17; Haffner 2019: n.p.). The reproduced façades are presented in the main galleries while smaller objects are displayed in the adjacent galleries. The curatorial focus in the Pergamon Museum is on the monumental façades, presented as architectural masterpieces, as Can Bilsel has pointed out. In de-contextualising and reproducing façades as displays to be presented in the environment of a major museum in Berlin, inside major galleries devoid of other, smaller exhibits or context, the reproduced monuments-turned-exhibits reflect the cultural-political debates and scholarly performance in the early 20th century Berlin rather than ancient sites, as Bilsel has argued (Bilsel 2012: 23; Loeseke 2019b). While drawing on Bilsel's interpretation, this study seeks to discuss in what way the supposed masterpieces might as well be considered as contextualising exhibits and explore how museum directors, from the opening of the museum onward, have attempted to contextualise the exhibits in various ways.

Pergamon Altar

The German scholarly lens through which the exhibits were reproduced becomes visible by comparing the final, current version of the Berlin "Pergamon Altar" in the current museum building with an earlier version that was on display in the so-called interim building (*Interimsbau*) that preceded the current Pergamon Museum building. A comparative examination of both versions, however, reflects quite well the curatorial and spatial framework that generate the monumental exhibits as ambiguous, multi-layered "cultural heritage". The ancient altar was in ruins when the German excavators arrived on the spot in modern-day Turkey (Bilsel 2012: 89-100). While the stairs of the final version of Berlin's Pergamon Altar that has been on display from the opening of the exhibition in 1930 to the present day, are built in full length stretching from one side of the Altar to the other, the stairs of the earlier version are arranged in such a way as to integrate the presentation of a reconstructed ancient mosaic on the gallery floor. Hence, the reproduced versions of a presumingly preserved cultural heritage have taken on different shapes at different stages of their reproduction history. However, while a model of the original altar is presented next to the reproduced monument, the circumstances and complexities around the reproduction process of the altar-exhibit are not critically addressed in the galleries.

Moreover, museum versions of the Pergamon Altar have reproduced only one façade of the ancient altar; a small model of what the ancient altar assumingly looked like was presented next to the altar façade before the gallery was temporarily closed. Moreover, the original fragments of the Gigantomachy frieze that originally decorated the walls of the ancient altar, are presented inversely on the museum walls that surround the reproduced altar façade. In fact, the reproduced façade in Berlin's Pergamon Museum provides the contextualising decorative frame for the original fragments of the frieze.

While the Pergamon Altar was in ruins when the excavation took place, the Byzantine Wall in the citadel of Bergamo, which had partly been built of fragments of the Gigantomachy and Telephos friezes, was destroyed by the German archaeologists in order to separate the Hellenistic fragments of the friezes from the later Byzantine Wall (Bilsel 2005: 16-17). The archaeologists subsequently pieced together the Pergamon Altar from Hellenistic fragments only. However, despite their respective Hellenistic, Roman or Mesopotamian origins, the exhibits of the Pergamon Museum, labelled as originating from the Ottoman Empire, share the same gallery space in the museum (Bilsel 2012: 18).

Ishtar Gate and Processional Way

The Ishtar Gate and Processional Way, like the Pergamon Altar, were in ruins when German architect and archaeologist Robert Koldewey saw them for the first time in Babylon (modern-day Iraq) (wall panel, main gallery of the Ishtar Gate). The excavations of the Ishtar complex in Babylon, led by Robert Koldewey, took place between 1899 and 1917. The fragmented glazed bricks were desalinated and pieced together; missing bricks were substituted by modern bricks, produced by workshops near Berlin (Bilsel 2012: 181; for context see 89-124, 159-188, 189-214). The museum houses the reproductions of parts of the Ishtar Gate presented along a part of the reproduced façade of the Throne Room of King Nebuchadnezzar II in the eastern gallery of the south wing, and parts of the Processional Way in the central axis of the wing.

Like the Berlin version of the Pergamon Altar exhibit, the reproduced versions of the Ishtar Gate and Processional Way represent only a small part of the ancient monumental

259

ensemble. What is labelled as the Ishtar Gate is, in fact, a reproduction of one of the smaller, outer gates of the entire complex. The corresponding inner gate of the ancient complex was not reconstructed; it is assumed that the inner gate was almost twice as high as the reconstructed smaller, outer gate, as is indicated by small model on display in the central gallery. The fragmented monuments were pieced together inside the museum building that, despite its own monumentality, limited the potential height and scope of the reproductions. The material infrastructure of the gallery space technically and conceptually transformed the fragmented monuments into tailored museum exhibits that fit the gallery space (Bilsel 2012: 213). More than that, the finds from the excavation site had been split. While the largest portion of the fragmented Ishtar ensemble is on display in Berlin, smaller reproduced parts were sold to other museums in Europe and the USA (Haffner 2019). The ancient Babylonian monument had been erected in three main phases, which included an early monochrome phase with animal decorations in relief, a polychrome phase without relief decorations, and a later polychrome phase with relief animals (Bilsel 2012: 189-214). In Berlin, the monumental Ishtar Gate and Processional Way on display in the main galleries were rebuilt according to the youngest, polychrome phase, while reproductions of small portions of the wall decorations from the earlier stages were on display in the smaller adjacent galleries of the museum before the temporary closure of the galleries. The polychrome reproduction of the Ishtar Gate and Processional Way is juxtaposed to the (misleadingly) monochrome reproductions of the Greek Pergamon Altar and Roman Miletus Market Gate. Such a contrasting presentation visually sets apart the (assumingly) monochrome façades of Greek and Roman origin from the polychrome reproductions of the Ishtar complex, generating an orientalising display that reinforces rather than challenges existing stereotypes about (assumingly) "European" vs. "Oriental" arts and architecture, as Can Bilsel points out (Bilsel 2012: 15-19). Furthermore, the reproduced monumental exhibits are presented as façades as opposed to entire buildings as the labelling as Ishtar Gate and Processional Way might suggest. Moreover, the façades are presented without any other; smaller objects are displayed together with them that might provide some context. Apart from some information about the assumed original purpose of the ancient monuments, the museum does not provide any further historical context about the object journey of the ancient monuments which turned iconic exhibits.

Such an emptied, de-contextualising presentation of façades—as opposed to entire buildings—reduces the former ancient monuments to purely architectural masterpieces, as Bilsel highlights. Such a framing, one could argue, further transforms the displayed "masterly" exhibits into typical, even iconic examples of "cultural heritage", produced and framed by the museum for the visitor's consumption. Such a typological production of cultural heritage not only claims to represent a certain pre-given "culture" that is being excavated, rescued from decay or loss, and preserved, inside the museum, for future generations of spectators, but also produces trophies from excavations undertaken during the times of the German Empire. Rather than a historical site or assumed ancient "culture", the displays hence reflect the German cultural politics of the time (Bilsel 2005: 17; Bilsel 2012: 23-28, 125-158, 207-214; Gaehtgens 1996: 72-74). More than that, the iconic displays demonstrate the German scholarly expertise of the late 19th and early 20th centuries as this study seeks to highlight. The museum's framing of what is on display remains ambiguous. Visitors are encouraged to explore both the (reproduced) monuments of ancient cultures and the reproductions of the ancient monuments, i.e. the iconic museum exhibits, as this study seeks to argue.

Modern Reconstructions

In some galleries, the original sculptures and reproduced façades from original fragments and substitutes are complemented by "suggested reconstructions" (Rekonstruktionsvorschlag) of façades as the excavators imagined them, as one of the museum labels indicates. These suggested reconstructions are built of modern material and provide a historicising context to original sculptures or decorative elements. In other cases, the imitations complement the reproduced façades pieced together from original fragments and modern substitutes. A third case is a combination of modern reconstructions of architectural ornaments and decorative friezes to evoke an assumingly authentic interior design of an ancient palace room (wall panels, main eastern gallery, and southern galleries).

Modern reconstructions include, for example, the inner gate of the ancient citadel of Sam'al (modern-day Zincirli in Turkey). The reconstruction covers the entire eastern gallery wall that is painted in a beige-yellow colour to imitate the original mud-brick walls of the citadel. Original basalt slabs with decorative reliefs cover the base of the gallery wall. Four colossal lion sculptures flank the inner and outer gate, respectively; one of the outer sculptures on display is a plaster copy (wall panel, western gallery).

Another example is the painted, almost monochrome modern reconstruction of a façade of the Parthian palace from Ashur, on display next to the reproduced façade of the Ishtar Gate in the main gallery.[8] A selection of fragments of original decorative elements from such a façade are presented on the wall next to the reconstruction (wall panel, main eastern gallery).

While the lower sections of the Babylonian Ishtar Processional Way are pieced together using original glazed brick fragments and modern substitutes, the upper parts are "suggested reconstructions". To complement the lower partly original reproduction, modern imagined reconstructions are blended in that suggest a decoration of stylised palm trees and ornaments.

One of the smaller galleries reconstructs the interior design of an Assyrian palace chamber with walls painted in oxblood. According to a wall panel, department director "Walter Andrae's declared aim was to give visitors as graphic and detailed an impression as possible of life at the Assyrian royal court" (wall panel, Assyrian palace chamber room). Andrae combined original artefacts with "copies from various Assyrian sites and periods", such as replicas of statues that serve as doorkeepers, as the panel indicates.[9] While the historicising interior design of this gallery dates back to the opening of the exhibitions in the 1930s, the "decorative friezes of rosettes and palmettes in blue, white and red colours" were added in 1957.[10]

Walter Andrae's curatorial concept to present the partly reproduced architectural monuments together with the modern reproductions might have been inspired by Wilhelm Bode's earlier concept of the "style room" that co-presented artworks, furniture and decorative architectural elements of the same epoch in one exhibition space in order to provide a historicising context to the exhibits, the artworks in particular (Bilsel 2012: 22, 152-157; Bakkor 2013: 77-81; Paul 1995: 12-15). However, the monumental façades, the Pergamon Altar or the Ishtar Gate and Processional Way, were pieced together from original fragments as well as modern substitutes, as described. Hence, the Berlin versions of the Pergamon and Ishtar façades serve as museum exhibits in their own right (Bilsel 2012: 22) and context for the original fragments they include. These ambiguous, highly staged exhibits are further contextualised by the modern reproductions after ancient monuments as imagined by the German excavators.

Paintings

Walter Andrae augmented this multi-layered display space even further by paintings in selected galleries, adding even more contextualising layers. Upon entering the galleries through the central axis, visitors are greeted by contemporary wall panels that "welcome [the public] to a different time" (wall panel, central axis), to "Assyrian Time", as a smaller label clarifies. The panels describe how "different cultures" have measured time in different ways and explore how "the Assyrians in Mesopotamia" developed a system of stele rows that bore the king's and other dignitaries' names to indicate each year. The wall panels further reproduce a "reconstruction drawing" by Walter Andrae who led the excavations in Ashur in the early 20th century and served as the director of the Ancient Near Eastern department at the Pergamon Museum from 1928 to 1952. The drawing depicts the stele rows of Ashur in the context of the ancient citadel of Ashur as imagined by Andrae.[11]

While Walter Andrae's reconstruction drawing and the introductory text on the wall panels indicate the ancient times and cultures of Ashur, the large paintings in the smaller galleries of the south wing quite ambiguously evoke various layers of time. The upper parts of the walls in the galleries adjacent to the central axis are covered by large-scale framed paintings. An undated painting in the western gallery of the south wing depicts remains of the ancient citadel in Sam'al in the foreground, and the Amanus Mountains in the background (museum label, western gallery). The site was excavated by a team of archaeologists led by Felix von Luschan and architect Robert Koldewey on behalf of the DOG and the (former) Royal Museums in Berlin during five expeditions from 1888 to 1902.[12]

Two other paintings, to give another example, are presented in the central northern gallery of the south wing and depict the remains of the ancient Ashur Temple. The larger painting shows the view from the Ziggurat of Ashur, a temple tower, with remains of monumental structures in the foreground and the banks of the Tigris River in the background. The smaller painting depicts the remains of a water basin in the courtyard of the temple in the foreground and the ziggurat in the background (museum label, central northern gallery).

These large paintings are oil paintings that were produced from 1931 to 1936 (wall paintings, signatures and labels). Commissioned by Walter Andrae (Abele 2010: 71; Bakkor 2011: 96), the former director of excavations and director of the ancient Near Eastern Department, the paintings were painted after photographs from the excavations the museum was involved in during the late 19th and early 20th centuries (museum label and wall panel). Andrae had planned to include paintings in the exhibition design of selected galleries as early as in the 1920s. A reproduction of a draft of the interior design of the Babylon Room by Walter Andrae from the late 1920s was temporarily on display in 2017.[13]

Most of the large paintings were produced by Elisabeth Andrae, Walter Andrae's sister.[14] While some of the paintings currently on display were signed by Elisabeth Andrae—E. Andrae or E. A.—her name is provided on only one label and one wall text. Moreover, the labelling as "copies" from photographs indicates that the paintings were not considered as works of art in their own right. Instead, they served as commissioned contextualising decorations. The paintings provide an overview of the remains of ancient sites from a slightly heightened point of view. All paintings in the galleries, but one, depict the ancient spots as abandoned sites where human beings are absent. Only on one painting in the west gallery can we see a small group of people in the centre in the background, almost hidden behind the remains of a monumental gate.

It is worth noting that the paintings produce a then-contemporary image of the remains of ancient sites, as opposed to, for example, a historicising image of ancient temples (Bakkor 2011: 96).[15] The paintings represent the ancient sites at the time the German scholars saw them for the first time. In other words, the sites of ancient remains are depicted as modern excavation sites.

The paintings hence support the curatorial approach in the main galleries to present de-contextualised masterpieces that were re-contextualised within the decorated galleries of the Berlin Pergamon Museum. The paintings create an almost immersive experience that invites the museum visitors to immerse themselves into the deserted sites as the excavators saw them at their time of arrival. While presented in the context of the historical landscape, the sites are depicted as de-contextualised, i.e. cleared of any machines or vehicles used for the excavations. Through the large-scale paintings, visitors might experience the depictions— as well as the reproduced fragmented façades—as cleared, purified sites of ancient masterpieces. Rather than representing ancient cultural artefacts within a historicising decoration as described above, the paintings in the respective galleries present the ancient sites as iconic "cultural heritage", i.e. as material "remains" of a glorious past to be (re-) discovered, excavated and preserved. More than that, in framing the historical spots as modern sites of excavation, the paintings highlight the task and scholarly challenge ahead of the excavators.

Photographic Images

Apart from the photographs of the Hittite sanctuary of Hattusa/Yazilikaya, which represent the remains of the ancient site, and the paintings after photographs from the excavation sites, the museum also presents reproductions of historical photographs. On a large wall panel in the gallery of the Ishtar Gate, three photographic images are presented next to a text under the headline "The Discovery of the Ishtar Gate". Next to this wall panel, a map indicates the excavation sites, the Berlin museums have been working at, and other historical sites in the Near East. The first photographic image dates from 1902 and shows excavations at the site of the Ishtar Gate, with a partly excavated wall section with one of the characteristic animal reliefs in the centre of the image and workers with a barrow in the foreground.[16] The second photograph shows the desalination of the glazed bricks of the Ishtar Gate and dates from the late 1920s.[17] The fragmented bricks, which had been excavated and brought to Berlin, are desalinated in numerous tubs arranged in two long rows. In the background, the photograph shows a man pouring water over the bricks. The third photograph demonstrates the next step in the process. Numerous brick fragments are laid out on wooden work benches in three long rows; six men are shown sorting the pieces.[18] The headline of the text next to the photographic images reads "Thousands of fragments in 536 crates". The text provides a summary of the expedition and excavation history, indicating that at the very beginning of the excavations in Babylon in 1899, the architect Robert Koldewey's attention was drawn to pieces of broken blue-glazed bricks. Subsequently, excavations were started in that area of the city in which they appeared particularly frequently.

However, instead of a complete building, the excavators initially found thousands of fragments of these distinctive glazed bricks. Only the two older construction phases below could be identified as a gate. Parts of these findings are displayed in room 6. Inscriptions discovered later confirmed that the excavators had found the remains of the Ishtar Gate of Nebuchadnezzar II (604 BC–562 BC).

After negotiations with the Ottoman Empire, the first fragments of glazed bricks came to Berlin in 1903. In accordance with the partage, i.e. division of finds, with the Iraqi directorate of antiquities, over 500 crates of brick fragments followed in 1927. They were pieced together with painstaking effort; missing bricks were substituted with modern ones (wall panel).

What are the key issues that this short, inevitably selective text attempts to highlight? How does the museum frame its role in the acquisition and appropriation process?

Interestingly, the text not only seeks to justify the museum's historical endeavours by emphasising the negotiations with the Ottoman Empire and the subsequent agreement about the division of finds with the Iraqi administration, but also acknowledges that instead of "complete buildings" the excavators found "pieces of broken [...] bricks". While the text further indicates that "missing bricks were substituted by modern bricks", the overall display does not explore in depth how the specific historical set-up of the display produced situated Berlin museum versions of ancient heritage. Instead, the reproduced façades on display are labelled as authentic ancient buildings, as the Pergamon Altar or Ishtar Gate (Bilsel 2012: 214-215). More than that, the text indicates that, while the first fragments were brought to Berlin in 1903, the majority of brick fragments only "followed" 24 years later. While the text does subtly hint to negotiations about the division of finds, the gap in time is not further explained, nor is this section of the objects' journey during this quarter of a century. To the contrary, the language used in the text attempts to render a neutral process of acquisition and appropriation—the fragments "came" to Berlin or "followed" in 1927— concealing potential conflicts between European scholars, excavators, and local authorities.

The text finally highlights the high number of glazed bricks—"thousands of fragments"—the excavators "found" in Babylon and transported to Berlin in the assumingly impressive number of "over 500 crates". Moreover, the text frames the process of piecing together the appropriated fragments of glazed bricks as a "painstaking effort". Such an emphasis of the high number of fragments and praise of the scholars' efforts effectively support the visual narrative as produced by the photographic images. Both photographic images and texts highlight the number of fragments brought together, emphasising the challenge ahead of the scholars to piece together the fragments, in the context of the Ishtar gallery that, in the form of the Ishtar Gate display, demonstrates the museum's scholarly achievements.

Crate Installation

This study of the museum's display concludes with the description of a crate with brick

267

fragments that is arranged in a show case in the centre of the gallery that houses the reproduced façade of the Ishtar Gate. The installation is placed in the northern centre of the gallery between the wall panel with the photographic images and the map on the one side and the reproduced façade on the other. According to the label, the crate on display is "one of the 536 original wooden crates in which the glazed brick fragments from Babylon were shipped to Berlin" (museum label). The wooden crate is filled with glazed blue brick fragments. Two labels, tucked to the two shorter sides of the crate, read "Babylon Ziegel" (Babylon bricks) and "blaue Ziegel" (blue bricks), respectively. A few brick fragments are loosely arranged next to the crate, in the show case.

The installation of the historical crate filled with brick fragments quite ironically indicates a key element of the material infrastructure of the acquisition and appropriation process. By highlighting both the fragmented remains and the transport of the finds to Berlin, the installation symbolises the transition from ancient fragment to museum exhibit and display as well as appropriating framework: in more detail, from the ancient remains to the excavated fragment, to a shipped material trophy of Empire and material for scholarly research, to the generation of "cultural heritage", to the piece of a collection, to a museum exhibit, to an iconic appropriated trophy of Empire, to the result of scholarly effort, to a popular tourist attraction, to a signifier of contested cultural heritage, and to a disputed piece of claims for restitution and/or a politically charged symbol of (various notions of) "shared heritage" (Bilsel 2005).[19]

Conclusions

The presentation of the crate with bricks points to the transitional, ambiguous, multi-valent epistemic structure of what the museum labels as Babylonian Ishtar Gate and Processional Way. In framing the contemporary reproductions as masterpieces, the scholars and museum directors involved in setting up the displays not only generate iconic museum exhibits, but also classify them as typical representations of an assumed material ancient "culture". Through the transformation of material remains into exhibits on display in specialist museums such as the Pergamon Museum, the scholars generate an academically framed "cultural heritage" that is assumed to be preserved, further studied and presented to the public. The reproduced displays in the Pergamon Museum—that keep reproducing their own subject matter—provide a rich case study to explore the museum's contribution to establishing a research framework that generates the very notion of the material "object" transformed into both an object of scholarly research and public awe.

While the museum-generated façades contextualise the material finds from the excavations through reproducing them as masterpieces and transforming them into exhibits, these exhibits are further contextualised by decorative elements. These decorative elements, however, co-constitute the museum displays, reframing the supposed masterpieces in an ambiguous way. While the assumingly de-contextualising framing of the "masterpieces" in fact contextualises the material finds in a reductive, aestheticising way, the decorative elements in some of the galleries undermine as well as highlight the curators' authenticating, historicising framing concept that transforms the material ancient remains into a cultural heritage on display. The different decorative layers the curators generate in fact highlight the supposed ancient masterpieces as the result of a major scholarly effort. The exposed scholarly practice of conceptualising and setting up a display not only transforms the material ancient remains into representations of an ancient "culture", but also identifies them as pieces of a collection that classifies types of objects that establish an interpretive research framework. It is this curatorial and museological shift from a historicising to a contemporary framing that constitutes the displays in the Pergamon Museum. Not only does the museum present what curators have reproduced as "masterpieces" of ancient "cultures", the museum but also highlights its own role in generating masterpieces that are crucial for shaping an emerging academic discipline.

However, instead of scrutinising and critically exploring the ambiguous, multi-layered nature of its historical display encompassing the reproduced façades, reconstructions, paintings, and historical photographs, the 21st century Pergamon Museum perpetuates the disputable historical curatorial approach. As this study has examined, the historical paintings from the 1930s copied historical photographs of the excavation sites from the early 20th century pointing at the (so-called) discovery and rescue of ancient remains by Berlin archaeologists and excavators. The photographic images, panel text and installation of the crate highlight the next steps in the process of appropriation—the shipping, processing and sorting of the assumingly rescued finds from the excavations. By framing such a material and scholarly appropriation as a "painstaking effort", the curators frame the reproduction of the Ishtar façades as the result of an impressive, awe-inspiring scholarly effort that legitimises the appropriating transformation of ancient remains into finds and then pieces of the museum's collection. Instead of challenging the biased approach of the historical displays, today's curators not only build on this historical visual narrative, but also, in fact, reinforce it through adding the historical photographic images, the wall panel text and the showcase of an original crate with brick fragments as explored in this study. As the examination of the display of reproduced façades, reproductions, paintings, photographic images, showcases, labels and of wall texts has demonstrated, excavators and museum curators have highlighted their scholarly contribution to rediscovering, reproducing and thus preserving "cultural heritage" from ancient "cultures". From the opening in the 1930s onward, the overall museum display has generated "expertise" and framed the museum as an institution of scholarly research. To this day, the museum website highlights the museum's historical as well as current close links to academia and emphasises their contribution to establishing the then-emerging academic disciplines of Archaeology or Assyriology, indicating the "early successes" in deciphering of a cuneiform script in the museum's collection (Gaehtgens 1996: 73).[20] However, while the museum curators have highlighted their scholarly and curatorial achievements, they have not critically addressed their own role in the appropriating process, nor transparently laid out the competing, potentially conflicting political, economic and scholarly motivations and interests of the various stakeholders involved in the excavations, forming of collections and staging of displays, as described above. While on display—in plain sight—the display's collaborative, competitive and value-laden generation of an interpretive framework that transforms ancient fragments into objects of a museum collection, remains a peculiarly blind spot within the Pergamon Museum's curatorial performance.

Such an exposure of the display as a constitutive research framework and appropriating academic practice, however, urges us to reassess the practice of generating displays as explored in this study. Not only do we need to reconsider the interpretation of the Pergamon as an "architecture museum" or "museum of ancient architecture"[21], as both the museum website and Can Bilsel suggest (Bilsel 2012: 207, 212). We further need to explore the role of displays in producing and framing potentially contested cultural heritage. More than that, we need to consider the displays themselves as a (potentially contested) cultural heritage. More research is needed to examine how displays have been instrumental in producing theoretical frameworks to reinterpret and, in fact, academically or intellectually appropriate the (material) remains of ancient sites in the name of scholarly research (Bilsel 2012: 27).

Empirical research is needed in order to clarify whether—or to what extent—the museum's self-perception and framing as a primarily scholarly institution undermines a critical assessment of its own role as well as other stakeholders' involvement in the generation of "expertise" and value-laden frameworks. To challenge (historical) visual narratives, museums might scrutinise and transparently reflect their historical and current scholarly practice of ordering, narrating and visualising (Bennett et al. 2017). How could museums and universities in the 21st century challenge their historiographical legacy, and examine the impact of (euro-centric) historiographical practice on the present, both in regards to the countries and societies the archaeological finds originate from, and the societies where the museum serves as a public space? How can we rethink exhibitions that help us explore the multi-layered, polycentric histories of what have been reproduced as cultural heritage by German scholars in the early 20th century? How can we complement research on entangled histories with a less euro-centric approach of comparative histories? How can we become more inclusive and consider the many voices and perspectives of "the public" that might include stakeholders in various countries and societies involved (Reeve 2018: 63-65, 68-69), i.e. visitors and wider audiences as well as museum directors, curators,

271

representatives of public funding bodies, private donors, influential members of friends schemes such as the DOG, or political activists that claim restitution (Bilsel 2005), to name just these?

Considering the image that the museum has framed—and keeps reframing—of its role as a scholarly institution, a first step might be to acknowledge that museums and displays are not—and have never been—neutral and value-free. While the Museum of the Ancient Near East in the Pergamon Museum has recently been involved in a number of collaborative research projects—for example, about the historical division of archaeological finds, the systematic cataloguing of objects and archival documents of the Babylon collection, and an Iraqi-German expert dialogue[22]—its exhibitions fail to transparently address the epistemic power of research frameworks to generate cultural heritage. In what way—and why—do museums produce, as opposed to represent cultural heritage? How could museums explore the polycentric notions of displays, exhibitions, museum-institutions, and curatorial contexts, as discussed in this article? How could museums—and universities—reconsider their own scholarly practice and their perception as primarily scholarly institutions? How could scholarly institutions transparently engage in the debate about "shared heritage", a controversial term that refers to the potentially contested "cultural heritage" museums which have been involved in producing and keep reproducing?

It seems that museums have yet to find out what their role in this process—and their new *raison d'être*—might be. "Sharing" an assumed cultural heritage—apart from ethical implications, for example, with regard to provenance research or policies of restitution and repatriation—inevitably includes a reconsideration of epistemic questions about "what" is on display, of what displays "do". We might "share" what has been framed as cultural heritage, but we should consider that we might share it from (historically) different, yet tangled perspectives and through potentially different, yet tangled motivations and interests. The discussion about ambiguities and blind spots of displays urges us to look more closely at the practice of scholarly or intellectual appropriation and re-interpretation, i.e. the conservation, reproduction, and presentation of artefacts in (European) museums, in short, at the production of cultural heritage, generation of interpretive frameworks and framing of institutional

272

expertise in and by museums and academia, from the 19th century to the present day.

Notes

1. Accessed May 31, 2019. https://www.smb.museum/en/museums-institutions/ vorderasiatisches-museum/collection-research/about-the-collection.html.

2. Accessed May 31, 2019. https://www.smb.museum/en/museums-institutions/ vorderasiatisches-museum/about-us/about-us.html.

3. Accessed May 31, 2019. https://www.smb.museum/en/museums-institutions/ vorderasiatisches-museum/about-us/about-us.html.

4. Accessed May 31, 2019. https://www.museums insel-berlin.de/home/ and https://www. museumsinsel-berlin.de/en/collections/ museum-of-the-ancient-near-east/.

5. Accessed May 31, 2019. https://www.smb.museum/en/museums-institutions/ vorderasiatisches-museum/collection-research/research.html.

6. Several galleries of the Pergamon Museum have been temporary closed due to refurbishment since 2013, among them are the gallery of the Pergamon Altar and smaller galleries of the south wing. Prussian Cultural Heritage Foundation, Masterplan Museumsinsel Website. Accessed May 31, 2019 https://www.museumsinsel-berlin.de/ en/buildings/ pergamonmuseum/.

7. Accessed December 12, 2017. http://www.smb.museum/en/about-us/history.html.

8. Accessed May 31, 2019. https://www.smb.museum/en/ museums-institutions/ vorderasiatisches-museum/about-us/about-us.html.

9. Accessed May 31, 2019. https://www.smb.museum/en/ museums-institutions/ vorderasiatisches-museum/collection-research/about-the-collection.html.

10. Accessed May 31, 2019. https://www.smb.museum/en/ museums-institutions/ vorderasiatisches-museum/collection-research/about-the-collection.html

11. Wall panel: "Reconstruction drawing by Walter Andrae depicting the stele rows of Ashur, Staatsbibliothek zu Berlin, SPK, Handschriftenabteilung." (National Library in Berlin, Prussian Cultural Heritage Foundation, department of manuscripts; English

translation by the author)

12. Accessed May 31, 2019. The University of Chicago. The Neubauer Expedition to Zincirli. https://zincirli.uchicago. edu/page/site-and-setting and https://zincirli. uchicago.edu/ page/previous-excavations.

13. Wall panel: "Entwurfszeichnung für die Einrichtung des Babylon-Raumes von Walter Andrae, Ende der 1920er Jahre. Draft of the interior design of the Babylon Room by Walter Andrae, late 1920s."

14. A few paintings were carried out by the studio of the painter Johann Walter-Kurau: Abele 2010: 71.

15. Historicising decorations and wall paintings, depicting landscapes and Ancient Egyptian temple decorations, can be found in the Egyptian Museum on Museum Island.

16. Museum label, image caption: "Grabungen am Ischtar-Tor, April 1902. Excavations at the Ishtar Gate, April 1902."

17. Museum label, image caption: "Entsalzen der Glasurziegel des Ischtar-Tores und der Prozessionsstraße, Ende der 1920er Jahre. Desalination of the glazed bricks of the Ishtar Gate and the Processional Way, late 1920s."

18. Museum label, image caption: "Sortieren der Ziegelbruchstücke, Ende der 1920er Jahre. Sorting of brick fragments, late 1920s."

19. For context, see the debate about notions of "shared heritage" or "world heritage" in regards to Berlin's new Humboldt Forum in the reproduced former royal palace, due to house the Ethnological and Asian Art Collections of the National Museums in Berlin (Mbembe 2018; MacGregor 2017; Opoku 2015).

20. Accessed May 31, 2019. https://www.smb.museum/en/museums-institutions/ vorderasiatisches-museum/collection-research/about-the-collection.html.

21. Accessed May 31, 2019. https://www.smb.museum/veranstaltungen/detail/im-fokus-die-deutschen-grabungen-und-das-pergamonmuseum-1.html.

22. Accessed May 31, 2019. https://www.smb.museum/en/museums-institutions/ vorderasiatisches-museum/collection-research/research.html.

□ Disclosure Statement

No potential conflict of interest was reported by the author.

□ Note on Contributor

Dr. *Annette Loeseke* is Lecturer in Museum Studies at New York University in Berlin. She has also worked as External Lecturer in Visitor Studies in the Master-of-Museology Programme at the Reinwardt Academy, Amsterdam University of the Arts. She was a senior visiting fellow at university College London in Qatar in January 2019, and a scholar-in-residence at Cornell University in Ithaca, NY in the summer of 2015. Her research interests include postcolonial museum studies, curatorial ecosystems and empirical visitor/stakeholder studies. Recent publications include the chapters "Transhistoricism. Using the Past to Critique the Present" (In *The Contemporary Museum*, edited by Simon Knell, London: Routledge, 2019), "Experimental Exhibition Models" (In *The Future of Museum and Gallery Design*, edited by Suzanne MacLeod, Tricia Austin, Oscar Ho et al., London: Routledge, 2018) and "Studying International Visitors at Shanghai Museum" (In *New Museum Practice in Asia*, edited by Caroline Lang, and John Reeve, London: Lund Humphries, 2018).

☐ References

Abele, K. 2010. Johann Walter (Walter-Kurau): 1869–1932. Doctoral Dissertation, Latvian Academy of Art, Riga. Accessed May 31, 2019. https://www.academia.edu/37309439/ Johann_Walter_Walter-Kurau_._1869_1932 _Summary_of_the_Doctoral_Dissertation. Riga_Latvian_Academy_of_Art_2010.

Bakkor, H. 2013. Zur Repräsentation von Geschichte und Kultur des Alten Orients in großen europäischen Museen: Die Analyse der Dauerausstellungen in den vorderasiatischen Museenim Louvre, British Museum und Pergamonmuseum. Doctoral Dissertation, Freie Universität, Berlin. Accessed May 31, 2019. https://refubium.fu-berlin.de/ bitstream/handle/ fub188/7995/Dissertation_Bakkor.pdf?sequence=1&isAllowed=y.

Bennett, T., et al. 2017. *Collecting, Ordering, Governing. Anthropology, Museums, and Liberal Government.* London: Duke University Press.

Bilsel, C. 2005. The Undoing of a Monument: Preservation as Critical Engagement with Pergamon's Heritage. *Future Anterior: Journal of Historic Preservation History, Theory, and Criticism* 2 (1): 12-21. Accessed May 31, 2019. http://www.jstor.org/stable/ 25834957.

Bilsel, C. 2012. *Antiquity on Display: Regimes of the Authentic in Berlin's Pergamon Museum.* Oxford: Oxford University Press.

Deutsche Orient-Gesellschaft. Accessed May 31, 2019. http://www.orient-gesellschaft.de/.

Deutsches Archäologisches Institut. Accessed May 31, 2019. https://www.dainst.org/en/dai/ meldungen.

Gaehtgens, T. W. 1996. The Museum Island in Berlin. In *The Formation of National Collections of Art and Archaeology*, edited by G. Wright, 53-77. Hannover/London: University Press of New England.

Haffner, D. 2019. Babylonische Löwen: Rezeption und Wanderungen. In *Von analogen und digitalen Zugängen zur Kunst*, edited by M. Effinger et al., 203-214. Heidelberg: arthistoricum.net.

Loeseke, A. 2019a. Transhistoricism: Using the Past to Critique the Present. In *The Contemporary Museum: Shaping Museums for the Global Now*, edited by S. Knell, 142-151. London: Routledge.

Loeseke, A. 2019b. From Sanctuary for Art and Science to Centre of World Culture? In *Museum Universalities in Western Cultural Capitals in the Nineteenth and Early Twentieth Century*, edited by H. Inglebert, and S. Kemp (forthcoming).

MacGregor, N. 2017. World Heritage and Ownership. October 16, 2017. Accessed May 31, 2019. https://humboldtforum.com/en/stories/ world-heritage-and-ownership.

Mbembe, A. 2018. Sie gehörenunsallen. Dekolonisation, wiekann das gelingen? Gesprächmit Achille Mbembe. March 7, 2018. Accessed May 31, 2019. https://www. zeit.de/2018/11/dekolonisation-achille-mbembe-philosoph/ komplettansicht?print.

Opoku, K. 2015. Looted Artefacts Now Declared a "Shared Heritage". September 9, 2015. Accessed May 31, 2019. https://www.pambazuka.org/arts/looted-artefacts-now-declared-%E2%80%9Cshared-heritage%E2%80%9D.

Paul, B. 1995. Collecting Is the Noblest of All Passions! Wilhelm von Bode and the Relationship Between Museums, Art Dealing, and Private Collecting. *International Journal of Political Economy* 25 (2): 9-32.

Reeve, J. 2018. Islamic Art, the Islamic World and Museums. In *The Contemporary Museum: Shaping Museums for the Global Now*, edited by S. Knell, 55-73. London: Routledge.

Social Innovations in Museum and Heritage Management

Carolina Jonsson Malm

Malmö University, 205 06 Malmö, Sweden. CONTACT Carolina Jonsson Malm: carolina.jonsson-malm@mau.se

Abstract: To shed light on heritage-based social innovation as a neglected area of research, this article presents the results of a multi-sited case study of innovative work within the Swedish cultural heritage sector. A theoretical framework on social innovation is applied to analyse how museums and other cultural heritage organisations work in novel ways to create social change. The six social initiatives selected as case studies addressed a diverse range of social needs: education, integration, health care, employment, urban development, conflict management and peacebuilding. The analysis focuses on the innovative aspects of the initiatives by examining and comparing the central components of the innovation processes. The study shows that the cultural heritage organisations are innovative in many ways, through new objectives, target groups, methods, activities and collaborations and also through new uses of heritage. The article also highlights some of the possible implications for heritage and heritage management when heritage is used as a means to achieve social goals and suggests some directions for further study.

Keywords: cultural heritage, social innovation, case studies, Sweden

Introduction

Recent years have seen a rapid growth in the understanding of the role which cultural heritage can play in society and its potential for social cohesion, economic growth and sustainable development. Recognising the importance of cultural heritage as a unique, valuable resource and a major asset, politicians and decision-makers globally are investing in the development and use of heritage—tangible, intangible and digital—in new and creative ways. There is a broad consensus that cultural heritage plays an important role as a source of innovation and change (European Commission 2018). However, innovation in the context of cultural heritage has manifold meanings, including technological, economic, entrepreneurial, environmental, political and social innovation.

The heritage sector is not usually associated with the term "social innovation". However, the educational and social practices of many museums and heritage organisations share similarities with social entrepreneurs and social enterprises through their common goal to deliver social benefits to communities. Though the concept of social innovation has recently received increased attention in human and social science research, it has drawn but limited attention in the fields of heritage and museum studies. Similarly, the concept of cultural heritage has rarely been focused on in social innovation studies. This motivates further investigation of how cultural heritage can be understood and used as a driver for social innovation.

To shed light on the cultural heritage sector as a neglected area of social innovation, this article presents the results of a study of innovative work within the Swedish cultural heritage sector promoting new forms of cross-sectoral heritage management aiming at social change. The study explores how a theoretical framework on social innovation can be applied to analyse how museums and other cultural heritage organisations work in creative and novel ways to creat social change. The guiding research question for the study thus concerns the objectives, methods and outcomes of this innovative work and why it can be considered innovative. It highlights the innovative aspects of heritage-based social innovation and pinpoints both the common and the unique elements of the actions.

Furthermore, the study provides insights into how heritage and heritage management can be reconceptualised in a social innovation framework and the implications of this reframing.

The article starts with a theoretical background of the study: introducing the field of social innovation studies and the field(s) of heritage and museum studies, and where and how they intersect. This is followed by an account of the multiple case study design from which the empirical data and results are derived. The results are then presented with a special focus on the innovative aspects of the studied cases. Thereafter, a discussion follows on how the results can be interpreted in an analytical framework on heritage-based social innovation. Finally, the main conclusions of the study are summarised and a reflection concerning how this research serves to advance the knowledge on innovative social actions in the heritage sector is presented.

Studying Social Innovation, Heritage and Museums

The common definition of social innovations is that they are new and original ideas aimed at meeting social goals. They are designed to address a societal challenge or meet a social need and create positive social impacts, such as improved quality of life, well-being, social inclusion, equality and empowerment (Moulaert et al. 2014). The innovative aspect of the actions can be to focus on a new social phenomenon and its complexities, to propose a new approach to an existing problem or to improve existing methods in novel ways. It may entail new ways of thinking, new processes and procedures, new techniques, new products, new collaborations, or new organisations, thus encompassing both material and immaterial dimensions. It is crucial that the innovation is not just an idea or a prototype, but is actually implemented in a social setting where it has a profound impact and eventually can replace common practice. However, most importantly is that the overall purpose of the innovation is to generate social profit, not primarily financial profit (Howaldt et al. 2018; Moulaert et al. 2014; Nicholls, Simon, and Gabriel 2015; Westley, McGowan, and Tjörnbo 2017).

Thus, the core element of social innovations is that they create social value in novel ways. However, there are also other common features of social innovations (Figure 1). For example, they are often of a collaborative nature, cross-sectoral and multidisciplinary. It is common to involve stakeholders and end-users in the development and implementation process—a process characterised by openness, mutualism and co-production (The Young Foundation 2012). Furthermore, social innovations can be divided into three categories that occur on three levels: grassroots, societal and systemic. Grassroots innovations are bottom-up initiatives responding to a pressing social need in a local context. Societal innovations address broader societal challenges and are directed towards society as a whole. Lastly, systemic innovations call for "fundamental changes in attitudes and values, strategies and policies, organisational structures and processes, delivery systems and services" (BEPA 2010: 8). A quite common challenge for social innovations is to scale up from community level to national and international level, and to transfer and adapt best practices to different contexts (Murray, Caulier-Grice, and Mulgan 2010). This is where research and research dissemination can play a crucial role in developing, testing and promoting useful models.

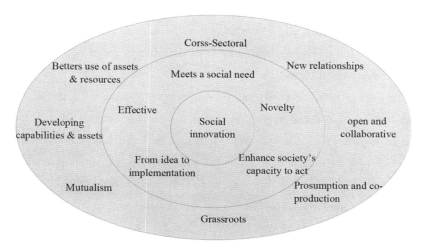

Figure 1   Core elements and common features of social innovation

The past two decades has seen an increased demand for innovative approaches in the discussions on how to meet current and future challenges, such as demographical changes, economic inequalities, political and democratic transformations, and technological developments, as well as human hardship caused by climate change. For instance, the European Union has incorporated the concept of social innovation into its drive towards an Innovative Union: one of its seven flagship initiatives to reach the Europe 2020 target of achieving smart, sustainable and inclusive growth (BEPA 2010).

Sweden is currently not a leading country in social innovation policy or practice. Indeed, social innovation there has just recently gained political recognition as a field of interest and a national strategic agenda on social innovation which is still being established (Gustafsson and Netz 2018; The Ministry of Enterprise and Innovation 2018). Behind this lack of activity is the long-standing belief that the Swedish welfare state caters for the social needs of its people, which renders philanthropy and initiatives from the private and civil sector unnecessary. However, since the late 1990s, the Swedish welfare system has been steadily deregulated and dismantled, fuelled by New Public Management ideology and global economic crises; this has opened up for new forms of involvement in the provision of social services. There is also a growing demand for more specialised and personalised social services and more inclusive forms of participation in social policy design and implementation (Pestoff 2009).

In the wake of the political and public interest for novel solutions to societal challenges, the scholarly field of social innovation studies has expanded significantly. Scientific studies on social innovation have sought to introduce, explore, define, classify, exemplify and problematise the concept of social innovation as an emerging social phenomenon, a theoretical construct, a methodological approach and a multidisciplinary field of research (Ayob, Teasdale, and Fagan 2016; Brundenius 2017; Cajaiba-Santana 2014; Grimm 2013; Jessop et al. 2014; Marques, Morgan, and Richardson 2017; Moulaert et al. 2017; Nicholls, Simon, and Gabriel 2015; Wittmayer et al. 2017).

Social innovation studies examine the process of innovation, what drives innovation, and how innovation and change take shape. This research is not only focusing on the new products, services, methods, organisations and other outcomes that result from the innovation, but also covering all the stages in the innovation process—from idea generation and definition of innovation goals to idea implementation and evaluation of the social impact on individuals, organisations and societies (Moulaert et al. 2014). These processes are mainly studied through single or multiple cases of social innovation in relation to various localities (such as cities, rural areas, communities, regions and nations), areas of activity (such as public services, academia, business sectors, social enterprises and civil societies) and types of organisations (such as schools, hospitals, homes, community centres, non-profits, innovation labs). In general terms, studies of social innovation processes in the cultural heritage sector, as in this article, are scarce. In comparison, studies of social innovations based on the arts and the creative industries, commonly referred to as artistic and cultural innovation or culture-led innovation, are far more common (for literature reviews, see André, Henriques, and Malheiros 2009; Fusco Girard, Baycan, and Nijkamp 2011; Tremblay and Pilati 2014). When heritage is mentioned, it is often presented as something opposed to innovation and creativity, thereby indicating that the field of social innovation has not yet caught up with the state of the art in heritage and museum studies.

Over the past two decades, the field of heritage studies has expanded across different disciplines in the human and social sciences (such as archaeology, anthropology, architecture, cultural studies, history, law, political science, sociology, geography and tourism). Like many other branches of the human and social sciences, it has also been affected by the critical turn, thus prompting more and more researchers to view heritage as dynamic and socially constructed rather than fixed and unchanging, and also as complex processes of power, ideology and identity rather than uncontested products of history and time (Smith 2012; Winter 2013; Witcomb and Buckley 2013). The field covers research that explores how the past is used in the present, what is preserved for the future and why, relations of power, cultural representation and the politics of belonging, are among other things (Graham and Howard 2008; Harrison 2012; Logan, Nic Craith, and Kockel 2016;

Silverman, Waterton, and Watson 2017; Smith 2006).

Museum studies, also referred to as museology, is an adjacent field of research, focusing specifically on the practices and policies of museums as cultural and educational institutions. The critical approach to museology, called the "new museology", is concerned with dismantling social hierarchies and exclusions, and transforming the museum from an elitist, authoritative and object-focused institution to an open, inclusive and visitor-centred experience (Bennett 1995; Black 2005; Carbonell 2004; Hooper-Greenhill 1992; Macdonald 2006; Marstine 2005; Message 2006; Vergo 1989). The new museology also involves a redefinition of the relationship between museums and their communities; thus, participatory practices and community empowerment have been central topics (Peers and Brown 2003; Watson 2007; Witcomb 2003).

The two critical schools within heritage and museum studies overlap in many ways, for example, sharing a common interest for cultural theory, critical analysis, practice-based research and action-oriented methods (Witcomb and Buckley 2013). A particularly interesting strand of literature examines the idea of heritage and heritage institutions as resources for economic, social and sustainable development (Albert 2015; Auclair and Fairclough 2015). In recent years, the recognition, development and use of heritage have been high on the political agenda. Cultural heritage is believed to have many positive effects on society, such as raising the attractiveness of urban and rural areas, enhancing the quality of life of the inhabitants, driving cultural tourism, boosting creativity and innovation, creating jobs, contributing to economic growth, stimulating education and learning, promoting community building and social cohesion, and preserving the environment (CHCFE 2015). As a consequence, there has been a surge of interest among researchers wanting not only to observe, describe and explain this trend, but also to find ways to bring research and practice closer together in order to develop practical applications and solutions to existing problems (for example, the activities at the Research Centre for Museums and Galleries at the University of Leicester in the UK or the Centre for Applied Heritage at Linnaeus University in Sweden).

A subfield within this way of conducting applied research is specialising in the social benefits of heritage and how actors in the heritage and museum sector can engage in social action, thereby actively contributing to social transformation in different areas of society. Examples of such areas are education (Westergren 2017; Zipsane 2008), health (Chatterjee and Noble 2016; Dodd and Jones 2014), social justice (Sandell 2007; Sandell and Nightingale 2012), conflict management and peace building (Sevcenko 2010), migration and integration (Holtorf, Pantazatos and Scarre 2019), urban planning (Labadi and Logan 2016; Söderström 2018), regional development and community building (Harrison 2010; Holtorf, Gustafsson, and Westergren 2011; Kearns, Kling, and Wistman 2011; Santos 2007), and many more. This article suggests that these efforts may be categorised as "socially applied heritage" and that studies on social applications of heritage are characterised by the combination of applied research and a critical approach, and by the desire to evaluate social actions, and explore new methods and analyse processes of social change. Considering these characteristics, it is perhaps surprising that this kind of research has not considered the concept of social innovation as a useful analytical framework. Fernández (2016: 3), archaeologist and social entrepreneur, is one of the few to make the argument that connections should be between social innovation and cultural heritage:

We encounter the concept of social innovation importing it from other areas and fields of knowledge. It is scarcely used in cultural heritage and this does not mean that this sector is not socially innovative—which it is—yet something much more serious: reflection on its importance is not taking place and no bridges are being built towards other areas of knowledge, sciences, fields, experiences that, on their part, are doing so. If heritage is to be connected to emerging grassroots movements, to the social, political and scientific realities of our time, it appears that we should start renovating our conceptual repertoire.

Drawing on these conclusions, this article aims to show the relevance of bringing social innovation studies and critical heritage and museum studies together, and how this would enrich and benefit the research. Firstly, it will deepen the understanding of heritage-based social innovation in the field of social innovation by offering a more dynamic approach to heritage. Secondly, it will provide new insights and methods for analysing innovating processes and solutions in museum and heritage management.

Material and Methods

Methodologically, the study seeks to combine perspectives from social innovation studies and critical heritage and museum studies in an analytical framework to explore the innovativeness of social initiatives using heritage as a resource. A social initiative is defined as an initiative by which an actor (in this case, heritage organisations and their partners) engages in actions that promote positive social changes and sustainable developments (Cajaiba-Santana 2014). The framework integrates the three components of heritage-based social innovations—society, innovation, and heritage—and describes their relationships. To understand the interrelationships, this article proposes a heritage-based social innovation model (Figure 2) that can be easily adapted and used by researchers in both scientific fields. In doing so, the study generates applicable theoretical insights that go beyond state of the art and provides a basis for further investigation.

Figure 2 A schematic model of the interrelationship between society, innovation, and heritage

As the model illustrates, heritage-based social innovations are characterised by using heritage in novel ways to create social change. If one of the three components is missing, the action can no longer be regarded as a heritage-based social innovation. It may be a social innovation not involving any heritage resources, a social action within the heritage sector without an innovative approach or a heritage innovation not addressing social needs. The model and the multidisciplinary approach—merging perspectives from social innovation studies (on innovativeness and social change) and critical heritage and museum studies (on the social potential of heritage and heritage organisation)—inform the research design and the multi-method approach.

The research design is based on a qualitative and empirical approach built around a multi-sited ethnographic study. Multi-sited ethnography, according to Marcus (1995), is a methodological approach in which the ethnographer undertakes research in and between several locations as part of a single study in order to analyse and understand different places, actors and actions. This approach builds on an understanding that the sites have many dimensions (physical, social, and virtual) and no clear boundaries. In conducting multi-sited fieldwork, the aim is not to write an all-encompassing account of each of the studied sites but to understand the specificities of each site, thereby highlighting the organisational and situational context. A further characteristic of multi-sited research is the idea of comparison. What do the sites have in common, and how do they differ? However, the findings from the selected case studies can be generalised only in part. The aim is not to synthesise but to juxtapose in order to emphasise different applications and possibilities. Hence, the generalisability of the study mainly lies in the exportability of the theoretical framework that can conceptualise and contextualise the case studies.

The study consists of six case studies representing different types of organisations, initiatives, and approaches. The case studies were selected to reflect the range of social initiatives carried out by museums and other heritage organisations. The selection and analysis process was done through a series of partially overlapping methodological steps. The first step was to identify social and cultural areas—as opposed to, for example, industrial, commercial, technological or environmental areas—where museums and heritage organisations are trying to make a difference and achieve social change. The mapping revealed that some of the most common targets for social change were the following: education, health care, housing, employment, rural development, urban planning, infrastructure, democratic governance, civic engagement, social justice, conflict management, peace building, integration, and community building.

In the next step, six social initiatives from six different areas were selected on the basis of the core elements and common features of social innovation listed above. A set of criteria was formulated and adapted to the heritage context specifying that the selected social initiatives should do the following:

(1) meet a social need or social challenge;

(2) value social goals over heritage management goals (such as preservation and knowledge about the past);

(3) focus on method development;

(4) involve cross-sectoral cooperation;

(5) foster active stakeholder and user participation;

(6) be deemed successful by the involved actors (meaning that the initiative is believed to have had a positive social impact).

The six case studies selected for further analysis were Jamtli Museum (education), Swedish for Immigrants at museums (integration), Rönningegården (health care), Långban Mine and Culture Village (employment), Stenstan Visitor Centre (urban development) and Bridging Ages (conflict management and peace-building). After the selection process, data were collected from the six case studies. The main methods for collecting data were direct observations; semi-structured and open-ended interviews; informal conversations; and textual analysis of project materials, such as project plans, websites, films, brochures, handbooks, evaluation reports and other documents, and also press coverage and footage from other sources. The data were compiled and compared with the aim of analysing in greater depth how social initiatives within the heritage sector can be understood using a social innovation framework. Hence, the analytical focus is on the innovative aspects of the actions. The analysis examines the central components of the innovation process, from defining innovation goals to evaluating outcomes (Moulaert et al. 2014). For each case study, a set of data and results is presented in tabular form (Table 1).

Table 1   Data to be analysed in the case studies

Key features of the innovation process	Innovative aspects
Problem statement	The social need or societal challenge that the social action seeks to address
Aims	The purposes and aims of the social action
Target groups	Beneficiaries of the social action
Heritage resources	Assets and resources used by the actors
Methods	Methodological approaches, means, tools, designs of the action, implementation processes, etc.
Collaborations	Actors involved by the heritage organisations
Activities	Practices implemented or performed within the social action
Outputs	Expected outputs of the social action

Results

In this section, the theoretical framework of social innovation and heritage is employed to analyse the innovative aspects and applications of six social initiatives within the Swedish cultural heritage sector. The case studies are not meant to be empirically comprehensive or fully comparable, but they can be seen as a kind of test cases for applying the framework of heritage-based social innovation and focus some of their specific features. After presenting the results, I will discuss the merits of the application.

Case 1: Jamtli Open Preschool

The first example is an open preschool at Jamtli, an open-air museum in northern Sweden. An open preschool is a place for small children (from zero to six years) accompanied by their parents or other adults. Children and adults get to know each other, participate in activities and play together. Trained preschool teachers are responsible for the planning of activities—like storytelling, singing, and games—which have both educational and social goals. It is free to visit open preschools and participate in the activities. The Swedish open preschool system can be regarded as a social innovation in itself as it corresponds to a societal need, especially for unemployed parents or those on parental leave wanting to meet other adults during the day. In this case study, the innovative aspect lies in the use of cultural heritage to develop the open preschool. All activities of the open preschool at Jamtli take place in the old buildings or in the outdoor environment at the open-air museum. Jamtli open preschool aims to make history come alive and to teach cultural history through playing and having fun in the framework of heritage learning (Christidou 2014). Moreover, it intends to provide access to cultural heritage for new audiences, both young and old, thus contributing to social inclusion and lifelong learning and strengthening democracy. The results from case study 1 are shown in Table 2.

Table 2   Results from case study 1

Key features of the innovation process	Innovative aspects
Problem statement	There is a need for socially inclusive learning activities for young children
Aims	To contribute to social inclusion and lifelong learning
Target groups	Preschool children and their guardians
Heritage resources	Indoor and outdoor areas in the open-air museum
Methods	Democratic early childhood education
Collaborations	Trained preschool teachers
Activities	Playing games
Outputs	A new service (a heritage-based open preschool)

Case 2: Swedish for Immigrants (SFI) at Museums

The next case study is SFI at museums: a national network for museums involved with SFI. SFI is a national Swedish language course offered to all categories of immigrants. It is funded by the municipalities, and is cost-free. The course also teaches illiterates how to read and write. Many Swedish museums are involved in SFI courses through collaboration with certified SFI instructors and arranging student activities. Some examples of activities are guided tours, workshops, movie screenings, creative writing, crafting, painting, cooking and baking. Though the primary goal is language proficiency, there are many other positive effects as the students also develop other skills, learn about history and cultural heritage, gain a greater understanding of the local community and Swedish society, and adopt new attitudes and values. The museums hope that the SFI collaboration will encourage students to continue visiting museums after the course has ended. As immigrants are an underrepresented group at Swedish museums, this collaboration is a means to reach this group and provide access to cultural heritage. The results from case study 2 are shown in Table 3.

Table 3   Results from case study 2

Key features of the innovation process	Innovative aspects
Problem statement	Newcomers in Sweden need language proficiency and access to culture
Aims	To contribute to integration and social cohesion
Target groups	Newcomers
Heritage resources	Museums' collections and expertise
Methods	Creative learning and intercultural communication
Collaborations	SFI instructors
Activities	Culture-based language exercises
Outputs	A new service (a creative and heritage-based language course for immigrants)

Case 3: Rönningegården

It has become more common for museums to collaborate with actors in the health care sector. Research has found that attending and participating in cultural activities have a positive impact on health and well-being. Using arts and culture in, for instance, rehabilitation and elderly care has proven to be very effective. This case study is centred on a nursing home called Rönningegården in the city of Mörbylånga. It is the first nursing home in Sweden to specialise in arts and cultural heritage. Everyday life in a nursey home can often be perceived as uneventful and monotonous, and staff are often more focused on the medical care than on the mental well-being of the residents. By using arts and culture, the staff can contribute to a more meaningful and satisfying life. The methods used at Rönningegården have been developed together with Kalmar County Museum in a long-standing collaboration with the city of Mörbylånga. The museum has provided training for the staff and helped them organise cultural activities and events. A common problem in elderly care is the generational gap between the older care recipients and the younger caretakers, which can lead to communication barriers and cultural differences. The museum provides historical knowledge and tools that help bridge that gap. The innovative methods are based on the residents' individual backgrounds, memories and interests. The residents participate in social and cultural activities of their own choice, thus not only building on existing knowledge and experiences but also learning new things. The results from case study 3 are shown in Table 4.

Table 4   Results from case study 3

Key features of the innovation process	Innovative aspects
Problem statement	Residents in nursing homes need more meaningful activities
Aims	To contribute to well-being and active ageing
Target groups	The elderly residents at a nursing home
Heritage resources	Historical knowledge and tools
Methods	Life story methodology and individual-centred care
Collaborations	Rönningegården and the city of Mörbylånga
Activities	Cultural activities and events
Outputs	A new service (heritage-based elderly care)

Case 4: Långban Mine and Culture Village

In recent years, Sweden has seen a significant increase in its number of immigrants and refugees. The responsible social authorities have not been able to cater to all their needs and help them to become established socially and economically. To facilitate integration and social engagement, many museums and heritage organisations have initiated new strategic collaborations. An example of such an initiative, one which received much attention, is the collaboration between Värmland Museum and Filipstad Municipality in west-central Sweden. This project explored how local history and heritage sites can be used as resources for social development. Newly arrived immigrants in Filipstad were offered internship positions in landscape and building preservation at the Långban Mine and Culture Village. Långban has been a mining town dating back to the 16th century, with well-preserved cabins, mining fields and a mineral exhibition. The main purpose of the internships was vocational training, professional development and validation of skills and competences for the participants, as well as social integration through knowledge exchange and intercultural communication. The project also contributed to the development of Långban as a meeting place for the local community and a tourist attraction for visitors. The key to success was the organisers' ability to engage a large part of civil society and important stakeholders and to create a common sense of ownership. The integration through employment model is now being spread to other parts of the country. The results from case study 4 are shown in Table 5.

Table 5   Results from case study 4

Key features of the innovation process	Innovative aspects
Problem statement	The unemployment rate for immigrants and refugees is too high
Aims	To contribute to social integration and economic empowerment for vulnerable groups
Target groups	Immigrants, refugees and the receiving community
Heritage resources	The historical environment of the old mining town
Methods	Heritage management training and intercultural communication
Collaborations	Filipstad Municipality and the Swedish Employment Agency
Activities	Internships in historic site and historic building preservation and restoration
Outputs	A new service (heritage-based job training) and a new product (a tourist attraction)

Case 5: Stenstan Visitor Centre

This case study is focused on Stenstan Visitor Centre in the city of Sundsvall in northern Sweden. The centre collaborates with Sundsvall Museum and is a mixture of art gallery, exhibition space and tourist information centre. It is focused on the architectural heritage of the city, with its prominent stone buildings and Art Nouveau style, which gives the city its distinctive appearance. The visitors learn about the urban heritage of Sundsvall and get a deeper understanding of how the city has changed over time. Visitors also have access to the Future Lab, which is an innovative hub for urban planning open to the public. Using the latest digital technology, games and interactive media—developed with leading technological companies—the Future Lab helps visitors envision how the city of Sundsvall might look in the future. The focus is on sustainability, urban regeneration and innovative solutions. Because the municipality of Sundsvall is behind the Future Lab, all visitors' responses and ideas are reviewed and considered by municipal officials. The purpose of the Future Lab is to involve the residents of Sundsvall in urban planning processes, the democratising of decision-making processes and in the promotion of active citizenship. It is a platform for open dialogue and discussion about the future development of the city, based on its history. The results from case study 5 are shown in Table 6.

Table 6   Results from case study 5

Key features of the innovation process	Innovative aspects
Problem statement	There is a need to involve the town residents in urban planning processes
Aims	To contribute to democratic urban development and civic engagement
Target groups	Town residents
Heritage resources	The urban heritage of Sundsvall City
Methods	Museum pedagogy and digital tools
Collaborations	Sundsvall Museum, Sundsvall municipality and tech companies
Activities	Digital future-making
Outputs	A new function (a public innovation lab)

Case 6: Bridging Ages

Bridging Ages is a non-profit organisation focusing on heritage education and social development. The organisation was founded in 2007 and is based in Kalmar in the southwest of Sweden, but it has an international scope and members all over the world. Its members have developed an approach called "the Time Travel method", which is a way to address the challenges of today using the experiences of the past. The method uses local heritage (stories, memories, traditions, artefacts, and historic sites) and role-plays to facilitate discussion and reflection on contemporary issues related to conflict, discrimination and inequality. Role-play is a way to explore the personal and social values of self and others, as it requires an examination of the issue from varying points of view within a collaborative learning framework. It can help culturally diverse communities to negotiate cultural differences and explore common ground. The method creates a safe space for people to get engaged in meaningful exchanges and to find a way forward together. The organisation's vision is to develop future heritage and the future society. Amongst others, the organisation collaborates with the Department of Arts and Culture in South Africa and has developed a nationwide educational programme focusing on history, colonialism, racism, reconciliation, and social justice. Similar projects have been undertaken in collaboration with social actors and authorities in Kenya, Uganda, Turkey, Serbia, Northern Ireland and the Baltic countries, to name a few. The results from case study 6 are shown in Table 7.

Table 7   Results from case study 6

Key features of the innovation process	Innovative aspects
Problem statement	Conflict, discrimination, and inequalities lead to instability and polarisation of societies
Aims	To contribute to social cohesion and peace
Target groups	Communities
Heritage resources	Local heritage
Methods	Time Travel Methodology and Conflict Transformation
Collaborations	Social actors from all over the world, such as schools, universities, cultural organisations, NGOs, communities, and national and local authorities

Continued

Key features of the innovation process	Innovative aspects
Activities	Heritage-based role-plays focused on discussion and reflection on contemporary issues
Outputs	A new organisation (a non-profit organisation for heritage education and social development)

Discussion

When analysing the six case studies, the focus was on the innovate aspects of the actions. What new social areas and problems did the heritage organisations focus on? Which new target groups did they wish to reach? What new methods and practices were developed? Which knowledge and perspectives came to influence the practices? What new products or services could the actors offer? Were new partnerships and collaborations formed? Did the innovation lead to the establishment of new functions and organisations? And maybe, most importantly, in this context, how was heritage used in new and innovative ways?

The selected case studies addressed a diverse range of social needs: education, integration, health care, employment, urban development, conflict management and peacebuilding. A common denominator amongst them was the desire to contribute to social development and empower communities or vulnerable groups, such as young children, the elderly and newcomers. Though different methods and approaches were used, the common focus was learning: from early childhood education, senior learning and language courses to heritage management training, museum pedagogy and role-play. The learning can be formal or non-formal and aims at developing knowledge and skills or adopting new attitudes, values and behaviour. Another characteristic of the methods used is that they all seek to foster participatory, collaborative and communicative learning processes where individual experiences become interconnected with collective narratives. There is also a strong emphasis on creativity, exploration, self-expression and meaning-making. In all of the case studies, the actors employed a future-oriented approach aiming at engaging the participants in imagining a better life. When looking across the case studies, it is evident that they all resonate with the methodological approach known as the heritage learning framework, which explores how heritage and heritage organisations can be of greater relevance to people and society (Christidou 2014).

Moreover, the analysis shows that many of the heritage-based innovations were made possible by new partnerships and collaborations. The museums and heritage organisations joined forces with professionals and organisations from other sectors, companies, local authorities and communities to develop methods for inter-sectorial cooperation and to find joint solutions to social problems. The results were not just new ways of doing things or new ways of working together, but in some cases also new ways of organising the work by establishing new functions or organisations. This shows that sometimes existing institutions and organisational structures are not enough and that new solutions might be needed at the systemic level (BEPA 2010).

This study is particularly interested in how heritage can be used in innovative ways to create social change. The heritage resources used in the case studies included both tangible and intangible heritage, such as buildings, objects, landscapes, urban areas, stories, traditions and cultural expressions. The focus was on using and developing heritage rather than preserving and restoring. This reflects the approach to heritage within critical heritage studies where heritage is seen as an extrinsic and social process that gives meaning to people today and that might mean something else tomorrow (Smith 2006).

However, to treat heritage as a resource for social development and to focus primarily on social goals rather than promoting the cultural values in themselves is not uncontroversial. Similar discussions have been going on for some time across the heritage sector regarding the use of heritage for financial gains and economic development (Graham, Ashworth, and Tunbridge 2000; Ho and McKercher 2004). Some argue that this practice is devaluing both heritage and heritage expertise, while others argue that promoting and demonstrating the societal value of heritage will benefit the whole sector.

Related to this issue is the concern that scientific and critical perspectives will be less important when heritage is used for social purposes and that history and heritage will be used unreflectively—or even misused. There is also the question of what happens when museums and other heritage organisations work primarily towards social goals. Do they become social service organisations rather than heritage organisations? What are the long-term implications for heritage management practices, such as collecting, preserving, researching, exhibiting and developing heritage? How will the changing practices affect the recruitment and training of heritage professionals when heritage management also includes providing social services? Another concern is what happens when museums and heritage organisations engage with social critique and political action, and, in a way, become activists (Janes and Sandell 2019). How will they know how to act and when? And finally, what is social value anyway? Who decides what is a positive social impact and for whom?

Conclusions

The article presents six case studies on innovative social actions in the heritage sector. These cases have served to illustrate the possibility of studying such initiatives in the framework of social innovation. This approach directs the attention to the innovative aspects of the actions and shows how museums and other heritage organisations can use their heritage resources, expertise and educational skills in combination with new audiences, cross-sectorial partnerships and participatory methods to create social change. In doing so, the organisations are not only enhancing the capabilities of vulnerable groups and diverse communities but also changing the way we understand heritage and heritage management. To gain a deeper understanding of the processes, impact and wider societal implications of heritage-based social innovation, further studies taking a similar approach would be beneficial. For example, what are the key factors when designing successful social actions? What are the main challenges? How can we promote innovativeness and social responsibility in heritage management? As stated earlier, the last few years have seen an increased demand for social innovations in the discussions on how to meet current and future challenges. There is reason to believe that the surge of interest in social innovation will continue and expand into more areas of society; consequently, the need for expertise in innovation creation and innovative solutions will increase as well. I believe that the heritage sector is an area where we can expect a boost in social innovation. To meet this demand and understand how we can adjust to accelerated social changes, we (both researchers and practitioners) need more knowledge on the mechanisms and implications of heritage-based social innovation.

Acknowledgements

This article was presented at the 2018 Association of Critical Heritage Studies (ACHS) Conference in Hangzhou in September 2018, where I organised a session called Applied Heritage Practices and Research Across Sectors to Create Social Change. I would like to thank my fellow speakers—Sandra Uskokovic, Boris Bakal, Ulrika Söderström, and Cornelius Holtorf—and the audience for their encouragement and feedback.

Disclosure Statement

No potential conflict of interest was reported by the author.

Funding

This work was supported by the Swedish Arts Council, Regional Council of Kalmar County and Kalmar County Museum.

Note on Contributor

Carolina Jonsson Malm received her PhD in History from Lund University in 2011. She recently completed her postdoc project on Applied Heritage at Linnaeus University and is currently a research advisor at Malmö University.

□ References

Albert, Marie-Theres (ed.). 2015. *Perceptions of Sustainability in Heritage Studies.* Berlin: Walter De Gruyter GmbH.

André, Isabel, E. B. Henriques, and Jorge Malheiros. 2009. Inclusive Places, Arts and Socially Creative Milieux. In *Social Innovation and Territorial Development,* edited by Diana Maccallum, Frank Moulaert, Jean Hillier, and Serena Vicari, 149-166. Farnham, England: Ashgate Publishing.

Auclair, Elizabeth, and G. J. Fairclough (eds.). 2015. *Theory and Practice in Heritage and Sustainability: Between Past and Future.* New York: Routledge.

Ayob, Noorseha, Simon Teasdale, and Kylie Fagan. 2016. How Social Innovation "Came to Be": Tracing the Evolution of a Contested Concept. *Journal of Social Policy* 45 (4): 635-653.

Bennett, Tony. 1995. *The Birth of the Museum: History, Theory, Politics.* London: Routledge.

BEPA (Bureau of European Policy Advisors). 2010. *Empowering People, Driving Change: Social Innovation in the European Union.* Luxembourg: Publications Office of the European Union.

Black, Graham. 2005. *The Engaging Museum: Developing Museums for Visitor Involvement.* London: Routledge.

Brundenius, Claes, Bo Göransson, and José Manoel Carvalho de Mello (eds.). 2017. *Universities, Inclusive Development and Social Innovation: An International Perspective.* Cham: Springer.

Bund, Eva, David-Karl Hubrich, Björn Schmitz, Georg Mildenberger, and Gorgi Krlev. 2013. *Blueprint of Social Innovation Metrics: Contributions to an Understanding of Opportunities and Challenges of Social Innovation Measurement.* Brussels: European Commission, DG Research.

Cajaiba-Santana, Giovany. 2014. Social Innovation: Moving the Field Forward. A

Conceptual Framework. *Technological Forecasting and Social Change* 82: 42-51.

Carbonell, Bettina Messias (ed.). 2004. *Museum Studies: An Anthology of Contexts.* Malden: Blackwell.

Chatterjee, Helen, and Guy Noble. 2016. *Museums, Health and Well-being.* Abingdon: Routledge.

CHCFE (Cultural Heritage Counts for Europe). 2015. *Cultural Heritage Counts for Europe: Full Report.* Krakow: The International Cultural Centre.

Christidou, Dimitra (ed.). 2014. *Implementing Heritage Learning Outcomes.* Östersund: Jamtliförlag.

Dodd, Jocelyn, and Ceri Jones. 2014. *Mind, Body, Spirit: How Museums Impact Health and Wellbeing.* Leicester: Research Centre for Museums and Galleries.

European Commission. 2018. *Innovation & Cultural Heritage—20 March 2018, Royal Museum of Arts and History, Brussels—Conference Report.* Luxembourg: Publications Office of the European Union.

Fusco Girard, Luigi, Tüzin Baycan, and Peter Nijkamp (eds.). 2011. *Sustainable City and Creativity: Promoting Creative Urban Initiatives.* Farnham, Surrey: Ashgate.

Graham, Brian, G. J. Ashworth, and J. E. Tunbridge. 2000. *A Geography of Heritage: Power, Culture, and Economy.* London: Arnold.

Graham, Brian, and Peter Howard (eds.). 2008. *The Ashgate Research Companion to Heritage and Identity.* Aldershot: Ashgate.

Grimm, Robert, Christopher Fox, Susan Baines, and Kevin Albertson. 2013. Social Innovation, an Answer to Contemporary Societal Challenges? Locating the Concept in Theory and Practice. *Innovation: The European Journal of Social Science Research* 26 (4): 436-455.

Gustafsson, Felicia, and Andreas Netz. 2018. *Social innovation i Sverige: Kartläggning av ekosystemet för social innovation.* Stockholm: Sweden's Innovation Agency.

Harrison, Rodney. 2010. Heritage as Social Action. In *Understanding Heritage in Practice,* edited by Susie West, 240-276. Manchester: Manchester University Press in association with the Open University.

Harrison, Rodney. 2012. *Heritage: Critical Approaches*. London: Routledge.

Ho, Pamela S. Y., and Bob McKercher. 2004. Managing Heritage Resources as Tourism Products. *Asia Pacific Journal of Tourism Research* 9 (3): 255-266.

Holtorf, Cornelius, Andreas Pantazatos, and Geoffrey Scarre (eds.). 2019. *Cultural Heritage, Ethics and Contemporary Migrations*. Abingdon, Oxon: Routledge.

Holtorf, Cornelius, Birgitta E. Gustafsson, and Ebbe Westergren (eds.). 2011. The Social Benefits of Heritage. *Museum International* 63 (1-2): 6-9.

Hooper-Greenhill, Eilean. 1992. *Museums and the Shaping of Knowledge*. London: Routledge.

Howaldt, Jürgen, Christoph Kaletka, Antonius Schröder, and Marthe Zirngiebl (eds.). 2018. *Atlas of Social Innovation—New Practices for a Better Future*. Dortmund: Sozialforschungsstelle, TU Dortmund University.

Janes, Robert R., and Richard Sandell (eds.). 2019. *Museum Activism*. London: Routledge.

Jessop, Bob, Frank Moulaert, Lars Hulgård, and Abdelillah Hamdouch. 2014. Social Innovation Research: A New Stage in Innovation Analysis? In *The International Handbook on Social Innovation: Collective Action, Social Learning and Transdisciplinary Research*, edited by Frank Moulaert, Diana MacCallum, Abid Mehmood, and Abdelillah Hamdouch, 110-130. Cheltenham: Edward Elgar Publishing.

Kearns, Peter, Sofia Kling, and Christina Wistman (eds.). 2011. *Heritage, Regional Development and Social Cohesion*. Östersund: JamtliFörlag.

Labadi, Sophia, and William Logan (eds.). 2016. *Urban Heritage, Development and Sustainability: International Frameworks, National and Local Governance*. London: Routledge/Taylor & Francis Group.

Logan, William, Máiréad Nic Craith, and Ullrich Kockel (eds.). 2016. *A Companion to Heritage Studies*. Chichester, West Sussex, UK: Wiley-Blackwell.

Macdonald, Sharon (ed.). 2006. *A Companion to Museum Studies*. Chichester: Wiley-Blackwell.

Marques, Pedro, Kevin Morgan, and Ranald Richardson. 2017. Social Innovation in Question: The Theoretical and Practical Implications of a Contested Concept. *Environment and Planning C: Politics and Space* 36 (3): 496-512.

Marstine, Janet. 2005. *New Museum Theory and Practice: An Introduction*. Malden: Blackwell.

Message, Kylie. 2006. *New Museums and the Making of Culture*. Oxford: Berg.

Moulaert, Frank, Abid Mehmood, Diana MacCallum, and Bernhard Leubolt (eds.). 2017. *Social Innovation as a Trigger for Transformations—The Role of Research*. Luxembourg: Publications Office of the European Union.

Moulaert, Frank, Diana MacCallum, Abid Mehmood, and Abdelillah Hamdouch (eds.). 2014. *The International Handbook on Social Innovation: Collective Action, Social Learning and Transdisciplinary Research*. Cheltenham: Edward Elgar Publishing.

Murray, Robin, Julie Caulier-Grice, and Geoff Mulgan. 2010. *The Open Book of Social Innovation*. London: National Endowment for Science, Technology and the Art.

Nicholls, Alex, Julie Simon, and Madeleine Gabriel (eds.). 2015. *New Frontiers in Social Innovation Research*. Basingstoke: Palgrave Macmillan.

Peers, Laura, and Alison K. Brown (eds.). 2003. *Museums and Source Communities: A Routledge Reader*. London: Routledge.

Pestoff, Victor. 2009. Towards a Paradigm of Democratic Participation: Citizen Participation and Co-production of Personal Social Services in Sweden. *Annals of Public and Cooperative Economics* 80 (2):197-224.

Sandell, Richard. 2007. *Museums, Prejudice and the Reframing of Difference*. London: Routledge.

Sandell, Richard, and Eithne Nightingale (eds.). 2012. *Museums, Equality and Social Justice*. London: Routledge.

Santos, Paula Assunção dos. 2007. *Museology and Community Development in the XXI Century*. Lisbon: Edições Universitárias Lusófonas.

Sevcenko, Liz. 2010. Sites of Conscience: New Approaches to Conflicted Memory. *Museum*

International 62 (1/2): 20-25.

Silverman, Helaine, Emma Waterton, and Steve Watson (eds.). 2017. *Heritage in Action: Making the Past in the Present.* Cham: Springer International Publishing.

Smith, Laurajane. 2006. *Uses of Heritage.* Abingdon: Routledge.

Smith, Laurajane. 2012. Editorial. *International Journal of Heritage Studies* 18 (6): 533-540.

Söderström, Ulrika. 2018. *Contract Archaeology and Sustainable Development: Between Policy and Practice.* Växjö: Linnaeus University Press.

The Ministry of Enterprise and Innovation. 2018. *Regeringens strategi för sociala företag: Ett hållbart samhälle genom socialt företagande och social innovation.* Stockholm: The Government Offices of Sweden.

The Young Foundation. 2012. *Social Innovation Overview: A Deliverable of the Project: "The Theoretical, Empirical and Policy Foundations for Building Social Innovation in Europe" (TEPSIE), European Commission 7th Framework Programme.* Brussels: European Commission, DG Research.

Tremblay, Diane-Gabrielle, and Thomas Pilati. 2014. Social Innovation through Arts and Creativity. In *The International Handbook on Social Innovation: Collective Action, Social Learning and Transdisciplinary Research*, edited by Frank Moulaert, Diana MacCallum, Abid Mehmood, and Abdelillah Hamdouch, 67-79. Cheltenham: Edward Elgar Publishing.

Watson, Sheila (ed.). 2007. *Museums and their Communities.* London: Routledge.

Westergren, Ebbe. 2017. Use the Past, Create the Future—The Time Travel Method, a Tool for Learning, Social Cohesion and Community Building. In *The Archaeology of Time Travel: Experiencing the Past in the 21st Century*, edited by Bodil Petersson, and Cornelius Holtorf, 89-112. Oxford: Archaeopress.

Westley, Frances, Katherine McGowan, and Ola Tjörnbo (eds.). 2017. *The Evolution of Social Innovation Building Resilience Through Transitions.* Cheltenham: Edward Elgar Publishing.

Winter, Tim. 2013. Clarifying the Critical in Critical Heritage Studies. *International Journal of Heritage Studies* 19 (6): 532-545.

Witcomb, Andrea. 2003. *Re-imagining the Museum: Beyond the Mausoleum.* London and New York: Routledge.

Witcomb, Andrea, and Kristal Buckley AM. 2013. Engaging with the Future of "Critical Heritage Studies": Looking Back in Order to Look Forward. *International Journal of Heritage Studies* 19 (6): 562-578.

Wittmayer, Julia, Bonno Pel, Tom Bauler, and Flor Avelino. 2017. Editorial Synthesis: Methodological Challenges in Social Innovation Research. *European Public & Social Innovation Review* 2 (1): 1-16.

Zipsane, Henrik, 2008. Lifelong Learning Through Heritage and Art. In *The Routledge International Handbook of Lifelong Learning,* edited by Peter Jarvis, 173-182. London: Routledge.

Challenges of Research on Trans-Boundary Cultural Heritage in Southern Africa

Munukayumbwa Munyima

University of Zambia, Institute of Economic and Social Research Plot 2631, Munali Road, Chudleigh, P. O. Box 30900, Lusaka, Zambia. CONTACT Munukayumbwa Munyima: m.munyima@unza.zm

Abstract: Despite neighbouring countries in Africa sharing common cultural heritage, they have faced challenges of how to jointly better manage these resources. Most of these challenges can be better understood and addressed by carrying-out collaborative research involving countries sharing the heritage. Through a review of literature and the author's work experience in the field of heritage management in Zambia and Southern Africa, factors that hinder research on cultural heritage have been discussed. From discussions at different fora and reports by heritage professionals, there seems to be consensus that not much research is being undertaken in the area of cultural heritage. As a contribution to this discourse, this article attempts to answer the following questions: To what extent does government policy affect transboundary research on cultural heritage? To what extent does politics affect cultural heritage research? Do internal and external conflicts affect research on cultural heritage? Do economic conditions influence resource allocation to cultural heritage research? Is the attitude of heritage managers affecting research on cultural heritage? It is concluded that to prioritise cultural heritage research,

Southern African countries will have to begin funding this area using locally generated resources, as opposed to dependence on international support.

Keywords: cultural heritage, collaborative research, heritage professionals, trans-boundary

Introduction

Many neighbouring countries in Africa share a lot of common heritage, both cultural and natural. To better manage this heritage requires that experts in this field must have a clear understanding of both intrinsic and extrinsic factors surrounding the significance of these resources. This understanding can only be made possible through research. Unfortunately, research is largely not considered a priority by many African governments and this is more so as it pertains to cultural heritage. Intergovernmental organisations such as the United Nations Educational, Scientific and Cultural Orgnaisation (UNESCO) have, in the recent past, collaborated with national institutions in the Southern African region to build capacity among heritage experts and also to promote heritage (Chirikure 2013: 1). However, this effort does not seem to have provided much help in the area of research. This is because the people responsible for managing heritage have not considered research as a priority. They have focused mainly on the protection, conservation and promotion of the heritage. Notwithstanding, all these interventions can be better executed from an empirically informed standpoint through research.

This article attempts to examine why despite all the effort being directed towards protection and management of cross-border cultural heritage, there is insufficient research carried out to help in planning for and managing these resources. The article identifies key factors that could be making research on cultural heritage difficult to undertake in the Southern African region. The thrust of the article will be on identifying key trans-boundary culture heritage in the Southern African region, examining factors that hinder research on cultural heritage, and finally suggesting ways in which cultural heritage research can be enhanced in Southern Africa.

Justification

For a very long time, heritage protection has been seen as a hindrance to development or civilisation (Mabulla and Bower 2010: 33-39; Munyima 1993: 37-38). This has been from a national development planning point of view. At cross-border level, the issue becomes even more complicated and yet cultural heritage, particularly the intangible aspects, including language, cuts across borders. As such, cultural heritage can play a significant role in promoting regional integration in Southern Africa. Therefore, the downplaying of the significance of cultural heritage is largely due to the fact that many people, including decision makers, do not understand and appreciate the importance of cultural heritage.

Understanding and appreciation of the heritage field can only be achieved by providing empirical information which will highlight the cultural, economic and educational value to countries that share these resources. This can only be possible through research. However, while research on heritage has not been the focus of most heritage resource managers, commissioning research that relates to cultural heritage domiciled beyond national boundaries in the Southern African region is bound to encounter a number of challenges. It is these challenges that this article attempts to identify and discuss their negative effect on heritage protection, management and promotion in the region. In so doing, it is hoped that this article will stimulate debate among heritage professionals. Debate that will lead to the development of measures is aimed at not only promoting research on cross-border heritage but also providing solutions for the collaborative management of these resources.

Method of Study

This article is largely based on the author's more than 20 years working experience in the field of cultural heritage in Zambia and sharing of similar experiences with cultural heritage professionals from other countries within Southern Africa. A review of literature on the subject of research in the field of cultural heritage in Africa and other parts of the world has also contributed to informing this article.

Discussions in this article are arranged in three main parts. The part that follows immediately below presents the main types of cultural heritage found across borders in the Southern African region. The next part identifies and discusses challenges that affect cultural heritage research in this region while the part that follows it discusses how to manage these challenges. The last part presents the conclusions.

Types of Trans-Boundary Cultural Heritage

Cultural heritage has been defined differently by many authorities in different countries (Alzahrani 2013: 9-10). The word "cultural" is derived from "culture", a term that has equally been defined differently by different scholars. In 1952, Kroeber and Kluckhohn were reported to have reviewed more than 164 concepts and definitions of the term, "culture" (Spencer-Oatey 2012: 1). Within the context of this article, the Southern African Development Cooperation (SADC) Protocol on Culture, Information and Sport (2001: 4) defines culture as:

The totality of people's way of life, the whole complex of distinctive spiritual, material, intellectual and emotional features that characterize a society or social group, includes not only arts and literature, but also modes of life, the fundamental rights of human being, value systems traditions and beliefs.

For the purpose of this study, however, cultural heritage shall be defined as "the entire corpus of material or non-material signs or elements, either artistic or symbolic as well as manifestations of civil works that have been handed down from one generation of humankind to another".

Having multiple definitions implies that cultural heritage can be divided into different classifications. In the present case, the cultural heritage that is found across borders in Southern Africa can be divided in two main classifications, namely movable and immovable cultural heritage, each of which can further be divided into another classification of tangible and intangible cultural heritage.

Movable and Immovable Cultural Heritage

Movable cultural heritage would include objects or structures (tools, artefacts, instruments, sculptures, weapons, utensils, vessels, fabrics, etc.) and beliefs, skills, expressions that can, respectively, be moved or moved with from one place to another. Immovable cultural heritage would include fixed features or spaces associated with cultural beliefs of local traditional communities (shrines, places of worship, burial sites, hunting/fishing grounds, workspaces, initiation sites, celebration arenas, architectural works, etc.).

Tangible and Intangible Cultural Heritage

Tangible cultural heritage could either be movable or immovable. Movable tangible cultural heritage would include objects or structures as listed above while immovable tangible cultural heritage would include natural feature such as rock outcrops, landscapes, plantations or trees as well as built structures associated with cultural beliefs or events (Jokilehto 2005: 2).

Intangible cultural heritage (ICH) has been defined as practices, representations, expressions, knowledge, skills—as well as the instruments, objects, artefacts and cultural spaces associated therewith—that communities, groups and, in some cases, individuals recognise as part of their cultural heritage. Intangible cultural heritage could be said to be transmitted from generation to generation and is constantly recreated by communities and/ or groups in response to their environments, their interaction with nature, and their history (UNESCO 2003: 5).

Prominent Cross-Border Cultural Heritage in Southern Africa

Many forms of cultural heritage are shared across borders in the Southern African region. A few of them such as the Makishi masquerade and the Gule Wamukulu are inscribed on the UNESCO Representative List. Makishi masquerade cultural heritage associated with the initiation of boys into adulthood belongs to the Luvale people that are found in the northwestern parts of Zambia and the bordering parts of Angola. Gule Wamukulu is an age-old cultural, but secret-society dance performed while wearing masks as a disguise. The dance is performed by the Chewa ethnic group that is found in Malawi, Mozambique and Zambia. Another prominent cross-border cultural heritage is the Nyaminyami, a mythological rock outcrop that has been submerged by water in the man-made Kariba dam. The Nyaminyami is observed by the Tonga ethnic group that is found in Zambia and Zimbabwe.

Perhaps the most common of all cross-border cultural heritage in Southern Africa is the Mbira (or thumb piano). In fact some sources indicate that this musical instrument, also known as *Kalimba, Karimba* or *Kanombyo* among ethnic groups of Southern Africa, is believed to be present in countries as far as West Africa (Holdaway 2008). Mbira is also known as *likembe* and *sanza* in the Democratic Republic of the Congo, *kadongo* and *akogo* in Uganda and *kalimba* in Kenya (Florek 2014).

Apart from the identifiable specific culture heritage described above, many ethnic groups in Southern Africa are found in more than one country. As such they share a compendium of common cultural heritage beliefs, materials and practices across the geographical boundaries of countries. One example is the San ethnic group that is found across the borders of Botswana, Namibia, and South Africa. These ethnic groups share a composite movable and immovable, tangible and intangible cultural heritage that includes rock engravings and paintings, contemporary art, handicrafts, dance, beliefs as well as music (Bolaane 2014: 11-12). Other ethnic groups that share similar cultural heritage across borders are the Chewa in Malawi, Mozambique and Zambia; the Subiya in Namibia and Zambia; the Tonga in Zambia and Zimbabwe as well as the Lunda of Mwata Kazembe in

Zambia and the Democratic Republic of the Congo.

Table 1 summarises the most common cross-border cultural heritage found in Southern Africa.

Table 1   Selected cross-border cultural heritage in Southern Africa

Name of cultural heritage	Classification 1		Classification 2		Country commonly found
	Movable	Immovable	Tangible	Intangible	
Gule Wamukulu	√	×	√	√	Malawi, Mozambique, Zambia
Makishi masquerade	√	×	√	√	Angola, Zambia
Mbira	√	×	√	×	Angola, Botswana, Malawi, Namibia, Zambia, Zimbabwe
Nyaminyami	×	√	√	√	Zambia, Zimbabwe
Culture heritage of the San ethnic group	√	√	√	√	Botswana, Namibia, South Africa
Cultural heritage of the Subiya ethnic group	√	√	√	√	Namibia, Zambia
Cultural heritage of the Chewa ethnic group	√	√	√	√	Malawi, Mozambique, Zambia
Cultural heritage of the Lunda ethnic group of Mwata Kazembe	√	√	√	√	Congo DR, Zambia

Research on all categories and sub-categories of trans-boundary cultural heritage in Southern Africa is bound to be affected by similar challenges. The next section discusses how these challenges affect research in this part of Africa.

Challenges of Cross-Border Cultural Heritage Research

Cross-border cultural heritage research is facing many challenges. To have a better understanding of these challenges will depend on two main facts. First, it is important to appreciate that geographical borders are the sovereign "interface" between countries (Henrikson 2010). They operate as filters to the exchanges taking place between countries and regional borders. Their degree of openness, which can evolve over time, depends, to a large extent, on the relationship between respective countries. In the case of the cultural heritage of cross-border ethnic groups, members of the local community have little control over how it is managed and what happens to it in the neighbouring country. Who decides what should be considered to be valuable cultural heritage and how it should be preserved? Who determines how much cultural heritage contributes to the development of the local community and the country at large? What would happen if, due to the influence of modernity, ethnic groups decided that they no longer wanted to protect their own heritage? All these questions can only be answered by conducting research.

While many neighbouring countries in Africa share some elements of cultural heritage, carrying out research on these trans-boundary resources is often a challenge. This is mostly because of the differences in governance structures and policies related to management of research in the area of heritage in each country. Experience has also shown that even where there are similarities in governance and research policies, researchers in the field of heritage still face challenges because of the lack of appropriate provisions for cooperation in the available bilateral or multilateral agreements. Why is this so? Preliminary investigations show that in Africa, researchers in the field of heritage are rarely involved in the consultation process of developing cooperative agreements between or among countries. In this regard, therefore, there arise a number of questions: How can researchers in the field of heritage be included in relevant transnational cooperation programmes? How can the process of engagement be made more inclusive at all levels? How is the problem of trans-boundary research on heritage being handled in other parts of the world?

Second, it is a well-known fact that the field of heritage protection has not been given sufficient resources when compared with other aspects of development such as education, health and social protection. To bring out the significance of heritage and how to manage it best, there is a need to carry out research. However, with so many needs competing for the few resources provided to the heritage sub-sector, research in this area particularly in Southern Africa has not been sufficiently supported. Chirikure (2013: 1) observes that due to scarcity of resources, institutions and/or departments that manage heritage are understaffed, and most of their staff are inexperienced. In this regard, many of them do not have the capacity to carry out research which will inform decisions regarding the heritage that they manage. While this has some truth, the main challenges that hinder cultural heritage research in this part of Africa have to do with government policies, political expedience, internal or external conflicts, as well as unfavourable economic conditions and, to a large extent, the attitude of heritage managers.

Government Policies

As a general principle emanating from the African Union (AU), Cultural Charter for Africa, Article 13 of the SADC Protocol on Culture, Information and Sport provides that:

State Parties shall establish policy guidelines for the preservation and promotion of cultural heritage of the region in all its multi-furious facets formulated in close collaboration with relevant stakeholders, and shall seek to harmonise such guidelines in the interest of mutually beneficial integration of the Region. (SADC 2001: 10)

Similarly, the African Charter for African Cultural Renaissance, a revised version of the Cultural Charter for Africa, encourages members of the AU to develop and manage cultural policies through in-depth renewal of regional approaches. Such approaches are those that would include innovations and intellectual engagement as well as those that would provide education, resources, improved specialist training, cultural research centres and exchange programmes to all African people (AU 2006). This Charter is particularly important to enhance cross-border research as it calls for all African states to promote and foster a mutual undersatnding that will resist any form of cultural exclusion of oppression in Africa and to defend minorities, their cultures, their rights and their fundamental freedoms. This includes the creation of an enabling environment that will enhance the creation, protection, production and distribution of cultural works within the context of the rest of the world.

However, all these regional and continental provisions have not been followed by supportive policies at the national level. It would appear, countries in the region still prefer to develop their cultural heritage related policies in isolation and without referring to the guidelines provided by the SADC Protocol. This situation is worsened by the fact that both the regional and continental bodies do not have mechanisms for ensuring compliance and neither do they have the power nor means to impose sanctions on noncompliant member states.

Despite the good intentions of the regional and continental bodies, their inability to ensure compliance by member states has made it difficult to achieve cooperation in a number of areas including research on cultural heritage. As a result of this failure, most of the legal frameworks on cultural heritage operating in many Southern African countries have not been regularly revised and therefore remain quite detached from modern principles that seek to preserve and promote cultural heritage in the most sustainable way. This could be attributed to the fact that many of these countries particularly in Southern Africa appear not to consider cultural heritage as a priority. This is evidenced by the fact that a number of existing bilateral and multilateral agreements do not provide explicit mechanism for joint cultural heritage preservation and promotion. For example, all Joint Permanent Commissions between Zambia and her neighbours, namely Angola, Botswana, Malawi, Mozambique, Namibia and Zimbabwe are only focused on defence, security, and economic activities to the exclusion of culture heritage. If cultural heritage is excluded in these agreements, at what stage can the affected countries begin to discuss cooperation in this area? It is this cooperation that would enable the affected countries to collaborate in setting standards that are going to facilitate and support research on the shared cultural heritage.

Political Expedience

In Southern Africa, the cultural heritage that receives some attention is that which is state prioritised either from the political or economic point of view. Cultural heritage that is prioritised from the political point of view is mainly that which signifies the party in government's authority. It is for this reason that since the turn of the 20th Century, cultural and natural heritage elements associated with the liberation struggles in many parts of Africa were institutionalised (Manetsi 2017: 24). However, from the political point of view, research on such elements is often supported when the anticipated out-come will enhance the standing of the political part in power. For example, at a campaign rally in an opposition stronghold, the Vice President of Zambia, Mrs Inonge Wina warned the electorates that they would not get any government support if they continued voting for opposition representatives[1].

In many Southern African countries, traditional leaders, as custodian of cultural heritage, bear an important role of safeguarding the culture and traditions of their respective ethnic groups. For this reason, these leaders carry distinguished authority and influence over their subjects who, in most cases, have varying political inclinations (Ntonzima and Bayat 2012). As such, the role of the chiefs is expected to transcend political boundaries within and in some cases across national boundaries. For example, Paramount Chief Gawa Undi of the Chewa ethnic group in the Katete district of Eastern Zambia has authority over chiefs across the border between Malawi and Mozambique. Therefore, he has authority over the cultural heritage of the Chewa ethnic group in all the three countries. The Paramount Chief's standing with those with political power in each of these countries will ultimately have ramifications on how research on the Chewa cultural heritage can be conducted, and politicians know this. With this knowledge, politicians have taken advantage of the relationship between traditional leaders and their subjects for political expedience by promising favours to those that support them politically and denying such to those that are neutral or have opposing views. According to Baldwin (2013: 795) the embeddedness of patrons (traditional leaders) with their subjects gives them the capacity to broker relationships between voters and politicians which in this case implies giving votes to those seeking political office in return for a favour in the distribution of public resources for the development of the community. In this case, traditional leaders that do not openly support the government of the day may be denied resources that would otherwise go towards research on the cultural heritage of their communities. This is all because many African politicians are pre-occupied with greed for authority and power, and will therefore only commit resources to areas that will enhance their hold to political power.

Internal and External Conflicts

Intolerance and poor management of diversities in ethnic, religion and cultural heritage issues that seem to be at variance with preferred positions of decision makers could be one of the main causes of conflict within and across borders on the African continent. Where there is conflict, it is difficult to carry out objective cultural heritage research without the host community being suspicious of your activities. McClelland (2016) makes similar observations over the EU referendum debate which has revealed the distance and mistrust between people and the political establishment, exposing suspicions of expert knowledge while confirming societal differences based on geography, demography and other socio-economic indicators.

As observed earlier in this article, some ethnic groups in the region have composite cultural heritage that transcends national boundaries. This implies that research on the cultural heritage of ethnic groups that spread across-borders cannot be objectively carried out when one side of the border is at war. For example, because of the conflict currently occurring in the Democratic Republic of the Congo, it will be difficult to carry out a meaningful research on the cultural heritage of the Lunda ethnic group of Mwata Kazembe whose culture spreads across the boundary into Zambia. It is for this reason that AU's Agenda 2063, provides frameworks for managing diversities at the national and continental levels. At the national level, "Aspiration 4, goal 13, priority area (1) Maintenance and Restoration of Peace and Security" requires development of policies and strategies at the national level for the management of ethnicity, exclusiveness and religious fanaticism (AU 2015).

The devastating effects of war on cultural heritage are visible in Iran, Syria and many other countries in the Middle East. This is because, these effects are often documented and are in public domain, a situation that is rarely the case when it comes to cultural heritage in Africa. To make matters worse, even the custodians of cultural heritage, in many cases, do not know what to do to protect the value and integrity of their heritage during conflict. In a study by Abara (n.d.: 383) results show that a lack of awareness for the need to secure and protect their own cultural heritage is common among custodians and practitioners in Africa. In this process, a lot of meaning and significance in cultural heritage resources is lost, hence making it a challenge for researchers to collect verifiable information.

During conflict, another challenge in the area of cultural heritage research is that of inadequate time to carry out thorough academic research, as there is always pressure to collect as much information as possible within the shortest possible time. In such instances, reputable researchers would not want to have their names associated with rushed up research. When this happens it gives room to consultant (commercial) researchers who often do not pay attention to detail and ethical issues and thereby compromising the quality of research. Referring to researchers in the field of archaeological heritage, for example, Raab, in Arazi (2009: 97), identifies pressure of fierce commercial competition as they reason why many contract archaeologists have little time to keep up with important research advances. In the process, Raab further observes, such researchers churn out reports that seldom contain information that is widely circulated or appears in peer-reviewed publications.

To help in improving the quality of interventions aimed at protecting and managing both cultural and natural heritage, particularly in conflict, post-conflict and natural disaster situations, the African World Heritage Fund (AWHF) was launched (World Heritage Committee 2005). The main objective of the Fund is to develop a strategy for dealing with the challenges faced by African countries in the implementation of the World Heritage Convention. Among the objectives laid down for the fund is to provide support and assistance for the conservation and management of heritage sites in Africa, particularly, but not restricted to those already inscribed on the World Heritage List (Kiriama 2014: 17).

Unfavourable Economic Conditions

The prevailing economic conditions of a country will have a direct effect on that country's ability to fund research on cultural heritage. As many countries in Southern Africa, with the exception of South Africa have, in the last decade, been struggling to achieve some meaningful economic development, the distribution of resources is skewed towards economic growth sectors such as agriculture, mining, commerce and, in a broader sense, tourism (Chirikure 2013: 2; Eveleigh 2013: 15). It is through the tourism sector that cultural heritage protection and management, including research, the subject of this article, are funded.

The question, however, is how much of the funds allocated to the tourism sector goes to cultural heritage research. In Zambia, for example, out of ZMK 38.65 billion (about USD 129 million) that was allocated to the tourism sector in 2013, less than ZMK 1 billion (about USD 3.35 million) was apportioned to a basket of four programmatic areas that included research on both cultural and natural heritage (Munyima 2013: 101-102).

For as long as the economic benefit of preserving cultural heritage is mostly indirect and very difficult to measure, public funding for heritage protection and management in many Southern African countries will continue to be marginal. With this scenario, many countries with low Gross Domestic Product (GDP) will have a challenge to take away resources from sectors that may have immediate and direct economic benefits and allocate them cultural heritage research and all the activities that go along with the research. With insufficient resources, cultural heritage researchers will most likely use any little they get to carry out their work without involving the local people. When this happens, the local people tend to be uncooperative and will not, in the best of situation, provide the necessary information required by the research and in the worst situation they will be hostile to the researchers.

Attitude of Heritage Managers

The attitude of heritage managers in many countries of Southern Africa also contributes to the challenges faced in cultural heritage research. This is in two ways. First, many heritage professionals will not look for solutions from within their country, region or African continent.

They will, instead, look for solutions from overseas and in most cases such solutions are not sustainable for the long term—regardless of whether the funding is from AWHF or any other funding source such as the Flanders government, they all have a lifespan. As a result, heritage professionals remain perpetually searching for more overseas donations to run their programmes, hence leaving with no time to carry out research. Second, some of the heritage managers are in the profession simply to make money. As observed by Chirikure (2013: 2), a number of heritage institutions in Southern Africa are struggling with the issue of governance. This, Chirikure further observes, is because the priority for most of the managers of these institutions is attending meetings and conferences abroad at the expense of improving the status of the heritage that they were employed to manage.

Solving Challenges of Research on Cross-Border Cultural Heritage

To address some of the concerns regarding the challenges of research on heritage, some countries have begun to take advantage of existing global programmes such as those under UNESCO to leverage international cooperation in this area. For example, in the area of ICH, with the support of UNESCO and the Flanders government of Belgium, the Southern Africa Intangible Cultural Heritage (SAICH) platform, comprising seven countries in this region, has begun cooperating to formulate standard guidelines and policies that will not only help in the safeguard and management of ICH in the Southern African region but also support research and academic undertakings among related institutions. The seven countries are Botswana, Lesotho, Malawi, Namibia, Swaziland, Zambia and Zimbabwe. To support the effort of these countries in the area of capacity building, the University of Zambia, with the assistance of UNESCO, through its request for International Assistance Programme, has in 2019 introduced a Bachelor's degree programme aimed at strengthening capacity of the country and others in the region to safeguard ICH and manage all related activities independently. A Master's degree programme is expected to be introduced as soon as the first cohort of undergraduates has graduated.

At the continental level, the AU's Agenda 2063 aspires (Aspiration 5) for an "Africa with a strong cultural identity, common heritage, values and ethics: inculcating the spirit of Pan Africanism; tapping Africa's rich heritage and culture to ensure that the creative arts are major contributors to Africa's growth and transformation; and restoring and preserving Africa's cultural heritage, including its languages". In this regard, both the AU and SADC ought to put affirmative action by each introducing a chair for culture to provide guidance and provide financial support for cultural heritage management and research, particularly, across borders. Further, to build capacity among heritage professionals, the SADC needs to put in place deliberate measures that will encourage more universities in the region to introduce courses in heritage management.

At the national level, the aspiration of the AU and provisions of the SADC Protocol on Culture, Information and Sport will not come to fruition if individual countries do not make an effort to formulate policies that will actuate Africa's cultural identity and promote the continent's common heritage. Such policies should provide for a mechanism through which local communities who are the custodians of our cultural heritage can be meaningfully involved in heritage conservation and management. This is because, while cultural heritage professionals' interest protects cultural heritage for sustainable utilisation and posterity, the local communities have a different perspective about this. To local communities, cultural heritage is a lifestyle, a place of work, a place of worship, a grazing area for domestic animals, a resting place of ancestor and many other perspectives (Chikumbi et al. 2009: 58).

Strong national policies on cultural heritage will not only encourage and facilitate the participation of local communities, but will also provide an enabling environment for heritage and academic institutions to lobby government and local private sector for support to cultural heritage management in general and cultural heritage research in particular.

As a way of reducing dependence on overseas support, African countries, through the AU, must endeavour to increase funding to the AWHF for the institution to provide the much needed financial and technical support for heritage management. The AWHF, if well supported, and as an African initiative, has the potential to positively impact on the volume and quality of trans-boundary cultural heritage research. With evidence-based information

322

on cultural heritage, heritage professionals will be in a better position to influence positive perceptions and depoliticise government decisions pertaining to this area.

Conclusions

That over the years, a significant amount of investment in heritage conservation has been made is not deniable. However, what is of concern is that a large portion of this investment has been supported and influenced from outside Africa. As a result, these investments have been directed only towards the funders' interests, and research has not been among them. Research is one of the surest ways to bring out the significance and intrinsic value of, particularly, cultural heritage so that it can be understood and appreciated and therefore supported by decision makers who have all along given a lip service to the field of heritage protection and management.

It has been established, in this article, that many aspects of cultural heritage in Africa are connected to living communities. Therefore, the involvement of these communities in deciding how their heritage is to be managed is cardinal to the success of heritage management in totality from documentation, research, protection and up to promotion. To this end, and given that a substantial amount of cultural heritage spreads across borders in Southern Africa, improved regional cooperation in this area will be the best way to pool resources for joint research activities.

While there have been significant challenges in carrying out cultural heritage research among countries in Southern Africa, introducing a "Chair" for culture at the SADC secretariat might help to stimulate affirmative actions towards the regional body's Protocol on Culture, Information and Sport at the national level. This is because challenges of research on cultural heritage can best be tackled by home-grown solutions. In all this, what is cardinal is to get private sectors involved in supporting the management and promotion of cultural heritage for sustainable utilisation.

The long term solution to the challenges of cultural heritage is to get African universities to introduce courses in heritage conservation and management using their local experience. Such courses should include disciplines such as planning, environmental studies, conservation research and heritage promotion for them to best prepare graduates for the task ahead. Training heritage experts at the highest levels will help to encourage critical thinking in the field of heritage which will, in turn, promote research. Findings of research will help heritage managers to generate home-grown best practices for managing African cultural heritage in the Southern African region.

Note

1. Lusaka Times, August 18, 2018.

☐ Acknowledgements

First, I thank the orgnaisers of the 2018 Association of Critical Heritage Studies (ACHS) Conference for the initiative to publish the conference proceedings as a book. Second, Ms. Gertrude Ngenda who, at short notice, agreed to proofread this manuscript in readiness for submission is greatly appreciated. Finally, I acknowledge the space and time that my employers, the University of Zambia and particularly those at my work station, the Institute of Economic and Social Research, provided for me to complete this work.

☐ Funding

My participation in the 2018 ACHS Conference was made possible by funding from the United Nations Educational, Scientific and Cultural Organisation (UNESCO) through their sponsorship of my PhD progamme and the Embassy of the Republic of China that provided me with an air ticket for a round trip to Hangzhou.

☐ Note on Contributor

Munukayumbwa Munyima is a research fellow in the Socio-cultural Research Programme at the University of Zambia's Institute of Economic and Social Research. He is a holder of Master of Letters in Cultural Anthropology from James Cook University and is currently a Sociology PhD candidate at the University of Zambia. His areas of interests are socio-economics, conservation and management of cultural resources, and tourism development. Previously, he worked for the National Heritage Conservation Commission in Zambia for a period of 18 years during which he served in positions that ranged from Conservation Anthropologist to Regional Director. He is an ICH expert and is currently leading a team of University of Zambia academics developing and implementing a Bachelor of Arts degree in ICH.

⬜ References

Abara, Julie Chinwe. n.d. The Challenges of Safeguarding and Securing Cultural Heritage Materials During Violent Conflict in Nigeria. In *Proceedings of the II International Conference on Best Practices in World Heritage: People and Communities*, 375-386. Madrid: Universidad Complutense de Madrid.

Alzahrani, D. A. 2013. The Adoption of a Standard Definition of Cultural Heritage. *International Journal of Social Science and Humanity* 3 (1): 9-12.

Arazi, Noemie. 2009. Cultural Research Management in Africa: Challenges, Dangers and Opportunities. *Azania: Archaeological Research in Africa* 44 (1): 95-106.

AU (African Union). 2006. African Union Charter for African Cultural Renaissance. January 24, 2006. Accessed May 22, 2019. https://au.int/sites/default/files/pages/32901-file-01_charter african_cultural_renaissance_en.pdf.

AUC (African Union Commission). 2015. Agenda 2063: The Africa We Want. Accessed May 22, 2019. http://www.un.org/en/africa/osaa/pdf/au/agenda2063-first10yearimplementation.pdf.

AWHF (African World Heritage Fund). 2013. World Heritage and Impacts of Development in Africa. Accessed May 22, 2019. http://awhf.net/wp-content/uploads/2015/10/Final-publication-Extractive-Industries.pdf.

Baldwin, Kate. 2013. Why Vote with the Chief? Political Connections and Public Goods Provision in Zambia. *American Journal of Political Science* 57 (4): 794-809.

BOLAANE, Maitseo. 2014. San Cross-Border Cultural Heritage and Identity in Botswana, Namibia and South Africa. *African Study Monographs* 35 (1): 41-64.

Chikumbi, Donald C., Nicholas M. Katanekwa, Anne Hege Simonsen, and Inger A. Heldal (eds.). 2009. Cultural Heritage, Celebrating 10 Years of Institutional Cooperation. Accessed May 23, 2019. https://core.ac.uk/reader/52074854.

Chirikure, Shadreck. 2013. Heritage Conservation in Africa: The Good, the Bad, and the Challenges. *Southern African Journal of Science* 109 (1/2): 16-18.

Eveleigh, Melissa. 2013. Stakeholder Research: Funding Analysis—Modes of Engagement. Accessed May 23, 2019. https://africalia.be/assets/files/ZIM-ARTS-CULTURE-FUNDING-STREAMS.pdf.

Florek, Stan. 2014. Mbira—Thumb Piano of Africa: Ancient instrument with a promising future, Australian Museum. Accessed November 29, 2017. https://australianmuseum.net.au/mbira-thumb-piano-of-africa.

Henrikson, K. Alan 2011. Border Regions as Neighbourhoods. In *The Ashgate Research Companion to Border Studies,* edited by Doris Wastl-Walter, 85-102. Farnham and Burlington: Ashgate Publishing Limited.

Holdaway, Mark. 2008. The Kalimba: A Brief History of an Ancient Instrument from Africa. Accessed November 29, 2017. http://www.kalimbamagic.com/newsletters/newsletter4.02/newsletter4.02_assets/KalimbaHistoryII.pdf.

Kariama, O. Herman. 2014. The Role of the African World Heritage Fund in the Conservation of African World Heritage Sites. In *The Management of Cultural World Heritage Sites and Development in Africa, Simon Makuvaza,* 17-32. New York and London: Springer.

Mabulla, Z. P. Audax, and John F. R. Bower. 2010. Cultural Heritage Management in Tanzania's Protected Areas: Challenges and Future Prospects. *CRM: The Journal of Heritage Stewardship* 7 (1): 27-45.

Manetsi, Thabo. 2017. State-Prioritised Heritage: Governmentality, Heritage Management and the Prioritisation of Liberation Heritage in Post-Colonial South Africa. Doctoral Disseration, University of Cape Town. Accessed May 22, 2019. https://open.uct.ac.za/bitstream/handle/11427/27334/thesis_hum_2017_manetsi_thabo.pdf?sequence=1&isAllowed=y.

McClelland, G. Andrew. 2016. The Management of Heritage in Contested Cross-Border Contexts: Emerging Research on the Island of Ireland. *The Journal of Cross Border Studies in Ireland* 11: 91-104.

Munyima, K. M. 1993. Heritage Protection and Development Planning. Master's Thesis,

James Cook University, Townsville.

Munyima, Munukayumbwa. 2013. Policy Pronouncements Versus Resource Allocation: The Case of 2010-2013 Tourism Sector Development in Zambia. *African Social Research* 57/58: 89-110.

Ntonzima, Lulamile, and Mohamed Sayeed Bayat. 2012. The Role of Traditional Leaders in South Africa—A Relic of the Past, or a Contemporary Reality? *Arabian Journal of Business and Management Review (OMAN Chapter)* 1 (6): 88-108.

SADC (Southern African Development Cooperation). 2001. Southern African Development Community, Protocol on Culture, Information and Sport. August 14, 2001. Accessed May 22, 2019. http://www.sadc.int/files/3213/5292/8362/ Protocol on_ Culture_ Information_and_Sport2001.pdf.

Spencer-Oatey, H. 2012. *What is Culture? A Compilation of Quotations*. Coventry: GlobalPAD, University of Warwick.

"Tolerance" in Urgent Need of Conservation: A Case Study of the Crumbling *Jaina* Heritage in Pakistan

Asif Mahmood Rana

Nusrat Jehan College, Chenab Nagar, Pakistan. CONTACT Asif Mahmood Rana: asifranaonline@gmail.com

Abstract: Respect for all forms of life is the essence of *Agamas*, the sacred *Jaina* texts. The *Jaina* practice of non-violence well embedded in time and space not only influenced some great emperors but successfully reduced the element of violence for some brief periods of time in Indian history. Right from the time of *Mahavira*, as some traditions point out, or from the 1st century BCE, as the remains at Sirkap suggest, Jains had been living in the areas that now constitute Pakistan. Post partition chaos and riots of 1980s and 1990s compelled Jains to move eastwards leaving their heritage abandoned. Completely or partially demolished *Jaina* heritage in Pakistan is analogous to the state of peace and tolerance in current societal trends of violence and intolerance. On the other hand, a few intact temples are the hope of presence of the other tradition. Conservation and restoration of this genre of abandoned heritage would, therefore, result in the restoration of "non-violent" thinking patterns in our society. The present article, based on a joint systematic survey of Nusrat Jahan College (NJC), Pakistan and School of Oriental and African Studies (SOAS), London, discusses the distribution and present state of *Jaina* Heritage across Pakistan and the current efforts to document and restore them.

Keywords: tolerance, non-violence, Jain heritage in Pakistan, art and architecture, extremism

Background

Right from the pre-historic times Indian subcontinent has been a land of tolerate communities except for a few short-lived events in a historic period. Archaeological remains of bronze age cultures of Indus and their precursors at Mehrgarh near Bolan river Balochistan lack tools of war and any signs of persecution or violence (Baloch and Mengal 2016: 17-24). Ancient Indian religions that still survive to the day i.e. Hinduism, Buddhism and Jainism have deep roots in the Proto-Historic Indus Valley Civilisation or even earlier as their claims propose (Jain 1974: ix). The followers of these religions share a common value i.e. *ahimsa* or the non-violence. Humbleness and meekness in acts of salutations with each other and kindness even towards animals of these religions still depict their respect for all forms of life. This value was taken up by the Jains in an extreme form i.e. they don't even kill the parasites that cause severe human diseases. The other *Jaina* value of non-attachment kept them away from acquiring lands and goods from others through any means that would have resulted in war and disorder. With such peace-loving values Jains have been playing an important role in inspiring Indian societies from ancient times to live peacefully. Even today the geographical zones where Jains live in considerable numbers present a relevantly tolerant social set-up. Their absence has produced opposite results to some extent.

Jainism is one of the most ancient religions of India following the *Sramana* tradition. Jains believe that their philosophy is the most ancient in India (Roy 1984: 4) and all others are derived or deviated from it. *Sramana* (against Vedic) is a non-theistic philosophy that prevailed in ancient India. Buddhists, Ajivikas and some minor or extinct groups along with the Jains follow this tradition. In ancient Indian literature Jains can be recognised as the nude *Sramanas* of *Rig Veda* who practiced meditation in the jungles, rejected *Vedas* and supremacy of *Brahmins*. As a consequence, they also rejected caste system of Vedic society and their pointless sacraments and practised high morals, the most important of which was *Ahimsa* (Huntington 2001: 32). *Parsvanatha*, the 23rd *tirthankara* of this religion had snake as his vehicle and guardian of his throne. Because of this relevance snake is considered to be sacred in Jainism and inspired by them sacred to other religions of India too. Hence, Jains recognise themselves to be the *Naga Sadhus* or the snake worshippers of *Puranas* and *Upanishads*. *Niggantha*, i.e. free from bonds, a term used in *Acaranga Sutra* and *the Kalpa Sutra*, or *Nirgranthas*, i.e. without any sacred book (Roy 1984: 4) are considered to be a mention of Jainas of ancient India. Jainism, as we know today, was founded by *Mahavira* who was the 24th *tirthankara* or the ford-maker of this religion, and a contemporary of Gautam Buddha. Jains consider their religion to be eternal (Roy 1984: 4) without a starting point or any end.

Historical Overview

Jainism as a religion as well as a philosophy has deep roots in present-day Pakistan. Speculative claims of some Jains supported by undeciphered (as most of the specialists believe) archaeological evidence, link *Jaina* practices of nudity, yoga and *ahimsa* with the Indus Valley Civilisation (2500 BCE–1600 BCE). The nude Harappan torso of a male (Chandra 1985: 22) and the male figure sitting in yogic posture surrounded by animals are believed to be of *Jaina* origin (Jain 1974: 107). Unfortunately there is no confirmation of the fact but it can be assumed that *Jaina* philosophy in one form or the other can be a continuity of Indus Valley Civilisation's traditions in a general sense. In the historic period there are a number of references about the presence of the present form of Jainism founded in the 6th century BCE by the 24th *tirthankara*, i.e. Vardhman Mahavira. Mahavira himself visited Bhera of Punjab, near the bank of Jhelum River on foot (Qaiser 2017: 72) where a 15th century CE *Jaina* temple still stands within the walled city of the city. Then he went to present-day Indian state of Gujarat that houses the most sacred and ancient pilgrimage sites of this religion crossing the Indus Valley and Tharparkar district of Sindh. Possibly a few in number, but there were some followers of Mahavira inspired by his teachings of non-violence and non-attachement in Punjab and Sindh at this early stage of the revived version of this religion. The next mention of these people is in the Greek invasion of Gandhara where Greek army encountered gymnosophists in Taxila (Sheikh 2015: 30). Taxila, somewhere around the 1st century of the common era was known as the city of hundred *Jaina* stupas of which only one have been identified by Sir John Marshall (Marshall 1918: 72). *Jaina* remains that stupas include newly discovered Chirana Padukas (Ahmad 2015: 40-42) found from Murti Temple District Chakwal present seconed stage of this ancient period when *Jaina* activities are predominent in northern parts of Punjab probably around 1st to 2nd century of the common era. There is no visible reason for whipping out of Jainism in the following centuries but we find almost no remains of this period so far in Punjab. Though their religion flourished and enjoyed prosperity in district Tharparkar (Flugel and Ahmad 2018: 26) where *Jaina* communities are affiliated with the greater *Jaina* trade class of Gujarat and Rajasthan (Rana 2019: 118). This period extents from the 8th century CE to the British period. Graceful *Jaina* temples in this district represent the zenith of architectural and artistic proficiency of the *Jaina* artisans and the wealth of the community living in this vicinity. *Jaina* activities in the fields of trade and commerce become evident in medieval times in which we find their mention in literary sources and remains of their temples in all the major cities of the Punjab located on trade routes (Flugel and Ahmad 2018: 26). This period extends to the partition of the subcontinent when Jain community altogether left Pakistan and abandoned their temples and homes. A few individual house-holds stayed in hope of better future but had to leave in the chaotic times during the riots of 1970s and 1990s.

This historical overview establishes the fact that there is an apparent continuity of *Jaina* occupation in present-day Pakistan and hence their role in moulding trends of social behaviours with their teachings of extreme non-violence cannot be denied. *Jaina* presence and contribution in the local and national political and social businesses remained prominent in the 3rd century BCE, i.e. the Mauryan period (Sheikh 2015: 30), Early Islamic occupation of the 8th century to the 10th century CE, Sultanate and Mughal periods in Taxila, Tharparkar and Punjab respectively. Later on, *Jaina* community settles down on the trade routes in Punjab and Sindh. Before 1947, they were about 1% of the total population (Flugel and Ahmad 2018: 28) in this region but played a much larger part in economic and social infrastructure as is evident from their present economic role in India despite of their small number. They took a huge number of the sculptures of their *tirthankaras*, sacred books and scriptures from their libraries on private air crafts and trains as they could in the chaos of partition of the subcontinent but left their immovable heritage in the form of temples, community halls and houses.

Built *Jaina* Heritage

Jaina built heritage of Pakistan includes *Jaina* places of worship, i.e. the *Derasars* of, the *Deravasi* or the idol worshipper sects of *Jains*, *Samadhis*, i.e. chapel-like buildings built in the memory of spiritual teachers, community halls of the *Sthanakvasi* sect and schools for boys and girls mostly in northern parts of Punjab.

Following the timeline of Jainism in Pakistan in the historical overview, built heritage of this religion can be categorised or the other way with respect to the typology one can do so. In the following pages location and condition of the *Jaina* edifices have been given in brief to understand their distribution pattern and what they have been through.

No material remains of the first phase of Jainism in Pakistan, i.e. the 6th century BCE belonging to the time of the 24th *tirthankara* are recognisable. Jain temple of *Sirkap,* Taxila can be declared as the earliest material remains (1st–2nd century CE) of this category that is now only in the form of a platform with ashlar masonry (Marshall 1918: 73). Dispersed blocks made of red sandstone, damaged sculptures of unrecognisable *Jaina* characters and a few architectural motifs are what archaeologists have so far recovered from *Murti,* Chakwal and displayed in Lahore museum's *Jaina* Gallery that belongs to a period later than *Sirkap.*

The remains related to the next phase of the *Jaina* heritage, i.e. of the medieval period

333

are standing in district Tharparkar of Sindh with elegance, though deteriorating day by day. Three temples representing three altogether different schools of architecture are in the village *Bhodesar* on the foot of *Karoonjhar* hills about 8 kms from Nagarparkar. Temple 1 of *Bhodesar* (Figure 1), standing on a raised platform is a huge monumental edifice made of local sandstone and granite, which belongs to 10th–11th century CE. Escaped from the persecution of human hands, the temple gave up before natural disasters, i.e. the earthquakes. Temple 2 of this vicinity is in a much better state. It exhibits a relevantly different form of architectural scheme probably the only example of this type in this region (Figure 2). Gauri and Virawah temples on Mithi-Islamkot road in the villages with the respective names are two other master pieces of art and architecture. Gauri Temple (Figure 3) that stands in solitary in the desert of Thar, is a huge complex with 24 chapels, 55 domes, hundreds of painted scenes and sculptures of subsidiary gods. A unique element of this temple is the extensive intact miniature painted scenes of devotees approaching *Parsvanatha* or *Godichi* to whom the temple has been dedicated, inside the dome of the porch in the form of concentric circles (Figure 4). No Jain visits the temple today and no offerings are made to the deity. However, the message of peace remains unchanged, though no one chooses to learn from it. Two more temples in *Karojain* near Nagarparkar and a magnificent *Jaina* Temple within the City of Nagarparkar locally known as *Bazaar Mandir* are some other identified *Jaina* temples of the region. *Bazaar Mandir* (Figure 5) displays many Gujarati and Rajasthani elements and inscriptions in Gujarati, and hence this temple is a key source to trace back the affiliation of the *Jaina* community of Tharparkar region.

All the *Jaina* temples of this region show notable association with Gujarati and Rajasthani school of art and architecture with conventional North-Indian temple tradition, i.e. the Nagara Style of temple architecture. Gujarati inscriptions from Bazaar Temple Nagarparkar and use of Gujarati books by the local Hindu Brahmins are enough evidence of the fact. Jain temples of Tharparkar are the only examples of this genre of architecture in Pakistan. Almost all of these edifices are in danger because of natural calamities and ignorance. Temple 1 of *Bhodesar* is about a thousand-year-old *tirtha* with Nagara style tower. About ten years

Figure 1   Temple 1, *Bhodesar*, Tharparkar (photo by the author 2016)

Figure 2   Temple 2, *Bhodesar*, Tharparkar (photo by the author 2016)

Figure 3　Gauri Temple, Tharparkar (photo by the author 2016)

Figure 4　Miniature painted scenes, inside the dome of the porch, Gauri Temple
(photo by the author 2016)

336

Figure 5   Sikhara of the *Bazaar Mandir*, NagarParkar (photo by the author 2018)

ago, the tower of the temple stood high in the beautiful landscape of Tharparkar, but due to earthquakes and no salvage projects in the past, most of the building and its elegant tower crumbled. At present a devoted team has been busy in restoring the temple. The state of preservation of the other *Jaina* temples of this region is not different. Paintings from the walls of these temples have been scratched. Sculptures have been mutilated in the process of *"purifying the land of the pure"*. Marbles from the floor have been removed. If the situation stays the same, Pakistan's heritage would lose one of its history's beautiful chapters.

The concluding chapter of architectural advancement of *Jaina* heritage left its colossal ruins both in the southern and the northern parts of the Western Punjab. This class of architectural remains represent later Mughal and Sikh building tradition. Elaborately decorated *Jaina* temple at *Rasulnagar,* District Gujranwala lost its charm in the last few decades completely. Rains and earthquakes along with the treasure finders have left no part of it. Beautiful frescos once covered all the walls and the ceilings of this temple. Frescos of the sanctum on the first floor became visible when debris and dust was removed. A beautiful scene of Shatrunjaya hills, the most sacred pilgrimage site of Jainism in Indian state of Gujrat, crowns the entrance of the sanctum from inside (Figure 6). In another scene, which has been repeated three times in different rooms of the same temple, two men arguing whether the fruit picking or the branch cutting would harm the tree or not have been painted. Unfortunately, a mindset does not even think whether cutting hands and legs of an innocent would harm him or not. With the waning of the stories on the walls of *Jaina* temples, these morals have also been fading away from our society. The three-storey building of *Rasulnagar's Jaina* temple follows Sikh architectural traditions of British period in the sub-continent with a few additions of *Jaina* tradition. The building sways during earthquakes and seeps from every side during rains; hence it has been closed for visitors by the local guardians.

Figure 6   Fresco depicting pilgrimage site, Sanctum wall *Rasulnagar* Temple, Gujranwala, (photo by Amjad Javed 2016)

Pipnakha, a small town in district Gujranwala, has a relevantly huge Jain temple that seems to be a Sikh Gurudwara at first glance. This building has a relatively better condition. It has been used as an office of local council of the government. To keep the building usable, it has been white-washed annually that has covered all the rich art beneath. Though the sanctum and the ambulatory and a few other chambers are still intact. Another beautiful but in a terrible state of preservation is a colossal *Svetambara Jaina* Temple in Bhabra Bazaar inside the old Narowal city. In the neighbouring small town of *Sankhatra*, in district Narowal two *Jaina* temples of the same category have been used by the locals, one as a residence and other as a shop. Bhera near Pind Dadan Khan and Pind Dadan Khan itself housed a large *Jaina* community before partition. Bhera is said to have been visited by the last *tirthankara* of Jain religion, i.e. *Mahavira* (Qaiser 2017: 72). A 15th century *Jaina* temple is inside walled city of Bhera and another allegedly a *Jaina* temple stands outside the walled city near the bank of Jhelum River. Only the brick structures of these two temples stand while all the artistic details have been withered completely. Kasur and Khanqah Dogran's temples are among the other *Jaina* temples of northern parts of the Western Punjab. In a house-size complex near Mohallah Shah Rukn e Alam of Kasur, two *Jaina* temples still stand. One of them is in the form of a brick building and belongs to the earlier decades of the 20th century. While the other with a beautiful white tower is a renovated temple in a relatively good condition. Khanqah Dogran's *Jaina* temple is a small three-storey temple with an octagonal tower. A jeweler's family lives in and takes good care of the building with most of the temple's pats intact.

Sialkot's Mohallah Saraey Bhaberiyan in the walled city near Kanak Mandi, Circular Road was a Jain Mohallah with a modern brick structure of a temple now being used as a primary school. Rawalpindi once had a large Hindu and *Jaina* population. Abandoned temples of these religions in Rawalpindi can give a rough estimate of their population. As the merchant class of Bhabra Jains were goldsmiths. That is why the Sooha Bazaar of major cities of Punjab are also known as Bhabra Bazaar and *Jaina* temples around these markets are more likely to exist. Same is the case with Rawalpindi and its *Jaina* community. In addition, *Jaina* library at Messi gate, Sadar, and community-run schools near old city also constitute the *Jaina* heritage of this vicinity. A demolished *Adinatha* temple in old *Anarkali* Lahore (Figure 7), reminds every visitor of the violent riots of early 1990s sparked all around the country as an outrageous reaction to the demolishing of the historical Baburi Mosque by extremist Hindus in India. During the documentation of the *Jaina* temples of Multan, two Muslim clerics came to the team. One of them asked that why the team was photographing the temple. The other replied that the team probably want to preserve our heritage.

Figure 7   Adinatha Temple, Anarkali Lahore (photo by the author 2016)

In Multan, a major in Southern Punjab known for its Saints and shrines, there are three confirmed *Jaina* temples of later British period with inscribed names, i.e. *Shri Parsvanatha Svetambara Jain Mandir, Choori Saraey* Bazaar, Near Bohar Gate Walled City of Multan, Digambar Jain temple in the same locality, and another Digambar temple in the cantonment, all representing very different architectural styles yet to be classified. The *Svetambara* temple is a three-storey huge complex with shops on Bazaar level, main temple building above the former level, and a third level that houses a secondary sanctum and residential rooms. It also has a fourth underground level that has long been abandoned. But the rest of the temple is in a good state of preservation despite the fact that a huge mob tried to attack the temple in 1992.

The locals told us the story. It was a cold morning in December 1992, when young children gathered in a building to learn the holy Quran from a pious Maulvi Sahib, i.e. a Muslim cleric. Before the sun appeared from the thick fog, a mob of vigilantes led by some radical mullahs headed towards that building in the *Choori Saraey* Bazaar of Multan. The mob were carrying sticks and metallic rods and chanted anti-Hindu slogans declaring them "infidels" and "enemies of Islam" as they approached it. Most of the mob were actually clueless as to why were they heading towards the said Bazaar and whom the few of his young students in front of the temple to stop them. The man neither wore an orange rob nor a white one that Hindu or Jain monks usually do. He was actually a Muslim *Maulvi Sahib*; the pious maulvi sahib, standed with his madrassa pupils, to defend the temple. It was in fact *Shri Parshwanath Svetambara Jain Mandir*, as inscribed on the top of the wooden door frame of the temple. The same *Maulvi Sahib* teaches young students of the locality right in the courtyard of this Jain Temple (Figure 8). All of his students would clean up the temple daily, even the *Jaina* deities on the walls painted with colours and gold water. In order to uproot the extremism and hatred against minorities, we need more of such pious *Maulvi Sahibs* and students.

Figure 8   Shri Parshwanath Jain Svetambara Mandir, *Choori Saraey* Bazaar, Walled City, Multan (photo by the author 2016)

Another prominent *Jaina* temple of this region, i.e. the Southern Punjab, is the temple of Dera Ghazi Khan that is architecturally the sister temple of *Svetambara* Temple of Multan mentioned above; hence they seem to belong to the same period of time, i.e. late British period. *Mandapa* or the central gathering hall with multi-cusped arcades, gallery all around this hall with painted panels depicting 14 sacred dreams of *tirthankara*'s mother and pilgrimage sites, a sanctum with narrow ambulatory and a five-band tower with bronze *kalasa* and niches are common in both the edifices. Though most of the paintings in the later temple have been white-washed by the family living in it.

Monumental Samadhi, i.e. a commemorative chapel, of *Atma Ram Gi* (Figure 9) with a Ghar Mandir (small temple) in Sabzi Mandi, Grand Trunk road Gujranwala city and of *Jin Kushal Suraj* (Flugel and Ahmad 2018: 26) in Derawar, district Bahawalpur are significant in *Jaina* history of the region as both of these distinguished intellectuals of this religion's *Svetambara* sect promoted education and Jain religion across Northern Punjab and Southern Punjab respectively.

Figure 9   Samadhi *Atma Ram*, Gujranwala (photo by Amjad Javed 2016)

Jaina heritage of district Tharparkar of Sindh is providentially under the guardianship of endowment fund trust for preservation of the heritage of Sindh and therefore is being conserved; hence it apparently has a relatively safe future. While *Jaina* temples in Punjab have almost all been allotted to the locals for residence who use *Gambhara*, the most sacred part of a Jain temple, as store rooms, *mandapas*, the prayer halls, stables (Jain Manzil Tehsil Bazaar, Walled City Lahore [Sheikh 2015: 30] or scrap yards, as is the case with the temple in Bagh Mohalla Jhelum city. Sense of responsibility among the locals and local administrative authorities is looked-for to preserve or record these disintegrating memorials lest they disappear completely from the memories too.

Intangible Heritage

As claimed by the Jains, their religion is considered to be the earliest of all the creeds and philosophies in India that seems to be partly accurate as the origins of *Jaina* fundamentals can be recognised in ancient Indian civilisations. The claims of such a remote antiquity of Jainism is a subject of great interest. Alexander's army witnessed gymnosophists or the naked philosophers in Taxila, who match no other Indian creed more than Jains (Sheikh 2015: 30). The Essenes of ancient Israel are also said to be influenced by Jainism. Their strict rules of meditation, white clothing, non-attachment with material life, etc., are the clues to prove the link with some evidence-based theories that Israeli tribes came to the region in the time of their diaspora before the dawn of Buddhism in Northern India.

Scenes portrayed on the walls and ceilings of *Jaina* monuments all over Pakistan have an unfathomable message of Peace, of mind and soul through non-attachment from the worldly bonds and non-violence, a memorandum that every religion educated its followers but regrettably almost everyone forgot. As a substitute of swords, trisulas, battle fields, and heaps skulls or skulls on spear heads as signs of victory, *Jaina* temples have been adorned with the *tirthankaras* in meditation position, noble men debating on the possibilities of not harming the animals and even not the plants, and the sceneries of the sacred *Jaina* pilgrimage sites, e.g. Mount Abu and Mount Girnar. The places where most of the *tirthankaras* attained moksha or liberation from worldly greed and bondages were the sign of their greatest victory after which they were called *Jinas*. Preferment of such art and the morals that Jain artisans and artists engraved and painted can reduce the component of

343

ferocity and immoderation from our society.

Currently the followers of Jainism are comparably few in number but the profound outcome of its ideology has undoubtedly influenced almost all the great religions and ancient civilisations of the world. For instance, *Ahimsa*, i.e. non-violence, is by some means a part of all prevailing creeds. Similarly meditation, fasting, loosening material bonds, putting on white robes or in some cases practicing full or semi-nudity, trying to minimise one's own desires, seeking for an eternal truth, salvation, *karmic* power and its consequences, giving reverence to spiritual leaders in different ways even long after their demise, pilgrimage to holy sites in the memory of some great spiritual events like the attainment of moksha or ascension to heavens, constructing buildings as local places for worship and keeping them clean and staying clean while visiting them, code of conduct for the worshippers and many other devotional practices and beliefs that can be observed in one form or the other in ancient and modern religions as well have roots in Jainism. For much of these practices, Jains claim credit of their origin (Jain 1974: 108, 109).

Increasing Intolerance

From the last four decades especially and since the partition of the subcontinent in general, the entities that opposed the creation of a new nation have been dominating in spreading hatred and promoting extremism. More precisely, right after the demise of the founder of Pakistan Mohammad Ali Jinnah then the prime minister of the Nation presented objectives resolution in 1949—a prelude to future constitution. His successor announced an inequality of rights among the citizens on the basis of religion. So, the government-lead discriminative legislation supported the extremists. Though their number is small, they are effective in different regions of the country. Present government has taken positive steps to control the situation and has been successful in doing so, but a long journey has yet to be covered in this regard. To boost up these peace-promoting activities, archaeological and heritage circles can play an important role. Through the conservation of *Jaina* temples their message of extreme non-violence can be re-introduced in the society along with the efforts to let the people know that they have common origins and mutually shared culture in remote past. The land they reside had been home to tolerate societies so much so that they even did not had the need to have arms and armies. This indicates that a tolerant society can divert a huge chunk of annual budget to the welfare and education of the locals rather than purchasing weapons to encounter terrorism and extremism. *Jaina* heritage has surely got the potential to tackle the worsening situation.

Conclusions

The present crumbling state of Jain-built heritage and the art depicted on it (that encourages "non-attachment", i.e. the basis of not harming others by means of suppression of greed for worldly benefits and resources), in fact, manifests the state of peace and tolerance in our society. The alternate tradition of violence and intolerance has been replacing it, and in many places, is responsible for the critical condition of this heritage's preservation.

Jaina heritage of Pakistan has been an ignored class of heritage. Recent studies on their temples and settling patterns have brought to light the importance of this genre. Still most of the art and descriptions on the *Jaina* temples of Pakistan are undeciphered yet. A class of heritage that belongs to a community of extremely non-violent behaviour can play the role of a buffer in our ever-increasing intolerant society. Conservation of *Jaina* heritage needs urgent attention followed by interpreting the art depicted on their temples, and propagating the philosophy of their teachings of peace and tolerance. This can result in multi-dimensional benefits. It would not only be a beautiful addition in the heritage sites of Pakistan in a state ready to be visited and get knowledge of the community that once lived in the region, but also be a source to spread their peace-loving thoughts, awareness about the links among the philosophies of subcontinental religions, the common message of tolerance etc. Sindh endowment fund for heritage has taken the initiative for the conservation of *Jaina* sites and department of archaeology, University of the Punjab has started artistic and architectural studies on them but the rate of deterioration of these sites is far higher than the work to preserve and study them.

◻ Acknowledgments

The present article is based on a systematic documentation of the *Jaina* heritage through a joint pilot project of Centre of *Jaina* Studies, SOAS University of London and Nusrat Jehan College, Chenab Nagar Pakistan, named "Exploratory survey of *Jaina* heritage in Pakistan" under the supervision of Dr. Peter Flugel (CoJS SOAS), Dr. Mirza Naseer Ahmad (NJC) and Mr. Muzaffar Ahmad (NJC). The author of this article worked as field in charge for this project.

◻ Disclosure Statement

No potential conflict of interest was reported by the author.

◻ Note on Contributor

Asif Mahmood Rana is a Pakistani National Archaeologist and scholar of comparative religions. He has recently completed his Master's in Philosophy from the Department of Archaeology University of the Punjab, Lahore Pakistan. His field of research was *Jaina* Art and Architecture. He did his Master's in History from University of the Punjab, Lahore Pakistan. He has attended a number of archaeological training workshops in different institutes in Pakistan. He has co-organised a number of short training courses in the field of archaeology, photography and archaeological drafting. He also has co-authored a field manual of archaeology in Urdu. He has presented a number of papers in local, national and international conferences and seminar on the subjects of Jainism, research methodology, primary sources for the narrative of the great deluge, etc. The author participated in a number of field projects including "Exploratory survey of *Jaina* heritage in Pakistan", excavations at Sheranwala Gate, Walled City of Lahore and Red Fort, Muzaffarabad AJ&K. He is currently working as Research Assistant in a private institute in the field of comparative religions.

□ References

Ahmad, Muzaffar. 2015. Newly Discovered Jaina Carana Padukas in Chel-Abdal Chakwal. *CoJS Newsletter* 10: 40-42.

Baloch, Jahanzeb, and Saeeda Mengal. 2016. The Role and Place of Mehrgarh in the Development of South Asian Civilizations. *Baluchistan Review* 34: 17-24.

Buhlar, J. G. 1903. *On the Indian Sect of the Jainas*. London: Luzac & Co.

Chandra, Pramod. 1985. *The Sculpture of India 3000 B.C.–1300 A.D.* Washington: National Gallery of Arts U.S.

Cousens, H. 1926. *The Architectural Antiquities of Western India*. Delhi: Cosmo Publications.

Flugel, Peter, and Muzaffar Ahmad. 2018. An Exploratory Survey of the Jaina Heritage in Pakistan. *Newsletter of the Centre of Jaina Studies* 13: 26-32.

Gupte, R. S. 1972. *Iconography of the Hindus, Buddhists and Jains*. Bombay: D. B. Taraporevala Sons and Co Private LTD.

Hassan, Sheikh Khursheed. 2008. *Pakistan: Its Ancient Hindu Temples and Shrines*. Islamabad: Department of Archaeology and Museums.

Huntington, S. L., and J. C. Huntington. 2006. *The Art of Ancient India*. London: Weather Hill Boston.

India Census Commissioner. 1941. *Census of India, 1941*. Delhi: The Manager of Publications.

Jain, Champat Rai. 1974. *Fundamentals of Jainism*. Meerut: Veer Nirvan Bharti.

Jarrige, J. F. 1995. *Mehrgarh: From Neolithic to the Indus Civilization*. Karachi: Department of Culture and Tourism, Government of Sindh, Pakistan.

Kalhoro, Zulifqar Ali. 2014. *Perspectives on the Art and Architecture of Sindh*. Karachi: Endowment Fund Trust for Preservation of the Heritage of Sindh.

Marshall, John. 1918. *A Guide to Taxila*. Calcutta: Suprintendant Government Printing India.

Nadiem, Ihsan H. 2001. *Thar: The Great Pakistani Desert Land, History, People*. Lahore: Sang-e-Meel Publications.

Nahar, Puran Chand. 1917. *An Epitome of Jainism*. Calcutta: H. Duby Ghulab Kumar Library .

Ojha, Mangha Ram. 1966. *Purana Parkar*. Sadia Naseem (Trans.). Jam Shoro, Sindh: Sindhi Adabi Board.

Qaiser, Iqbal. 2017. *Ujrrey Daraan De Darshan*. Lahore: Punjabi Adabi Board.

Rai, Lala Lajpat. 1925. *Historical Facts About Jainism*. Bombay: The Jain Association of India.

Raikes, Captain Stanley Napier. 1856. *Memoir on the Thurr and Parkur: Districts of Sind*. Bombay: Education Society's Press, Byculla.

Rana, Asif Mahmood. 2019. Jaina Temple Nagarparkar: Art and Architecture. Master's Thesis, University of the Punjab.

Roy, A. K. 1984. *A History of Jains. New Delhi: Gitanjali Publishing House*. New Delhi: Gitanjali Publishing House.

Sheikh, Majid. 2015. Harking Back: Jain Temples of Lahore and the "naked sages". November 22, 2015. Accessed July 7, 2019. https://www.dawn، com/news/1221387.

Singhvi, L. M. 2002. *The Jain Declaration on Nature*. Boston: Harvard University Press.

Stevenson, Sinclair. 1915. The Heart of Jainism. In *The Religious Quest of India*, edited by J. N. Farquhar, 43-65. London: Oxford University Press.

Linguistic Representations of "Home" in a French-Kanak Children's Book: New Perspectives on Intangible Cultural Heritage

Séverine Julie Didier

School of Arts, Humanities & Social Sciences, University of Tasmania, Australia.
CONTACT Séverine Julie Didier: Severine.didier@utas.edu.au

Abstract: The object of my research is the intangible cultural heritage (ICH) carried by the "*home*" ("*chez soi*" in French) of indigenous people from New Caledonia and Australia, through a selection of local picture books for children. My cognitive–linguistic methodology considers the transmission of cultural representations through words and books that were written by indigenous authors from those countries, as an ICH. Those books have emerged in a "glocal" context—that is the encounter of local and global tendencies generated by the phenomenon of globalization—in the 21st century. This article depicts how the cultural representations associated to the meaning of "*home*" and "*chez soi*" can be preserved but also transformed in one story, leading to a potential ethno-decentration of readers. I combine a semantic analysis and a discourse analysis for this purpose. By investigating the renewal and the preservation of the semantic and the discursive meanings of "*home*", I demonstrate how the Semantics of Argumentative Possibilities (SAP) theory can reveal the cultural innovative vs. conservative paradigm, relevant to intangible cultural heritage. Lastly, my study proves that the ideology of *"home"* conveyed by those books originates in the suggestive structure of the text, which conceals multiple interpretative paths.

Keywords: intangible cultural heritage, Semantics of Argumentative Possibilities (SAP), home, Australia, New Caledonia, emergent children's literature

Introduction

Reflecting on linguistic and cultural heritage strategies in children's media, this article questions the preservation of language-culture diversity and the revival of local identities in a global world. Drawn from an interdisciplinary theoretical framework, the analysis' unique positioning—at the crossroads of linguistics, literature and intercultural communications— offers innovative perspectives in the area of Cultural Heritage Studies (CHS). The highlights of my PhD research (Didier 2015) on Intangible Cultural Heritage in Emergent Children's Literature (case of the meaning *"home"*/*"chez soi"* in a French-Kanak Children's book) seem relevant to mention, especially considering the results of the referendum that recently took place on November 4, 2018 in New Caledonia: voters were given the chance of remaining part of France or becoming an independent country and 43.6% voted in favor of independence[1]. This underlines an identity conflict in New Caledonia which remains significantly divided despite the political agreement of "Nouméa Accords" (1998) aiming at decolonization and reconciliation of both cultures and languages, toward "one common destiny".

While the 21st century has witnessed the development of bilingual indigenous books for children in all the Francophone and Anglophone regions of Oceania, the countries of Australia, New Zealand and New Caledonia were the prominent ones in terms of emergent children's literature. With that in mind, this article will deal more particularly with one children's book from New Caledonia where the preservation of Kanak local cultures and languages has been strongly encouraged. The support of French-Kanak authors since 2000 has clearly been aligned with the ideology of the *Nouméa Accords* promoting a local cultural revival. Yet, I would like to show how a discourse analysis can enlighten those ideologies and identity re-constructions. Indeed, my article aims to depict some specific analytical tools which give more tangibility to intangible feelings, ideas, values, and representations.

From a linguistic framework based on the Semantics of Argumentative Possibilities (SAP) (Galatanu 2000, 2007), I investigate intangible cultural heritage (ICH) in languages by examining:

- the power of cultural co-text and context to influence discursive meaning;
- the power of discursive meaning to transform not only socio-cultural and cognitive representations but also the meaning of the words, which name and denominate the social and the human.

"The role of language in assigning new meanings and values to heritage objects and to meanings of words referring to those objects" (Galatanu 2000, 2007) will be at stake. In this perspective, I will explore more particularly ICH as a process of transformation and preservation of identity representations in discourses of emergent children's literature.

Looking at promoting cultural diversity, I argue that local-global books for children (so to say, locally/home-made, while opening local rituals to global audiences) have a significant potential of heritage, and that this potential is encrypted in the text. I postulate that those linguistic heritage strategies can be deconstructed by a linguistic model and I consider a local-global methodology for this purpose. This argument will be developed in the first part.

From the example of *Mèyènô* (Ponga 2004), a bilingual Kanak contemporary book written by an indigenous author of New Caledonia, I will show more specifically how the SAP theory can be used:

- Firstly, to reveal the cultural *renewal vs. preservation* paradigm that characterizes the process of ICH. The application of this theory is based on the word *"home"* (*"chez soi"* in French), more particularly on the *renewal vs. preservation* of its semantic and discursive meaning.

- Secondly, to disclose the local-global structure of heritage stories and its power to re-shape the representations of the Self and the Other.

Firstly, this article will summarize the implications of ethnolinguistic representations of home and ICH for intercultural children's books and their readers. My hybrid methodology will be clarified through significant examples of my PhD research. Secondly, focusing on children's literature, and particularly the tale of *Mèyènô*, I will explore the textual rites of passage and the discursive-semantic mask(s) disclosed within the story: those powerful semantic strategies contribute to create new meanings (re-semantization) in the reader's mind. Those new meanings specifically cover new local-global meanings which can develop a local-global reader's identity, or at least a local-global interpretative skill for young readers. Thus, I will exemplify how *chez soi* becomes a semantic and narrative schema granted with parabolic, transformative and heritage potential. We shall discover in what ways emergent literature particularly unveils this regenerative home ideology by projecting the image of a cultural revival for indigenous communities.

Ethnolinguistic Representations of Home and Intangible Heritage in Children's Books

Semantic Approach of Intangible Cultural Heritage: The Meaning of Home in "Glocal" Books

Different translations of *home* exist from one language to another, and the semantic fields of such words do not exactly overlap. Indeed, *home* is a tangible signifier linked to a potential signified that it is an intangible representation. *Home* projects a linguistic worldview, which conceals a field of local articulations' probabilities. In cognitive ethnolinguistics, Bartminski (2009: 23) explains that a linguistic worldview is "not a reflection" but a "language-entrenched interpretation of reality". According to cultural geography, "place and self exist but must be given social relevance through interpretation and contextualization" (Birkeland 2005: 148), which notably happens through words and discourses. For Bartminski, the concept of *house/home* "is universal because it constitutes the center of a person's world, the place from which the person views reality [...]. But it is also culture-specific because cultures mould it according to historical circumstances and within a given system of values" (2009: 149). I explore here the implications of the contemporary renewed linguistic representations of *chez soi (home)* in French for ICH. Looking specifically at the preservation of diversity and the revival of local indigenous cultures—Kanak society in particular—I consider global-local or "glocal" (Robertson 1997), cross-cultural and cultural-natural continuums.

Indeed, globalization has enhanced the assertion of local voices, cultural representations and identities: "local" means here "particular" and "contextual" as opposed to "universal" and "decontextualized". Indeed, two interrelated phenomena have emerged. Firstly, "glocalization" describes the complementary and interpenetrative processes of globalization and localization as one. Glocalization was popularized by Robertson (1997) who extended this concept from its financial focus to a social approach. Secondly, "modern liquidity" is a concept explored by Bauman (2000) since the 1990s: it describes the modern and inflating dissolution of the frontiers which define human space and time, notably affecting people's cultures and identities. Both phenomena can account for the intensified human and non-human transformations of the postmodern world. For instance, increasing contacts between people from different countries have not only created physical and virtual "hypermobilities" (Adams 1999), but also new liquid and glocal identities, landscapes and representations which linguistics can show, as I postulate in this article—from my PhD manuscript (Didier 2015). I examine localization as a process of appropriation and identification to a specific culture, particularly via re-semantization in a glocal narrative: such glocal media gives both global access to local cultures and local access to a global culture.

The growth of global communications has particularly expanded the scope of local potential meanings. The new profiles of local identities—in my case, the indigenous and

Kanak ones—reflect blurred concepts related to identity spaces, such as *culture* or *home/ chez soi*. Birkeland (2005: 57) argues that the new identities and representations of home are rebuilt during journeys, out of home. In a western perspective, representations of local identities are traditionally associated to isolation and separateness from the global world. Hence, they relate to fixed conceptions of culture and home. On the contrary, postmodern local identities are essentially potential and intersubjective. They integrate plurality and difference within sameness, the other within the self. So more than local, I postulate that they have become glocal identities. In other words, new local voices appear "non-authoritarian, open-ended and process-oriented" (Birkeland 2005: 28; referring to Flax 1990) so that they depict a "continual becoming of self" (Birkeland 2005: 16). However, this new local, intersubjective and interconnected conception of self and place seems to have always existed in Oceanian indigenous cultures, although western discourses have represented those societies as isolated (Hauo'fa 2001). Thus, in the postcolonial context, indigenous new local identities are depicted by a return to their lost or stolen identity and home. In this revival purpose, indigenous people such as the Kanak are willing to raise their voice globally via glocal communication tools, and witness the passage from oral to written traditions. Thus, the case of indigenous emergent children's literature as vehicle of heritage needs to be explored in the context of these broadscale transformations. Considering that "re-inscribing place with a new meaning needs place-writing" (Birkeland 2005: 148), this article investigates the example of the meaning of *chez soi* and its articulation in a children's book from New Caledonia: *Mèyènô* (Ponga 2004) written in both French and A'jië by a Kanak author. The analysis was exclusively textual—it was not focused on the book's pictures. My study of the semantic renewal of *chez soi* uncovers a transformative process that combines identity-making, cross-cultural representations and ICH. Innovative linguistic lenses that I have customized this context reveal how these sociocultural processes are inscribed in children's books and ultimately, potentially impact on young readers.

Two main crossroads define my linguistic approach: cognitive poetics and cognitive ethnolinguistics; semantics and pragmatics. On the one hand, the cognitive aspect covers here the interrelation of experiential meanings, cultural key words (Wierzbicka 1997) and narratives. On the other hand, semantics deals with decontextualized meanings: I defined what I called "a global meaning" (decontextualized meaning) of "*chez soi*" from lexicographic definitions. For instance, Le Lexis (2002) defines "*chez soi*" as "the localization in the residence, the country or civilization, the literary or artistic work of someone"; "the presence of something in the physique, in the behavior of someone, or, possibly, an animal" (my translation). The discursive and local actualization of this global definition was then reviewed as a contextualized meaning that I called "local meaning": this was relevant to pragmatics. Here, local and global meanings simultaneously describe conceptual meaning.

Ethnodecentration and Home-Remaking via Local-Global Children's Literature

Home is a linguistic map and "the map is not the territory" for "everyone has a different map of the world". Those sayings depict the distinction between representations and reality, signified and signifier. People use words (signifier) as linguistic maps to express and regenerate subjective realities (signified). Since multiple experiences of the same concept co-exist, reality remains intersubjective although individuals and groups often believe their vision to be universal and/or superior to others: societies have always known this phenomenon as *ethnocentrism*. With respect to human and non-human interactions, anthropocentrism depicts the tendency to perceive reality only from a human perspective.

Ethnocentrism and anthropocentrism can inform our attachments to identity, values, and belief systems. They reveal the illusion of a secured self or ego, also associated to a still ground: "There is an experience that there is no absolute, static or solid ground under one's feet. The ground exists, but it is not absolute, and has shifting meanings. People move on a floating ground and ground things on a moving earth." (Birkeland 2005: 28; referring to Clifford and Marcus 1986) Thus, as an experiential meaning, *home* shifts as we walk on moving grounds for "the experience of place is grounded in the experience of the body" (Birkeland 2005: 9).

355

Impermanent and transgressive representations of *home* are all the more strengthened by the daily effects of modern liquidity. This accounts for significant and increasing uncertainties. Feelings of displacement and self-disconnection (Bauman and Bury 2007) lead us to redefine permanent markers on moving grounds, "We keep hoping that identities will come our way because the rest of the world is so confusing: everything else is turning, but identities ought to be some stable point of reference which were like that in the past, are now and ever shall be, still points in a turning world" (Hall 1997: 22).

Contingent to identities, meanings are also expected to be stable grounds. Nevertheless, like maps, they are bound to evolve to reflect human experiences. Out of fear of losing ourselves, attachment to still points accounts for extreme protective attitudes, behaviors and ideologies. Fear of change can however be thwarted by learning how to change. Intercultural studies are particularly focused on *decentration* strategies as an attempt to lift oneself "beyond the natural tendency to distance the other" (Dittmar 2004: 4-8, my translation).

Looking at cultural differences, *ethnodecentration* can be conditioned by new rituals through cross-cultural mediation. I argue that transcultural or *local-global* books, so to say locally/homemade but still opening local rituals to global audiences, also contain this potential. For example, the Kanak author proves the authentic and local anchor of *Mèyènô*. Moreover, the bilingual French-Kanak narrative mirrors the postcolonial context defined by the Noumea Accord (1998). This political agreement aims at decolonization and reconciliation of both cultures and languages, toward one common destiny. At the instigation of Kanak Language Academy and Tjibaou Cultural Center, workshops gathered indigenous authors and non-indigenous illustrators around picture books. Then *Mèyènô* and the collection of Kanak Tales were born.

The reality projected by those stories is that within sameness, repetition and continuity, life itself is a manifestation of change, becoming, and innovation. ICH and its alternative conceptions drawn from indigenous studies (Harrison and Rose 2010) are rooted on this dialogic principle, which integrates natural and cultural, human and non-human elements.

Dialogic heritage appears as a regenerative, sustainable process based on rituals and their transgression. Therefore, I argue that *local-global* books like the collection of Kanak Tales potentiate dialogic heritage. *Mèyènô* uncovers indeed a multiple, dividual and dialogic *home* as an in-between place that integrates *home* and *homes* themselves, and *not-home*; human, nature and ancestors. In short, *Mèyènô* narrates the journey of a boy to the sea where his ancestors live. The first part depicts his coming of age, guided by his grandfather, until he leaves home, following the river. While the end discloses both characters' re-integration in the ancestral home, the mutual growth of *Mèyènô* and his grandfather will continue in the sea. Moreover, *Mèyènô*'s transformation as a lizard, his totem, marks his transgression and rebirth. Henceforth, he has the new ability to go back and forth through the river that links his two homes: earth and sea, life and death.

Liminality has a large interpretative potential here that most likely underlines a renewal pattern and a dialogic identity embodied in the island's landscape (Seixo 2004). Prominent in emergent literature through spiraled patterns, the regenerative schema universally symbolizes rebirth, continuity and ancestrality (Perrot 2005). That is to say, the only constant reality is change: this principle accounts for phenomenology's cross-disciplinary applications. Hence, my linguistic perspective of heritage dynamics potentially intertwines with several fields for they share the search for what reality is and who we are. Questioning the meaning of *home* certainly raises these fundamental issues of redefining reality and the self in terms of relation. In this way, "difference refers to a difference that exceeds binary opposites and which moves towards non dualist ideas of difference" (Birkeland 2005: 8).With that in mind, the shifting meaning of *home*, I postulate, informs self-construction *with* and/or *different from* the Other. Identity negotiation is based on opposition/integration of individual/collectivity, local/global. So conceptual meaning's negotiation is essentially glocal, for it displays the dialogue *universal vs. particular,* which generates the dynamics of heritage. In other words, meaning (re)construction is governed by a heritage process of repetition and innovation. Through the lens of children's literature.

Global subjectivity, (…) is characterized by its neutrality and fluidity. This is not to say that global signs and symbols have no meaning but that "sharedness" allows these meanings to become generalized. The fluidity of the global sign is given substance when grounded on (…) local rock: local landscape, local bodies, and the ideologies embedded in them. (Gutierrez 2013: 23)

Applied to linguistics, this idea divulges the local, discursive actualization of a global potential meaning covered by a signifier such as *home*. In my case, using the term glocal, I focus notably on the cross-cultural representations between non-western, indigenous local visions and western, non-indigenous, global representations involved in emergent children's literature. I prefer the specific term *local-global* to accentuate local and "horizontal" communications (Graham 2009) emerging from a local community and being accessible to the global world.

My research demonstrates that such literature holds glocal semantic-pragmatic clues and strategies. Those interpretative paths potentiate the reader/public and the writer/narrator with a glocal competence relevant to ethnodecentration. Applied to transcultural learning via local-global media, I consider glocal learning to focus on the ability to:

- (re)create local visions accessible locally and globally;
- understand and create glocal representations;
- be aware of glocal intersubjectivities: the transparency and opacity of local meanings.

I argue that this competence can be indeed encrypted through discursive interpretative paths, informed by the process of semantic deconstruction and reconstruction. Thus, the reader constructs meaning "from the kit of parts supplied by the writer" (Oatley 2003: 167). That is to say, texts incorporate rituals or kits, which govern the initiatory process of meaning-making or interpretation. My aim is to enlighten them in order to reveal the transformative, intangible power of words, particularly significant in the case of *home*.

Methodology Development: Cognitive Poetics in Linguistics

SAP Theory

At the intersection of discourse analysis and semantics, my research originally aimed at discovering intangible and cross-cultural representations in children's literature. In this purpose, I intended to expand the current methodology of SAP (Galatanu 2012). Since the late 1990s, Galatanu has developed this "semantic-pragmatic interface being the simultaneous revelation of two states of the same linguistic phenomenon (linguistic significance and discursive meaning)" (Galatanu 2012). SAP's approach to semantics is interactive, argumentative and conceptual (cognitive), mainly applicable to verbal interactions and textual variations. SAP particularly examines shifting lexical meanings: this phenomenon called *semantic kinetics* arises from the communicative and cognitive aspects of language (Galatanu 2011: 175). I will focus on the meaning of the lexical entity *"chez soi"* as a potential that SAP clarifies according to three stratums (Galatanu 2011: 174-175): the core (semantic categorization's features or essential properties), the stereotypes associated to words[2] and "argumentative probabilities" (AP), which articulates those associations. The analysis of discursive meaning is a construction of hypotheses based on the "argumentative deployment" (AD) in the text: AD can either correspond to the AP or transgress them by creating new associations, which can be explained culturally or by an original situation.

In French, the closest translation from the English noun *home* is *chez soi* composed of two words: firstly, *soi* is a personal reflexive pronoun which means *self*; secondly, *chez* comes from the Latin *casa*, signifying *house,* or *maison* in French. So the semantics of *chez soi* proves the presence of a subject within a defined place. *Soi*, which I describe as X for my SAP analysis, is situated and lives in a defined place which is his/hers, while this place defines the self: it can be a house, a region, a country, a body, a group of people, etc. The self is assimilated to an inner space, distinct from an outsider other, whom I describe as Y. The exclusive self's representation stands out in the lexicographic definitions of *chez soi*. Built from dictionaries, my SAP lexical meaning description of *chez X* can be summarized according to the following Core-stereotype basic structure:

Core (base): [Space of the Same (X/self and demultiplication of X/self) HENCE different from the space of the Other (Y/other(s)/Diverse/away and demultiplications of Y)]
Stereotypes (base): [X's spirit/mind or personnality, in X's body HENCE X's behavior and feelings, X's creation, in a geographical and sociocultural space] (my translation)

Besides, the analysis of the narrative reveals new liminal elements added to the global meaning of *chez X*: they manifest as XY, underlining a liquid or dissolved threshold between the self and the other, which accounts for a liminal *home*. In *Mèyènô*, I show that XY elements include water, birds, trees, the totem-lizard and ancestral beings. Those elements contaminate the meaning of *chez X* and catalyze its expansion. The local core meaning of *chez soi* has notably shifted from an exclusive space toward an inclusive process:

Modified core (base): [Space of the Same (X/self and demultiplication of X/self) HENCE integration of the space of the Other (Y/other(s)/Diverse/away and demultiplications of Y)]

Paradoxically, Y and XY elements can appear as various components of X: for example, "natural and spiritual elements $(X_1, X_2, X_3...)$" were added to the stereotype "social space of X". *Chez X* becomes a maturation process, originated in the self and extending towards the other. This process particularly arises from a will power to develop through knowledge transmission, learning and experiencing the unknown:

Modified core (base): [Will to extend and transmit the Space of the Same (X/self and demultiplication of X/self) to/with the Other]

However, *Mèyènô*'s will dissolves into a collective will and/or cultural laws (obligations), but also into an uncontrollable desire moved by natural laws (necessity). Thus, the local representation of *chez X* becomes a natural-cultural growth path. It involves subjective values, teaching and learning about the self-other-place as a whole. Besides, semantic kinetics manifested in stereotypes, creating new associations such as: home HENCE change/transformation/maturation.

Non-occurrence and Cognitive Poetics

Exploring emergent children's literature in Oceania, I noticed the common absence of the words *chez, maison* (house) or *home* although the corpus was obviously governed by an omniscient ideology of *home*. Therefore, I searched for the schema of *home* implicitly contained within the story, mainly via parabolic projections such as metaphors. The hidden word-schema was named *non-occurrence* in order to expose its contractive, invisible or intangible presence. Subsequently, *non-occurrence* has developed toward Cognitive Poetics (CP) theories in order to explore that suggestive structure of discourses, in which polyphony and emotions are allegedly rooted. Indeed, this structure appears as the perfect nest for meaning's regeneration. The shifting meaning of *home* was especially explored via *conceptual blending* and the *parabolic mind* (Turner 1996) to emphasize the superposition of mind and landscape. From interwoven conceptual and experiential realities emerges *home* in imagined landscapes and "embodied geographies" (Teather 1999). Therefore, narratives potentiate the representations of all the participants involved in storytelling (Oatley 2003).

My methodology was then applied to the case of *non-occurrent chez X*, in the prototypical local-global narrative *Mèyènô* (French text). The objective was to demonstrate the paradoxical phenomenon of meaning of *regeneration vs. preservation*: its significant role in the process of human and non-human heritage, notably its potential to convey heritage parables, initiations and ideologies via poetic-cognitive strategies.

Intangible Heritage of the Meanings of Home

As an instrumental case study, my work exemplifies a specific problem: how to make tangible, using the combination of two theories (SAP and CP), the relatively intangible and potentially encrypted phenomenon of cultural heritage in poetic narratives. Experiential and affective meanings form the intangible heart of heritage (Harrison and Rose 2010). Indeed, ICH examines meanings related to places and objects: what we think, do and feel become heritage (Ruggles and Silverman 2009; Harrison et al. 2010). Accordingly, the semantic reconstruction of "*chez X*" in *Mèyènô* illustrates how intangible cultures are transmitted and renewed, notably via narrative re-appropriation and representation of social place.

In this way the global semantic meaning of "*chez X*" itself shows a large potential semantic field encompassing numerous stereotypes such as *family, community, culture, country* (my translation). As stated by Thaler and Jean-Bart (2008: 27, my translation):

"Home", which is the focus of human sciences (…) remains however a concept whose frontiers remains hardly be defined since it covers an extended semantic field and shows a large and rich network of connotations (…). Those connotations vary not only from a culture to another but also within one culture, because "home" is the center of fundamental challenges concerning the representations of geographical, physical but also psychic and ideological environment.

Therefore, *home* appears as a major symbolic or parabolic concept, which manifests in every aspects of reality. Parable is a key poetic-cognitive instrument that I explore via linguistic *non-occurrences* in order to understand identity's ideologies. I display how narrative emotions are involved in the interpretative potential carried by words. Like *chez soi*, "referring to a building or a place, however, home refers to the quality of feelings associated with that place" (Nel and Lissa 2011: 10), so *home* embodies and becomes intangible heritage. In fact, my SAP global semantic description of *chez X* underlines emotional elements, notably the following stereotype and AP:

Stereotype: [Emotional stablity of X: place where X feels comfortable, at ease]
AP: [Home HENCE comfortable, happy, secured, not afraid, etc.] (my translation)

I have used such *normal* stereotype and AP to evince the non-occurrent linguistic presence of *chez soi* in *Mèyènô*. Additionally, non-occurrent/co-occurrent semantic kinetics of *chez soi* formed *transgressive*, interpretative layers of meaning. Together, normal and transgressive layers conceptualize the heritage potential of local, experiential meanings associated to a place and culture.

Initiatory Semantics of Home/Chez Soi in Children's Literature

Home–away–home Scenario as a Rite of Passage

A powerful, highly connoted ideology is carried by the representations of *chez soi/home*, particularly in children's literature. According to Anne Rusnak, "the specificity of this literature accounts for its building on the structure *home–away–home*". She explains: "the young character leaves his home and his family in search of adventure, which happens away, then he returns home, transformed and more mature, and the narrative ends." (Rusnak 2008: 53, my translation)

Home/away, chez soi/ailleurs, form the binary axis of *rite of passage* narratives. Indeed, this *initiation* genre depicts specifically the protagonist's growth. Typically, the youngster's leaving home marks the beginning of a circular journey. Far from home, the quest induces his/her learning, decentration and transformation. After many vicissitudes emphasized by the crossing of thresholds, the quest leads to an ultimate passage: the return home through a creative action (Stephens 2011). Moreover, the character itself and his/her home have been transformed, underlining an achieved autonomy and accomplishment. The character's re-incorporation in his original but extended place can also epitomize a successful initiation consistent with Van Gennep's theory in anthropology (1960). Mimesis generated by the encounter of the protagonist and the reader brings the latter to a potential initiation and self-development.

As shown by Thaler and Jean-Bart (2008: 29, my translation), "if the famous saying 'travel shapes youth' tells the truth, then one has to accept the idea that 'home' never defines a universe with fixed frontiers but that those frontiers constantly move and that 'home' expands according to the discoveries and the evolutions of the self". The mutual extension of home and identity described here via journeys can be linguistically documented by SAP semantic kinetics of *home/chez soi* and *not-home/pas-chez soi* within initiation narratives. This phenomenon of meaning regeneration is profoundly linked to self-renewal: not only in the significant case of *home*, but also concerning any signifier or text, the enunciator/narrator is inscribed in his/her own discourse by which reality and subjectivity are re-invented. Similarly, readers' interpretations reshape reality. Writing and reading consequently blend (Oatley 2003). This accounts for narrative complexity, which appears prominent in transcultural literature and indigenous discourses because their strong poetic and suggestive structure accentuates polyphony (Poirier 2008).

At the crossroads of those trends, my case study deals with emergent indigenous children's literature as transcultural and glocal media: complexity might indeed reach its highest level here. Moreover, the combination of intercultural communication and self-development through rite of passage scenarios potentiates ethnodecentration. Stephens (2011) uses those arguments to emphasize "robust" representations of cultural diversity, contrasting with weak and western ones. In my case, the expansion of the interpretative, intercultural potential is documented on the extended potential meaning of *chez soi*.

Linguistic Model Development Towards Local-Global Communications and Poetic Meaning

The initiatory structure of narratives channels the expansion of glocal, potential meaning. Nevertheless, ongoing debates about authorship in emergent children's literature address the issue of authenticity (Bradford 2003; Jouve 2011): local communities must remain at the center of their heritage by developing local-global communications.

Hence, SAP appears as an excellent theory to explore the interactive potential of local-global texts. Moreover, cognitive poetics enhance what I called the *masked meaning* or more technically *non-occurrence* in order to explore the parabolic, poetic, initiatory and suggestive dimensions of semantics. The parabolic SAP analysis of "*chez X*" contributes to understand potential articulations of intersubjectivity and glocal identity related to a place. Meanings and representations can consequently be explored in multiple, simultaneous, and alternative dimensions that I define as *co-occurrence*. Indeed, the textual non-occurrence of *home* expands its co-occurrence. A significant non-occurrent, co-occurrence of "home" and "not-home" stretches within *Mèyènô* as a repetitive binary pattern of [Home NEVERTHELESS not-home] (SAP, my translation). This paradigm highlights liminality.

Local-global strategies notably witness this discursive mask effect, highly prominent in traditional narratives and myths (Levi-Strauss 1979). Permanent and/or dynamic, shared/ specific, explicit/implicit, conscious/unconscious, visible/hidden, preserved/renewed, binary representations point out the mask as a dividual figure (Poirier 2008), which instantiates the passage from one face to another and their coexistence. Universal vehicle of transformation, the mask fundamentally represents identity negotiation between opacity and transparency (Levi-Strauss 1979). In this fashion, cultural heritage is transmitted from ancestors to human beings through masks, which can also manifest as dreams or totems (Herold 1992: 7, 45). For instance, in *Mèyènô,* the lizard is the leading figure and the boy's totem: it indicates his belonging to a clan as a home. Since Réséda Ponga, the author, is an initiated *passer* who can wear such a mask, the narrative becomes a potential vehicle of heritage. It aims at teaching readers the re-appropriation of traditional knowledge.

The mask's basic paradigm (*opacity vs. transparency*) and its articulations can be documented on the one hand, by the normal or transgressive actualization of stereotypes (schemas and scenario included) within the semantic meaning's description and on the other hand, by *non-occurrences*: for example, *home* usually implies emotions, notably love and safety, whereas *not-home* is associated with fear and danger. Thus, the sentence "far from home, you are safe" instantiates a transgressive stereotype: [not-home, HENCE, safety] or [home, HENCE, danger/fear] (SAP). Non-occurrence of [home, HENCE, safety] and [danger/fear HENCE return home] is exemplified by this introductory part of *Mèyènô* (my translation):

Nôe met a huge lizard in the bush and escaped very fast.
She ran to her grandmother who told her a story.

The escape of Nôe indicates a danger associated to an unknown animal in a *not-home* space, contrasting with *home* that the grandmother and her storytelling symbolize here.

Indeed, as shown by Thaler and Jean-Bart (2008: 28, my translation), "travel", "journey" or "adventures" are stereotypes of "non-chez soi"/"not-home". In my analysis, the opposition "home vs. away" manifests on both semantic and discursive grounds: in the global semantic description of *chez soi* as a differential space, and in the transgressive actualization of its stereotypes in *Mèyènô*. For instance, [home NEVERTHELESS "worried"] (SAP, my translation) describes the grandfather's increasing emotion of *worry* while he waits for *Mèyènô's* return. Since *worry* transgresses the stereotypes "comfortable/ feel at ease" usually associated to "home" (my translation), the paradigm [home NEVERTHELESS not-home] is here discursively reconstructed, underlining a liminal place and a potential change of home and self.

Additionally, "home vs. away" sheds light on "domi-centric" and "domi-fugal" representations, which outline two ambivalent *homes*. Firstly, to go or to stay home projects *home* as a "refuge" and a center which brings a feeling of safety. Secondly, "escaping home reflects the fear of home" and/or "the excitement of the promised adventure from the external world" (Thaler and Jean-Bart 2008: 28, my translation). Those contrasting aspirations and emotions usually mirror children and young adults' transformations. Referring to Jean-Michel Adam (1999; Heidmann and Adam 2010), I also demonstrate that both trajectories depict the ICH's dynamics based on sustainable cultural development. Firstly, centripetal, domi-centric, compressive movements potentially depict identity and cultural preservation. This is documented with SAP by normal stereotype actualizations. Secondly, alternative actualizations of stereotypes demonstrate centrifugal, domi-fugal, expanding movements, which emphasize the variations of norms and cultural innovation. Besides, not only does my SAP analysis instantiate both domi-centric and domi-fugal movements in *Mèyènô*, but it also correlates them with opposite attitudes toward the Other. In children's literature, both attitudes are addressed by Hisaoka (2013) through the pivotal concepts of *identity-with* and *difference-from* (James et al. 1998: 202): *identity-with* shelters collaborative values, a participative or intersubjective self and an integrated difference whereas *difference-from* underlines individualism, an exclusive self, separated from others. Then according to Thaler and Jean-Bart (2008: 28, my translation):

> The geographic space is organized from the home vs. not-home opposition, for if individualism is emphasized by anthropocentrism, ethnocentrism and egocentrism, it is also influenced by a "domi-centric" vision of space, that is to say a consciousness of space articulated around a familiar place whose representations are associated with the ideas of identity, safety (physical and psychological) and self-fulfillment.

"Domi-centric" representation of space can be, however, renegotiated through variable degrees of collaboration/exclusion, and witness domi-fugal or domi-centric trajectories. Similarly, the meaning of *home* can be normalized and/or expanded in/by discourses. Conservative or transgressive tendencies to identity-remaking are revealed in this way.

My analysis of *Mèyènô* specifically evidences the blend of a normalized and/or expanded non-occurrent, linguistic representation of *chez X*. Consequently, a contradictive *home* is implicitly emphasized by the superposition of trajectory, center, and domi-fugal or domi-centric moves. Above all, linguistic clues indicate a potential parable: the narrative seems to carry a liminal French-Kanak identity disclosed by contradictory ideologies of the Self. Indeed, while modern Western cultures are embodied by an exclusive Self, indigenous cultures demonstrate an inclusive and dividual Self (Poirier 2008: 78) also found among

Asian cultures, as explained by Stephens (2013) in the context of children's books. Another potential parable would be the passage from an old, stereotyped, westernized representation of local identities, to a new, postmodern, and glocal one. The latest potentiates the reconstruction of the Other that is non-exclusive, in an ethno-decentered perspective.

Home as a Trajectory in Emergent Literature

Meaning-making can happen through diverse media. The case of emergent children's literature as a local-global media intertwines meaning-making, "community-making" (Sell 2004), "making self" and "making place" (Birkeland 2005). In a postcolonial context, literature emerges from oral traditions as a cultural restoration and identity re-appropriation. This revival through experiential writing is salient in Aboriginal Australia and among the Kanak in New Caledonia. Indigenous emergent literature often depicts *home* as a subjective geography and trajectory. This vision echoes the act of dwelling, defined as "a process where the space in which human beings live becomes a personal space or a personal world: a home" (Birkeland 2005: 9). Dwelling clarifies here the process of home-making that I describe in terms of localization, *semiotization* and appropriation of a self-in-place. Thus, "with a focus on the becoming rather than the being", Birkeland argues that "from talking about dwelling in places, we might talk about dwelling-as-path" (2005: 16). Eventually, home as a trajectory incorporates the difference. Highlighted in *Mèyènô* with new local stereotypes such as "home HENCE change/difference" (my translation), this shift of meaning echoes the shift toward the "feminine" that Birkeland calls forth: "Place can potentially be a feeling of being at home in our body–place in a way where difference is allowed for. I think this would be a sense of home where difference is met with wonder." (2005: 148) Moreover, dwelling is specifically instantiated by the *return home* in literature, which notably emerges in Bartminski's cognitive ethnolinguistics of *home* concepts: "Returning home is interpreted as returning to oneself. I am my own home, you are your own home. One cannot escape or abandon the home so understood." (Bartminski 2009: 159) In other words, one cannot run away from oneself. Home and the self thus become either a prison or an instrument of liberation and fulfilment. As such, the *return home* can symbolize indigenous potential liberation, decolonization, re-traditionalization and cultural revival (Attwood 2011; Kolig 2004; Maddock 2004).

Last but not least, *home* as a center and trajectory mirrors the *routes vs. roots* paradigm that characterizes indigenous societies of Oceania (Jolly 2001). The initiatory meaning of *home* carried by indigenous children's literature has in fact always existed in oral traditions. For instance, storytelling in the Yolngu indigenous community in Australia is addressed by Fiona Magowan: "The ability to condense long journeys over vast tracts of land through telling stories is a means of journeying from place to place and from one group to another in practice and in the imagination." (Magowan 2001: 44) So traditional narratives fundamentally remain rites of passage stories embodied in experiential landscapes. Therefore, traditional stories are superposed maps: they enclose multiple layers of meaning re-created by contexts and co-texts, cultural practices and places, individuals and groups. This network forms a complex system moved by ancestrality, the heart of heritage. Emergent literature is rooted in those oral traditions. Thus, I have proven that *Mèyènô* conceals such layers, as routes and roots, which were revealed by the pragmatic-semantics of *home*.

Conclusion: Conservative-Innovative Heritage Strategies and Multipolarized Home

As expected, a powerful, highly connoted ideology is carried by the representations of home in the text, as it is generally the case in children's literature. Yet, my discourse analysis has also confirmed that the story of *Mèyènô* uncovers a multiple, dividual and dialogic representation of home as an in-between place that integrates home and homes but also home and not-home: human, nature and ancestors.

Looking specifically at the preservation of diversity and the revival of local communities (Kanak society in particular), I investigated loca-global continuums rooted in the linguistic structure of the contemporary media that were produced by those societies.

This study has illustrated how the parabolic, local-global structure of the text:

- expands its interpretative potential;
- potentiates a local-global dialogue;
- offers paths of interpretation, nevertheless secured by contextual cultural knowledge and initiations.

To summarize, my linguistic analysis of *chez soi* within *Mèyènô* has evidenced the transformative power of this text, especially because it potentiates the discussion between the representations of the Self/Sameness and the Other/Difference. In this way, the text mixes local (Kanak) and global worldviews, which contributes to the preservation of local representations as well as the renewal of those representations in the process of interpretation from "global" reader: the dialogical connexion between "local and global" visions becomes possible through the story. This was documented on the one hand, by a co-constructed and integrative French-Kanak representation of *chez soi,* also articulated as a multi-layered linguistic schema/scenario. Linked to the "dividual self ", the dividual and liminal *chez soi* indicates a new representation of "home" which might be a local, Kanak one; whereas exclusive images of self and *chez soi* remain normal and preserved according to the lexicographic meaning of *"chez soi"* (that is the decontextualized meaning from the perspective of a French, non-Kanak reader).

Moreover, I have shown the ideology of *chez soi* inscribed within a poetic intercultural narrative. I have displayed semantic-discursive strategies that can either transform or preserve the representations of the meaning of *chez soi*. This contributes to understand, shape and initiate identity representations (here, the Kanak culture), from one's language (here, French).

In *Mèyènô*, the shift from *difference-from* to *identity-with* patterns induces an ever expanding *chez soi*, and witnesses the polyphonic narrative that conceals two alternative attitudes toward stereotypes: participation-detachment, respectively linked to preservation-innovation and to domi-centric–domi-fugal binary motions and emotions. However, those contrasts are often blurred. This is notably instantiated by a binary *chez soi* emerging between life and death. As follows, back and forth movements in the story mirror uncertain, liquid and interactive identities governed by conservative and innovative heritage strategies.

Accordingly, interaction gathers contradictive viewpoints depicted by co-occurrent *chez soi* patterns. Once transformed into a lizard, *Mèyènô* becomes a totem or a mask that, indeed, instantiates dialogue, sustaining oppositions into continuums: roots and routes, human and non-human; land and sea; space and time; visible and invisible; imagination and reality; global and local. One still point eventually appears in this turning world: the original *chez soi*. Its key words could be integration, dialogue and renewal. Ultimately, the rebirth of *Mèyènô* is a return home, to his true essence: the mask—totem and water element—enhances fluid decentration, continuous transformation and learning. Here, the representation of an alternative *chez soi* potentiates the parable of dialogic heritage, along with glocal and liquid identities. Last but not least, narrative interpretative paths are secured by initiations, the only condition to open indigenous rituals to western readers, allowing glocal, cross-cultural learning.

In fact, those paths bring in the sustainable and glocal potential of linguistic meaning. That involves the coexistence of universalism and particularism at the core of heritage. Meaning-making is moved by a heritage process of preservation and innovation via alternative strategies of silence and revelation, which my study has disclosed. Hence, the shifting meaning of *chez soi* confirms that "there is no absolute comprehension of another cultural experience, only degrees" (Marcus and Fischer 1986: 64). One can move closer to those foreign representations through *initiatory* local-global narratives. Besides, semantic modifications might stabilize within a given group and expand the semantic heritage of *chez soi*. Drawing on *Le Lexis'* definition, "localization" and "presence *in* (…)" could move toward an open process of *becoming with*. *Chez soi* might indicate interstitial dynamics; an expanding network of interconnections *between* multiple probabilities of residence(s)/ country(ies)/body(ies) (…) of someone, as a dividual self. Echoing the original home of the mother's womb, *chez soi* emerges as a source and vehicle of growth; the channel of the becoming self. Instead of delimiting the self, *chez soi* might entangle or tune with the self. Shifting from object to subject, *chez soi* could eventually be described as a living body-place and the essential nurturing environment for self-development. In fact, in the perspective of a contingent self, *chez soi* becomes potential, intangible and multipolarized. Defined as "living at home abroad or abroad at home—ways of inhabiting multiple places at once" (Pollock et al. 2002: 11), *cosmopolitanism* seems to emerge from my analysis. Accordingly, *Mèyènô* can show a "cosmopolitan heritage practice (…) as one that expands the community of the present to include the community of the past" (Byrne 2009: 249). The multipolarized home could also relate to a multipolarized identity reflected through the recent referendum in New Caledonia.

Finally, in the light of the glocal semantics of *home*, I have explored how language can shape systems of thoughts and beliefs by creating new visions. I have emphasized how identity discourses can use poetics to transform society's representations, especially people's attitude toward difference. The positive association of difference and reciprocity can be reinforced by local-global media so that *home* as *culture* do "account for the difference" (McGrane 1989; quoted by Robertson 1997: 72) but not so much "of ", as *with* "the other". Opening indigenous worldviews, this vision draws a sustainable path for human and non-human heritage. It sheds light on our responsibility to re-invent the rituals that define our *home*.

In further research I have investigated the possible applications of glocal narratives and glocal models for learning languages and cultures. Moreover, other types of local-global media can be explored as well as the extension and the application of SAP to the analysis of the text and pictures (semiotic components). Regarding the SAP model, my PhD research has shown that it remains particularly relevant for new local-global narratives created in various communities, such as Kanak but also Aboriginal societies in Australia, which I would like to explore further. Yet, SAP can be applied to any language, discourse or context: the potential for research development here is endless.

Notes

1. Despite the failure of the motion, New Caledonians will, under the terms of the Nouméa Accord, have the opportunity to vote again in 2020 and (if that vote fails as well) in 2022 if one third of the Congress of New Caledonia—the local legislature—agree to allow those votes to be held.

2. Galatanu defines stereotypes here as an "open set of associations of the core elements with other representations, which constitute blocks of internal argumentations" (2011: 175, my translation).

❑ Acknowledgement

This work is based on the results of my PhD research at Macquarie University, Australia and Université de Nantes, France (2015).

❑ Disclosure Statement

No potential conflict of interest was reported by the author.

❑ Funding

PhD Research funding by Macquarie University International Research Excellence Scholarship (Australia).

❑ Note on Contributor

Dr. *Séverine J. Didier* is Associate Lecturer in French at the University of Tasmania in Australia. She holds a PhD in International Studies—Arts, specialized in European Languages and Cultures (Macquarie University, Australia) as well as Doctorate in Language's Science specialized in Semantics and Discourse Analysis (Université de Nantes, France). Her PhD deals with "The transmission of intangible cultural heritage through children's literature. Semantic-discursive modeling of *'home'* and *'chez soi'* in the narrative *Mèyènô*" (Ponga 2004). Prior to her PhD, Dr. Didier obtained three Masters Diplomas in International Business, in Marketing but also in Literature, Languages and Communications for Research with a specialization in French as a Foreign Language.

□ References

Adam, J. M. 1999. *Linguistique Textuelle des Genres de Discours aux Textes*. Paris: Nathan.

Adams, J. M. 1999. The Social Implications of Hypermobility. In *OECD Project on Environmentally Sustainable Transport. The Economic and Social Implications of Sustainable Transportation*, 95-134. Paris: OECD publications.

Attwood, B. 2011. Aboriginal History, Minority Histories and Historical Wounds: The Postcolonial Condition, Historical Knowledge and the Public Life of History in Australia. *Postcolonial Studies* 14: 171-186.

Bartminski, J., and J. Zinken. 2009. *Aspects of Cognitive Ethnolinguistics*. London: Equinox Pub.

Bauman, Z. 2000. *Liquid Modernity*. Cambridge: Polity Press.

Bauman, Z., and L. Bury. 2007. *Le Présent Liquide—Peurs Sociales et Obsession Sécuritaire*. Laurent Bury (Trans.). Paris: Seuil.

Birkeland, I. J. 2005. Making Place, *Making Self: Travel, Subjectivity and Sexual Difference*. Aldershot: Ashgate.

Bradford, C. 2003. "Oh How Different!": Regimes of Knowledge in Aboriginal Texts for Children. *The Lion and the Unicorn* 27 (2): 199-217.

Byrne, D. 2009. A Critique of Unfeeling Heritage. In *Intangible Heritage*, edited by L. Smith, and N. Akagawa, 229-252. London: Routledge.

Clifford, J., and G. E. Marcus. 1986. *Writing Culture: The Poetics and Politics of Ethnography: A School of American Research Advanced Seminar*. Berkeley: University of California Press.

Didier, S. J. 2015. The Transmission of Intangible Cultural Heritage in Children's Literature. Semantic-Discursive Modelling of "Chez Soi" ("Home" in French) in the Narrative *Mèyènô* (Ponga 2004). Doctoral Dissertation, Macquarie University, sydney and University of Nantes.

Dubois, J. 2002. Chez Soi. In *Larousse de la Langue Française: Lexis*, 330-331. Paris:

Larousse/VUEF.

Galatanu, O. 2011. Les Valeurs Affectives des "MarqueursDiscursifsIllocutionnaires" en Français et en Anglais. In *Marqueurs Discursifs et Subjectivité*, edited by S. Hancil, 173-190. Rouen: PURH.

Galatanu, O. 2012. De la Menace Illocutionnaire aux Actes Illocutionnaires "Menaçants". Pour une Sémantique de l'Interaction Verbale. *Studii de Lingvistica* 59 (2) : 59-79.

Graham, L. R. 2009. Problematizing of Technologies for Documenting Intangible Culture: Some Positive and Negative Consequences. In *Intangible Heritage Embodied*, edited by D. F. Ruggles, and H. Silverman, 185-200. New York: Springer.

Gutierrez, A. K. 2013. Metamorphosis: The Emergence of Glocal Subjectivities in the Blend of Global, Local, East, and West. In *Subjectivity in Asian Children's Literature and Film: Global Theories and Implications*, edited by J. Stephens, 19-42. New York: Routledge.

Hall, S. 1997. The Local and the Global: Globalization and Ethnicity. In *Culture, Globalization and the World System: Contemporary Conditions for the Representation of Identity*, edited by A. D. King, 19-39. Minneapolis, Minnesota: University of Minnesota Press.

Harrison, R., and D. B. Rose. 2010. Intangible Heritage. In *Understanding Heritage and Memory*, edited by R. Harrison, D. B. Rose, and T. Benton, 238-245. Manchester: Manchester University Press in association with the Open University.

Harrison, R., D. B. Rose, and T. Benton. 2010. *Understanding Heritage and Memory*. Manchester: Manchester University Press in association with the Open University.

Heidmann, U., and J. M. Adam. 2010. *Textualité et Intertextualité des Contes: Perrault, Apulée, La Fontaine, Lhéritier.* Paris: Editions Classiques Garnier.

Herold, E. 1992. *The World of Masks*. Prague: Hamlyn.

Hisaoka, M. 2013. Cooperation and Negociation, Formation of Subjectivity in Japanese and Australian Picture Books. In *Subjectivity in Asian Children's Literature and Film: Global Theories and Implications*, edited by J. Stephens, 59-78. New York: Routledge.

James, A., C. Jenks, and A. Prout. 1998. *Theorizing Childhood*. Cambridge: Polity Press in association with Blackwell.

Jolly, M. 2001. On the Edge? Deserts, Oceans, Islands. *The Contemporary Pacific* 13 (2): 417-466.

Jouve, D. 2011. L'Auteur de Littérature de Jeunesse en Nouvelle-Calédonie: un Auteur dans Tousses Etats. In *L'Auteur pour la Jeunesse, de l'Editionà l'Ecole*, edited by J. F. Massol, and F. Quet, 121-139. Grenoble: Ellug, ENS de Lyon.

Juniper, E. 2001. A New Oceania: An Interview with Epeli Hau'ofa. *Antipodes* 15: 22-25.

Kolig, E., and H. Muckler. 2002. *Politics of Indigeneity in the South Pacific: Recent Problems of Identity in Oceania*. Münster, Germany: Lit Verlag.

Levi-Strauss, C. 1979. *La Voie des Masques*. Paris: Plon.

Maddock, K. 2002. Revival, Renaissance, and the Meaning of Modern Constructions in Australia. In *Politics of indigeneity in the South Pacific: Recent Problems of Identity in Oceania*, edited by E. Kolig, K. Maddock, and H. Mueckler, 25-46. Münster, Germany: Lit Verlag.

Magowan, F. 2001. Crying to Remember: Reproducing Personhood and Community. In *Telling Stories: Indigenous History and Memory in Australia and New Zealand*, edited by B. Attwood, and F. Magowan, 41-60. Wellington: Bridget Williams Books Limited.

Marcus, G. E., and M. M. J. Fischer. 1986. *Anthropology as Cultural Critique: An Experimental Moment in the Human Sciences*. Chicago: University of Chicago Press.

McGrane, B. 1989. *Beyond Anthropology: Society and the Other*. New York: Columbia University Press.

Nel, P., and L. Paul. 2011. *Keywords for Children's Literature*. New York: New York University Press.

Oatley, K. 2003. Writing and Reading: The Future of Cognitive Poetics. In *Cognitive Poetics in Practice*, edited by G. Steen, and J. Gavins, 151-173. London: Routledge.

Perrot, J. 2005. *Mythe et Transmission de l'Identité Kanak*. Citrouille: ASLJ.

Poirier, S. 2008. Reflections on Indigenous Cosmopolitics—Poetics. *Anthropologica* 50: 75-85.

Ponga, R., and L. Lagabrielle. 2004. *Mèyènô: Conte Kanak en Français—A'jië.* Noumea, New Caledonia: Grain de Sable Jeunesse and Ngan Jila Tjibaou Cultural Centre.

Robertson, R. 1997. Social Theory, Cultural Relativity and the Problem of Globality. In *Culture, Globalization and the World System: Contemporary Conditions for the Representation of Identity,* edited by A. D. King, 69-90. Minneapolis, Minnesota: University of Minnesota Press.

Ruggles, D. F., and H. Silverman. 2009. *Intangible Heritage Embodied.* New York: Springer.

Rusnak, A. 2008. Le "Home": un Espace Privilégiéen Littérature de Jeunesse Québécoise. In *Home Words: Discourses of Children's Literature in Canada,* edited by M. Reimer, 51-66. Waterloo: Wilfrid Laurier University Press.

Seixo, M. A. 2004. Littérature Post-coloniale et Globalisation—Sur Quelques Textes de la Littérature du Pacifique. In *Littératures d'émergence et mondialisation: Théorie, société et politique,* edited by S. Faessel, 25-37. Paris: Editions In Press.

Sell, R. D. 2004. What's Literary Communication and What's Literary Community. In *Littératures d'émergence et mondialisation: Théorie, société et politique,* edited by S. Faessel, 39-45. Paris: Editions In Press.

Stephens, J. 2011. Schemas and Scripts: Cognitive Instruments and the Representation of Cultural Diversity in Children's Literature. In *Contemporary Children's Literature and Film: Engaging with Theory,* edited by K. Mallan, and C. Bradford, 12-35. New York: Palgrave Macmillan.

Stephens, J. 2013. *Subjectivity in Asian Children's Literature and Film: Global Theories and Implications.* New York: Routledge.

Teather, E. K. 1999. *Embodied Geographies: Spaces, Bodies and Rites of Passage.* New York: Routledge.

Thaler, D., and Alain Jean-Bart. 2008. Les Représentations du *"Home"* dans les Romans Historiques Québécois Destinés aux Adolescents. In *Home Words: Discourses of Canadian Literature,* edited by M. Reimer, 31-45. Waterloo: Wilfrid Laurier

University Press.

Turner, M. 1996. *The Literary Mind*. New York: Oxford University Press.

Van Gennep, A. 1960. *The Rites of Passage*. Chicago: University of Chicago Press.

Wierzbicka, A. 1997. *Understanding Cultures Through Their Key Words: English, Russian, Polish, German, and Japanese*. New York: Oxford University Press.

Staying in Academia or Facing the Public: University Museums in China Today

WANG Shaohan

Institute of Archaeology, University College London, 31-34 Gordon Square, London
WC1H 0PY UK. CONTACT WANG Shaohan: shaohan.wang.15@ucl.ac.uk

Abstract: The early university museums in China seem to be conceived with a strong academic emphasis. Curators in most university museums are museologists or heritage professionals who actively participate in university teaching and academic research. However, the contribution of today's university museums is not limited to their academic remit. In 2011, the State Bureau of Cultural Relics and the Ministry of Education in China published a notification on developing university museums. This document emphasises that university museums not only complement academic research and higher education, but also make important contributions to public engagement and social responsibility. This demonstrates the increasing attention paid towards the public function of university museums, which raises a question for curators of such museums: how can university museums balance their role within and outside the academic world, with a situation of limited human and financial resources? Drawing on a comparative analysis of the Sichuan University Museum and the Arthur M. Sackler Museum of Art and Archaeology at Peking University, this article attempts to discuss the academic and social roles of university museums in China today.

Keywords: university museums, publicly facing institutions, parent universities, academia, identity

Introduction

University museums can contribute to the academic research and education of their parent universities. In 1914, Jian Zhang, a famous Chinese industrialist of the early 20th century, established the first university museum in China, the Nantong Museum. This museum was developed around the botanical garden of the Tongzhou Normal University with a major purpose of providing practical training opportunities to the students. This academic function naturally became its main concern. Since then, an increasing number of university collections have become valued as irreplaceable teaching resources in China. In some museums curators themselves also actively participate in the teaching and research of the universities.

Entering the late 20th century, the role of university museums was debated by academics globally. In 1999, Kelly published her work on the study of higher education museums, galleries and collections (HEMGCs) management approaches in UK. The management of university museums from the perspectives of functions, purposes, management structures and stakeholders were analysed with examples. She argues that HEMGC has two roles: one within the academic world and the other as a public role. For universities, HEMGC not only assesses the academic research and high-level education for specific areas, but also provides interdisciplinary experiences to students from other areas (Kelly 1999). In fact, university museums use interdisciplinary collaboration to demonstrating its value in interdisciplinary research/teaching (Kelly 1999). This argument could be supported by the cooperation of the Yale Centre for British Art (YCBA) with the Yale School of Medicine in 1999, which aimed at improving the observational skills of medical students (Friedlaender 2016; Dolev, Friedlaender, and Braverman 2001).

Kelly's suggestion on engaging wider audiences is not limited to interdisciplinary cooperation. As an outcome of the International Management Seminar in Higher Education hosted in 2000, she further argued that university museums have the ability to attract the general public of all ages and social classes (Kelly 2001: 9-12). In other words, they are windows that allow their parent universities to reach out the wider world.

The International Council of Museum (ICOM) also shows great concern to the topic. One volume of *MUSEUM International* (Volume 52, Issue 2 and 3 etc.) was published on the theme of "university museum" in 2000. University museums worldwide were discussed and examined from various perspectives by international museologists. Willumson, one of the contributors has studied the change in university museum audiences since the 1980s. He believes that due to the "shirking" of financial support, university museums were trying to cater to the needs of audiences outside the university to find new funding sources (Willumson 2000). This phenomenon became one of the underlying reasons that lead university museums to the way of becoming a public-facing institution.

Discussions on the transformation of university museums in China focus on providing practical advice to university museums on how to expand their public functions (Liu and Zhang 2012; Ye 2012), whilst maintaining their academic importance. Shan (2015) argued that university museums in China are usually supported by academic departments with relevant majors. The expansion of the public function of university museums is not simply a new fad but also turns them into a more comprehensive academic basis for museology (Shan 2015). From another aspect, university museums are unique cultural landscapes for universities (Shan 2015). Museologists based in universities and the high credibility of the parent institutions are natural resources that enable the development of university museums (Shan 2015).

One might argue that this public function is embodied in the birth of Chinese university museums since the Nantong Museum did provide access to the general public. In fact, since the early establishment of some large university museums such as the Ashmolean Museum, the sense of public service has been part of their management strategy, embodied by providing limited access to the public (MacGregor 2001). However, does enabling limited public accessibility equate to a university museum which fully fulfills its public functions?

This article will use the Sichuan University Museum and the Arthur M. Sackler Museum of Art and Archaeology at Peking University as case studies to address the recent change of university museums. In addition, another question that will be discussed is if a university museum does have a public function, how it balances this with its academic role.

Defining University Museum

The term "museum" is generated from the ancient Greek "Μουσεῖov" (Mouseion), the place where gods and goddesses of history, poetry, dance and other arts meditate (Wittlin 1949). With the development of museum theories, the definition of museums has become more specific and complex. In 2007, the ICOM published its newest museum definition and included the intangible heritage of humanity and its environment into it:

A museum is a non-profit, permanent institution in the service of society and its development, open to the public, which acquires, conserves, researches, communicates and exhibits the tangible and intangible heritage of humanity and its environment for the purposes of education, study and enjoyment.

What about university museums? How could we define a "university museum"? It is beyond doubt that "university museum" is a special type of museum. Similar to public museums, university museums are also a complex phenomenon (Wittlin 1949). They are not only diverse in collections and display methods, but their functions and roles within and outside universities also vary. Thus, it might be difficult to accurately define what is a university museum. Wittlin (1949) regarded university museums as a "presentative type of collection that may form part of a learned society or research station of any kind". It recognises intellectuals as the main audience group and reflects the research function of university museums. This definition clearly reflected the character of early university museums in Europe. In the 19th and the early 20th century, university museums were established with the objective of assisting academic research and university education (Merriman 2001). According to the research of Merriman (2001: 57), university collections at that time were fundamental requirements of teaching and research in most universities. The wide use of collections promoted the development of university museums (Merriman 2001). Today, however, their function is changing and they are transforming from academic collections to public institutions. Based on the discussions in the 2000 Institutional Management Seminar in Higher Education, Kelly (2001) argues that university museums are "preeminent" in assisting scholarship as well as benefiting the public. Their primary function also determines that till now most university museums are with no or limited facilities/services designed for audiences outside of the universities.

Another museologist, Warhurst (2015), provides a more literal meaning of the term. Different from Wittlin, Warhurst's definition is more focused on the physical identity of university museums. He argues that university museums are museums or collections which are established and administrated by "parent universities". This definition emphasises the interaction between the university museums and their parent universities. From this aspect, we could see university museums as a type of cultural facility/institution within universities which are usually classified by disciplines, such as archaeology, zoology or nature science. The majority of collections kept in those museums are usually from the fieldworks conducted by relevant faculties. They reflect the contributions made by the parent universities in disciplinary development. Furthermore, the unique identity of a parent university could be presented by its university museum through exhibiting and interpreting the collections. This fact is a key point that differentiates university museums from other types of museum.

University Museums in China[1]

After university museums were first introduced to China in the early 20th century, there was a boom in the 1960s and today. Currently there are over 160 university museums in China. Although their developmental trajectories vary considerably, one similar aspect is the increasing attention paid to developing public functions. Entering the 21st century, expanding audience groups seems to be drawing more attention from many university museum curators. Benefiting the general public seems to have become an important function of Chinese university museums. Efforts to engage wider audiences have been taken by museums, such as the Sichuan University Museum and the Arthur M. Sackler Museum of Art and Archaeology at Peking University. To understand the past development, current condition and future strategy of the two university museums, the method used in this research took the combination of textural document research and semi-structured interview. The textural documents mainly cover literatures contributed by Chinese scholars and the online materials provided by the two university museums. Semi-structured interview is a commonly used method when collecting data from people. One manager from each university museum was invited in this research as an interviewee.

The Sichuan University Museum is one of the earliest established university museums in China. In 1919, the West China Union College (now called the West China Centre of Medical University of Sichuan University) established the first university museum in southwest China. Initially founded by an American missionary, D. S. Dye, this museum introduced modern western museum theories and management systems into China (Smalley 2012). During the early period of the West China Union College Museum, it focused on assisting academic research in ethnography, anthropology and natural history. A collection of over 6000 objects belonging to the museum were stored in the Hard College. After Dr. David Crockett Graham became the curator in 1932, while remaining active in academic fields, the museum started to extend its influence to the wider public (Liljestrand 1934). The relocation of the museum to the library building provided permanent display areas for the collections. The new exhibition attracted more and more interests from the society (Xu 2016: 305). Later in the 1940s, Dekun Zheng, the new curator of the museum, saw the potential for using the museum collections in mass education and opened the museum to the public (Xu 2016: 314).

In the 1980s, the university started to take actions in disengaging the museum from the Institute of History. The administration authority of the Sichuan University Museum was then moved from department to central university control in 1984. This change transformed the museum into an independent institution and a more comprehensive plan for the museum was developed. In addition to assisting university teaching and research, more academic achievements were acquired by the museum members in wider subjects. During the interview, Manager A from the museum mentioned that being an independent institution meant that the museum needed to directly serve the development plan of the university. The university acknowledged the growing importance of the museum, not only in improving academic capacity but also in arousing social awareness. To some extent, the change promoted the transformation process of the museum from a traditional university museum to a public-facing institution. Six exhibition rooms were then established for the museum with the support of the Ministry of Education. With the expansion of exhibition areas, the audience capacity of the museum was impressively enlarged. Five thematic exhibitions were designed by the museum managers, including folklore, ethnology and rock carving art. Manager A regarded the change of the exhibition strategy, from following a comprehensive history to developed thematic exhibitions, as another change brought about by the administrative movement. In addition, to provide better public accessibility, the use of new exhibition methods improved the visiting experience. The wider public were regarded as stakeholders and were involved in the exhibition design from the start. A public-facing institution is a place run for all people to use. Its services are designed for the need of the wider public. In the past, although people outside the university were welcomed to visit the Sichuan University Museum, their desires and needs were seldom considered by the museum's managers. From this, it can be seen that it was after becoming independent, that the museum first became equipped to take on a public function.

Its public function was further explored and increasingly valued after 2005, when the museum moved to its current location. Special activities and courses were designed for different audience groups, including local communities, school children, and local forces. Manager A believes that the funding the university gets from the government is public money. And that, therefore, it is the responsibility of the university to fulfill its social role. As the university is the major funding source for the museum, meeting the university's needs is also important to the museum. In other words, it is also the responsibility of the museum to reach the wider public and contribute to the process of fulfilling the social responsibility of the university. What worried Manger A is that the museum's limited staff could hardly support the dual role of the museum. Most professional managers in the museum are from the School of History and Culture who are also heavily engaged in academic research and university teaching. Their dual roles mean they work under enormous pressure. Concentrating on just the museum management is almost impossible for these professionals. The lack of professional staff has become a major challenge at the museum.

A different scenario exists at the Arthur M. Sackler Museum of Art and Archaeology at Peking University which is under the administration of the School of Archaeology and Museology. Established in 1986, the museum is the first archaeology museum in China. Evolving the wider public is in their development plan since the establishment. However, the original intention of the donor, Arthur M. Sackler, was to build a platform for academic exchange between China and the US. Thus, assisting academic activities is still the major concern of the museum. Collections in the museum include objects donated by Sackler, as well as the early collections of the past Yenching University and the early Peking University. In fact, Peking University has a long history of collecting relics and specimens. A number of objects stored in the museum were collected from the previous excavations and investigations of Peking University.

Manager B from the museum explained the aims of the museum during the interview as: firstly, preserving, protecting, displaying, studying and interpreting the collections; secondly, constantly researching new knowledge; and thirdly, sharing their academic achievements with the world. These aims clearly present the dual role of the museum as an academic contributor together with a public-facing institution. Since the official opening of the Arthur M. Sackler Museum of Art and Archaeology at Peking University in 1993, audiences outside of the university get the opportunity to access the museum and its collections. Similar to the Sichuan University Museum, the wider public provide comprehensive audience groups to the museum. The permanent exhibition introduces audiences to the development and achievements of the School of Archaeology and Museology which highlight the identity of the department. As mentioned by Manager B, what makes the museum distinct is that the museum regards enhancing the public's understanding of archaeology and art as a major mission. By focusing on certain topics, the exhibitions in the Arthur M. Sackler Museum of Art and Archaeology at Peking University try to help visitors to understand more about how archaeological studies are conducted and how artistic works could be understood from an academic perspective. This exhibition strategy forms one of the key characters which distinguishes public-facing university museums from public museums.

It is worth noting that a public-facing university museum is not the same as a public museum. Using exhibitions to introduce the history and the development direction of certain disciplines is a method which help university museums position themselves and distinguish themselves from public museums. Exhibitions in public museums usually focus on general education about a culture, a technology, a site or certain historical periods, etc. Attention is seldomly paid to the understanding of relevant disciplines. However, universities are at the foremost position of disciplinary developments. As a contributor, a public-facing university museum has the ability and should take the responsibility in introducing the dynamic development of different disciplines to the general public. This aim is not necessarily realised by designing a thematic exhibition; on the contrary, it should be concerned in various exhibitions and illustrated with the combination of different collections as it is a progressive process.

The engagement of the wider public in exhibition preparation further underlines their position as stakeholders in the museum. Fulfilling the public function and building a reputation is not the only benefit of engaging the public. The participation of the general public, from different ages and social strata, also brings new ideas and energy to the museum. In 2017, the museum designed an exhibition named "Inside and Outside of the

Wall (墙 内 外)". This exhibition was based on the results of the community archaeology project conducted in the Pingliangtai Site. Local communities were invited into the project not only as participants but also as contributors to the exhibition. It encourages the wider public to relocate themselves as participants instead of spectators while visiting the exhibition. As a consequence, the exhibition addressed questions such as "what is the link between archaeology and the current world?" and "what can archaeologists contribute to this link?" From my point of view, this exhibition made a vivid description of the development of Chinese archaeology from "studies into the past" to "influencing the future" in a way which audiences from all background could understand.

Similarly, the Arthur M. Sackler Museum of Art and Archaeology at the Peking University is also facing the problem of a lack of professional staff. Manager B mentioned that to lessen the work pressure, the museum encourages museology students to participate in the exhibition designs. This also allows the students to practise the theories they have learned in their lectures, as well as to further explore and examine public engagement methods while running exhibitions.

A Time of Change

One of the factors that could affect the development of university museums is how universities regard and treat them. The reason why university museums need to follow the instruction of their parent universities comes from the position of university museums. In China, a university is the major, or the only sponsor of its museum. To acquire more financial support, university museums must ensure their work and plans follow those of their parent universities. In addition, since university museums are the ones that located inside universities, their sustainable development must be ensured by their parent universities. In other words, the universities have the right and responsibility to "direct" their museums.

Charles Saumarez Smith, in his article "Museums, Artefacts, and Meanings", argues that the history of museums can be characterised by a "process of transformation from a private collection into a public institution" (Saumarez Smith 1997: 7). Unlike public museums, all collections preserved inside university museums could still be regarded as "private" to some extent. Physically, those collections are owned and managed by their parent universities. That is to say, universities have the right to decide whether their collections will be kept within the university and its departments.

Universities nowadays in China are encouraged by academics and the government in becoming knowledge bases for a wider public. Based on Altbach and Peterson's discussion on modern universities' function in 2007, Gu (2011) argues that under global challenges, modern universities are now in the transformation from "elite education" to "mass education", and then to "universal education". While intergrading into society and the wider public, establishing a cultural field and spiritual home for the public has become the new mission for universities nowadays in China (Gu 2011). In 2012, the Ministry of Education together with the Ministry of Finance proposed their ideas on enhancing the innovate capacity of universities, in which universities are encouraged to take on their role in social services. In response to this document, universities, such as the Peking University, established their MOOC (massive open online course) website, which aim at reforming teaching methods and benefiting the wider public through providing self-learning opportunities. Within this new tendency, university museums nowadays are rarely institutions only for intellectuals.

Parent universities create a living environment for their museums and provide them with financial, technical and employment support. In other words, the development of university museums depends greatly on their parent universities. Thus, as unique resources for universities, they logically become another front in realising the new identity of Chinese universities. They follow the instructions of the governing sectors and fulfill the developing purposes of their parent universities. From this aspect, it seems reasonable to conjecture that facing a wider public is an essential development for many university museums. This principle could also be generated from the role of universities as institutions with social responsibility and is emphasised by universities' various developing "impact" agendas.

Regarding the cultural assets they preserve as well as their exhibitions and interpretative ability, university museums are put at "the heart of the evolving Higher Education sector" (MacDonald et al. 2013: 2-3). They are places for universities to present their heritage and academic traditions. By engaging with communities, schools and even international audiences, university museums provide opportunities for the public, from different ages and social backgrounds, to enjoy a life-long education experience in higher education institutions. As a consequence, these changes of university museums "provide public relations value to the university's external image" (Boylan 1999: 53) and bring an intangible asset—prestige to universities.

According to this research, the history of the Sichuan University Museum presents a process of reconsideration of its position in the university. The contribution of university museums in enhancing their parent universities' social influence has been valued. Compared with purely academic institutions such as academic departments and faculties, university museums can be more easily approached by the general public. Besides the relatively separate space, university museums have the ability to integrate and demonstrate the heritage and academic achievements of the university through exhibitions and activities, with the help of collections and supplements. Thus, there is a possibility for the general public to understand the identity of a university while exploring exhibitions or attending workshops in the museums. In addition, online exhibitions and education projects for the general public and school children also contribute to enhancing the wider social influence of universities.

Another feature developing in university museums in China is the need for external financial support. Although university museums are fully funded by their parent institutions in China, financial support can be very limited. According to the investigation, of 49 university museums in 2014, only 5 of them could get 1 million yuan per year from their parent universities; 23 of them could get annual funding of 500 thousands to 1 million yuan; 13 of them could get 100 thousands to 500 thousands yuan per year; the remaining 8 university museums could only get annual funding below 100 thousands yuan (Xie, Zhang, and Sha 2016). This annual funding is not only for exhibitions but also includes the daily maintenance expenses. Those university museums with less funding could hardly ensure the daily opening of their exhibition halls (Xie, Zhang, and Sha 2016). For the sake of enlarging collections, extending outreach and developing exhibitions, university museums need to find external grants and financial supports. The example of the Sichuan University Museum might demonstrate the need for external financial support to some museums. Manager A from the Sichuan University Museum argued that the museum's development was at the mercy of its limited funding. The annual funding provided to the Sichuan Museum was usually not enough for designing new exhibitions. The funding shortfalls and the desire to develop urged the Sichuan University Museum to search for external financial help. Exhibitions, such as "Thomas Torrance and the West of Sichuan", are held with external financial help from foundations. While studying the funding bodies for university museums in UK, one common criterion is the ability of university museums in reaching the wider public. This phenomenon has caused the transformation of British university museums to public-facing institutions (Wang 2014). In China, the external funding bodies could also have the similar desire for more influence amongst a wider community. The expansion of audience groups in university museums could help fulfill their desire.

Balancing and Negotiating

The case studies of the Sichuan Museum and the Arthur M. Sackler Museum of Art and Archaeology at Peking University demonstrate the tendency of university museums to become increasingly public-facing institutions. This phenomenon raises a question for university museum curators: how university museums can balance their role inside and outside the academic world, within an environment of increasingly limited human and financial resources. There is no conflict between the role of university museums as public-facing institutions and that of academic institutions. It seems that the public function and the academic function could be regarded as the outer side and inner side of a university museum. The two roles of university museums can be complementary to each other. On the one hand, the academic function of university museums can benefit their public function by enriching and extending their academic content. On the other hand, the engagement of the wider public can enhance the reputation of a university museum and encourage external support from authorities which might promote the advancement of academic services.

Yet not all museum professionals take such a positive attitude. In 2012, Liu and Zhang discussed in their article the current challenges and difficulties of university museums in China. From their perspective, currently even the function of assisting university education and research has not been fully fulfilled by Chinese university museums (Liu and Zhang 2012). Thus, it might not be the time for Chinese university museums to extend their scope to the wider public (Liu and Zhang 2012).

Indeed, after decades of development, university museums in China are facing difficulties. The current condition of university museums in China is similar to that of British university museums during the 1980s. At the annual conference of Museum Association in 1986, Warhurst argued that university museums in England were suffering from a triple crisis (Warhurst 1986: 137). In the words of Merriman (2002) : "1) a crisis of identity and purpose; 2) a crisis of recognition (by university and wider society) ; 3) a crisis of resources." With the pressure of transforming from a strictly academic institution to one with dual purpose, university museums in China are now facing a similar situation.

University museums have the responsibility to decide what they want to be. It is true that, as discussed above, the need for universities could largely influence the development of their museums. Whether or not a university museum should add functionality and engage the wider public as stakeholders, ought to be decided by the resources it has. The engagement of a wider public is not simply opening the gates and designing interesting activities which could absorb audiences of all backgrounds and ages. University museum managers need to understand the needs of their audiences as the foundation for forming a development plan (Kelly 2001: 12). In addition, a reasonable assessment is required, when considering expanding audience groups as this process which needs support from professionals and could largely increase the operating costs of a university museum. As mentioned above, the need for absorbing external funding is one of the potential reasons that lead university museums to enrich functionality. However, university museums need to understand that it is not the public function itself that brings external funding to the institution. The criteria of external funding bodies are related to the ability of a university museum to interpret its collections and institutional heritage as well as what it could offer to the external funding sources.

At both the Sichuan University Museum and the Arthur M. Sackler Museum of Art and Archaeology at Peking University, difficulties could be found in realising their public function. Practically, these two university museums are making every effort to balance their dual role. The academic function of the two university museums could be divided into three contents: assisting academic research of the university as well as external institutions, academic contributions from the staff, and functioning as a professional teaching base. Preserving collections is a traditional way of realising the academic function. Furthermore, their academic function could be presented via the exhibitions in the museums. As academic institutions administrated by universities/academic departments, exhibitions in these two museums indicate the differences of university museums from public museums. Their permanent exhibitions usually include two topics: academic achievements and academic traditions. The interpretations used in exhibitions usually explain more profound understandings and the developmental process of certain objects/matters. Meanwhile, as a public-facing institution, those profound understandings are illustrated in simple terms to be understood by audiences from all backgrounds. Thus, the scheme of these exhibitions requires comprehensive skills and requires support from archaeologists, heritage professionals and museologists which addresses the first difficulty: a lack of staff. While working in the museums, they have another position as academic fellows in the institution they belong to. This dual identity imposes huge pressure on them. What makes it worse is that the number of professional positions in a university museum is very limited. Take the Arthur M. Sackler Museum of Art and Archaeology at Peking University, for example, there are four official staff in the museum who need to plan over ten activities per year.

The current solution of the Arthur M. Sackler Museum of Art and Archaeology at Peking University is to encourage undergraduate and postgraduate students from museology courses to participate in the work.

It might be true that through the participation of academic staff, university museums could fulfill a role as an independent academic institution. However, there are university museums that believe their contributions to the academic world could be realised in another way. Dr. Merriman, the Director of the Manchester Museum[2], supports this idea[3]. The way in which the Manchester Museum engages in academic work is different from most university museums in China, such as the Sichuan University Museum and the Arthur M. Sackler Museum of Art and Archaeology at Peking University, where museum curators and managers are professionals and academics in particular areas. In the interview with Dr. Merriman, he argued that, in the case of the Manchester Museum, participating in academic research directly is not the most efficient way to fulfill the academic function.

The Manchester Museum is within the central administration of the University of Manchester. It is an active member of the unit called Library and Cultural Institutions of the university (which includes the university library, the Manchester Museum, the Whitworth Art Gallery, Jodrell Bank Visitor Centre) and a major partner museum of the Arts Council. The major financial support for the museum comes from four sources: the University of Manchester, the Higher Education Funding Council of England (HEFCE), the Arts Council and the City Galleries. Commercial incomes obtained through shop, café and providing space for weddings and meetings is also an important source of income for the museum.

As part of the university, it is the responsibility of the Manchester Museum to fulfill the goals of the university: international and high-level research, and great teaching and public engagement (or social responsibility). Thus, in terms of satisfying the goals and purposes of the university, contributing to academic research, university education and public engagement is essential to the museum. Moreover, the dedication of the museum to serving the wider public also could satisfy the criterion of HEFCE and the goals of the Arts Council.

The staff at the Manchester Museum are not academics and managers are not employed on academic contracts. In other words, the museum does not directly contribute to the Research Excellence Framework of the university. Dr. Merriman and his team think it is more efficient for their staff to have a role in facilitating research by others. Thus, the museum's role in academic research could be centred in supporting and getting research done based on the collections. On the contrary, the museum directly contributes to the teaching framework. There are about 120 university courses taught by the museum members.

The museum's role and the main reason why the university values them are in the third goal around public engagement and social responsibility. Nowadays, engaging a wider public and demonstrating the impact of research are important in the development plan of the University of Manchester. Thus, designing exhibitions based on new research and helping academic colleagues demonstrate the impact of their work are important in the work plan of the museum. Moreover, the governing sector of the University of Manchester believes that it is more efficient to support a new academic department than to devote their university museum to academic research. Thus, the primary work of the museum staff is not academic. However, they still contribute to the academic sector by supporting academics inside the university and beyond.

Working behind the scenes also could be a way assisting university museums fulfill multiple and complementary roles. However, to some extent, the idea of Dr. Merriman puts the two roles, assisting academic and public-facing, into a binary opposition. The way Manchester Museum choose weakened its influence in academia. This fact is the biggest difference between the Manchester Museum and the university museums in China nowadays. The practical approaches taken by the Sichuan University Museum and the Arthur M. Sackler Museum of Art and Archaeology at Peking University all show that they are trying to harmonise between providing public cultural opportunities and assisting wider academic work. The dual role turns university museums into a more comprehensive base for museum studies. However, not all the museums have the ability to conduct independent research, especially the universities which do not have museology courses. As argued above, there are various ways for university museums to fulfill their academic function. The example of the Manchester Museum gives an excellent example for university museums in China on how to assist and promote academic research efficiently by being a service institution.

Conclusions

There are a large number of Chinese university museums, galleries and collections, while the case studies used in this article relate to the minority who are involved in engaging the public. Although the majority of university collections are not open to the public, some of them might still have connections with the public or the desire to expand their role to benefit wider audiences. By studying more public-facing university museums in China, this article attempts to address a potential developing trend of those university museums in the 21st century.

Currently, university museums in China have reached an era of change. The first change could be the attitudes of museum professionals and university governing sectors towards university museums. The difficulties university museums came across seem to generate an increasing concern over the resourcing, dual role and future of Chinese university museums from museum professionals (Shan 2015). Universities such as Sichuan University and Peking University have started to reconsider the position and potential contributions for their museums.

The second change could be the extension of university museum functions to a wider public. The past few decades have witnessed the function of university museums in China being continually extended so as to benefit wider audience groups. In the development strategies of Chinese university museums, it seems that how to balance their dual role in contributing to academic work and engaging a wider public is in an ongoing area. Using representative data collected by semi-structured interviews and textual research, this article demonstrates the development trajectories and strategies of university museums in China.

Based on case studies, this article argues that the main reasons for the changes in Chinese university museums are the requirements of parent universities and the need for external funding sources. Furthermore, this article also tries to give examples on how university museums in China could balance their dual role.

The impact of trying two different things, and of having dual role can be seen in the challenge that Chinese university museums face in clearly identifying their identity and position. University museum managers need to be aware that becoming a public-facing institution does not mean they need to acquire the same function as a public museum. Instead of providing general knowledge to the wider public, university museums should speak for their parent universities and for relevant disciplines. For example, the British Museum interprets world history with its extraordinary collections. However, its exhibitions seldom touch one topic, what is archaeology/history. In fact, such exhibition topics could hardly be found in most public museums. However, university museum exhibitions could fulfill the gap. With loans and their own collections, the Arthur M. Sackler Museum of Art and Archaeology at Peking University has designed several exhibitions about their achievements in archology. With discoveries from different areas and tools used in excavations/investigations, those exhibitions explain "archaeology" to their audiences as a dynamic process. Audiences could produce a deep understanding of "what is archaeology?" and "who are archaeologists?" by themselves. Furthermore, comparing archaeological exhibitions in different university museums, the characters of each institution/university could be clearly formed in audiences' minds, expressing the identities of relevant institutions and universities by exploring their heritage.

It is important to point out that to realise the universities' desire in enhancing social awareness, university museums do not necessarily need to be restricted to certain forms. Universities with a small quantity of collections and a limited budget could build a "mini university museum" in independent space, such as corridors, with glass showcases. The significance of university museums is not presented by architectures or permanent exhibition areas. What matters is the cultural enrichment delivered by their collections and exhibitions. With limited space and collections, "new university museums" could also fulfill the requirements of universities by demonstrating the university's history or significant research projects and by providing cultural opportunities to the public via their exhibitions.

Notes

1. In accordance with the ethical agreements, the interviewees in both museums will remain anonymous. Manager A is a member of staff from the Sichuan University Museum, and Manager B is from the Arthur M. Sackler Museum of Art and Archaeology at Peking University.
2. The Manchester Museum is owned by the University of Manchester.
3. An interview with Dr. Merriman was conducted in 2014 regarding the topic.

☐ Acknowledgements

I am infinitely grateful to those who have helped me during this research. Without their help, support and guidance of the following people, I would never have been able to finish this research.

- Associate Professor Tim Williams and Associate Professor Yijie Zhuang who undertook to act as my PhD supervisor and guided me patiently.
- Professor Wei Huo, Professor Xiangguang Sone, Mz. Hong Cao, Dr. Nich Merriman who supported me during the research and provided me useful information regarding the development of the university museums in China.
- The managers from the Sichuan University Museum and the Arthur M. Sackler Museum of Art and Archaeology at Peking University who kindly helped me in understanding the development of their museums.

☐ Disclosure Statement

No potential conflict of interest was reported by the author.

☐ Note on Contributor

WANG Shaohan is a PhD candidate in the Institute of Archaeology at University College London. She received her BA from Shandong University and her MPhil in Archaeological Heritage Management and Museum Studies at St Edmund's College, Cambridge University. Her research interests include heritage management, World Heritage theories, Silk Road heritage and cultural memory. Her current project centres on the transboundary coordinating strategies for nominated serial properties, using "Silk Road: The Routes Network of Chang'an-Tianshan Corridor" as a case study.

□ References

Altbach, Philip G, and P McGill Peterson. 2007. *Higher Education in the New Century: Global Challenges and Innovative Ideas*. Rotterdam: Sense Publishers.

Boylan, Patrick J. 1999. Universities and Museums: Past, Present and Future. *Museum Management and Curatorship* 18 (1): 43-56.

Dolev, Jacqueline C., Linda Krohner Friedlaender, and Irwin M. Braverman. 2001. Use of Fine Art to Enhance Visual Diagnostic Skills. *JAMA* 286 (9): 1020-1021.

Friedlaender, Linda K. 2016. Enhancing Observational Skills: A Case Study. Collaboration Between a University Art Museum and Its Medical School. In *Museums and Higher Education Working Together: Challenges and Opportunities*, edited by Anne Boddington, Jos Boys, and Catherine Speight, 147-158. New York: Routledge.

Gu, Hailiang. 2011. The Development of Humanity and Social Science in Universities: Observation and Reflection Based on Social Responsibility. *Theoretical Front In Higher Education* 4: 4-8. [顾海良 . 2011. 高校社会科学发展的使命——基于 "社会责任" 的观察与思考. 高校理论战线 4: 4-8.]

ICOM (International Council of Museum). 2007. ICOM Statutes. Accessed February 12, 2018. http://archives.icom.museum/statutes.html.

Kelly, Melanie. 1999. *Management of Higher Education Museums, Galleries and Collections in the UK*. Bath: International Centre for Higher Education Management, University of Bath.

Kelly, Melanie. 2001. *Managing University Museums. Education and Skills*. Paris: Organisation for Economic Cooperation and Development Publications.

Liljestrand, S. H. 1934. A Resume of Border Research and Researchers: Presidential Address. *Journal of the West China Border Research Society* 6: xiii-x.

Liu, Shiyi, and Qin Zhang. 2012. The Challenges and Difficulties of Contemporary University Museums. *Folk Art and Literature* 10 (2): 25. [刘仕毅，张琴 . 2012. 浅谈当代大学博物馆的困境. 群文天地 10 (2): 25.]

MacDonald, Sally, Kate Arnold-Forster, and Neil Curtis. 2013. *Impact and Engagement: University Museums for the 21st Century.* Dundee: University Museums Group and University Museums in Scotland.

MacGregor, Arthur. 2001. *The Ashmolean Museum: A Brief History of the Institution and Its Collections.* London: Ashmolean Museum & Jonathan Horne Publications.

Merriman, Nick. 2001. University Museums: Problems, Policy and Progress. *Archaeology International* 5: 57-59.

Merriman, Nick. 2002. The Current State of Higher Education Museums, Galleries and Collections in the UK. *Museologia* 2: 71-80.

Saumarez Smith, Charles. 1997. Museums, Artefacts, and Meanings. In *The New Museology*, edited by Peter Vergo, 6-9. London: Reaktion Books.

Shan, Jixiang. 2015. Reflection on Enhancing the Social Affinity of University Museums. *International Museum* Z1:128-132. [单霁翔. 2015. 增加高校博物馆社会亲和力的思考. 国际博物馆Z1: 128-132.]

Smalley, Martha Lund. 2012. Missionary Museums in China. *Material Religion* 8 (1):105-107.

Wang, Shaohan. 2014. University Museums in England. MPhil Dissertation, University of Cambridge. Unpublished.

Warhurst, Alan. 1986. Triple Crisis in University Museums. *Museums Journal* 86 (3):137-140.

Warhurst, Alan. 2015. University museums. In *Manual of Curatorship: A Guide to Museum Practice*, edited by John M. A. Thompson, 111-118. London: Routledge.

Willumson, Glenn. 2000. The shifting audience of the university museum. *Museum International* 52 (2): 15-18.

Wittlin, Alma Stephanie. 1949. *The Museum Its History and Its Tasks in Education.* London: Routledge and Kegan Paul Ltd.

Xie, Xiang, Xin Zhang, and Di Sha. 2016. A Discussion on the Current Condition and Problem of University Museums. *Journal of Natural Science Museum Research* 2: 22-29. [谢祥, 章鑫, 沙迪. 2016. 高校博物馆发展现状、问题及对策探讨. 自然科学博物馆研究 2: 22-29.]

Xu, Jian. 2016. We Were Never Alone: The Early University Museums Group in China. *In Great Foundations: An Intellectual History of Early Chinese Museums*, 294-346. Beijing: Science Press. [徐坚. 2016. 道不孤也：早期大学博物馆群体//徐坚. 名山：作为思想史的早期中国博物馆史，294-346. 北京：科学出版社.]

Ye, Chen. 2012. The Differences Between Management Systems of University Museums in Western Countries and China. *Magnificent Writing* 36: 320. [叶晨. 2012. 论中外大学博物馆机构设置的差异. 华章36: 320.]

Gender and Human Rights Within UNESCO's International Heritage Discourse: A Case Study of the Convention for Safeguarding the Intangible Cultural Heritage

Vanessa Whittington

Institute for Culture and Society, Western Sydney University, Locked Bag 1797, Penrith NSW 2752, Australia. CONTACT Vanessa Whittington: V. Whittington@westernsydney.edu.au

Abstract: Human rights discourses have significant relevance to contemporary understandings of heritage and its conservation, particularly in the context of the key international conventions for safeguarding the world's cultural heritage promulgated by UNESCO. The right to heritage is recognised as a human right falling under the right to culture or cultural identity. However, states are the primary bodies responsible for heritage identification and conservation, and may prefer to preserve the heritage of dominant social groups. Heritage identification and management by states, including nomination of items for inclusion on the Representative List (RL) of the Convention for Safeguarding the Intangible Cultural Heritage (CSICH), thus has the potential to compromise the cultural rights of marginalised social groups, including women. Limited existing research and original research discussed herein reveal a dearth of heritage associated with women on the RL. However the problematic gender dynamics of this discourse goes beyond simple representativeness to encompass the ways in which women and their heritage are portrayed when included. The RL typically seeks to maintain existing social relations, including gender relations, with negative implications for women's human rights set out in the UN Convention on the Elimination of All Forms of Discrimination Against Women (CEDAW).

Keywords: gender, human rights, world heritage, intangible cultural heritage, UNESCO

Introduction

It has been argued that culture is a key component of social systems that "operate to produce, reproduce and maintain [gender] inequality" (Dairam 2015: 370). In this article I contend that international heritage conservation practices promulgated by the UNESCO through key instruments such as the 2003 Convention for Safeguarding the Intangible Cultural Heritage (CSICH), play a role in this process.

The relevance of gender and human rights paradigms to the interdisciplinary field of heritage, particularly at the international level, is increasingly recognised as an important emerging area of inquiry (Labadi 2007; Logan 2007, 2012 and 2014; Moghadam and Bagheritari 2007; Reading 2015; UNESCO 2014a). For example, Moghadam and Bagheritari (2007) raised concerns about the human rights dimensions of the CSICH and possible negative implications for women's rights as set out in the United Nations (UN) 1979 Convention on the Elimination of All Forms of Discrimination Against Women (CEDAW). In the same year Labadi (2007) published a quantitative analysis of the key values of properties inscribed on the World Heritage List (WHL) up to this point, identifying the predominance of a hegemonic masculinity and the marginalisation of heritage associated with women. However, apart from work done by Labadi and an analysis of dance-based inscriptions on the CSICH by Pietrobruno (2015), there has been limited systematic empirical study or in depth qualitative analysis of the gender dynamics of UNESCO's key instruments for safeguarding world cultural heritage.

This article reports the findings of research that set out to address this gap, by analysing all "elements" on the CSICH's Representative List (RL) for the five years from 2011–2015, to identify their gender associations. I couple this with a discourse analysis of selected nomination files inscribed over the same period, recognising discourse as a set of semiotic "practices that systematically form the objects of which they speak" (Foucault 1972: 49).

My research thus goes beyond a simplistic focus on gender-based inclusion or exclusion to investigate the gender dynamics of Convention listings as modes of representation, including whether representations of women are in alignment with the human rights guaranteed in CEDAW. In so doing I treat culture as an expression of the broader social, economic and political forces that constitute it rather than a "privileged" domain (UNESCO 2016) necessary for collective identity, to which the principles and standards of civil society do not apply.

Methodology

This article employs an interdisciplinary mixed qualitative and quantitative approach. The key qualitative methodology is discourse analysis; however it is contextualised by a literature review, and supplemented by a quantitative analysis of RL inscriptions. The use of mixed methods is recommended by key proponents of discourse analysis to strengthen its validity, by introducing a historical, political or sociological dimension (Van Dijk 1993; Wodak 2001b; Fairclough 2003) to the analysis of discourse.

The study of discourse as a specific form of language use shaped by situational rules and context owes much to the work of the French theorist Michel Foucault (Foucault 1972), who understood discourse as enacting operations of power. I supplement a more generalised discourse analysis of the gendered nature of the RL based on these insights, with a strategic application of Critical Discourse Analysis (CDA). CDA is a branch of discourse analysis that seeks to reveal the way that meaning, and very often social inequality, is "expressed, signalled, constituted [and] legitimized" (Wodak 2001a: 2) by language in use, both written and spoken. It is useful for revealing the particular linguistic devices that construct inequality, drawing these dynamics out and making them explicit. However I favour a strategic rather than extensive use of CDA, as technical and at times cumbersome explanations of linguistic devices can detract from the accessibility and readability of the text, restricting it to "the closed world of the initiated" (Billig 2008: 795), and undermining its social activism agenda.

Although there is not scope to discuss this at length, a number of scholars have recognised heritage as a discursive practice and applied discourse analysis to the study of heritage (Hall 1997, cited in Wu and Hou 2015: 40; Waterton et al. 2006; Waterton 2010). Smith (2006) famously coined the term Authorised Heritage Discourse (AHD) to refer to what she argued was a dominant paradigm within national and international heritage systems,"that privileges monumentality and grand scale, innate artefact/site significance tied to time depth, scientific/aesthetic expert judgement, social consensus and nation building" (Smith 2006: 11). She later linked this discourse to the marginalisation of "dissonant and subaltern heritage" (Shackel, Smith, and Campbell 2011: 291). Both Smith and Waterton (2010) have also employed CDA to deconstruct the AHD: Waterton, for example, has utilised it to highlight the western character of texts such as the World Heritage Convention (WHC) and CSICH.

Ruth Wodak, a linguist and key proponent of CDA, explains that this approach is commonly employed to analyse power dynamics related to constructions of gender, race, media discourses and identity. Typical modes of analysis include examining texts to reveal hidden power relations that understate the responsibility of powerful social actors (Van Dijk 1993), including through deliberate vagueness. It can also be used to reveal the ways that discourse becomes a segregated structure, in which some voices are not heard, and thereby enacts a "persuasive marginalisation of the 'other'"(Van Dijk 1993: 265). In addition, discourse analysis can highlight the way that texts rely for meaning not only on what is made explicit, but also on what is implicit or assumed (Fairclough 2003: 11). Each of these modes of analysis is strategically employed in this article to argue that; on the whole, the CSICH enacts a form of gender dynamics that detracts from women's status and rights.

Gender and World Cultural Heritage

Before moving on to a discussion of research findings, it is important to unpack terms such as "culture" and "gender" and to introduce some of the key literature on gender and international heritage discourse within the interdisciplinary field of critical heritage studies.

The United Nations Committee on Economic, Social and Cultural Rights refers to culture as a "living process, historical, dynamic and evolving" (2009: 3). This notion of culture as dynamic rather than fixed is closely related to the changing notion of the human subject in contemporary critical theory. Rather than monolithic, unitary and based on the model of the self-determining white male individual, post-structuralist and post-modernist theorists note that identity and subjectivity are constituted by multiple points of difference, including gender, class, ethnicity, race, sexuality and post-coloniality (Mikula 2008; Grosz 1990; Rothfield 1990).

If culture is regarded as a distinctive yet changing set of features of a society or group, it has been argued that gender, like kinship, is a key factor constituting cultural identity (Rubin 1975). However rather than being primarily biologically determined, "second wave" feminism pointed to gendered socialisation practices to argue that gender is not innate but socially constructed (Mikula 2008). The concept of the social construction of gender is closely linked to the feminist critique of essentialism, a form of biologism that views certain qualities and characteristic as the natural result of being born either male or female (Grosz 1990).

Essentialism is a component of gender stereotyping that cultural theorist Stuart Hall describes, in a discussion of racial stereotyping, as a process of reducing identities to a few exaggerated, simplified traits "as part of the maintenance of social and symbolic order", a practice that occurs "where there are gross inequalities of power, with this [p] ower... directed against the subordinate or excluded group" (Hall 1997: 258). Parallel developments in feminist theory viewed the construction of gender as evident not only in personality and behaviour, but also in the production of sexed bodies. Such thinkers questioned the validity of binary thinking such as the sex/gender distinction (Butler 1990), arguing that the body is also discursively produced and that "gender is the knowledge that establishes meaning for bodily differences" (Scott 1988: 2). In fact, "third wave" feminist theorists such as philosopher Linda Nicholson (1994: 101) have argued that the term woman itself does not have a fixed meaning, but rather must be understood as contextual, historical, and comprising "intersecting similarities and differences" between those thus classified.

It is now recognised that there is "no single globally applicable idea of gender" (Blake 2015a: 6). For example men in cultures such as the Aka of Central Africa take a significant role in caring for infants and women take the primary role in hunting (Hewlett 2005). Other cultures have more than two recognised genders, such as Hijras or "eunuch-transvestites" in India, who are viewed as a third gender. In a Western context, queer and trans-theory questions the validity of understanding gender in terms of the dichotomy of male/female and suggests that bodies may be more than one gender, rejecting the reduction of personhood to "binarized truth regimes" (Noble 2013: 278). While the concept of gender is no longer regarded as a simplistic analytical category, anthropologist Dorothy Hodgson argues for its ongoing usefulness in "signifying the dynamic, cultural, historical and political" meanings of terms such as "women, human and rights...across time and space" (Hodgson 2011: 4).

At odds with this contemporary understanding of gender are representations of gender on the RL, which, as will be discussed, depict stereotypical notions of masculinity and femininity. The observation that heritage discourse can reinforce traditional beliefs about gender identity has been made by a number of heritage scholars, including Sophia Labadi (2007), Laurajane Smith (2008) and Anna Reading (2015). Smith argues that gender inequality in heritage is both a cause and an effect of gender inequality in the broader society, reflecting the intrinsic connections between political and social systems and the realm of culture. She identifies two significant ways in which this inequality impacts on heritage, the first relating to the neglect within registers of conserved heritage of "places of significance to women's history and experience" and the second relating to "the degree to which the stories told at heritage places and museums... convey and legitimize gender stereotypes of men and women" (Smith 2008: 162).

Similarly, Reading argues that heritage and gender are best understood in terms of how "changing constructions of masculinity and femininity interact with what is valued and included as heritage", reinforcing some identities while marginalising others (Reading 2015: 401). According to Reading, memorialisation of important male figures in history has "arisen out of a framing of the past and of heritage that prioritises the activities of ... men in political and military life" (Reading 2015: 402) in the formation of the identities of nation states.

Within this context, Deputy Director of UNESCO's Heritage Division, Mechtild Rössler, has observed that "very few sites on the World Heritage List are directly related to the history and lives of women" (Rössler 2014: 68). Rössler cites Sophia Labadi's 2007 article investigating dominant and marginalised forms of representation on the WHL as evidence of this bias. Labadi examined the values of 106 sites which were nominated for inclusion on the WHL between 1977 and 2002, concluding that "men from the middle and upper classes" were one of the most frequently mentioned attributes, while heritage associated with women was barely represented. Labadi suggested that a myth of masculinity formed part of the image of national identity within these properties, stressing "the monumentality and importance of sites in order to provide an image of the nation as heroic, grand and powerful" (Labadi 2007: 160), and that within this discourse women were marginalised as "'the other', the weaker gender" (Labadi 2007: 162).

Rössler attributes the lack of visibility of women on the WHL to the marginalisation of gender in cultural policy and the impact of societal power relations between genders in determining what is valued as heritage. She recognises that not only the predominantly material cultural heritage represented on the WHL, but also the intangible heritage safeguarded by the CSICH, is potentially problematic from a gender perspective. This is because cultural practices, spaces and their access can be gender defined, and the transmission of heritage gender specific, "strengthening social reproduction, its gender relations and stereotypes" (Rössler 2014: 67). However, Moghadam and Bagheritari go further and raise concerns that an instrument such as the CSICH could have a negative impact on the human rights of women and girls. This is primarily because of the "discriminatory or harmful nature of some 'social practices and rituals'" (Moghadam and Bagheritari 2007: 10), a domain of intangible heritage that the Convention seeks to safeguard.

Moghadam and Bagheritari also identified the tension that can exist between collective cultural rights and women's international human rights. Furthermore, they claimed that CEDAW's call for a change of traditional gender roles of women, including in society and the family, in order to achieve gender equality (Article 5), is incompatible with the CSICH's "gender neutral language", making it "vulnerable to manipulation or dismissal of women's participation and rights" (Moghadam and Bagheritari 2007: 16). Janet Blake has also observed that the CSICH "is silent on the specific issue of gender in Intangible Cultural Heritage (ICH) production and performance", when the opposite approach is required to address the marginalisation of women within their own communities (Blake 2015a: 6).

While this Convention does not mandate or even encourage such an approach to avoid "positive discrimination" (UNESCO 2004: 1), its Operational Directives were amended in 2016 to request that state parties "ensure gender equality in the planning, management and implementation of safeguarding measures" (UNESCO 2016: 181) at the national level. However, a number of limitations to these amendments, including not extending the gender equity requirement to elements nominated for recognition on the CSICH's RL and Urgent Safeguarding List, are likely to reduce their effectiveness. It is arguable that the historic failure of these Directives to address the issue of gender has contributed to the dearth of women's intangible heritage identified in the quantitative analysis provided below.

Quantitative Findings: Gender Representation on the CSICH RL

One hundred and twenty-four elements were inscribed on the CSICH RL in the period 2011 to 2015 and all were examined. Table 1 and Figure 1 show that practices on the RL in which both sexes had a significant role were marginally more common than those identified as primarily male, with 41% and 38% of elements respectively characterised in these ways. However in three of the years surveyed primarily male practices were marginally more common than those characterised as shared. Only 9% of inscriptions (n=11) were characterised as primarily female, in the sense that women were the primary practitioners and were responsible for the element's transmission.

Table 1   Gender associations of elements inscribed on CSICH RL, 2011–2015

Year	No. of inscriptions	Primarily male practice	Primarily female practice	No gender association	Shared practice
2011	18	7 (39%)	1 (6%)	0 (0%)	10 (55%)
2012	27	12 (44%)	2 (7%)	5 (19%)	8 (30%)
2013	25	5 (20%)	3 (12%)	6 (24%)	11 (44%)
2014	31	12 (39%)	4 (13%)	3 (9%)	12 (38%)
2015	23	11 (48%)	1 (4%)	1 (4%)	10 (44%)
Total	124	47 (38%)	1 1 (9%)	15 (12%)	51 (41%)

Source: RL of the Convention for Safeguarding the Intangible Cultural Heritage, UNESCO, 2016

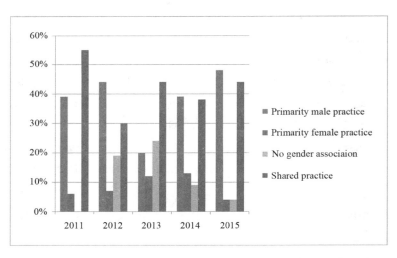

Figure 1   Gender associations of elements inscribed on CSICH RL, 2011–2015
Source: RL of the Convention for Safeguarding the Intangible Cultural Heritage, UNESCO, 2016

While it might have been anticipated that heritage associated with women would have equal prominence on the RL, as it purports to deal with representative practices, this analysis demonstrates that heritage associated with men was significantly more common than that associated with women. Although heritage in which both genders had a significant role also figured prominently in the RL, as will be discussed below, the gender stereotyped nature of these practices, and the more prominent role given to men in many shared practices, undermines the significance of this from a gender equity perspective.

Qualitative Findings: Case Studies from the RL

Shared Practices

The predominance of shared practices on the RL and the identification of some practices that were exclusively female give women a limited degree of visibility on the RL, however this does not mean that the CSICH can be regarded as egalitarian from a gender perspective. This is because many of the shared practices, and indeed the primarily female practices, express gender-prescribed roles of lesser value and/or ascribe value to women based on criteria not applied to men within that cultural context, such as beauty or skill as a "housewife".

For example, one of the main components of Sefrou Cherry Festival (Morocco), inscribed on the RL and classified as a shared practice, is a beauty pageant in which each year's Cherry Queen is chosen (Figure 2). The selection criteria for the Queen, chosen from the "prettiest young girls from all over Morocco" are "beauty, slenderness, higher studies and general knowledge" (Moroccan Government 2012). Female value is reduced to criteria such as youth, slenderness and beauty, a form of "sexual objectification" associated with "body shame", low self-esteem and eating disorders for women unable to meet these standards (Tylka and Sabik 2010: 18).

413

Figure 2   Sefrou Cherry Queen, Morocco, 2010

Source: CSICH RL (UNESCO 2016), © Conseil municipal de Sefrou, 2010, with the permission of UNESCO

Similarly, the Slava Celebration of family patron saint day, Serbia, another shared practice, ascribes the "dominant role" to the "oldest male member of the family", referred to as "the host" (Serbian Government 2014). The role of the host is to greet the guests, cut and break the Slava cake and be first to say a prayer for prosperity. Figure 3 shows male family members participating in the priest's blessing of the cake in an area of the home suitable for public gatherings, while Figure 4 depicts a woman, perhaps the "host's wife", alone in a kitchen making the Slava cake or other food for the occasion. The "host's wife", whose subordinate status in indicated by being defined in relation to her husband through the use of the possessive apostrophe, prepares and decorates the cake and makes dough ornaments, but does not otherwise have a significant role in formal proceedings.

Figure 3 Male family members and a priest with the Slava cake

Source: CSICH RL (UNESCO 2016) ©Ethnographic museum in Belgrade, 2013, with the permission of UNESCO

Figure 4 Female family member preparing food for Slava celebration

Source: CSICH RL (UNESCO 2016) ©Ethnographic museum in Belgrade, 2013, with the permission of UNESCO

This element's nomination file describes it as achieving the "maintenance of existing social relations...based primarily on kinship, friendship, and neighbourhood ties" (Serbian Government 2014). The "maintenance of existing social relations" is assumed to be a social good; however within this discourse only one voice is heard, obfuscating that what is also maintained is existing gender relations, with women as the silenced and subordinated "other". At the same time the nomination file and text summarising the element on the CSICH website emphasise the important role women play in transmitting knowledge of this ritual within the family, giving them particular responsibility for reproducing these relations.

The view expressed by the Serbian Government is reminiscent of that of state representatives meeting during the Convention's development to discuss women's ICH, who associated women's gender roles with "essential realms of culture...indispensable in maintaining familial and cohesive social relations[1]" (UNESCO 1999: 2). There is an underlying assumption within this discourse that preserving existing "familial and social relations" is desirable to all, regardless of their nature or the role of women within them. However CDA would suggest the existence of an obfuscated male subject to whom such gender roles are "indispensable".

As a consequence of women's role of intergenerational transmission within the family, the same meeting claimed that "women...effectively counter eroding influences, thus ensuring greater continuity of local cultural expressions" (UNESCO 1999: 4). The term "eroding influences" is left deliberately vague, free to constitute anything the absent male subject decides. Women are given responsibility for maintaining culture as a static form, with forces of change viewed as a wholly negative "eroding influence", rather than having the potential to renew and positively transform practices which may, in their traditional form, present human rights concerns.

Primarily Female Practices

As part of this research I also identified and examined elements on the RL that could be classified as primarily female practices in the 2011–2015 period. These represented a minority of inscriptions, 11 in total, and most were associated with traditional gender-based domestic activities such as food preparation, and home-based weaving and embroidery. In this context, the DPR of Korea's nomination file for Kimchi-making promotes a traditional view of the role of women as "housewives" and "mothers" who should be concerned with their "kitchen-practice". All of the "nation's housewives" are identified as this element's major practitioners, since "acquiring the skill of Kimchi-making is one of the processes to go through to become a good mother". The use of the verb "is" makes the importance of Kimchi-making to the status of being a "good mother" unequivocal, while the desirability that a woman should be a "good mother" is taken as given, this text relying on implicit assumptions for its meaning in the way described by Fairclough (2003).

The nominating state makes it clear that Kimchi-making is valued because it "lays the foundations for social cohesion and unity" (DPR of Korea 2015). Again, there is an assumption that "social cohesion" is a desirable goal, regardless of its reliance on gender based stereotypes and inequality. Women of the DPR of Korea are thus given responsibility for maintaining both social cohesion and national identity by continuing to perform the traditional roles of housewife and mother through Kimchi-making. This practice carries a heavy representational burden, potentially limiting women's capacity for exercising agency in determining their participation.

The rites and craftsmanship associated with the wedding costume tradition of Tlemcen, Algeria, is another practice identified as primarily female, noting that it is not just the craft practice but the social practices associated with it that are highlighted in the nomination file. The rituals associated with the wedding costume are intended to perpetuate a system whereby "women [are] called upon to ensure the continuity of the community by procreating after their marriage". Who is calling upon women to act in this way is left vague and unstated; just as the inevitability of marriage and childbirth is not called into question, but is an underlying assumption within this discourse. The nomination file discusses how this practice is reinforced by girls attending the marriages of community members and observing that wearing the costume is "a sign of belonging to the community" (Algerian Government 2012). This element and its associated social practices thus bring significant social pressure to bear upon girls and women to conform to the socially sanctioned roles of wife and mother, or face community ostracism.

Primarily Male Practices

Unlike the primarily female practices discussed above, primarily male practices on the RL are numerous, many of which are performances (song, dance, etc.) undertaken in public space before an audience. In contrast, elements identified with women are more likely to be performed in the private domestic sphere, strengthening a traditional public/private dichotomy. Many of these activities reinforce masculine identities associated with sporting skill (Spanish Riding School, Vienna), athleticism (Lad's dance, Romania) and militaristic traditions and link masculinity with heroism (Daredevils of Sassoun, Armenia), bravery and "chivalry" (Al-Ayyala, Oman, and United Arab Emirates [UAE]).

For example Al-Ayyala, a traditional performing art of the Sultanate of Oman and the UAE , involves men performing a martial style dance, with the female contribution provided by "girls" who "stand and toss their long hair from side to side" to signify their "faith in their protection by the chivalrous male performers" (Oman and UAE Governments 2014). Although many of these elements reinforce stereotypical masculine gender identities, Al-Ayyala is noteworthy in its reference to the antiquated notion of chivalry. This concept, based on assumptions of female passivity and victimhood on the one hand and male heroism on the other, is starkly out of keeping with international human rights norms of gender equality.

In some instances, women are specifically excluded from participation in an element, as in Al-Ayyala, Alardah and Alnajdiyah (dance, drumming and poetry) of Saudi Arabia. This element's nomination file states that "women are not present at public performances", but "may participate [within the home] as costume makers" (Saudi Arabian Government 2015). The use of the verbal phrase "are not present" makes the prohibition of women's public participation clear; however the subject prohibiting this is notably absent, obscuring the role of powerful social actors in making such a prohibition. In contrast, use of the modal auxiliary verb "may" indicates that their participation as costume makers is optional, and that they have the capacity to exercise choice in this regard, unlike their prohibition from public performances, where choice is unavailable. The use of the auxiliary verb "may" also suggests that women's participation in this element is relatively unimportant, and that the practice would continue without their involvement.

Similarly, for the Leuven age set ritual repertoire, Belgium, "a rite of passage in a man's life centring on the ten years leading up to his 50th birthday", "the only conditions for participation are to be a man and to be born in the same year" (Belgian Government 2011) (Figure 5). There is no comparable ritual for the women of Leuven, whose involvement consists of playing a supportive role to the male participants.

Figure 5   The all-male participants in the Leuven age set ritual, Belgium, 2011
Source: CSICH RL (UNESCO 2016), © Karel Rondou, 2009, with the permission of UNESCO

Discussion and Conclusion

In this article I set out to explore whether UNESCO's doctrinal heritage Conventions such as the CSICH have a gender bias, and whether the CSICH lends itself to the inscription of practices that are not in keeping with women's human rights. In determining whether a gender bias exists, I have taken a dual focus on the extent to which UNESCO's key instruments for safeguarding the world's cultural heritage include heritage associated with women, and to which women could be viewed as the primary practitioners, and the ways in which gender is represented in this discourse.

The findings of both the quantitative and qualitative components of this research clearly demonstrate a gender bias within the CSICH, in the sense that practices dominated by men significantly outnumber those in which women are the primary practitioners. As a more recent Convention, which purports to protect human rights and safeguard representative heritage, greater inclusion of women's intangible heritage could be anticipated.

While the most common category identified was practices shared by both men and women, giving women some visibility on the CSICH, roles performed by women were frequently subsidiary and supportive, rather than central public performative roles. With some exceptions, the intangible heritage on the RL involving women perpetuates their restriction to the traditional roles of women as wife and mother, arising from and reinforcing essentialist notions of female identity as innately and biologically determined. In many of these elements, maternity and the care of children is not viewed as a "social function" as understood in Article 5 (b) of CEDAW, but rather a biological imperative arising from women's essential nature.

Women are also given particular responsibility for maintaining existing social (and gender) relations, a practice that could be termed "cultural reproduction" (Bourdieu 2006), thereby ensuring community cohesion based on a static notion of cultural identity and perpetuating their own subordination. The significance attached to these roles suggests that states have an investment in perpetuating them as they are viewed as integral to collective national identity. Consequently, a clear tension exists between collective cultural and national identity and the individual human rights of women within this discourse. Moghadam and Bagheritari's concern that the CSICH could be detrimental to women's human rights is borne out in this analysis in the restricted roles and essentialist stereotypes perpetuated in all of its domains. This state of affairs is not in keeping with Article 5 (a) of CEDAW, which calls on States Parties "to modify the social and cultural patterns of conduct of men and women" (United Nations 1979), to enable "the creation of a social environment through which society will accept and recognise women's right to equality" (Dairam 2015: 389).

Torggler et al. (2013), in their Evaluation of UNESCO's Standard-Setting Work of the Culture Sector, identify "integrating UNESCO's Global Priority Gender Equality into relevant ICH-related policies, legislation, development planning, safeguarding plans and programmes, etc." as a clear priority for the organisation. Despite this, they name it the "'elephant in the room'...[that] nobody wishes to acknowledge" for fear that a large proportion of ICH would be excluded if a more rigorous assessment were conducted. The authors conclude that the CSICH's Intergovernmental Committee, assisted by UNESCO, "should work towards defining more clearly where the limits lie between what can be identified as ICH for the purposes of the Convention and what should not" (Torggler et al. 2013: 17).

While it is clear that ICH is to some extent gender based, and that this does not in itself constitute discrimination (Blake 2014b), signals that an element may be directly discriminatory and therefore unsuitable for listing include prohibitions against participation on the basis of gender, where a comparable form of participation is not available for the excluded gender, and where other forms of state sanctioned gender based discrimination also exist. By prohibiting women's involvement on an equal basis with men, such elements risk preventing women from participating in all aspects of cultural life contrary to Article 13 (a) of CEDAW.

A culturally relativist argument that would defend such exclusions on the basis of different cultural norms alone is inconsistent with universalistic human rights principles enshrining women's rights as absolutes (Dairam 2015; Bennoune 2016). While domestic heritage policy is a product of the social and cultural systems of nation-states and reflects domestic gender relations, there is an onus on an agency such as UNESCO to reflect international human rights norms in selecting items for listing on these Conventions.

However the politicisation of listing processes, reflected in the rise in political appointments to UNESCO committees and the diminishing role of experts, suggests a poor prognosis for addressing gender equity, both in the short and longer term (Meskell 2013; Kuutma 2018). This is borne out in the limitations to the 2016 gender revisions to the CSICH Operational Directives, recommended by Torggler et al. (2013), discussed herein, suggesting that culture remains a "privileged" realm with UNESCO's international heritage discourse (UNESCO 2016).

Note

1. These "realms" are said to include "language, codes of ethics, behavioural patterns, value systems, and religious beliefs" (UNESCO 1999: 2).

Acknowledgements

The author would like to thank Professor Emma Waterton and Associate Professor Denis Byrne for comments on an earlier draft of this article, and Dr. Steve Brown, who was the supervisor of the dissertation on which this article is based.

Disclosure Statement

No potential conflict of interest was reported by the author.

Data Availability Statement

The data supporting this article were held by the author and can be made available upon request.

Note on Contributor

Vanessa Whittington is a PhD Candidate of the Institute for Culture and Society, Western Sydney University. Her Doctoral research, "Moved to Care for Country? Visitors, Landscape, Affect and the Role of Heritage Interpretation", investigates visitor responses to recognised places of Aboriginal cultural heritage in Australian national parks. This article is based on a dissertation completed in 2017 as part of a Master's of Museum and Heritage Studies Degree, Sydney University. Vanessa also has a Master's (Hons) in Women's Studies from the University of New South Wales, Sydney, and has worked in policy and research roles for Australian government and non-government agencies with a human services, social justice, and social policy focus.

□ References

Algerian Government. 2012. Rites and Craftsmanship Associated with the Wedding Costume Tradition of Tlemcen. Nomination file No. 00668. Accessed April 5, 2016. http://www.unesco.org/culture/ich/en/RL/rites-and-craftsmanship-associated-with-the-wedding-costume-tradition-of-tlemcen-00668.

Baksh, Rawwida and Wendy Harcourt. 2015. Introduction: Rethinking Knowledge, Power and Social Change. In *The Oxford Handbook of Transnational Feminist Movements*, edited by Rawwida Baksh, and Wendy Harcourt, 1-47. Oxford: Oxford University Press.

Beitz, Charles. 2003. What Human Rights Mean. *Daedalus* 132 (1): 36-46.

Belgian Government. 2011. Leuven Age Set Ritual Repertoire. Nomination file No. 00404. Accessed April 5, 2016. http://www.unesco.org/culture/ich/en/RL/leuven-age-set-ritual-repertoire-00404.

Bennoune, Karima. 2016. Report of the Special Rapporteur in the Field of Cultural Rights to Human Rights Council. A/HRC/31/59, United Nations General Assembly. Accessed April 10, 2016. http://www.ohchr.org/EN/Issues/CulturalRights/Pages/SRCulturalRightsIndex.aspx.

Billig, Michael. 2008. Nominalizing and De-Nominalizing: A Reply. *Discourse and Society*, 19 (6): 829-841.

Blake, Janet. 2014a. Gender and Intangible Heritage. In *Gender Equality, Heritage and Creativity*, edited by Penelope Keenan, Keiko Nowacka, and Lynne Patchett, 48-60. Paris: UNESCO Publishing.

Blake, Janet. 2014b. Seven Years of Implementing UNESCO's Intangible Heritage Convention—Honeymoon Period or the "Seven Year Itch"? *International Journal of Cultural Property* 21 (3): 291-304.

Blake, Janet. 2015. Human Rights Dimensions of Gender and Intangible Cultural Heritage. *Human Rights Defender* 24 (2): 5-7.

Bourdieu, Pierre. 2006. Cultural Reproduction and Social Reproduction. In *Inequality: Classic Readings in Race, Class, and Gender*, edited by David Grusky, and Szonja Szelenyi, 257-271. Colorado: Westview Press.

Butler, Judith. 1990. *Gender Trouble: Feminism and the Subversion of Identity.* New York: Routledge.

Dairam, M. Shanthi. 2015. CEDAW, Gender and Culture. In *The Oxford Handbook of Transnational Feminist Movements*, edited by Rawwida Baksh, and Wendy Harcourt, 367-393. Oxford: Oxford University Press.

DPR of Korea Government. 2015. Tradition of Kimchi-Making in the Democratic People's Republic of Korea. Nomination file No. 01063. Accessed May 20, 2016. http://www.unesco.org/culture/ich/en/RL/tradition-of-kimchi-making-in-the-democratic-people-s-republic-of-korea-01063.

Fairclough, Norman. 2001. Critical Discourse Analysis as a Method in Social Scientific Research. In *Methods of Critical Discourse Analysis*, edited by Ruth Wodak, and Michaek Meyer, 121-138. London: Sage Publications.

Fairclough, Norman. 2003. *Analysing Discourse: Textual Analysis for Social Research.* London: Routledge.

Foucault, Michel. 1972. *The Archaeology of Knowledge.* A. M. Sheridan (Trans.). London: Tavistock Publications.

Grosz, Elizabth. 1990. Contemporary Theories of Power and Subjectivity. In *Feminist Knowledge: Critique and Construct*, edited by Sneja Gunew, 59-120. London and New York: Routledge.

Hafstein, Valdimar. 2014. Protection as Dispossession: Government in the Vernacular. In *Cultural Heritage in Transit: Intangible Rights as Human Rights*, edited by Deborah Kapchan, 25-58. Philadelphia: University of Pennsylvania Press.

Hall, Catherine. 1992. *White, Male and Middle Class-Explorations in Feminism and History.* Cambridge: Polity Press.

Hall, Stuart. 1997. The Work of Representation. In *Representation: Cultural Representations and Signifying Practices*, edited by Stuart Hall, 15-71. London: Sage Publications.

Hewlett, Barry. 2005. The Cultural Nexus of Aka Father-Infant Bonding. In *Gender in Cross-Cultural Perspective*, Fourth Edition, edited by Caroline Brettell, and Carolyn Sargent, 37-48. New Jersey: Pearson Education Inc.

Hodgson, Dorothy. 2011. Introduction: Gender and Culture at the Limit of Rights. In *Gender and Culture at the Limit of Rights*, edited by Dorothy Hodgson, 1-14. Pennsylvania: University of Pennsylvania Press.

Kuutma, Kristin. 2018. Inside the UNESCO Apparatus: From Intangible Representations to Tangible Effects. In *Safeguarding Intangible Heritage: Practices and Politics*, edited by Natsuko Akagawa, and Laurajane Smith, 80-95. Oxon: Routledge.

Labadi, Sophia. 2007. Representations of the Nation and Cultural Diversity in Discourses on World Heritage. *Journal of Social Archaeology* 7 (2): 147-170.

Logan, William. 2007. Closing Pandora's Box: Human Rights Conundrums in Cultural Heritage Protection. In *Cultural Heritage and Human Rights*, edited by Helaine Silverman, and D. Fairchild Ruggles, 33-53. New York: Springer Press.

Logan, William. 2012. Cultural Diversity, Cultural Heritage and Human Rights: Towards Heritage Management as Human Rights-based Cultural Practice. *International Journal of Heritage Studies* 18 (3): 231-244.

Logan, William. 2014. Heritage Rights—Avoidance and Reinforcement. *Heritage & Society* 7 (2): 156-169.

Meskell, Lyn. 2013. UNESCO's World Heritage Convention at 40: Challenging the Economic and Political Order of International Heritage Conservation. *Current Anthropology* 54 (4): 483-494.

Mikula, Maja. 2008. *Key Concepts in Cultural Studies Palgrave Key Concepts*. Hampshire: Palgrave Macmillan.

Moghadam, Valentine, and Manilee Bagheritari M. 2007. Cultures, Conventions, and the Human Rights of Women: Examining the Convention for Safeguarding Intangible Cultural Heritage, and the Declaration on Cultural Diversity. *Museum International* 59

(4): 9-18.

Moroccan Government 2012. Sefrou Cherry Festival. Nomination file No. 00641. Accessed October 20, 2016. http://www.unesco.org/culture/ich/en/RL/cherry-festival-in-sefrou-00641.

Nicholson, Linda. 1994. Interpreting Gender. *Journal of Women in Culture and Society* 20 (1): 79-105. Accessed May 5, 2016. http://openscholarship.wustl.edu/wgss/22.

Noble, Bobby. 2012. Trans. In *Rethinking Women's and Gender Studies*, edited by Catherine Orr, Ann Braithwaite, and Diane Lichtenstein, 277-293. Routledge: New York.

Oman and United Arab Emirates Governments. 2014. Al-Ayyala, a Traditional Performing Art of the Sultanate of Oman and the United Arab Emirates. Nomination file No. 01012. Accessed May 20, 2016. http://www.unesco.org/culture/ich/en/RL/al-ayyala-a-traditional-performing-art-of-the-sultanate-of-oman-and-the-united-arab-emirates-01012.

Pietrobruno, Sheenagh. 2015. Social Media and Whirling Dervishes: Countering UNESCO's Intangible Cultural Heritage. *Performing Islam* 4 (1): 11-33.

Reading, Anna. 2015. Making Feminist Heritage Work: Gender and Heritage. In *The Palgrave Handbook of Contemporary Heritage Research*, edited by Emma Waterton, and Steve Watson, 397-410. London: Palgrave Macmillan.

Reddy, Gayatri and Serena Nanda. 2005. Hirjas: An Alternative Sex/Gender in India. In *Gender in Cross-Cultural Perspective*, Fourth Edition, edited by Caroline Brettell, and Carolyn Sargent, 278-285. New Jersey: Pearson Education Inc.

Rössler, M. 2014. Gendered World Heritage? A Review of the Implementation of the UNESCO World Heritage Convention 1972. In *Gender Equality, Heritage and Creativity*, edited by Penelope Keenan, Keiko Nowacka, and Lynne Patchett, 60-73. Paris: UNESCO Publishing.

Rothfield, Philipa. 1990. Feminism, Subjectivity and Sexual Difference. In *Feminist Knowledge Critique and Construct*, edited by Sneja Gunew, 121-144. London and New York: Routledge.

Rubin, Gayle. 1975. The Traffic in Women. In *Toward an Anthropology of Women*, edited by Rayna R. Reiter, 157-210. New York: Monthly Review.

Saudi Arabian Government. 2015. Alardah Alnajdiyah, Dance, Drumming and Poetry in Saudi Arabia. Nomination file No. 01196. Accessed April 20, 2016. http://www.unesco.org/culture/ich/en/RL/alardah-alnajdiyah-dance-drumming-and-poetry-in-saudi-arabia-01196.

Scollon, Ron. 2001. Action and Text: Towards an Integrated Understanding of the Place of Text in Social (Inter)action, Mediated Discourse Analysis and the Problem of Social Action. In *Methods of Critical Discourse Analysis*, edited by Ruth Wodak, and Michael Meyer, 139-184. London, Sage Publications.

Serbian Government. 2014. Celebration of Family Saint Patron's Day. Nomination file No. 01010. Accessed May 7, 2016. http://www.unesco.org/culture/ich/en/RL/slava-celebration-of-family-saint-patrons-day-01010.

Shackel, Paul A., Smith Laurajane, and Campbell Gary. 2011. Labour's Heritage. *International Journal of Heritage Studies* 17 (4): 291-300.

Smith, Laurajane. 2008. Heritage, Gender and Identity. In *The Ashgate Research Companion to Heritage and Identity*, edited by Brian J. Graham and Peter Howard, 159-178. Aldershot: Ashgate Publishing.

Taylor, Mary N. 2009. Intangible Heritage Governance, Cultural Diversity, Ethno-nationalism. *Focaal—European Journal of Anthropology* 55: 41-58.

Torggler, Barbara, Ekaterina Sediakina-Rivière, and Janet Blake. 2013. *Evaluation of UNESCOs Standard-setting Work of the Culture Sector, Part I—2003 Convention for the Safeguarding of the Intangible Cultural Heritage, Final Report*. Paris: UNESCO.

Tylka, Tracy, and Natalie Sabik. 2010. Integrating Social Comparison Theory and Self-Esteem within Objectification Theory to Predict Women's Disordered Eating. *Sex Roles* 63: 18-31.

UN (United Nations). 1979. Convention on the Elimination of all Forms of Discrimination Against Women. Accessed May 8, 2016. http://www.un.org/womenwatch/daw/cedaw/.

UNESCO. 1999. Annotated Agenda, International Symposium on the Role of Women in Transmission of Intangible Cultural Heritage. Accessed March 8, 2016. http://www.unesco.org/culture/ich/doc/src/00157-EN.pdf.

UNESCO. 2001. Synthesis Report—Activities in the Domain of Women and Intangible Heritage, International Editorial Meeting and Future Activities in the Domain. Accessed March 8, 2016. http://www.unesco.org/culture/ich/doc/src/00160-EN.pdf.

UNESCO. 2003. Convention for the Safeguarding of the Intangible Cultural Heritage. Accessed April 10, 2016. http://www.unesco.org/culture/ich/en/convention.

UNESCO. 2004. Final Report—Expert meeting "Gender and Intangible Heritage", 8-10 December 2003. Accessed March 3, 2016. http://www.unesco.org/culture/ich/doc/src/00125-EN.pdf.

UNESCO. 2014a. Heritage-Overview. In *Gender Equality, Heritage and Creativity*, edited by Penelope Keenan, Keiko Nowacka, and Lynne Patchett, 32-48. Paris: UNESCO Publishing.

UNESCO. 2014b. Operational Directives for the Implementation of the Convention for the Safeguarding of the Intangible Heritage. Accessed April 3, 2016. http://www.unesco.org/culture/ich/doc/src/ICH-Operational_Directives-2.GA-EN.pdf.

UNESCO. 2016. Operational Directives for the Implementation of the Convention for the Safeguarding of the Intangible Heritage. Accessed October 8, 2016. http://www.unesco.org/culture/ich/en/directives.

UNESCO n.d. Representative List, Convention for Safeguarding the Intangible Cultural Heritage. Accessed April 11, 2016. http://www.unesco.org/culture/ich/index.php?lg=en&pg=00559.

United Nations Committee on Economic, Social and Cultural Rights. 2009. General Comment No. 21 Right of Everyone to Take Part in Cultural Life. Accessed October 9, 2016. http://hrlibrary.umn.edu/gencomm/escgencom21.html.

Van Dijk, Tuen. 1993. Principles of Critical Discourse Analysis. *Discourse and Society* 4 (2): 249-283.

Waterton, Emma. 2010. *Politics, Policy and the Discourses of Heritage in Britain*. New York: Palgrave Macmillan.

Waterton, Emma, Laurajane Smith, and Gary Campbell. 2006. The Utility of Discourse Analysis to Heritage Studies: The Burra Charter and Social Inclusion. *International Journal of Heritage Studies* 12 (4): 339-355.

Wodak, Ruth. 2001a. What CDA is About—A Summary of its History, Important Concepts and its Developments. In *Methods of Critical Discourse Analysis*, edited by Ruth Wodak, and Michael Meyer, 1-13. London: Sage Publications.

Wodak, Ruth. 2001b. The Discourse-Historical Approach. In *Methods of Critical Discourse Analysis*, edited by Ruth Wodak, and Michael Meyer, 63-93. London: Sage Publications.

Wu, Zongjie, and Hou Song. 2015. Heritage and Discourse. In *The Palgrave Handbook of Contemporary Heritage Research*, edited by Emma Waterton, and Steve Watson, 37-48. Hampshire: Palgrave Macmillan.

Yuval-Davis, Nira. 1997. *Gender and Nation*. London: Sage Publications.

The U.S.-Mexico Border in Visual Art by Chicanas/os: Transcending National Barriers of Cultural Heritage

Eva Zetterman

University of Gothenburg. CONTACT Eva Zetterman: eva.zetterman@gu.se

Abstract: This article investigates contemporary visual art in the USA by Chicanas/os in which the U.S.-Mexico border is the common denominator. The aims of the investigating are: 1) how references to the border are expressed in different ways, 2) how different kinds of references to the border imply expressions that transcend conceptions of the U.S.-Mexico border as a dividing barrier, and 3) how various conceptualizations of the border bring forth understandings of a bi-national/transcultural heritage that reach across the border and into its both sides. By applying a combination of content analysis, visual semiotics and social semiotics and drawing from border history and the concept borderlands, a found selection of 30 artworks in different material and techniques are organized into five thematic clusters. These clusters of visual themes and conceptualizations of the border reveal that: 1) a continuity with the past is created through polyvalent visual signs and symbols that adjust themselves to the theme of any composition; and 2) that temporal and spatial links between colonial pasts, U.S.-Mexico border history and present conditions in the borderlands bring forth visual expressions of a bi-national/transcultural heritage that transcend and challenge the U.S.-Mexico border as a national barrier of cultural heritage.

Keywords: visual art by Chicanas/os, the U.S.-Mexico border, the borderlands, border art, re-cycling visual elements, signs and symbols

Introduction

This article examines visual art made in the USA by Chicanas/os, a subgroup among Mexican Americans. As a minority group in the USA, Mexican Americans express and identify with their Mexican ancestry in different ways and in various degrees. So do Chicanas/os, who also contest and oppose a hegemonic national U.S. identity as White Anglo-Saxon Protestant (WASP) and who claim an identity as "brown" and with mixed Mexican and Indian ancestry (Acuña 2011). In the 1960s, when Mexican Americans began to claim their self-defined identities as Chicanas/os by mobilizing in the Chicano Movement for affirmation and empowerment, visual art became an important tool applied for spreading political and ideological messages (Castillo, McKenna, and Yarbro-Bejarano 1991). Since the Chicano Movement 1965–1985, the subject matter in visual art by Chicanas/os often deals with Mexican ancestry, history and socio-cultural circumstances of Mexicans and Chicanas/os in present USA (Goldman 1994; Goldman and Ybarra-Frausto 1991). This article focuses on visual expressions with historical perspectives that refer to the U.S.-Mexico border and the history of the border.

The history of the present U.S.-Mexico border goes back in time to the mid 19th century, when the Mexican-American war (1846–1848) ended with the signing in 1848 of the Treaty of Guadalupe with a new borderline between Mexico and the USA drawn on the map further south. As a consequence, almost half of the geographical territory of Mexico was incorporated into the USA, which today become the states California, Arizona, New Mexico, Texas, Nevada, Utah and parts of Wyoming and Colorado (Acuña 2011; Castillo 1992). The moved borderline meant that Mexicans living in what had been the northern parts of Mexico suddenly became U.S. nationals without having chosen this themselves, Mexican communities situated on separate sides of the new border were divided, and U.S.

nationals in the new minority group Mexican Americans and their descendants became considered as second-class citizens in U.S. society (Acuña 2011; Castillo 1992). In short, the new borderline that was drawn on the map further south became a dividing barrier by which families were split, community ties were broken, and border-crossers from Mexico became considered as illegal immigrants (Acuña 2011).

The aim of this article is to investigate visual art created by Chicanas/os in which the U.S.-Mexico border is the common denominator for signifying and meaning-making processes. The signifying processes I am interested in are how references to the border are expressed in different ways and how these different ways of referring to the border imply expressions of the border that transcend conceptions of the present U.S.-Mexico border as a dividing barrier. I am also interested in how conceptualizations of the border from various perspectives bring forth understandings of a bi-national/transcultural heritage that spatially and temporally reaches into both sides of the border and thus expands across the border.

Material and Methods

For the investigation presented in this article I have applied a combination of different analytical methods and theoretical perspectives. I have collected examples of Chicana/o visual art by traveling in the USA, visiting mural sites, art museums, exhibitions and galleries, searching through exhibition catalogues, books, articles, and various websites. This research process has resulted in a large body of art on which I have applied content analysis (Rose 2007), with a systematic search for examples of artworks in which the U.S.-Mexico border is the common denominator and by coding and identifying shared visual elements. For identifying the border as the common denominator, I focused on several aspects of the artworks, such as subject matter including content and titles, and visual elements including symbols and signs. By this analytical process, I was able to find an empirical material consisting of a collection of 30 examples of Chicana/o artworks in which the U.S.-Mexico border is the common denominator. The found examples are created at different times, and by different Chicana/o artists and artist groups. The earliest example is from the late 1960s, the latest from the early 2010s. The artworks are made in a multitude of media, techniques and material, including paintings, posters, prints, mixed media works, murals, performances, video still, woven tapestry and installation/sculpture.

For analysing and interpreting the artworks, I applied a combination of visual semiotics and social semiotics. In close-readings of individual artworks, I applied visual semiotics for analysing denotations and connotations of visual elements, signs and symbols referring to the border (Rose 2007; Barthes 1999), while social semiotics opened up for connecting signifying and meaning-making processes in the artworks to broader but still site-specific historical and socio-cultural contexts (Leeuwen 2008). By these analytical steps, I could organize the empirical material into thematic clusters representing shared visual characteristics and signifying themes. I have interpreted shared signifying themes as representing certain conceptualizations of the border. Each thematic cluster thus mediates different perspectives by which the border is conceptualized. These different perspectives by which the border is conceptualized imply understandings of bi-national/transcultural heritage that expand across the border both as a physical barrier and a national boundary and thus spatially and temporally reach into both sides of the border.

The combination of analytical methods described above has been applied together with interacting theoretical perspectives. One theoretical perspective is border history (Acuña 2011; Castillo 1992), which I find important since the change of the border's geographical location had a fundamental impact on both the socio-cultural circumstances of Mexican communities divided by the border and the socio-cultural circumstances of Mexican Americans as a minority group in the USA. With this article I argue that the collected examples of artworks visually express the impact on generations of Mexican Americans and Chicanas/os by the border's new geographical location with the Treaty of Guadalupe.

The other theoretical perspective applied in this investigation is the borderland, which is a common concept in theorizing the U.S.-Mexico border. In Border Studies, the borderland is defined as a historical as well as a spatial whole with cross-boundary economic ties and social interactions between diverse border communities (Wastl-Walter 2016; Mignolo 2000). In Chicana/o Studies, scholars have stressed the connections in the borderlands by people, memories, bodies, and identities (Anzaldúa 1987; Pérez 1999; Saldívar 1997; Acuña 2011). In writings by Gloria Anzaldúa and Emma Pérez for example, the borderland is theorized as a zone from which to re-conceptualize history as a narration by a multiplicity of voices and as a space for intellectual consciousness and psychological awareness from which to acknowledge differences, accept contradictions and to construct identities that transgress singular identifications (Anzaldúa 1987; Pérez 1999).

The combination of U.S.-Mexico border history and definitions of the concept borderland from Border Studies and Chicana/o Studies have been guiding me through the research process with finding and coding examples of artworks, analysing and interpreting individual artworks, organizing the found examples into thematic clusters, and naming visual themes and conceptualizations of the border. The combination of theoretical perspectives has also guided me through the process of interpreting the visual themes and conceptualizations of the border in regard to layers of transnational, bi-national and cross-national cultural heritage.

Found Visual Themes and Border Aspects

The empirical material with thirty examples of visual artworks by Chicanas/os in which the U.S.-Mexico border is the common denominator has been organized into five thematic clusters. Each thematic cluster represents a visual theme that mediates a certain aspect of the border. Some examples of artworks, however, include visual elements shared with examples of artworks organized into other thematic groups. This means that some artworks represent more than one visual theme and thus mediate more than one aspect of the border than the thematic cluster into which they are organized. In such cases, when an artwork can be considered as belonging to more than one thematic cluster, I have made a choice of thematic cluster that sometimes is based on the most apparent visual elements and sometimes on the conceptualization of a certain aspect of the border. This means that one specific artwork is sometimes described in more than one thematic group. The organization of the empirical material into five thematic clusters is presented as a result below. Only 10 of the discussed 30 artworks are represented in this article with visual illustrations. When a title of an artwork is mentioned in the text with no visual illustration, a reference is made to a textual source where a visual illustration of the artwork can be found.

Changed Identities-Border Effects

Five examples of artworks in which the U.S.-Mexico border is the common denominator relate to issues of new and changed identities that are expressed by a combination of visual and textual elements. One artwork (Figure 1) is a mixed media work by Malaquias Montoya with the title *The Treaty of Guadalupe, 1848* (1998) (Keller 2002a: 26).

Figure 1   Malaquias Montoya, *The Treaty of Guadalupe, 1848* (1998), mixed media.
© Malaquias Montoya (photo by Craig Smith)

436

In the upper part of the image is "1848", the year of the Treaty of Guadalupe, written with large numbers in black, followed by the words "In the Name of Almighty God". In the central and lower part of the image, two textual fragments from the Treaty of Guadalupe are inserted. To the right is a historical map of Mexico, which reveals how much further north the geographical territory of the Mexican nation-state stretched before 1848, far into the southern parts of the USA. Montoya's *The Treaty of Guadalupe, 1848* is visually documenting the impact of the Treaty of Guadalupe as a historical document, with the changed border, the incorporation of northern Mexico into the U.S. South-West, and the foundation of the U.S.-Mexico borderlands. Its main topic is the changed national/cultural identity of the geographical territory of northern Mexico to the U.S. South-West.

Two artworks deal with changed identities of people/individuals, *Who's the Illegal Alien, Pilgrim?/Quién es el extranjeroilegal, peregrino?* (1981) by Yolanda López (Davalos 2008: 54; Keller 2002b: 90), and *We Are Not A Minority* (1978) by the art collective Congresso de Artistas Chicanos en Aztlán (Dunitz and Prigoff 1997: 172). The composition in both follows the composition in political draft posters from the First and Second World Wars, in which Lord Kitchener and Uncle Sam are pointing their fingers toward the spectators/audiences with the aim to persuade young men to join the army in Great Britain and the USA respectively. The artwork *We Are Not A Minority* (1978) (Figure 2) is a street mural in East Los Angeles.

Figure 2   Congresso de Artistas Chicanos en Aztlán, *We Are Not A Minority* (1978), street mural. © Congresso de Artistas Chicanos en Aztlán (photo by Eva Zetterman)

In the mural is the pointing finger attached to a facial portrait of Che Guevara and beside him is a text written in large letters claiming that "We Are Not A Minority". The design of the letters with symbolic choices of colours, shapes and fonts, is referring to Mexican culture; the "A" for example is in the shape of a pyramid. The combination of visual and textual elements in the mural is a visual message created of affirmation and empowerment in line with the Chicano Movement in the 1970s. My interpretation of the signifying process of the mural is a message saying: "We are not a minority, we are indigenous inhabitants of this land/geographical territory, who were transformed from being Mexican to American. It is the country that has changed its identity, and we are thus not immigrants, nor a minority."

The artwork *Who's the Illegal Alien, Pilgrim?/Quién es el extranjeroilegal, peregrino?* (1981) (Figare 3) by Yolanda López is a printed poster. In this image is the gesture with the pointing finger to the audience done by a man with Indian/Aztec features, a representation based on a portrait of a male friend by López (Davalos 2008: 54-55).

Figure 3   Yolanda López, *Who's the Illegal Alien, Pilgrim?* (1981), offset lithograph.
© Yolanda M. López (photo from SFMOMA Archive)

On the man's chest is the text "Who's the Illegal Alien, Pilgrim?" written in large black letters and in one of his hands he holds a document with the text "Immigration Plans". As Karen Mary Davalos points out in her book about Yolanda López, this poster was created for a campaign about immigration rights, organized by the Committee on Chicano Rights in San Diego (Davalos 2008: 53). As such, the poster critically questions whose identities; it is fair to give a status as illegal. The poster suggests that Mexican Americans should not be considered illegal because they have inhabited the geographical location of the U.S. South-West since long before the 1848 Treaty of Guadalupe. Both *Who's the Illegal Alien, Pilgrim?* and *We Are Not A Minority* deal with consequences of the new border which meant changed national identities of Mexicans into Mexican Americans and changed sociocultural status of Mexican Americans as a minority group in the present USA.

Additional artworks in this group of examples are two performance by Guillermo Gómez-Peña, who was born in Mexico City but since the late 1970s live in California. One of these performances is *El Guerrero de la Gringostroika/The Warrior of Gringostroika* (1992) (Gómez-Peña 1993: 139; Gómez-Peña 1996: 31).

In one photograph (Figure 4) documenting Gómez-Peña performing as the character *The Warrior of Gringostroika*, the performer is seen wearing a costume typical for Mexican mariachi orchestras, having a wrestler mask over his head similar to the mask of the Mexican community activist Superbarrio, and on his chest he has written the words "Please don't discover me". The character *The Warrior of Gringostroika* is from a multi-media performance series in a large project "The Year of the White Bear" and thus situated within a series of performances that Gómez-Peña's enacted in protest to the global celebration in 1992 of the 500th anniversary of Christopher Columbus' "discovery" of the American continent (Gómez-Peña 1993). As such it is a critical comment to the Spanish colonialization in the early 16th century of the pre-colonial geographical territory of the Aztecs, Mayas, Zapotecs and several other indigenous groups that eventually became Mexico.

Figure 4   Guillermo Gómez-Peña, *El Guerrero de la Gringostroika/The Warrior of Gringostroika* (1992), performance. © Guillermo Gómez-Peña (photo from BAW/ TAF Archives)

The second performance by Gómez-Peña is *Temple of Confessions* (1995), staged together with performance artist Roberto Sifuentes in several enactments at the Ex-Teresa Arte Alternativo in Mexico City (Gómez-Peña and Sifuentes 1996).

In one photograph (Figure 5) documenting this performance is Gómez-Peña seen sitting on a chair with a sign that is tied to a rope around his neck and hanging in front of his chest, and on the sign he has written "There Used to be a Mexican Inside this Body" (Gómez-Peña 1996: 8). These two performances both express transformations of national and sociocultural identities by two kinds of historical cultural processes. One of which is a process of geographical territories changing their identities by new national borders, the other is a process when brown bodies move across these national borders.

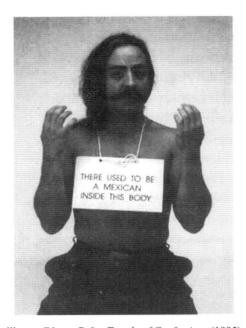

Figure 5   Guillermo Gómez-Peña, *Temple of Confessions* (1995), performance.
© Guillermo Gómez-Peña (photo from BAW/TAF Archives)

The identity issues brought up in these artworks concern changed and transformed identities by historical events. One of the historical events referred to is when the geographical territory of what later became Mexico was "discovered" in the early 16th century by Hernán Cortéz and his Spanish soldiers, which leads to the transformation of the Aztec territory of Anahuac into a Spanish colony (Townsend 2000). The second historical event referred to is the Mexican-American war in the mid 19th century and the signing in 1848 of the Treaty of Guadalupe, by which the borderline between Mexico and the USA was redrawn on the map further south and the northern parts of Mexico became incorporated into the USA. As a consequence of these historical events, geographical territories changed their cultural/national identities, from Aztec to Spanish, from Spanish to Mexican, and from Mexican to American. By these new national identities of geographical locations, the national identities of the people living in these locations changed. In the examples of artworks that express transformations of national and cultural identities of both geographical territories and groups of individuals, the border is not only conceptualized as a zone in line with how the borderland is understood in Border Studies, as a spatial and temporal whole, but also in line with understandings by Anzaldúa and Pérez of the concept the borderland (Anzaldúa 1987; Pérez 1999), as a space from which to construct identities that transgress singular identifications.

Creating Genealogies—Connecting Sides of the Border

Four examples of artworks in which the U.S.-Mexico border is the common denominator include portraits of historical individuals by which a creation of genealogies is crafted across the border. One of these examples is *The del Rey Mural* (1968) by Antonio Bernal, a street mural painted on one of the exterior walls of El Teatro Campesino Cultural Center in Del Rey, California (Barnet-Sánchez 1996: 22). According to art historian Shifra Goldman, the murals on El Teatro Campesino belong to some of the earliest murals of the Chicano Movement in the 1960s (Goldman 1996: 26).

On one exterior wall (Figure 6) are a group of individuals depicted standing in full-figure beside each other in a straight line. These figures represent a selection of historical individuals from two important and powerful social movements, one in Mexico, the Mexican Revolution in the 1910s, and one in the USA, the Civil Rights Movement in the 1960s. The first three figures that represent the Mexican Revolution include the mythical figure Adelita and the two legendary revolutionaries Pancho Villa and Emiliano Zapata (Goldman 1996: 26). Then follows five figures representing the Civil Rights Movement in the USA, including both Mexican American and African American Civil Rights activists, such as César Chavez of the United Farm Workers, Reies López Tijerina of the Federal Alliance of Land Grants, Malcolm X of the Black Panther Party and the African-American leader Martin Luther King (Goldman 1996: 26). By the selection of these historical individuals is a genealogy created of both social movements and historical role models, by which temporal and spatial links are established across the border, bridging nations and connecting geographical areas.

Figure 6   Antonio Bernal, *The del Rey Mural* (1968), mural. © Antonio Bernal
(photo by Robert Sommer)

A second example in this group of artworks is the street mural *Ghosts of the Barrio* (1974) (Figure 7) by Wayne Healy (Dunitz and Prigoff 1997: 171).

Figure 7   Wayne Healy, *Ghosts of the Barrio* (1974), mural. © Wayne Healy
(photo by Eva Zetterman)

In this street mural, painted on the exterior wall of a domestic house in the East Los Angeles's housing project Ramona Gardens, are four homeboys/gang members depicted sitting on the outdoor stairs of the house. On each side of them stand three ghostlike figures from the past in Mexico representing their cultural ancestors, to the left a mestizo soldier from the Mexican Revolution, to the right an Aztec warrior and a Spanish conquistador. In discussing this artwork, the artist Wayne Healy has explained that the composition with the selection of figures creates a visual narrative of warfare, by which a genealogical link is established between the four homeboys in Los Angeles and their historical ancestors in Mexico, by which gang wars in the East Los Angeles barrios become connected to the Mexican Revolution and the Spanish conquest in the past (Healy 1997: 171).

A third example in this group of artworks is the painting *Veteranos: A Legacy of Valor* (2000) (Figure 8) by Ignacio Gómez (Keller 2002a: 281).

Figure 8   Ignacio Gómez, *Veteranos: A Legacy of Valor* (2000), acrylic painting.
© Ignacio Gómez (photo by Craig Smith)

In this painting are four Chicanos portrayed as American soldiers, each representing a war in which the USA was involved in the 20th century: World War I, World War II, the Korean War and the Vietnam War. As Chicano historian Rodolfo Acuña has noted, in the Vietnam War for example, Chicanos distinguished themselves both by receiving the greatest number of congressional medals and by providing the largest number of military personnels in relation to their representation in the general population, while their casualty rates were much higher than among other ethnic groups in the USA (Acuña 1981). Gómez's painting is paying homage to Chicanos serving as soldiers in U.S. wars. The four Chicano soldiers are portrayed as if their upper bodies are rising through the U.S. national flag that is depicted as a porous intangible cloud. Behind them rises a monumental facial portrait of an Aztec warrior above them in the background. By the visual element of an Aztec warrior, the Chicano soldiers are related to their Mexican ancestry and a pre-colonial past. A genealogical link is thus established between the four Chicanos fighting as U.S. soldiers in 20th century wars and their Aztec predecessors, fighting against Spanish soldiers in Tenochtitlán during the Spanish conquest of Anahuac in the early 16th century.

A fourth example in this group of artworks is the large street mural *Raices/Roots* (1995) (Figure 9) on West Maple Avenue in Lompoc, California, painted by Leonardo Nuñez and students from Lompoc High School (Dunitz and Prigoff 1997: 133).

Figure 9 Leonardo Nuñez and students from Lompoc High School, *Raices/Roots* (1995), mural.
© Leonardo Nuñez (photo from Lompoc Mural Society)

The composition of the mural is divided into two parts, the left side representing Mexico, the right the USA. On each side are facial portraits of role models/heroes from the two nations depicted against the blue sky as angelical heads floating in the air. The division of the composition into two national parts by the U.S.-Mexico border in middle central part of the image is symbolically represented by a brown eagle flying in the air against the blue sky and by a large pre-colonial pyramid. These two symbols represent a historical/cultural heritage that goes back in time before the arrival of the Spaniards in the 16th century (Townsend 2000; Miller and Taube 1993: 139-140). The pyramid represents the multitude of pre-colonial cultures before the Spanish conquest (Miller and Taube 1993). The brown eagle is a Mexican/Aztec symbol from the legend of the Aztecs' mythical homeland Aztlán and in the 19th century, when the Spanish colony New Spain became the independent nation-state Mexico, the eagle was included as a central visual element in the Mexican flag (Miller and Taube 1993: 82-83). In the lower central part of the mural, in front of the pyramid, is the border represented by a fence and beside the fence is a family with a father, a mother and a child struggling to get through the fence on their journey as migrant border-crossers from Mexico to the USA.

The examples in this group of artworks bring forth role models by portraits of individuals from both sides of the border by which genealogies are created across the U.S.-Mexico border and by which both sides of the border are tied together and connected. The two sides of the border is thus visually mediated in line with how Anzaldúa (1987) has verbally described the US-Mexico borderlands, as a Siamese twin, sharing the same body but each with their own individual identity. The crafting of historical genealogies temporally and spatially connects the two sides of the U.S.-Mexico border and implies conceptualizations of the border as one historical and spatial whole, in which its borderlands are a space where people, memories, bodies and identities are interconnected in a historical web of transcultural bonds.

Barbed Wire and Migrant Families on the Run—the Border as Barrier

Ten examples of artworks in which the U.S.-Mexico border is the common denominator include two dominant visual elements referring to the border, the barbed wire and to a migrant family on the run. One of these ten examples is the large street mural *Raices/Roots* (1995) described above, in which both the barbed wire and a migrant family on the run are included as visual elements.

In five artworks, the barbed wire of the U.S.-Mexico border is included as a dominant visual element that covers a major part of the composition in a grid-like pattern. These five artworks are *¡Cesen Deportación!* (1973), a print by Rupert García (Castillo, McKenna, and Yarbro-Bejarano 1991: 35), *Undocumented* (1981) (Keller 2002a: 229) and *Una Familia* (1990) (Keller 2004: 60), both prints by Malaquias Montoya, *California Dreaming* (1997), a print by Jacalyn López García (Keller 2002a: 227; Keller 2004: 6), and *Amor Indocumentado/Undocumented Love* (1986) (Figure 10), a painting by José Antonio Burciaga (Mesa-Bains and Ybarra-Frausto 1986: 20).

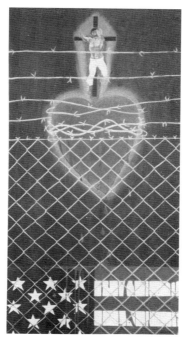

Figure 10   José Antonio Burciaga, *Amor Indocumentado/Undocumented Love* (1986), acrylic painting. © José Antonio Burciaga (photo from Mexican Museum, San Francisco)

In the painting *Amor Indocumentado* is the fence represented by horizontal strings of thorns followed by barbed wire in a grid-like pattern and combined with various Roman-Catholic symbols, such as the crucifix of Jesus Chirst, his crucified body, the thorns, the holy blood and the sacred burning heart. As spectators of this image, we are situated on the Mexican side of the border, looking through the fence to the U.S. side of the border. On the other side of the fence is a man running toward us, with his arms stretched out in our direction and his body attached to a crucifix. Below the crucifix is a large red heart from which blood is dropping down on the American flag in the lower part of the image behind the fence.

A migrant family on the run is the main motif in four artworks in this group of examples. These four artworks are the painting *La Familia* (1999) by Jesús Rangel (Keller 2002b: 220), the painting *La Sagrada Familia en Aztlán* (1994) by Rosa M. (Keller 2002a: 27), the painting *Hollywood via Tijuana* (1994) by Richard Duffy (Keller 2002a: 31), and the print *Liberty on the Run* (2010) by Lalo Alcatraz (Justseeds Artists' Cooperative 2012). In all of these artworks is the visual depiction of the family on the run based on the original traffic sign of a running family with a father, a mother and a child, which can be seen along highways north of the U.S.-Mexico border, warning car drivers to watch out for border-crossers from Mexico. In this group of artworks is the border referred to as a dividing barrier, either by being represented as a materialized separating fence, or by being represented as a migrant family on the run as an effect of the border as a barrier between Mexico and the USA.

Reclaiming National Icons—the Border Becoming Porous

Seven examples of artworks in which the U.S.-Mexico border is the common denominator refer to two national icons by appropriating visual elements from their iconography, the U.S. Statue of Liberty and the Mexican Virgin of Guadalupe. One of these examples is Alcatraz's print *Liberty on the Run* (2010) (Figure 11), mentioned above.

Figure 11   Lalo Alcatraz, *Liberty on the Run* (2010), print. © Lalo Alcatraz
(photo from Justseeds Artists' Cooperative)

In this image of a family on the run, the Statue of Liberty is referred to by the torch that one of the two adult family members holds in his/her hand and by the three family members' hair, which is depicted in a punk style, giving their heads a zigzagged silhouette. As noted above, the visual composition of the three family members is based on the common traffic sign warning car drivers to watch out for border-crossers from Mexico. By the combination with references to the Statue of Liberty, the image becomes a representation of a Mexican migrant family on the run that has crossed the border with great difficulties and now risks deportation, maybe even their lives, by running as "illegals" into the self-proclaimed nation-state of "freedom" and "liberty". The title of the image *Liberty on the Run* further suggests that the image is a sarcastic visual representation of a running family that is the Statue of Liberty's own family, whose three family members now run as Mexican "illegal" immigrants into the U.S. in search of "freedom" and "liberty".

A second example in this group of artworks is the print *Cruzando el Milenario* (1999) (Figure 12) by Tony Ortega (Keller 2002b: 176).

Figure 12   Tony Ortega, *Cruzando el Milenario* (1999), silkscreen.
© Tony Ortega (photo by Craig Smith)

In this image is a representation of the Statue of Liberty depicted in the foreground as a silhouette with golden lines. Through the silhouette is an adult couple with a man and a woman seen walking hand-in-hand into the desert. By the silhouette of the Statue of Liberty as a ghostlike shape in front of the couple, she can either symbolize a metaphorical map by which the couple can guide themselves through the desert by following her golden lines, or she can personify a guardian angel that will protect them on their dangerous journey into the desert.

In two examples in this group of artworks is the representation of the Statue of Liberty mixed with visual elements referring to common national icons in Mexico, which transforms her into a representation of a national icon with a Mexican identity. One of these is the print *La Libertad II* (the Liberty II) (1987) (Figure 13) by Ester Hernández (Keller 2004: 182; Keller 2002b: 240).

Figure 13   Ester Hernández, *La Libertad II* (the Liberty II) (1987), etching and aquatint.
© Ester Hernández (photo by Craig Smith)

In this image a young female artist is seen standing on a ladder that is leaning against the Statue of Liberty. Standing on the top of the ladder, the female artist is cutting out pieces from the Statue of Liberty and remodeling her shape into a monumental stone sculpture of the Aztec moon deity Coyolxauhqui. The representation of Coyolxauhqui in Hernández' print is based on a pre-colonial stone disc, *El Cuerpo de Coyolxauhqui* (the body of Coyolxauhqui), found in Mexico City in 1978 and today kept in the Templo Mayor Museum in central Mexico City (Townsend 2000: 153, 160; Miller and Taube 1993: 68-69). The second of these is the artwork *La Virgen de Guadaliberty* (1999) (Figure 14), a print by Nephtalí de León (Keller 2004: 170; Keller 2002a: 239).

Figure 14   Nephtalí de León, *La Virgen de Guadaliberty* (1999), serigraph.
© Nephtalí de León (photo by Craig Smith)

In this image, the Statue of Liberty is referred to by her classic standing pose with one arm lifted in the air and a selection of visual elements from her iconography, such as the torch that she holds in her right hand above her head, the document representing the U.S. *Declaration of Independence* that she holds in her left hand, and the crown on her head with the rays forming a halo. But in León's print are visual elements from the iconography of the Virgin of Guadalupe added to the representation of the Statue of Liberty, such as Guadalupe's pink dress, her green mantle, the crescent moon held by an angel below her feet, and the mandorla behind her. This change of symbolic visual elements transforms the Statue of Liberty as a symbolic national icon of the USA into a representation of the Virgin of Guadalupe, which is the master signifier of the Mexican nation-state (Lafaye 1976).

452

A fifth example in this group of artworks is a cotton tapestry titled *Proyecto para la bandera de una colonia mexicana* (project for the flag of a Mexican colony) (1987) (Figure 15) by Adolfo Patiño (Roque 1995: 29). The Patiño's tapestry shows an American flag, but the stars are replaced with three large versions of the Virgin of Guadalupe.

Figure 15 Adolfo Patiño, *Proyecto para la bandera de una colonia mexicana* (1987), cotton tapestry. © Adolfo Patiño (photo from shrill_eflags Archive)

Each version is depicted in one color, either green or white or red. These colors are the colors of the national flag of Mexico, which together with the representations of the Virgin of Guadalupe symbolically transform the U.S. national flag into a "mexicanized" version of the U.S. flag. As in the previous two examples of artworks in which the Statue of Liberty is visually transformed in a national signifier of Mexico, the visual change of the U.S. flag indicates that the geographical territory that the flag is meant to represent has changed its identity, and this identity is now becoming a national hybrid. The conceptualization of the border in the three artworks *La Libertad II*, *La Virgen de Guadaliberty* and *Proyecto para la bandera de una colonia mexicana* is a border that as a national boundary between two nation-states has become porous and starting to leak "mexicaness" into the USA.

The last two examples in this group of artworks are ironic representations of the Mexican national icon the Virgin of Guadalupe. One of these examples is the mixed media print *The Virgin of Guadalupe Got Her Green Card* (2001) (Figure 16) by Isabel Martínez (Keller 2004: 7).

Figure 16   Isabel Martínez, *The Virgin of Guadalupe Got Her Green Card* (2001), serigraph. © Isabel Martínez (photo by Craig Smith)

In this print the Virgin of Guadalupe is represented as a happy young woman smiling to the spectator and in one of her hands she holds her green card, showing it to the spectator as if it is her most valuable document, since it allows her to stay in the USA as a "legal" immigrant.

The second example is the print *La Virgen de Guadalupe as Wanted Terrorist* (2010) (Figure 17) by Ester Hernández (Román-Odio 2013: 107).

Figure 17   Ester Hernández, *La Virgen de Guadalupe as Wanted Terrorist* (2010), print. © Ester Hernández (photo from Dignidad Rebelde Archive)

In this print is the Virgin of Guadalupe represented as an "illegal", even dangerous immigrant. The composition of this image with a combination of textual and visual elements appropriates the composition of historical posters of wanted criminals. In the upper part of the image is a text written in black letters as a headline that reads: "Wanted terrorist, La Virgen de Guadalupe." In the central part of the image below are two representations of the Virgin of Guadalupe as a veiled woman inserted as photographs, one frontal, the other in profile. In the lower part of the image is the second text inserted in which Guadalupe is described as "considered powerful and dangerous". The combination of these visual and textual elements turns the representation of the Virgin of Guadalupe into a symbolic personification of Mexico whose connotations of a "mexicaness" is so powerful that she poses a threat to the U.S. hegemonic identity as WASP, which becomes in danger.

The artworks in this group of examples referring to the Statue of Liberty and the Virgin of Guadalupe as national signifiers apply a visual strategy of appropriation by which visual elements from their traditional iconography are changed, replaced and have undergone contextual shifts, turning their meaning-making processes into new signifying directions. By reclaiming the two master signifiers of the USA and Mexico by changing visual elements from their iconography, their identities as national master signifiers change, and so do the national identities of the nations that they are supposed to represent. This suggests a conceptualization of the U.S.-Mexico border by which the border has gone from a dividing barrier to becoming instable and porous and a border through which "mexicaness" is continuously leaking into the USA.

Imaginary Alternative Futures—Opened and Erased Borders

Four examples of artworks in which the U.S.-Mexico border is the common denominator either represent or refer directly to the border. One example is a published statement on a poster to a site-specific performance along the U.S.-Mexico border, *End of the Line* (1986) by the art group Border Art Workshop/Taller de Arte Fronterizo (the BAW/TAF). In addition to *End of the Line*, BAW/TAF has enacted several other series of site-specific performances along the U.S.-Mexico border, such as *Border Realities* (1985) and *Border Sutures* (1990) (Sheren 2010: 59). These site-specific performances have been documented in several photographs, but here I instead include as an artwork the statement to the performance *End of the Line* that in 1989 was published in the artists' magazine *The Broken Line/La Linea Quebrada* as a poster with written words, saying "The reason we Mexicans are so successful in crossing the border is that we've refined it to an art form" (Cortés 2007: 325). A declared intention by BAW/TAF with *End of the Line* was to challenge media conceptions of the U.S.-Mexico border as a zone of war or conflict and instead create a sense of "no-border" (Fusco 1989: 61). Situated within the context of the site-specific performance *End of the Line* with the intention of creating a sense of "no-border, the published statement turns the border into a conceptualized zone giving space for practicing artistic and creative performative skills".

A second example in this group of artworks is the site-specific performance *Tijuana-Niagara* (1987–1988) (Figure 18) by two members in the art group BAW/TAF, Guillermo Gómez-Peña and Emily Hicks.

Figure 18   Guillermo Gómez-Peña and Emily Hicks, *Tijuana-Niagara* (1987–1988),
performance. © Guillermo Gómez-Peña and Emily Hicks
(photo from BAW/TAF Archives)

With this performance they traveled along the U.S.-Canadian border in a mobile "temple of kitsch" (Gómez-Peña 1996: 91). In photographs documenting this performance, Emily Hicks is variously seen wearing a long blond wig, a black veil covering her face, and having a wrestler's mask over her head that is similar to the mask of the Mexican community activist Superbarrio, with whom BAW/TAF collaborated (Fusco 1989: 57). In one photograph where she is wearing a wrestler's mask, she is seen sitting on the floor on the top of a large map of the American continent. The map on the floor is placed in front of the camera so that from a spectator's angle it is presented upside-down, with South America in the north and Canada in the south (Lippard 2000: 218; Gómez-Peña 1991: 45). On the map is Emily Hicks sitting with her legs spread wide apart and right in front of her crotch rises a Mickey Mouse figure. These performative acts with the map contribute to a symbolic transformation of the geographical territory of USA by which USA is turned into a Disney-land and Mickey Mouse into a phallic toy for female masturbation. In addition, due to the title of the performance, *Tijuana-Niagara*, the nation-state USA becomes invisible. What is left is a hyphen into which USA has dissolved into a waste border region between the nation-states of Canada and Mexico.

A third example in this group of artworks is the site-specific performance *Erasing the Border* (2012) (Figure 19) by Ana Teresa Fernandez (Public Delivery 2018).

Figure 19   Ana Teresa Fernández, *Erasing the Border* (2012), performance.
© Ana Teresa Fernández (photo from Ana Teresa Fernández Archive)

This performance was staged at the U.S.-Mexico border where the border fence between Tijuana and San Diego meets the Pacific Ocean. Video-stills documenting this performance show how Ana Teresa Fernández is standing on the Tijuana side of the border and painting the fence with a bright blue color. This physical as well as corporeal and tangible enactment turns the materiality of the fence into a visual impression by which it dissolves into the air and turns into a segment of the blue sky above.

A fourth example in this group of artworks is the site-specific installation/sculpture *Border Door* (1988) (Figure 20) by Richard Lou (Keller 2002a: 225).

Figure 20   Richard Lou, *Border Door* (1988), installation/sculpture.
© Richard Lou (photo by Jim Elliott)

For this installation/sculpture, Richard Lou literally placed a freestanding door hinged on a frame on the U.S.-Mexico border a few miles from the Tijuana International Airport (Latorre 2012: 3). With the only material signs left of the border in the form of a framed half-opened door and traces of barbed wire, this artwork turns the border into a material manifestation of a barrier that has been broken and gradually crumbles. Conceptualized as a line drawn on a map, it has dissolved into a by-gone memory.

In these examples of artworks are representations of or references to the border done in ways by which the border is transformed into new kinds of border representations. The U.S.-Mexico border is represented in these artworks as opened, even invisible, or broken, erased and dissolved. This suggests conceptualizations of the border in imaginary alternative futures in which the border has materially evolved into new and open forms.

Conclusions

The empirical material in this investigation consists of 30 examples of artworks by Chicanas/os in which the U.S.-Mexico border is the common denominator. The artworks are created in different times, by different artists, and in various techniques and materials, such as murals, paintings, posters, prints, mixed media works, performances, video stills, woven tapestry and installation/sculpture. The artworks thus show a great variety in regard to visual composition, combination of visual elements, repetition of signs, choice of symbols, combination of metaphors and mixing of spatial and temporal contexts. This variety in the artworks has opened up to a great diversity in how references to and conceptualizations of the border are expressed.

Because of the many different ways and forms by which references to the border are expressed in the artworks, they were organized into five clusters with shared visual themes. These visual themes were interpreted as representations of changed cultural and national identities, as crafting genealogies by portraits of strategic choices of role models, as representations of the border as dividing barrier by a repetition of the fence and migrant families on the run, as reclaiming national icons by appropriating representations of the Statue of Liberty and the Virgin of Guadalupe, and as multi-faceted expressions of new forms of the border in imaginary alternative futures. The clusters into which the artworks were organized were also interpreted as mediating various conceptualizations of the border, such as the border as a moved line on the map giving rise to new identities, the border as a stopping barrier dividing families and communities, the border as a barrier that can be crossed, the border with two sides that are connected, the border as porous and leaking "mexicaness" into the USA, and the border as opened and invisible, even erased, deleted, and materially dissolved.

The various conceptualizations of the border are expressed in ways by which continuity with the past is created through polyvalent visual signs and symbols that adjust themselves to the theme of any composition. These visual signs and symbols draw from multiple sources that temporally reach back in time to the Aztec Empire before the arrival of the

Spaniards in early 16th century. By creating a dialogue in the present with the past and connecting the two sides of the border are conceptualizations of a bi-national/transcultural heritage created that transcend and challenge the U.S.-Mexico border as barrier. The recycling of visual signs and symbols with contextual temporal shifts also brings forth conceptualizations of bi-national/transcultural heritage that expand spatially across the U.S.-Mexico border and reach into its both sides. The artworks thus visually represent temporal and spatial links between colonial pasts, U.S.-Mexico border history and present conditions in the borderlands.

The recycling in the artworks of visual elements, signs and symbols with contextual shifts reloads their visual connotations with new meanings. These meaning-making processes have opened up for new signifying conceptualizations of both the U.S.-Mexico border and its border history. Though all the artworks in one way or the other draw on the borderland concept, on border history and on the effects of the new borderline by which families were split, community ties were broken and border-crossers from Mexico to the USA were considered as illegal immigrants, this cycle is also turned around, giving rise to new and changed visual and conceptual effects. The artworks not only express the consequences of the changed national/cultural identity of the U.S. South-West, by which the national/cultural identities of Mexicans, Mexican Americans and Chicanas/os are transformed. The artworks also express how new national/cultural identities of groups of individuals, Mexicans, Mexican Americans and Chicanas/os, and give rise to new understandings of the national/cultural identity of the USA. The national/cultural identity of the geographical territory of the USA is thus slowly transformed and becoming "mexicanized".

◻ Disclosure Statement

No potential conflict of interest was reported by the author.

◻ Funding

This work was supported by the Faculty of Humanities, University of Gothenburg, Sweden.

◻ Note on Contributor

Eva Zetterman is an Associate Professor in Art History and Visual Culture and is affiliated to the University of Gothenburg in Sweden, where she mainly teaches on courses in Gender Studies and Cultural Studies. She received her PhD in 2003 with the dissertation "Frida Kahlosbildspråk—ansikte, kropp&landskap: Representation avnationalitet" [Frida Kahlo's Imagery—Face, Body & Landscape: Representation of Nationality], which has been published in three editions (2003, 2007 and 2011). Her later researches include contemporary Nordic/Swedish visual art, Chicana/o visual culture, museum studies and curatorial practices. These researches have been published as articles in various journals, such as American Studies in Scandinavia (2016) and Culture Unbound (2015), and as chapters in several books, such as En ny frihet—sjutton konstnärer: Hundra år i Göteborg [A New Freedom—Seventeenth Artists: Hundred Years in Gothenburg] (2018), Curating Differently: Feminisms, Exhibitions and Curatorial Spaces (2016), Globalizing Art: Negotiating Place, Identity and Nation in Contemporary Nordic Art (2011), and Representation och regionalitet: Genusstrukturer i fyra svenska konstmuseisamlingar [Representation and Regionality: Gender Structures in Four Swedish Art Museum Collections] (2011). Her present research areas are street art, performance art and visual historiography.

References

Acuña, Rodolfo F. 2011. *Occupied America: A History of Chicanos*. Boston: Longman.

Anzaldúa, Gloria. 1987. *Borderlands/La Frontera: The New Mestiza*. San Francisco: Aunt Lute Press.

Barthes, Roland. 1999. Rhetoric of the Image. In *Visual Culture: The Reader*, edited by Jessica Evans, and Stuart Hall, 33-40. London: Sage Publications.

Castillo, Richard Griswold del. 1992. *The Treaty of Guadalupe Hidalgo*. Oklahoma: University of Oklahoma Press.

Castillo, Richard Griswold del, Teresa McKenna, and Yvonne Yarbro-Bejarano (eds.). 1991. *Chicano Art: Resistance and Affirmation, 1965–1985*. Los Angeles: Wight Art Gallery and University of California Los Angeles.

Cockcroft, Eva Sperling, and Holly Barnet-Sánchez (eds.). 1996. *Signs Form the Heart: California Chicano Murals*. Venice, CA: Social and Public Art Resource Center; Albuquerque: University of New Mexico Press.

Cortés, Alejandro Navarrette. 2007. Symbolic Production in Mexico in the 1980s. In *La Era de la Discrepancia—The Age of Discrepancies: Arte y Cultura Visual en México—Art and Visual Culture in Mexico, 1968–1997*, edited by Ana Laura Cué, and Rodrigo Fernández de Gortari, 289-325. Mexico City: Museo Universitario de Ciencias y Arte.

Davalos, Karen Mary. 2008. *Yolanda M. López*. Los Angeles: UCLA Chicano Studies Research Center Press.

Dunitz, Robin J., and James Prigoff. 1997. *Painting the Towns: Murals of California*. Los Angeles: RJD Enterprises.

Fusco, Coco. 1989. The Border Art Workshop—Taller de Arte Fronterizo: An Interview with Guillermo Gómez-Peña and Emily Hicks. *Third Text* 3 (7): 53-76.

Goldman, Shifra M. 1994. *Dimensions of the Americas: Art and Social Change in Latin America and the United States*. Chicago and London: University of Chicago Press.

Goldman, Shifra M. 1996. How, Why, Where, and When it all Happened: Chicano Murals of California. In *Signs from the Heart: California Chicano Murals*, edited by Eva Sperling Cockcroft, and Holly Barnet-Sánchez, 23-53. Venice, CA: Social and Public Art Resource Center; Albuquerque: University of New Mexico Press.

Goldman, Shifra M., and Tomas Ybarra-Frausto. 1991. The Political and Social Contexts of Chicano Art. In *Chicano Art: Resistance and Affirmation, 1965–1985*, edited by Richard Griswold del Castillo, Teresa McKenna, and Yvonne Yarbro-Bejarano, 83-95. Los Angeles: Wight Art Gallery, University of California Los Angeles.

Gómez-Peña, Guillermo. 1991. A Binational Performance Pilgrimage. *The Drama Review* 35 (3): 22-55.

Gómez-Peña, Guillermo. 1993. *Warrior for Gringostroika*. Saint Paul: Graywolf Press.

Gómez-Peña, Guillermo. 1996. *The New World Border: Prophecies, Poems & Loqueras for the End of the Century*. San Francisco: City Lights.

Gómez-Peña, Guillermo, and Roberto Sifuentes. 1996. *Temple of Confessions: Mexican Beasts and Living Santos*. New York: Powerhouse Books.

Healy, Wayne Alaniz. 1997. Ghosts of the Barrio. In *Painting the Towns: Murals of California*, edited by Robin J. Dunitz, and James Prigoff, 171-177. Los Angeles: RJD Enterprises.

Justseeds Artists' Cooperative. 2012. *Migration Now: A Print Portfolio of Handmade Prints Addressing Migrant Issues From Justseeds and CultureStrike*. Pittsburgh, PA: Justseeds Artists' Cooperative.

Keller, Gary D. (ed.). 2002a. *Contemporary Chicana and Chicano Art—Artists, Works, Culture, and Education*, Vol. I. Tempe, Arizona: Bilingual Press.

Keller, Gary D. (ed.). 2002b. *Contemporary Chicana and Chicano Art—Artists, Works, Culture, and Education*, Vol. II. Tempe, Arizona: Bilingual Press/Editorial Bilingüe.

Keller, Gary D. (ed.). 2004. *Chicano Art For Our Millennium: Collected Works from the Arizona State University Community*. Tempe, Arizona: Bilingual Press/Editorial Bilingüe.

Lafaye, Jacques. 1976. *Quetzalcóatl and Guadalupe: The Formation of Mexican National*

Consciousness 1531–1813. Chicago and London: University of Chicago Press.

Latorre, Guisela. 2012. Border Consciousness and Activist Aesthetics: Richard Lou's Performance and Multimedia Artwork. *American Studies Journal* 57: 1-20. Accessed August 30, 2018. doi 10.18422/57-05. http://www.asjournal.org/archive/57/216.html.

Leeuwen, Theo van. 2008. *Introducing Social Semiotics*. London and New York: Routledge.

Lippard, Lucy R. 2000. *Mixed Blessings: New Art in a Multicultural America*. New York: The New Press.

Mesa-Bains, Amalia, and Tomas Ybarra-Frausto. 1986. *Lo Del Corazón: Heartbeat of a Culture*. San Francisco: The Mexican Museum.

Mignolo, Walter D. 2000. *Local Histories/Global Designs: Coloniality, Subaltern Knowledges and Border Thinking*. Princeton, NJ: Princeton University Press.

Miller, Mary, and Karl Taube. 1993. *The Gods and Symbols of Ancient Mexico and Maya*. London: Thames & Hudson.

Pérez, Emma. 1999. *The Decolonial Imaginary: Writing Chicanas into History*. Bloomington and Indianapolis: Indiana University Press.

Public Delivery. 2018. Archive: Ana Teresa Fernandez. Accessed August 30, 2018. https://publicdelivery.org/tag/ana-teresa-fernandez/.

Román-Odio, Clara. 2013. *Sacred Iconographies in Chicana Cultural Productions*. New York: Palgrave McMillan.

Roque, Georges. 1995. Espejos Clasificados: Estética de la Copia. *Artes de Mexico: La Falsificación y sus Espejos* 28: 26-31.

Rose, Gillian. 2007. *Visual Methodologies: And Introduction to the Interpretation of Visual Materials*. London: Sage Publications.

Saldívar, José David. 1997. *Border Matters: Remapping American Cultural Studies*. Berkeley and Los Angeles: University of California Press.

Sheren, Ila N. 2010. Coco Fusco and Guillermo Gómez-Peña's Cage Performance and La PochaNostra's Mapa Corpo: Art of the (Portable) Border. *Hemisphere: Visual Cultures of the Americas* 3 (1): 58-79. Accessed August 30, 2018. https://digitalrepository.unm.

edu/hemisphere/vol3/iss1/3.

Townsend, Richard F. 2000. *The Aztecs*. London: Thames and Hudson.

Wastl-Walter, Doris (ed.). 2016. *The Ashgate Research Companion to Border Studies*. London and New York: Routledge.

Constructing Landscape History Using the Timeline Method: Case Study of the Landscape in Chengdu Plain, China

ZHENG Hao

Research School of Humanities and the Arts, College of Arts & Social Sciences, Australian National University, Canberra, Australia. CONTACT ZHENG Hao: Hao.zheng@anu.edu.au

Abstract: Historical research is an indispensable aspect of contemporary landscape study. It not only provides a cogent landscape planning context for future potential modification, but also endows the landscape with unique emotional identification. In this article, a new approach which emphasises the relationship between historic processes and the transformation of landscape is developed to delineate the trajectory the landscape history of Chengdu Plain. This approach does not focus solely on historic events, but explores an integration of historical elements, exterior circumstance, and cultural transformation. A timeline graph replaces pure narrative as an essential element in the construction of the landscape history. The case study of Chengdu Plain illustrates this approach to the representation of landscape history. It is an approach that emphasises the holistic effects of different historical elements defined by the timeline graph, including: climate, ecology, civilisation, cultural flow, and multiple keystone processes.

Keywords: landscape history, Chengdu Plain, timeline, keystone process

Introduction

Chengdu Plain located in the southwest of China is an alluvium plain formed by the Ming River and the Tuo River. It covers 7340 km² of land between Longquan ridge, Longmeng ridge and Qionglai ridge. It includes the Dujiangyan Irrigation System, and is centred on Chengdu, the capital of Sichuan Province. This land has been intensively cultivated by farmers since the Zhou Dynasty (1046 BCE–256 BCE). It has been one of the most vital crop production areas in China for more than two thousand years. As a result, a distinct and specific landscape has evolved and people have built a close relationship with it. Elders learn about this landscape by their daily cultivation and new generations are continuously introduced to it by members from their kinfolks (Morphy 1995: 204). It is a process known as "Lin Pan" in which local people reach a harmonious coexistence with nature (Xue and Zhu 2013). The principal feature of "Lin Pan" is that several houses are stied in a plot of tall and dense trees, surrounded by the cultivated land. Many scholars have discussed the landscape or "Lin Pan" in Chengdu Plain in relation to its population structure, organised form, ecological system, and cultural genesis (Fang 2012; Fang and Zhou 2011; Xue and Zhu 2013; Shu 2011; Shu, Zhao, and Chen 2015; Zheng 2015). By contrast, this article focuses on the various historic events, via a synthetical timeline, to track the process of this landscape.

The Development of Historical Study in Landscape

As "complex integrations of nature and culture" (Relph 1976: 3), the agricultural landscape is endowed with a strong and irreplaceable sensual and emotional experience for the local farmers. These farmers who perennially work on the land build a profound attachment to it "muscles and scars bear witness to the physical intimacy of the contact" (Tuan 1990: 97). In the perspective of local peasants, the boundary of self and scene, object and subject is blurred (Pearson 2006: 11). To some extent, landscape is "the familiar domain of our dwelling" (Ingold 2002: 191) because people, especially these insiders, have become an inalienable part in it. It is, as Tuan (1990: 93) suggests "home, the locus of memory, and the means of gaining a living" due to its intimate relationship to past and future. Today, although there are still studies about landscape morphology or landscape ecology which focus on the material or natural attributes, the study of landscape has primarily shifted to the role of culture in landscape making (Relph 1976). Cosgrove (2004) argues that landscape acts to "naturalize" what is deeply cultural. In this way, landscapes, albeit have a tangible area with physical items, can be understood as "the story of different but sequential cultures occupying the same space, and creating their own succession of places" (Flores 1994: 12), or a contextual phenomenon which is embedded in a spatial and temporal or geographical and historical world (Marcucci 2000).

The dualism of nature and culture in landscape implies that there will always be a dimension of landscape that lies "beyond science" (Cosgrove 2004: 65). This proposition is repeated by O'Keeffe (2016: 9) who claims that even the concept of nature is culturally constituted. These arguments extend the study of the landscape to the avenues of history and literature as well as memory and poetry. History of landscape is not a novel concept, but the information about landscape is seldom recorded between the 18th century and 20th century, thereby causing people to ignore the effect of history on the landscape (Jackson 1984). Today, the study of history divides into two different streams: technology and humanity. In the realm of technology, landscape history is adopted to analyse the changes about the ecosystem, to predict the future potential modification, and finally to produce a cogent landscape planning context. Landscape history is regarded as a tool and the historical alteration records can be traced back to 10000 years ago, albeit most of these are great weather changes or natural calamities (Christensen 1989; Marcucci 2000). By contrast, in the field of humanity, some western scholars study people's daily activities, cultural identities, and political conflicts in the landscape history perspective, to reveal a human basis in the formation of the landscape. Overall, landscape history, on one hand, deciphers the traditional historical alteration records. On the other hand, it offers an interpretation of how identity is constructed and how "the spatial manifold containing nature, culture and imagination" (Cosgrove 2004) is formed.

Furthermore, landscape history is also important for outsiders like tourists. In the perspective of the outsiders, the landscape is not only a notion, a pictorial representation, and a privileging of sight, but also a way of seeing that has its own history (Cosgrove 1998). In the rural area, although aesthetic appreciation is attractive to some extent, many outsiders are enthralled by the "lure of the local", which is an appreciation of "historical narrative as it is written in the landscape or place by the people who live or lived there" (Lippard 1997: 7). Lewis (1985: 122) also points out that besides these physical features of landscape and terrain, onlookers or outsiders "are always aware of the men and women who have lived in these parts and of the history which they have shaped ". As a conclusion, even the landscape may have different quality or characteristics over time, history of landscape is so crucial for everyone who immerses in it because "the scenery is never separated from the history of that place, from the feeling for the lives that have been lived there" (Williams 1975: 72).

The Approach of Landscape History

Yet, previous study of landscape history does not lead to a certain method of landscape history. To date, the approaches which link historic events and landscape are still obscure. Jackson (1984: xi) reminds us that the landscape history is not just "little more than the local history with a spatial dimension thrown in for good measure"; conversely, it should illustrate "how it was formed, how it has changed, and who it was, who changed it". The separated study of history and landscape should be replaced by an integrated approach which concerns the reciprocal effects between landscape and historic events. In this sense, Marcucci (2000) presents a clear and pragmatic method to elucidate landscape history, which firstly confirms a specific area, then excavates the keystone processes in history, and finally unites all items in a holistic system.

The first stage of Marcucci's method related to historical geography offers an exterior circumstance as well as interior variables. For the landscape in Chengdu Plain, its history is obviously in a context of traditional agricultural development and Chinese peasant's temporary or perpetual fight against nature. Hence, its exterior circumstance is the weather,

470

topographical, and ecological condition for cultivation.

The second stage in Marcucci's method aims to illustrate the complex and multiple landscape processes and answers how these processes develop and why them happen. Here, the definition of keystone processes is "the ones that are influential in the evolutionary trajectory of the landscape" (Marcucci 2000: 72). Other factors pertinent to the keystone process are the spatial and temporal scale. For spatial scale, these keystone processes could be only detected when observers adopt a proper scale. It is noteworthy that if either a small or large scale is adopted, numerous or finite keystone processes will be found which lead to some confusion. Furthermore, the temporal span could also affect the results of keystone processes since climate change or geographical features show their incremental impacts on the landscape both shortly and continuously while cultural or political factors produce transitory but intensive influences. For example, in the case of Long Pond study (Pennsylvania, US), the timeline goes back to 100 centuries ago so that climate changes are palpable, whilst more weight is put on landscape changes in this century to reflecting the cultural and other anthropogenic disturbances (Marcucci 2000).

After confirming an appropriate scale, the following procedure is to use taxonomy to divide the diversified keystone processes. Smith and Hellmund (1993) attributed all new structures and new functional characteristics in the landscape to the flow of energy and the movement of materials. This argument emphasises the material aspect but ignores the cultural attribution as well as human initiatives, attempting to use a positivist way to interpret all kinds of phenomena. Nevertheless, it provides a rudimentary thought for future keystone process study. Later, more comprehensive categories for landscape changes were proposed: geomorphological processes, climate change, colonization patterns and growth of organisms, local disturbances of individual ecosystems, and cultural processes (Forman and Godron 1986; Nassauer and Faust 2013; Marcucci 2000). In these categories, the first two are foundation variables in the view of Forman and Godron (1986) because they both are long-term influences related to crustal movement and species migration. However, this claim seemingly somewhat falls into the trap of primordial natural determinism which is echoed in chronological history books such as Braudel's *Mediterranean* (1949) and is criticised by O'Keeffe (2016) due to it overlooking human activities. Overall, albeit some scholars attempt to divide landscape history into seemingly scientific categories, they overlook that all items are interwoven and reciprocally affected. Except for geomorphological processes and climate change, it is more sensible to include all other items into a category named human activities.

The third stage is to include all the items into a holistic system rather than presenting separated elements. Cosgrove asserts that "landscape is an integration of natural and human phenomena over a certain area"; in this case, the scholars tend to reach a consensus that landscape is a phenomenon in which every item is closely woven and linked (Rössler 2000; Nassauer 1995; Patterson 1994).When people experience landscape, although the places may be known by their most impressive and manifested cultural or natural features, people actually step into a matrix of time and place in which culture and nature are perceived simultaneously (Lozny 2008). Additionally, another important point concerning the holistic system is that it could express all items in a sequence which coincides with cultural development since every culture is the legacy of previous ones, affected and inculcated by earlier events (Marcucci 2000). In the case of the Chengdu Plain, the holistic system of landscape history is not only just the identification of successive cultures but also constructing a tight relationship between these cultures and their traces in the landscape. Here, some physical environmental features are intentionally ignored until they are connected with human activities or literature description, since all traits will gradually emerge from the background only when "the cultural system and the related economy make it so" (Marcucci 2000).

Landscape History of the Chengdu Plain

In the case of Chengdu Plain, different historic events, processes, and elements are enumerated in a chronological order. The first type of elements is what we have previously named—exterior circumstance—climate, topographical and ecological condition. Certainly, although these are exterior elements, they interact with interior landscape forms and cultural development.

The Exterior Circumstance

Hinsch (1988) generalises the climate changes in Chinese history and states that, in the New Stone Age, the weather was extremely warm, while it cooled down after 1500 BCE and reached its lowest point around 1000 BCE; then from the 11th century to the beginning of the 18th century, there was a long-term chilly period; and after that, the temperate weather re-emerged and lasted to the present. This weather trajectory results in a distinct representation in landscape, particularly agricultural landscape. Shu (2011) points out that in prehistoric times, ancient people in Chengdu Plain abandoned fishing and hunting, and changed to cultivation in response to climate variation. Yuan (2006) reiterates this argument by claiming that ancient Chinese people planted multiple crops rather than one specific category so that they could adapt to different weather conditions and improve their survival rate. In the cultural aspect, Fu (2011) speculates that Baodun culture and Sanxingdui civilisation were disrupted due to extremely chilly weather in 2000 BCE and 1000 BCE respectively. The topographical condition of Chengdu Plain is relatively stable, and the most significant feature is that several ridges cross this fertile plain. This topography to some extent cuts the informational and cultural communication between inside and outside until the beginning of the 20th century, which leads to a mystery in landscape and culture. On the other hand, it weakens the ecological resilience in the face of stress of some disasters such as wars or flooding. The typical example of this weak resilience can be found in Ming and Qing Dynasties, in which government had to organise two enormous migrations to revive the population decrease caused by wars (Chen 2005). For the ecological condition, because Chengdu Plain was secluded from outside, the interior ecological system is self-governed and seldom affected by surroundings.

The Keystone Processes

The second type of elements are keystone processes. Before we propose these keystone processes, a suitable temporal scale should be determined. For Chengdu Plain, Guo (1989) argued that the emergence of millet could be traced back to the middle of New Stone Age,

473

which means that at that time, ancient people had settled down. Based on this, the temporal scale should span over 8,000 years. In such a span, the interior climate is in compliance with the whole Chinese climate changes, fluctuating between being chill to warm but temperate on the whole (Hinsch 1988). By contrast, the ecological processes of Chengdu Plain are affected by climate and human activities simultaneously. Nevertheless, the change pattern still complies with the rule in landscape ecology which starts with perforation and ends with attrition (Forman 1995). Then a crucial category of keystone processes is various human activities. It is obvious that farming is the most dominant activity in this landscape. According to the historical record in chorography and evidence in archaeological sites, ancient people firstly resided in upper reaches of Ming River due to the regular flooding and backward agricultural technology, and only planted some upland crops such as millet (Tong 1979). After hundreds of years, the Du Yu Clan migrated into Chengdu Plain from Yunnan Province, established the Du Yu Dynasty (ca. 1100 BCE–700 BCE), as well as imported new agricultural technology to local people (Meng 1989). In the later Kai Ming Dynasty (ca. 666 BCE–316 BCE), because of the gradual progress in irrigation technology and the accumulation of cultivation experience, paddy fields replaced upland fields and became dominant (Shu 2011; Zheng 2015). Paddy fields continued to the end of the last century when the mixed plants such as tea trees or rapeseeds began to be planted to meet the demand of the market economy. The evolution of agriculture significantly altered the texture of the landscape: the virgin forest completely vanished (Figure 1), the land was modified by human labour, and countless ditches were built. Overall, by the cultivation, cultural elements become the theme of the landscape (Figure 2).

Wars are another inextricable human activities that change the landscape. There are three main war periods in history which happened in the Southern Song Dynasty (1127 CE–1279 CE), Yuan Dynasty (1206 CE–1368 CE) and the first half of the 20th century. The first war period in Southern Song Dynasty resulted in the emergence of "equally dividing field system" (均田制), which greatly increased the initiatives of farmers and expanded the

Figure 1 Virgin forest in the ancient landscape (Shu 2011: 110)

Figure 2 Contemporary landscape with artificial modifications (Google Earth Pro 7.3, 2017)

scale of farmland. In this case, numerous pools, mass cultivation, and intricate net of irrigating ditches were produced while the population witnessed a considerable increase (Figure 3).

Figure 3   The landscape after "equally dividing field system" (均田制) (Shu 2011: 112)

The second war period at the end of Yuan Dynasty lasted for a relatively long period and the whole Chengdu Plain fell into a state of depression. To revive the economy, the emperor of the Ming Dynasty (1368 CE–1644 CE) issued a proclaimation which gave the ownership of land to the cultivators. In this context, farmers got not only their own land which could be inherited by descendants but also a sense of security and guarantee for the future. As a result, many farmers left their former settlements to cultivate the wilderness, which caused large settlements to be split into several scattered small groups (大分散小集中) —the prototype of "Lin Pan" (Shu, Zhao, and Chen 2015) (Figure 4).

The third war period is the Second World War and the civil war which follows it. In this period, because Chengdu Plain was surrounded by several ridges, it became a relatively safe area and provided food to support frontline army. In this case, the government endeavoured to improve the yield by imparting new technology and encouraging people to expand

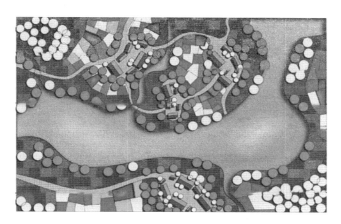

Figure 4   The prototype of "Lin Pan" (Zheng 2015: 34)

planting. However, according to Duan's (2005) analysis, crop growth was mainly caused by the increase in the coverage of cultivated land, while the average yield still stagnated. Due to the exploitation of barren land, the "Lin Pan" became the dominant landscape pattern in every corner of cultivated land while forest further shrank.

It is also noteworthy that migrants with different cultural backgrounds affect the landscape notably. There are three major waves of immigration before the 20th century—migration of Du Yu, first massive migration from Huguang (以湖广填四川), second massive migration from Huguang (以湖广填四川) (Shu 2011). The first and earliest migrant group is Du Yu from Yunnan who brought new agricultural technology to Chengdu Plain. The second and third migration occurred as a result of official policies aiming to boost the population after wars. They also have a similar constitution of migrants: people came from Hunan, Hubei, and north area of Guangxi moved into Chengdu Plain according to the encouragement of government. These two groups of migrants brought and merged their distinct culture into the mainstream, while modifying the landscape simultaneously. For example, Diaolou and Tulou which are special architecture styles derived from the race of Hakka, were found in the centre of Chengdu Plain. Hakkas also have the custom of planting cypresses as an "iron hedge" on the periphery of the house, which is different from aboriginal planting such as bamboo (Long 2013: 34). Another typical example is that migrants from Guangdong and Hunan built guild halls and ancestral temples in the centre of their settlements as places to discuss issues and worship ancestors.

The trend of migration somewhat stagnates in the second half of the 20th century because of the erection of the household registration system (户籍) which insulates farmers from city folks. At the beginning of the 21st century, due to the urbanisation and economical discrepancy between eastern and western parts of China, a counter-migration emerged in which massive young people left Chengdu Plain and arrived in the eastern part of China as well as metropolises to embark on their careers. This counter-migration rapidly weakened labour in Chengdu Plain, and caused a loss of cultivated land. As a result, the landscape showed more natural characters in this high artificial plain.

Recently, another noticeable phenomenon is found in the rural villages throughout China: in many villages, local people are prone to build their new properties on the periphery of villages, leaving the centre of the village in utter desolation. Xue (2001) coins the term "inner-decaying village" to delineate it while most scholars now are inclined to adopt the term "hollow village" (Chen, Feng, and Jiang 2001; Jiang and Luo 2014; H. Long, Li, and Liu 2009). According to a survey in 2017, 88.24% of villages in Chengdu Plain are "hollow villages" in varying degrees (Xie and Zheng 2017). The cause of "hollow village" is complex, but most scholars see it as the ramification of counter-migration (Wang, Yao, and Chen 2005; L. Xue 2001). The impact of "hollow village" on the landscape is that when villagers retreat from those remote and somewhat inaccessible lands, regarding them as worthless, what used to be farmland became abandoned wasteland. Just as Adams (1990: 92) states "rural landscape is the battleground between humans and nature". In the past, people clear a forest to sow and reap. Now, the forest returns as humans retreat.

Additionally, Dujiangyan (irrigation system) which benefits agriculture for more than 2000 years is a significant construction which marked human being's ability to transform the landscape. According to "The Classic of Mountains and Seas" (《山海经》), after the erection of Dujiangyan, farmers sowed in summer and winter regularly while lush crops grew in

Chengdu Plain (Anonymous 2000). This description illustrates that water has been a safe resource since the Qin Dynasty (1616 CE—1911 CE) and floods can be controlled. Dujiangyang makes it possible for people to earn a livelihood and settle down in one area as well as decreasing farmers' reliance on rivers and streams. Hence, it is not an exaggeration to argue that Dujiangyan is the indispensable substratum of later landscape with dense ditches and a scattering of "Lin Pan". Besides, Dujiangyan, along with its designer Li Bing, has become deeply embedded into the culture of Chengdu Plain. People have built many temples to memorialise Li Bing since the Qin Dynasty, and in the legends and fairy tales, Li Bing is exalted to the position of the god of Chengdu Plain who will protect this land forever (Luo 1988). Another cultural manifestation is that people learn to live and farm in harmony with nature from the experience of Dujiangyan which achieves great success through similarity to natural conditions instead of construction of dams. This culture has long term effect on the landscape. People always seek to be harmony with nature, and believe that if harmony is achieved, nature will repay them. Overall, Dujiangyan immediately creates a stable, manageable, and reliable environment for farming and other agricultural activities. In this case, local people no longer need to struggle for survival. Obliquely, Dujiangyan nurtures cultivation culture, water culture, tea culture, and recreation culture which affect people's reformation of the landscape in turn.

Other keystone processes are much more recent. At the beginning of the 1990s, the first rural tourism spot in China emerged in the Chengdu Plain. After that, the scale of rural tourism expanded speedily, and now rural tourism has become the main recreation for local people. Rural tourism, on one hand, offers a novel industry and considerably improves the income of farmers; on the other hand, alters landscape unconsciously. Some western scholars accentuate the possible benefits of rural tourism to landscape in terms of preserving food traditions and local produce (Daugstad 2008; Fleischer and Tchetchik 2005); increasing investment from public-sector, private-sector, and voluntary-sector (Garrod, Wornell, and Youell 2006); and sustainable development (Mitchell and Hall 2005; Lane 1994). By contrast, Chinese scholars are more prone to argue that although rural landscape drives the local economy, it has detrimental effects not only at a physical level such as contaminated water, soil, and air (Yang and Cao 2017), but also at a cultural level like Genius Loci (Xu 2007). For the Chengdu Plain, rural tourism changes the landscape in these aspects: (1) massive tourism service facilities are built in the centre of villages, which engenders a central pattern in landscape; (2) the landscape becomes a kind of commodity which needs to cater to tourists, and cultural custom turns into a stage performance (Huang 2014); (3) traditional agricultural landscape fades away, and elements from modern garden and park such as pools, fountains, and grassland emerge; (4) due to village transformation, the new landscape loses its variety, and becomes monotonous (Xu 2007).

In early 2006, the Central Committee of CPC issued the first document on the construction of a new socialist countryside proposal, and under the guidance of the document, Chengdu government proposed "three centralized layers planning" (Chengdu Municipal People's Government 2011) and instigated construction of the new countryside in the whole Chengdu Plain. According to the public document, in 2020, there will be more than 400 new villages in Chengdu Plain, and in 2025, the number will reach at least 500 (Chengdu Municipal Office 2017). The aim of this policy is to decrease the gap between the city and the village, and improve rural living standard (Wang, Yao, and Chen 2005). This policy affects nearly all of the settlements and changes the landscape of Chengdu Plain noticeably—new rural communities witness a visible increase and replace the old rural communities, pastoral landscape and rural idyll (Yu 2006b). In terms of Chengdu Plain, myriad tiny settlements are totally removed while large concentrated communities are formed. Government ask farmers to leave their old houses, move to the new uniform communities, accept and adapt to the new landscape which is designed by urban planners and architects, and gives priority to aesthetics. In this case, urban landscape elements such as large squares and fountains are introduced to the villages while the original landscape which features ditches, timber forests and tombs is on the verge of disappearance (Yu 2006a).

Summarily, in the landscape history of Chengdu Plain, farming activities, wars, migration, and Dujiangyan Irrigation System are four historical human activities

480

involving keystone processes. These processes interweave with the specific climate and geomorphological conditions, and generate distinct cultivation culture, water culture, tea culture, and recreation culture, and finally, a distinct landscape "Lin Pan" gradually forms. However, the recent keystone processes—rural tourism and new countryside construction, changed the landscape noticeably, which is characterised as being uniform, duplicate, commoditized and urbanised.

The Timeline Graph

It is sensible to arrange all of the keystone processes into a holistic system rather than enumerating them separately (Marcucci 2000). Therefore, a timeline graph is adopted to illustrate all these landscape periods, climate changes, ecological processes, civilisation, cultural flow, and keystone processes contemporaneously (Figure 5). In this timeline, all the historical information is layered while a logarithmic time scale which gives great weight to the recent events but traces back to 10000 years ago is used (Marcucci 2000: 74).

From the timeline, it is clear that there are seven different landscape periods in Chengdu Plain: virgin forest; cultivation commenced; cultivation expanded; a specific form of agriculture emerged; "Lin Pan" form; nursery garden emerged; and new countryside. For every period, the corresponding climate changes, ecological process are presented in this graph. Additionally, cultural flow and civilisation show a tight relationship between local people and landscape—how they occupy, exploit, manage, and maintain this land. As an agricultural area, farming activities are the main clue through the whole historical narration. In terms of the other keystone processes, in most of landscape history, Dujiangyan Irrigation System plays an indispensable role, which expresses the close and long-term correlation between the keystone process and landscape. By contrast, wars, migration, urbanisation, rural tourism, and new countryside construction produce short-term but striking changes to the landscape.

Discussion

The above discussion provides a grand narrative of the landscape history of Chengdu

481

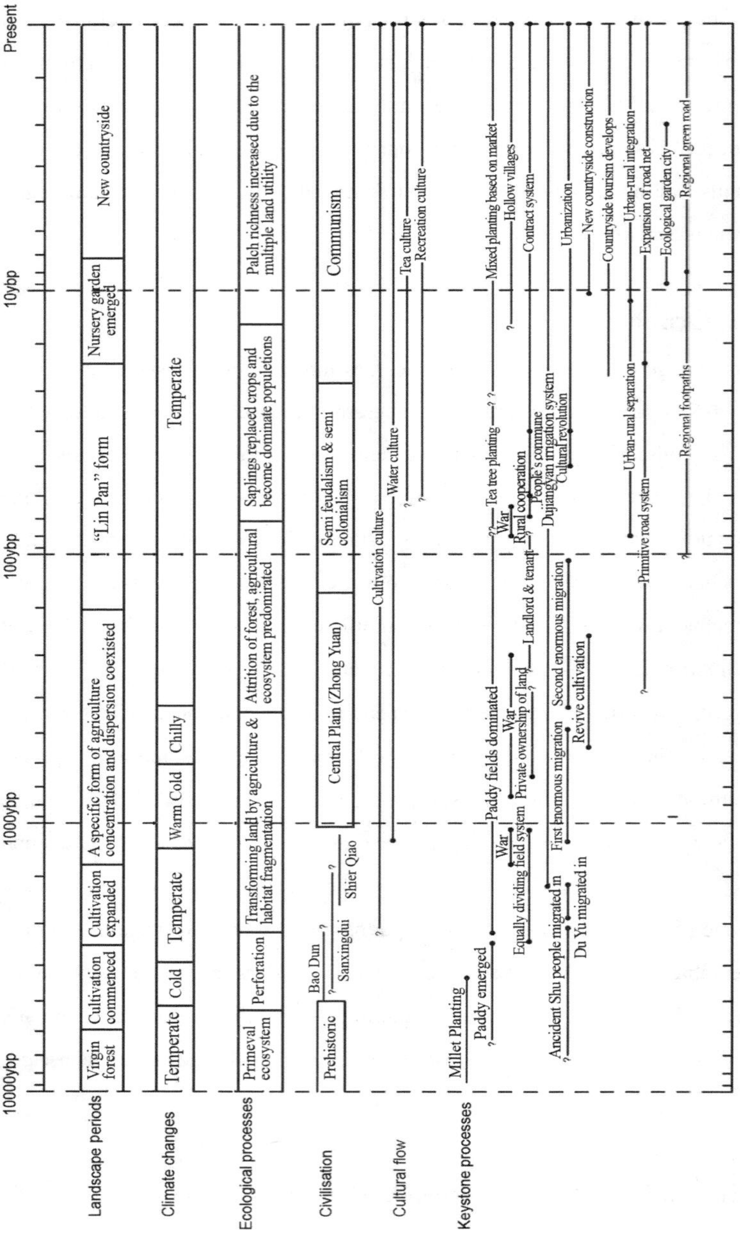

Figure 5   Timeline of landscape periods, climate changes, ecological processes, civilisation, cultural flow, and keystone processes in Chengdu Plain

Plain with a record of almost every momentous event. A method derived from positivism is adopted to decipher the trajectory of landscape development. Due to this prerequisite, landscape history somewhat accentuates the absolute correspondence between keystone processes, landscape representation, and typical features. However, history is an open process, filled with contingencies; it continues to present and affect people's recognition and action (Ryan 1996). In other words, ordinary people are never the blank background of events or processes, instead, they develop and ascribe new meaning to histories without cease. In this case, although every item is arranged in a holistic system, the timeline graph still has an intractable defect which is unduly stressing broad historical significance and generalisable typicality. This defect is universal and has been revealed when Greenblatt (2013) firstly proposed the new historicism as a complement to conventional historicism. New historicism scholars argued that the root of this flaw is that conventional historical narration regards common people as blank figures without any emotion or even name, and staying far away from daily life and events (Gallagher and Greenblatt 2000; Fu 2008). In the notion of the new historicism, the timeline graph and its corresponding landscape history are not so persuasive and somewhat lack the concern for ordinary people.

Conclusions

Awareness of the past is an important element in the love of place; it stresses the roots of people and enhances loyalty simultaneously (Tuan 1990: 99). In this article, the landscape history of the Chengdu Plain is constructed via a timeline graph. Ancient events, as well as some recent activities, are included in a holistic timeline, and the aim is to seek the typical traits of landscape and delineate the trajectory of landscape development. It may be scientific and sensible in a large scale; however, when we put it on the individual, this history becomes impotent. As new historicism criticises, many cracks emerge in the edifice of this history. To some extent, landscape history is just like a landscape painting, drawn by literature narrative from archaeology, ecology, and anthropology, which can never touch the real but give people an illusion of the past.

⧠ Acknowledgements

I thank Prof. Ken Taylor for comments on an earlier version of the manuscript. I would also like to show my gratitude to Prof. Bo Shu for sharing his work in agricultural landscape in Chengdu Plain.

⧠ Disclosure Statement

No potential conflict of interest was reported by the author.

⧠ Funding

The author received no specific funding for this work.

⧠ Note on Contributor

ZHENG Hao is a PhD candidate in Research School of Humanities and the Arts at Australian National University. His work focuses on landscape history, landscape conservation, and cultural landscape.

References

Adams, William Hampton. 1990. Landscape Archaeology, Landscape History, and the American Farmstead. *Historical Archaeology* 24 (4): 92-101.

Anonymous. 2000. *The Classic of Mountains and Seas*. Anne Birrell (Trans.). London: Penguin Classics.

Chen, Liansheng, Wenyong Feng, and Lihong Jiang. 2001. The Analysis of Rural Settlement Hollowizing System of the Southeast of Taiyuan Basin. *Acta Geographica Sinica* 4: 437-446. [程连生，冯文勇，蒋立宏. 2001. 太原盆地东南部农村聚落空心化机理分析. 地理学报4: 437-446.]

Chen, Shisong. 2005. *Great Diaspora: The Historic Interpretation of Yi Hu Guang*. Chengdu: Sichuan People's Publishing House.

Chengdu Municipal Office. 2017. The Advice about Instigation of the Construction of the New Countryside. Accessed February 10, 2019. http://gk.chengdu.gov.cn/govInfoPub/detail.action?id=87550&tn=6.

Chengdu Municipal People's Government. 2011. The Planning of the National Modern Agricultural Area (2011–2015). Accessed February 9, 2019. http://www.moa.gov.cn/ztzl/xdnysfq/fzgh/201301/t20130121_3204190.htm.

Christensen, Norman L. 1989. Landscape History and Ecological Change. *Journal of Forest History* 33 (3): 116-125.

Cosgrove, Denis E. 1998. *Social Formation and Symbolic Landscape*. Madison: University of Wisconsin Press.

Cosgrove, Denis E. 2004. Landscape and Landschaft. *German Historical Institute Bulletin* 35 (Fall): 57-71.

Daugstad, Karoline. 2008. Negotiating Landscape in Rural Tourism. *Annals of Tourism Research* 35 (2): 402-426.

Duan, Yu. 2005. *Sichuan in the Resistance to Japan*. Chengdu: Bashu Press.

Fang, Zhirong. 2012. Basic Study on the Linpan Culture at Western Sichuan Plain. Doctoral

Dissertation, Chongqing University. [方志戎. 2012. 川西林盘文化要义. 博士学位论文，重庆大学.]

Fang, Zhirong, and Jianhua Zhou. 2011. Population, Cultivated Land and the Self-Organization of Traditional Rural Settlement—With the Case of the Linpan Settlement System (1644–1911) in Chuanxi Plain. *Chinese Landscape Architecture* 27 (6): 83-87. [方志戎，周建华. 2011. 人口、耕地与传统农村聚落自组织——以川西平原林盘聚落体系(1644—1911)为例. 中国园林 27 (6): 83-87.]

Fernand, Braudel. 1949. *La Méditerranée et le Monde Méditerranéen à l'époque de Philippe II*. Paris: Armand Colin.

Fleischer, Aliza, and Anat Tchetchik. 2005. Does Rural Tourism Benefit from Agriculture? *Tourism Management* 26 (4): 493-501.

Flores, Dan. 1994. Place: An Argument for Bioregional History. *Environmental History Review* 18 (4): 1-18.

Forman, Richard TT. 1995. Some General Principles of Landscape and Regional Ecology. *Landscape Ecology* 10 (3): 133-142.

Forman, Richard TT, and M Godron. 1986. *Landscape Ecology*. New York: Jhon Wiley & Sons.

Fu, Jielin. 2008. A Study on New Historical and Cultural Poetics by Greenblatt. Doctoral Dissertation, Shandong University, Jinan [傅洁琳. 2008. 格林布拉特新历史主义与文化诗学研究. 博士学位论文，山东大学，济南.].

Fu, Shun, Fengsheng Li, Zhaokun Yan, and Yuerong Zheng. 2011. The Relationship Between the Development of Ancient Shu Culture and Climate. *Journal of Sichuan Normal University (Natural Science)* 34 (3): 417-421. [付顺，李奋生，颜照坤，郑月蓉. 2011. 成都平原全新世气候变迁与古蜀文化演进相关性研究. 四川师范大学学报（自然科学版）34 (3): 417-421.]

Gallagher, Catherine, and Stephen Greenblatt. 2000. *Practicing New Historicism*. Chicago & London: University of Chicago Press.

Garrod, Brian, Roz Wornell, and Ray Youell. 2006. Re-conceptualising Rural Resources as Countryside Capital: The Case of Rural Tourism. *Journal of Rural Studies* 22 (1): 117-128.

Greenblatt, Stephen. 2013. Towards a Poetics of Culture. In *The New Historicism*, edited by H. Aram Veeser, 17-30. London & New York: Routledge.

Guo, Shengbo. 1989. Brief Review of the Historical Agricultural Geography of Sichuan. *Collections of Essays on Chinese Historical Geography* 3: 111-125. [郭声波. 1989. 四川历史农业地理概论. 中国历史地理论丛 3: 111-125.]

Hinsch, Bret. 1988. Climatic Change and History in China. *Journal of Asian History* 22 (2): 131-159.

Huang, Qixin. 2014. Rural Toursim: Commercialization, Authenticity and Development Strategy of Cultural Ecotourism. *Journal of Northwest A&F University (Social Science Edition)* 14 (4): 133-136. [黄其新. 2014. 乡村旅游:商品化、真实性及文化生态发展策略. 西北农林科技大学学报（社会科学版）14 (4): 133-136.]

Ingold, Tim. 2002. *The Perception of the Environment: Essays on Livelihood, Dwelling and Skill*. London: Routledge.

Jackson, John Brinckerhoff. 1984. *Discovering the Vernacular Landscape*. New Haven & London: Yale University Press.

Jiang, Shaojing, and Pan Luo. 2014. A Literature Review on Hollow Villages in China. *China Population, Resources and Environment* 24 (6): 51-58.

Lane, Bernard. 1994. Sustainable Rural Tourism Strategies: A Tool for Development and Conservation. *Journal of Sustainable Tourism* 2 (1-2): 102-111.

Lewis Jones, B. 1985. Cynefin: The Word and the Concept. *Nature in Wales* 4 (1/2): 121-122.

Lippard, Lucy R. 1997. *The Lure of the Local: Senses of Place in a Multicentered Society*. New York: New Press.

Long, Chan. 2013. How Immigration Culture Affect the Continuous Life of Landscape Elements in Lin Pan in Chengdu Plain. Master's Thesis, Sichuan Agriculture University, Chengdu. [龙婵. 2013. 移民文化对川西林盘景观生命存续性的影响. 硕士学位论文，四川农业大学，成都.]

Long, Hualou, Yurui Li, and Yansui Liu. 2009. Analysis of Evolutive Characteristics and Their Driving Mechanism of Hollowing Villages in China. *Acta Geographica Sinica* 64

(10): 1203-1213. [龙花楼，李裕瑞，刘彦随. 2009. 中国空心化村庄演化特征及其动力机制. 地理学报 64 (10): 1203-1213.]

Lozny, Ludomir R. 2008. Place, Historical Ecology and Cultural Landscape: New Directions for Applied Archaeology. In *Landscapes Under Pressure*, 15-25. London: Springer.

Luo, Kaiyu. 1988. The Relationship Between Dujiangyan Irrigation System and Shu Culture. *Sichuan Cultural Relics* 3: 32-38. [罗开玉. 1988. 论都江堰与蜀文化的关系. 四川文物 3: 32-38.]

Marcucci, Daniel J. 2000. Landscape History as a Planning Tool. *Landscape and Urban Planning* 49 (1-2): 67-81.

Meng, Mo. 1989. *The Historic Documents of Sichuan*. Chengdu: Sichuan People's Publishing House. [蒙默 .1989. 四川古代史稿. 成都：四川人民出版社.]

Mitchell, Morag, and Derek Hall. 2005. Rural Tourism as Sustainable Business: Key Themes and Issues. In *Rural Tourism and Sustainable Business,* 3-14. Clevedon, UK: Channel View Publications.

Morphy, Howard. 1995. Landscape and the Reproduction of the Ancestral Past. In *The Anthropology of Landscape: Perspectives on Place and Space*, edited by Hirsch Eric, and O'Hanlon Michael, 184-209. Oxford University Press.

Nassauer, Joan Iverson. 1995. Culture and Changing Landscape Structure. *Landscape Ecology* 10 (4): 229-237.

Nassauer, Joan Iverson, and Chris Faust. 2013. *Placing Nature: Culture and Landscape Ecology*. Washington, D.C.: Island Press.

O'Keeffe, Tadhg. 2016. Landscape and Memory: Historiography, Theory, Methodology. In *Heritage, Memory and the Politics of Identity*, 15-30. London: Ashgate Publishing Company.

Patterson, Thomas C. 1994. Toward a Properly Historical Ecology. In *Historical Ecology: Cultural Knowledge and Changing Landscapes,* 223-237. Santa Fe, United States: School of American Research Press.

Pearson, Mike. 2006. *In Comes I: Performance, Memory and Landscape*. Exeter: University of Exeter Press.

Relph, Edward. 1976. *Place and Placelessness*. London: Sage Publications.

Rössler, Mechtild. 2000. World Heritage Cultural Landscapes. *The George Wright Forum* 17 (1): 27-34.

Ryan, K. 1996. *New Historicism and Cultural Materialism: A Reader*. London and New York: Arnold.

Shu, Bo. 2011. Research on the Agricultural Landscape of Chengdu Plain. Doctoral Dissertation, Southwest Jiaotong University, Chengdu. [舒波. 成都平原的农业景观研究. 博士学位论文, 西南交通大学, 成都.]

Shu, Bo, Yuanxing Zhao, and Yang Chen. 2015. Analysis on Influence of the Land System on Rural Clusters Space Form in Chengdu Plain. *Sichuan Building Science* 41 (4): 88-91. [舒波, 赵元欣, 陈阳. 2015. 土地制度对成都平原农村聚落形态的影响. 四川建筑科学研究 41 (4) : 88-91.]

Smith, Daniel S, and Paul Cawood Hellmund. 1993. *Ecology of Greenways: Design and Function of Linear Conservation Areas*. London: University of Minnesota Press.

Tong, Enzheng. 1979. *The Ancient Bashu*. Chengdu: Sichuan People's Publishing House. [童恩正. 1979. 古代的巴蜀. 成都：四川人民出版社.]

Tuan, YiFu. 1990. *Topophilia: A Study of Environmental Perceptions, Attitudes, and Values*. New York: Columbia University Press.

Wang, Chenxin, Shimou Yao, and Caihong Chen. 2005. Empirical Study on "Village-Hollowing" in China. *Scientia Geographica Sinica* 25 (3): 257-262. [王成新, 姚士谋, 陈彩虹. 2005. 中国农村聚落空心化问题实证研究. 地理科学 25 (3): 257-262.]

Williams, Raymond. 1975. *The Country and the City*, Vol. 423. London: Oxford University Press.

Xie, Yan, and Xungang Zheng. 2017. Research on the Degree of Village Hollowness in the Suburbs of Chengdu Plain. *Journal of Sichuan Agricultural University* 35 (3): 439-444. [谢艳, 郑循刚. 2017. 成都平原区城镇近郊村庄的空心化程度研究. 四川农业大学

学报 35 (3): 439-444.]

Xu, Qing. 2007. On the Landscape Crisis in Rural Tourism Development. *Chinese Landscape Architecture* 6: 83-87. [徐清. 2007. 论乡村旅游开发中的景观危机. 中国园林 6: 83-87.]

Xue, Fei, and Zhan-qiang Zhu. 2013. The Research of Linpan Culture Landscape Conservation. *Chinese Landscape Architecture* 29 (11): 25-29. [薛飞，朱战强. 2013. 川西林盘文化景观保护研究. 中国园林 29 (11): 25-29.]

Xue, Li. 2001. Study on the Inner Decaying Village and the Countermeasures with Jiangsu Province as the Case. *City Planning Review* 6: 8-13. [薛力. 2001. 城市化背景下的 "空心村" 现象及其对策探讨——以江苏省为例. 城市规划 6: 8-13.]

Yang, Long, and Kun Cao. 2017. The Investigation of the Impact of Rural Tourism on Natural Landscape—The Case of Chengdu. *Tourism Overview* 6: 209-210. [杨龙，曹锟. 2017. 关于农家乐对当地自然环境影响的调查——以成都为例. 旅游纵览 6: 209-210.]

Yu, Kongjian. 2006a. The New Countryside Construction Under Ethic Perspective. *Impact of Science on Society* 3: 26-31. [俞孔坚. 2006a. 伦理学视野中的新农村建设："新桃源" 陷阱与出路. 科学与社会 3: 26-31.]

Yu Kongjian. 2006b. Three Proposals for Preventing the Potential Damage by Building the New Countryside and Protecting the Local Cultural Landscape and the Industrial Heritage. *Chinese Landscape Architecture* 8: 8-12. [俞孔坚. 2006b. 关于防止新农村建设可能带来的破坏、乡土文化景观保护和工业遗产保护的三个建议. 中国园林 8: 8-12.]

Yuan, Jin. 2006. Research on Economic Forms from 2500 BC to 1500 BC in Central Plains. *China Relics*, October 27, 2006. [袁靖. 2006. 公元前2500年—公元前1500年中原地区经济形态研究. 中国文物报2006-10-27.]

Zheng, Hao. 2015. The Research About the Settlement Landscape in Chengdu Plain. Master's Thesis, Southwest Jiaotong University, Chengdu. [郑昊. 2015. 成都平原农村聚落景观研究. 硕士学位论文，西南交通大学，成都.]

图书在版编目（CIP）数据

文化遗产新探：跨界话语研究＝New Approach to Cultural Heritage: Profiling Discourse Across Borders: 英文/程乐，杨建平，蔡建明主编. — 杭州：浙江大学出版社，2020.12
ISBN 978-7-308-20435-4

Ⅰ. ①文⋯ Ⅱ. ①程⋯ ②杨⋯ ③蔡⋯ Ⅲ. ①文化遗产－世界－文集－英文 Ⅳ. ①K103-53

中国版本图书馆CIP数据核字(2020)第139735号

文化遗产新探：跨界话语研究
New Approach to Cultural Heritage: Profiling Discourse Across Borders
程 乐 杨建平 蔡建明 主编

责任编辑	包灵灵
文字编辑	徐 旸
责任校对	董齐琪
封面设计	十木米
出版发行	浙江大学出版社
	（杭州市天目山路148号　　邮政编码　310007）
	（网址：http://www.zjupress.com）
排　　版	杭州林智广告有限公司
印　　刷	浙江省邮电印刷股份有限公司
开　　本	880mm×1230mm 1/32
印　　张	15.75
字　　数	655千
版 印 次	2020年12月第1版　2020年12月第1次印刷
书　　号	ISBN 978-7-308-20435-4
定　　价	68.00元